CREATING

100 PROJECTS

FOR

CODING

BEGINNERS

HTML / CSS / JavaScript / Bootstrap / jQuery

A Journey through 100 Projects with 216 Tasks
in HTML, CSS, and JavaScript

BY SANGHYUN NA

Creating 100 Projects for Coding Beginners

- "Start from Scratch: A Journey through 100 Coding Projects for Beginners"

- "The Code Novice's Path: 100 Projects to Mastery"

- "Bootstrapping Coders: 100 Projects to Jumpstart Your Journey"

- "Climbing the Coding Ladder: 100 Beginner Projects to Reach the Top"

- "Novice to Notable: 100 Coding Projects to Transform Your Skills"

Experience a total of 216 coding tasks!

"Unlock the world of coding with 'Creating 100 Projects for Coding Beginners'. This comprehensive guide empowers you, providing step-by-step instruction through 100 unique projects. Explore the exciting realm of coding, gaining hands-on experience while building your skillset. Perfect for aspiring coders, your journey to mastery starts here."

"Dive into 'Creating 100 Projects for Coding Beginners', a resource designed to make your coding journey both engaging and practical. Over 100 projects, learn essential programming concepts, solve real-world problems, and build a solid foundation. This book is your roadmap to becoming a confident and capable coder."

"Embark on your coding adventure with 'Creating 100 Projects for Coding Beginners'. This invaluable guide lays out a clear path, through 100 practical projects, to acquiring coding proficiency. Cultivate hands-on skills, solve intricate problems, and turn from a novice into an adept coder with every project you complete."

PROJECT 100 + CODING 216

How to download 235 task files related to 100 projects:

1. Open page 276 of this book.
2. Enter the word(d...r) in the center of the top picture into the asterisk(*) place in step 3.
3. Input the following address into the URL field of Chrome or Edge, then press enter.

dolor

http://www.mij.co.kr/*****/235task-files.zip   (or)

mijkor.dothome.co.kr/*****/235task-files.zip

4. Once the download is complete, unzip the files, open the folder in Visual Studio Code, and utilize them.

TO : Yunyeob, Aron, Haim, and Siwoo (they are our future)

"Per the KDP's Paperback Guidelines, which state a page limit of 828,
the following 19 coding tasks aren't included.
However, rest assured, the files will still be provided."

015_TEMPERATURE CONVERTER2
038_BMI CALCULATOR2
047_CURRENCY CONVERTER2
050_VIRTUAL DICE ROLL3_USE_BOOTSTRAP
053_COUNTDOWN TIMER2
054_RECIPE FINDER2
058_MEMORY GAME2
060_HANGMAN GAME3_USE_BOOTSTRAP
061_DAILY PLANNER3
061_DAILY PLANNER1_USE_BOOTSTRAP
061_DAILY PLANNER2_USE_BOOTSTRAP
061_DAILY PLANNER3_USE_BOOTSTRAP
063_MY PORTFOLIO2
064_TASK TRACKER2
066_E-COMMERCE SITE3_USE_BOOTSTRAP
072_QUIZ APP2
073_LIBRARY MANAGEMENT3_USE-BOOTSTRAP
084_VIRTUAL PET GAME2
095_TASK MANAGEMENT2

Welcome to My HTML Page!

- Home
- About
- Contact

My First Article

This is my first article. It's great to have you here!

More Information

Here is some more information for you.

Click me

Created by ChatGPT. Copyright 2023.

```
<!DOCTYPE html>
<html>
<!-- First project for coding beginners! Starting is half the battle.
Let's keep going~~ -->
<head>
    <title>My HTML Page</title>
    <style>
        body {
            background-color: lightblue;
        }

        h1 {
            color: white;
            text-align: center;
        }
```

1

```
        p {
            font-family: verdana;
            font-size: 20px;
        }
    </style>

</head>a

<body>
    <header>
        <h1>Welcome to My HTML Page!</h1>
    </header>
    <nav>
        <ul>
            <li><a href="#"
onclick="myFunction2()">Home</a></li>
            <li><a href="#"
onclick="myFunction3()">About</a></li>
            <li><a href="#"
onclick="myFunction4()">Contact</a></li>
        </ul>
    </nav>
    <main>
        <article>
            <h2>My First Article</h2>
            <p>This is my first article. It's great to have you
here!</p>
            <img src="image1.jpg" alt="My Image" width="500"
height="400">
        </article>
        <aside>
            <h3>More Information</h3>
            <p>Here is some more information for you.</p>
        </aside>
    </main>
    <button onclick="myFunction()">Click me</button>
    <footer>
        <p>Created by ChatGPT. Copyright 2023.</p>
    </footer>
    <script>
        function myFunction() {
            alert("These projects can help you build your skills in
HTML, CSS, and JavaScript. Remember, the key is to start small
and gradually take on more complex projects as you become
more comfortable with coding. Enjoy your learning journey!");
        }

        function myFunction2() {
            alert("Welcome to My Homepage!!!");
        }
```

```
        function myFunction3() {
            alert("I am Freeman. I am Web Developer. I am
Traveller.");
        }

        function myFunction4() {
            alert("abcdef@naver.com   <= Please contact me
anytime.");
        }
    </script>
</body>

</html>

<!-- These projects can help you build your skills in HTML, CSS,
and JavaScript. Remember, the key is to start small and gradually
take on more complex projects as you become more comfortable
with coding. Enjoy your learning journey! -->
```

4

```
<!DOCTYPE html>
<html lang="en">
<!-- You can comment out by pressing the Control (Ctrl) and
Slash (/ or ?) keys simultaneously. -->

<head>
    <meta charset="UTF-8">
```

```html
    <title>My HTML Page</title>

    <!-- In the project for coding beginners, we won't create
separate style and JavaScript files, but will record everything on a
single page. -->

    <!-- <link rel="stylesheet" href="styles.css"> -->
    <style>
      body {
          background-color: lightblue;
      }

      h1 {
          color: white;
          text-align: center;
      }

      p {
          font-family: verdana;
          font-size: 20px;
      }
    </style>

    <!-- <script src="script.js"></script> -->

</head>

<!-- The goal of this project is to experiment with using more
than 30 different HTML tags in various ways. -->

<body>
    <header>
        <h1>Welcome to My HTML Page!</h1>
    </header>
    <nav>
        <ul>
            <li><a href="#section1">Section 1</a></li>
            <li><a href="#section2">Section 2</a></li>
            <li><a href="#section3">Section 3</a></li>
        </ul>
    </nav>
    <main>
        <section id="section1">
            <h2>Section 1</h2>
```

5

```html
        <article>
            <p>This is an article in section 1.</p>
            <figure>
                <img src="image2.jpg" alt="My Image"
width="300" height="200">
                <figcaption>This is my image.</figcaption>
            </figure>
        </article>
    </section>
    <section id="section2">
        <h2>Section 2</h2>
        <video controls width="300" height="200">
            <source src="video1.mp4" type="video/mp4">
        </video>
    </section>
    <section id="section3">
        <h2>Section 3</h2>
        <audio controls>
            <source src="song.mp3" type="audio/mpeg">
        </audio>
    </section>
    <hr>
    <form action="/submit" method="post">
        <label for="fname">First name:</label><br>
        <input type="text" id="fname" name="fname"><br>
        <label for="lname">Last name:</label><br>
        <input type="text" id="lname" name="lname"><br>
        <label for="email">Email:</label><br>
        <input type="email" id="email" name="email"><br>
        <label for="birthday">Birthday:</label><br>
        <input type="date" id="birthday"
name="birthday"><br>
        <input type="submit" value="Submit">
    </form>
</main>
<hr color="blue">
<aside>
    <h3>Side Content</h3>
    <p>This is some side content.</p>
    <table border="block">
        <tr>
            <th>Header 1</th>
            <th>Header 2</th>
        </tr>
```

6

```html
        <tr>
            <td>Data 1</td>
            <td>Data 2</td>
        </tr>
    </table>
</aside>
<footer>
    <p>Created by ChatGPT. Copyright 2023.</p>
    <address>Contact: <a
href="mailto:example@example.com">example@example.com</
a></address>
    </footer><br>
</body>

</html>
```

The time remaining until December 31, 2023!

Remaining days : 168

Remaining hours : 07

Remaining minutes : 40

Remaining seconds : 43

Ah, time! Please stop~~

8

```
<!DOCTYPE html>
<html>

<style>
  p {
    display: inline-block;
  }
</style>

<body>
  <h2>The time remaining until December 31, 2023!</h2>
  <label for="days">Remaining days : <p
id="days"></p></label><br>
  <label for="hours">Remaining hours : <p
id="hours"></p></label><br>
  <label for="minutes">Remaining minutes : <p
id="minutes"></p></label><br>
  <label for="seconds">Remaining seconds : <p
id="seconds"></p></label><br>

  <h3>Ah, time! Please stop~~</h3>
  <!-- If you change the numbers of the year, month, and day
below, it will tell you the remaining time in real-time.
  Take note that since the index for January starts at 0, December
should be written as 11 instead of 12. -->
  <script>
```

```
function countdown() {
  let now = new Date();
  let eventDate = new Date(2023, 11, 31); // Month is 0-
based in JavaScript

  let currentTime = now.getTime();
  let eventTime = eventDate.getTime();

  let remainingTime = eventTime - currentTime;

  let seconds = Math.floor(remainingTime / 1000);
  let minutes = Math.floor(seconds / 60);
  let hours = Math.floor(minutes / 60);
  let days = Math.floor(hours / 24);

  hours %= 24;
  minutes %= 60;
  seconds %= 60;

  hours = (hours < 10) ? "0" + hours : hours;
  minutes = (minutes < 10) ? "0" + minutes : minutes;
  seconds = (seconds < 10) ? "0" + seconds : seconds;

  document.getElementById("days").textContent = days;
  document.getElementById("hours").textContent = hours;
  document.getElementById("minutes").textContent =
minutes;
  document.getElementById("seconds").textContent =
seconds;

  setTimeout(countdown, 1000);
}

countdown();

</script>
</body>

</html>

<!-- In JavaScript, months are zero-based. This means January is
0, February is 1, and so on, up until December, which is 11. So, if
you want to target the 31st of December, 2023, you should use
new Date(2023, 11, 31), not new Date(2023, 12, 31). -->
```

9

```
<!-- The script code above and below are the same. -->

<!-- function countdown() {
  let now = Date.now();
  let eventTime = new Date(2023, 11, 31).getTime();

  let timeLeft = eventTime - now; // in milliseconds

  let seconds = Math.floor(timeLeft / 1000 % 60);
  let minutes = Math.floor(timeLeft / 1000 / 60 % 60);
  let hours = Math.floor(timeLeft / (1000 * 60 * 60) % 24);
  let days = Math.floor(timeLeft / (1000 * 60 * 60 * 24));

  document.getElementById("days").textContent = days;
  document.getElementById("hours").textContent = hours;
  document.getElementById("minutes").textContent = minutes;
  document.getElementById("seconds").textContent = seconds;

  setTimeout(countdown, 1000);
}

countdown(); -->
```

Remaining Time Calculator

Choose a date:

2023-12-25 📅

Start countdown

Remaining days : 162

Remaining hours : 07

Remaining minutes : 26

Remaining seconds : 30

Time and tide wait for no man.

Time is money.

Lost time is never found again.

The sands of time wait for no one.

Time heals all wounds.

11

```
<!DOCTYPE html>
<html>

<style>
 * {
   text-align: center;
 }

p {
   display: inline-block;
```

```
  }
</style>

<!-- Made it so that the user can directly select the year-month-
day. -->

<body>
  <h2>Remaining Time Calculator</h2>

  <label for="datePicker">Choose a date:</label><br>
  <input type="date" id="datePicker"><br>
  <button id="startCountdown">Start countdown</button><br>

  <label for="days">Remaining days : <p
id="days"></p></label><br>
  <label for="hours">Remaining hours : <p
id="hours"></p></label><br>
  <label for="minutes">Remaining minutes : <p
id="minutes"></p></label><br>
  <label for="seconds">Remaining seconds : <p
id="seconds"></p></label><br>
  <hr>
  <h3>Time and tide wait for no man.</h3>
  <h3>Time is money.</h3>
  <h3>Lost time is never found again.</h3>
  <h3>The sands of time wait for no one.</h3>
  <h3>Time heals all wounds.</h3>

  <script>
    let countdownInterval;

    document.getElementById("startCountdown").addEventListene
r("click", function () {
      let selectedDate = new
Date(document.getElementById("datePicker").value);

      // correct timezone offset
      selectedDate.setMinutes(selectedDate.getTimezoneOffset() -
selectedDate.getMinutes());

      if (selectedDate) {
        if (countdownInterval) {
          clearInterval(countdownInterval);
        }
```

```
       countdown(selectedDate);
     } else {
       alert("Please select a date.");
     }
   });

   function countdown(eventDate) {
     countdownInterval = setInterval(function () {
       let now = new Date();

       let currentTime = now.getTime();
       let eventTime = eventDate.getTime();

       let remainingTime = eventTime - currentTime;

       let seconds = Math.floor(remainingTime / 1000);
       let minutes = Math.floor(seconds / 60);
       let hours = Math.floor(minutes / 60);
       let days = Math.floor(hours / 24);

       hours %= 24;
       minutes %= 60;
       seconds %= 60;

       hours = (hours < 10) ? "0" + hours : hours;
       minutes = (minutes < 10) ? "0" + minutes : minutes;
       seconds = (seconds < 10) ? "0" + seconds : seconds;

       document.getElementById("days").textContent = days;
       document.getElementById("hours").textContent = hours;
       document.getElementById("minutes").textContent =
minutes;
       document.getElementById("seconds").textContent =
seconds;
     }, 1000);
   }
  </script>
</body>

</html>

<!-- // correct timezone offset
```

```
selectedDate.setMinutes(selectedDate.getTimezoneOffset() -
selectedDate.getMinutes());

JavaScript's Date object handles timezone conversions. When you
provide an input of type "date", the value is returned in the
format "yyyy-mm-dd". JavaScript takes this value as a UTC date
(with time set to 00:00:00). But when you create a new Date
object in JavaScript, it considers the local timezone of your
machine and hence a discrepancy is introduced.

The solution is to manually set the time part of the selected date
to your local time. This way you can remove the time zone offset.
-->
```

My Book List

Book Title:

Sapiens

Author:

Yuval Noah Harari

Add Book

- RICH DAD POOR DAD by ROBERT KIYOSAKI
- PALE BLUE DOT by CARL SAGAN
- THE SELFISH GENE by RICHARD DAWKINS
- Sapiens by Yuval Noah Harari

```
<!DOCTYPE html>
<html>
<head>
    <title>Book List</title>
</head>
<body>
    <h1>My Book List</h1>

    <form id="book-form">
        <label for="title">Book Title:</label><br>
        <input type="text" id="title" name="title"><br>
        <label for="author">Author:</label><br>
        <input type="text" id="author" name="author"><br>
        <input type="submit" value="Add Book">
    </form>

    <ul id="book-list">
        <!-- Books will be added here -->
    </ul>

    <script>
    document.getElementById('book-
form').addEventListener('submit', function(event) {
        event.preventDefault();
```

15

```
        let title = document.getElementById('title').value;
        let author = document.getElementById('author').value;

        let bookItem = document.createElement('li');
        bookItem.textContent = title + ' by ' + author;

        document.getElementById('book-
list').appendChild(bookItem);
      });
    </script>
</body>
</html>
```

```
<!DOCTYPE html>
<html>
<head>
 <title>Book List</title>
 <style>
  body {
    font-family: Arial, sans-serif;
    background-color: #f4f4f4;
    margin: 0;
    padding: 0;
  }
  h1 {
    color: #444;
    background-color: #ddd;
    padding: 10px 0;
    margin: 0;
    text-align: center;
  }
  #book-form {
    margin: 20px 0;
    padding: 10px;
    background-color: #fff;
    color: #444;
  }
```

```css
label {
  display: inline-block;
  width: 150px;
  color: #666;
}
input[type=text] {
  margin: 5px 0;
  padding: 5px;
  width: 200px;
}
input[type=submit] {
  margin-top: 10px;
  margin-left: 10px;
  padding: 5px 10px;
  background-color: #ddd;
  cursor: pointer;
  border: none;
}
#book-list {
  list-style: none;
  padding: 20px;
  margin: 0;
}
.book-item {
  background-color: #fff;
  margin-bottom: 5px;
  padding: 10px;
  border: 1px solid #ddd;
  position: relative;
}

.delete-btn,
.complete-btn {
  margin-left: 10px;
  padding: 3px;
  border: none;
  cursor: pointer;
}

.delete-btn {
  background-color: #f44336;
  color: white;
}
```

```css
    .complete-btn {
      background-color: #4CAF50;
      color: white;
    }

    .book-item.completed {
      text-decoration: line-through;
    }
  </style>
</head>

<body>
  <h1>My Book List</h1>

  <form id="book-form">
    <label for="title">Book Title:</label><br>
    <input type="text" id="title" name="title" autofocus><br>
    <label for="author">Author:</label><br>
    <input type="text" id="author" name="author"><br>
    <input type="submit" value="Add Book">
  </form>

  <ul id="book-list">
    <!-- Books will be added here -->
  </ul>

  <script>
    const bookForm = document.getElementById('book-form');
    const titleInput = document.getElementById('title');
    const authorInput = document.getElementById('author');
    const bookList = document.getElementById('book-list');

    bookForm.addEventListener('submit', function (event) {
      event.preventDefault();

      const title = titleInput.value;
      const author = authorInput.value;

      addBookToList(title, author);
      titleInput.value = '';
      authorInput.value = '';
      titleInput.focus();
    });
```

```
function addBookToList(title, author) {
  const bookItem = document.createElement('li');
  bookItem.className = 'book-item';

  // const bookText = document.createTextNode(title + ' by '
+ author);
  const bookText =
document.createTextNode(`${title}  by   ${author}`);
  bookItem.appendChild(bookText);

  const deleteBtn = document.createElement('button');
  deleteBtn.textContent = 'Delete';
  deleteBtn.className = 'delete-btn';
  deleteBtn.addEventListener('click', function () {
    bookList.removeChild(bookItem);
    saveListToLocalStorage();
  });

  const completeBtn = document.createElement('button');
  completeBtn.textContent = 'Completed';
  completeBtn.className = 'complete-btn';
  completeBtn.addEventListener('click', function () {
    bookItem.classList.add('completed');
  });

  bookItem.appendChild(deleteBtn);
  bookItem.appendChild(completeBtn);

  bookList.insertBefore(bookItem, bookList.firstChild);
  saveListToLocalStorage();
}

function loadListFromLocalStorage() {
  const books = JSON.parse(localStorage.getItem('books')) ||
[];
  for (let book of books) {
    addBookToList(book.title, book.author);
  }
}

function saveListToLocalStorage() {
  const books = [];
  for (let i = 0; i < bookList.children.length; i++) {
    const bookItem = bookList.children[i];
```

20

```
        const titleAuthor = bookItem.firstChild.textContent.split('
by ');
        const book = { title: titleAuthor[0], author:
titleAuthor[1] };
        // books.push(book);    // ascending order
        books.unshift(book);    // descending order
      }
      localStorage.setItem('books', JSON.stringify(books));
    }

    loadListFromLocalStorage();
  </script>
</body>
</html>

<!-- In this corrected code:
Delete and Complete buttons are created for each book item.
These buttons are styled for better visibility.
When the Delete button is clicked, the book item is removed from
the list and the list in the local storage is updated.
When the Complete button is clicked, the 'completed' class is
added to the book item, which applies a line-through style to it.
After a book is added to the list, the list in the local storage is
immediately updated. This ensures that the list in the local
storage is always up-to-date, even if the page is reloaded before it
is unloaded.
The loadListFromLocalStorage function is called when the script
runs to load the list from the local storage.
Please note that this code still does not remember the completed
status of the books. To add this feature, you would need to modify
the saveListToLocalStorage and loadListFromLocalStorage
functions to save and load this information. -->
```

Donald Trump's Resume

Name: Donald Trump

Date of Birth: June 14, 1946

Education

The Wharton School of the University of Pennsylvania - Bachelor's degree in Economics

Business Experience

President of The Trump Organization from 1971–2017

Executive producer and host of The Apprentice from 2004–2015

Political Experience

45th President of the United States from 2017–2021

Hide/Show Business Experience

```
<!DOCTYPE html>
<html>
<head>
    <title>Donald Trump's Resume</title>
    <style>
      body {
          font-family: Arial, sans-serif;
      }
    </style>
</head>
<body>
    <h1>Donald Trump's Resume</h1>
    <p>Name: Donald Trump</p>
    <p>Date of Birth: June 14, 1946</p>

    <h2>Education</h2>
    <p>The Wharton School of the University of Pennsylvania -
Bachelor's degree in Economics</p>

    <h2 id="business-header">Business Experience</h2>
    <div id="business-content">
       <p>President of The Trump Organization from 1971–
2017</p>
       <p>Executive producer and host of The Apprentice from
2004–2015</p>
    </div>

    <h2>Political Experience</h2>
```

22

```
<p>45th President of the United States from 2017–2021</p>

    <button id="toggle-button">Hide/Show Business
Experience</button>

    <script>
        document.getElementById('toggle-button').onclick =
function() {
            let content = document.getElementById('business-
content');
            let header = document.getElementById('business-
header');
            if (content.style.display === 'none') {
                content.style.display = 'block';
                header.style.display = 'block';
            } else {
                content.style.display = 'none';
                header.style.display = 'none';
            }
        }
    </script>
</body>
</html>
```

23

```
<!-- 'U+2013' and 'U+002D' are both Unicode code points, which
represent different characters in the Unicode standard:
1. 'U+2013' represents the En Dash (–). The en dash is used in
writing or typography to indicate a range of values, or a
relationship or connection between two things.

2. 'U+002D' represents the Hyphen-Minus (-). The hyphen-minus
character is a common, multipurpose character used in a lot of
places, most notably in mathematics to represent the subtraction
operator, and in writing as a hyphen or dash to join words or
separate syllables.

While they might look similar visually, they have different uses
and meanings in typography and text encoding. It's also worth
noting that not all fonts treat these characters the same way, so
the visual difference between the two can sometimes be quite
noticeable depending on the font used. -->
```

```
<!doctype html>
<html lang="ko">

<head>
    <title>My Online Resume</title>
    <meta charset="utf-8">
    <link rel="stylesheet" href="css/resume.css">

    <style>
        table {
            width: 80%;
            border: 1px solid #464646;
            border-collapse: collapse;
        }

        thead {
            background: #c0bdbd;
```

```
        }
      th,
      td {
          border: 1px solid #9f9d9d;
          padding: 5px;
          font-size: 0.8em;
      }
    </style>
</head>

<body>
    <div id="container">
      <aside>
        <div id="namecard">
            <img src="images/1997mypicture.jpg" alt=""
width="150px">
            <h1>Richard King</h1>
            <p>Every day is the best day of my life</p>
        </div>
        <div id="detail">
            <p>New York, USA</p>
            <p>google9876@gmail.com</p>
        </div>
        <div id="sns">
            <h2>Facebook</h2>
            <h2>YouTube</h2>
            <h2>Instagram</h2>

        </div>
      </aside>
      <div id="main">
        <section>
            <h2 class="subtitle">Let me introduce
myself.</h2>
            <p>I have a strong interest in <br><mark>front-
end web technologies, back-end programming</mark>, and
            book production.</p>
            <p>I am currently at my son's house in the United
States.</p>
        </section>

        <section>
            <h2 class="subtitle">Experience</h2>
```

```html
        <ul>
            <li>Web Design
                <ul>
                    <li>HTML </li>
                    <li>CSS </li>
                    <li>JavaScript</li>
                </ul>
            </li>
            <li>Back-end Tech.
                <ul>
                    <li>PHP </li>
                    <li>Database </li>
                    <li>Hosting</li>
                </ul>
            </li>
            <li>BOOK
                <ul>
                    <li>Coding Project </li>
                    <li>Animal & Plant Tale</li>
                    <li>Steel CNC Cutting Guidebook</li>
                </ul>
            </li>
        </ul>
</section>

<section>
    <h2 class="subtitle">Skills</h2>
    <ul>
        <li>Plasma Cutting </li>
        <li>English, Japanese, Korean </li>
        <li>Home Renovation</li>
    </ul>
</section>

<section>
    <h2 class="subtitle">Education</h2>
    <table>
        <caption>Educational Background</caption>
        <thead>
            <tr>
                <th>school</th>
                <th>major</th>
                <th>term</th>
                <th>status</th>
```

26

```html
            </tr>
          </thead>
          <tbody>
            <tr>
              <td>Kings College</td>
              <td>Computer Engineering</td>
              <td>2000.9 ~ 2004.8</td>
              <td>finish</td>
            </tr>
            <tr>
              <td>Graduate School</td>
              <td>Computer Science</td>
              <td>2006.3 ~ 2008.2</td>
              <td>finish</td>
            </tr>
          </tbody>
        </table>
      </section>
    </div>
  </div>
</body>

</html>

<!-- This coding is an upgrade of Kyunghee Ko's coding. -->
```

27

```
<!DOCTYPE html>
<html>
<head>
    <title>Image Gallery</title>
    <style>
        body {
            display: grid;
            grid-template-columns: repeat(auto-fill, minmax(200px,
1fr));
            grid-gap: 10px;
            padding: 10px;
            box-sizing: border-box;
        }

        .image {
            width: 100%;
            height: 0;
```

```
            padding-bottom: 100%;
            background-position: center;
            background-repeat: no-repeat;
            background-size: cover;
        }
    </style>
</head>
<body>
    <script>
        for (let i = 0; i < 100; i++) {
            let img = document.createElement('div');
            img.className = 'image';
            img.style.backgroundImage =
'url(https://placekitten.com/' + (200 + i % 10) + '/' + (200 + i %
10) + ')';
            document.body.appendChild(img);
        }
    </script>
</body>
</html>
```

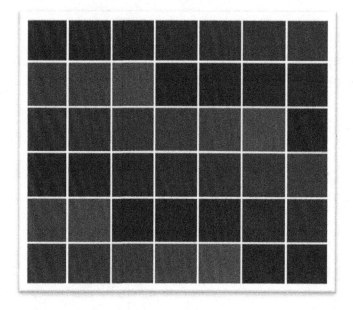

30

```
<!DOCTYPE html>
<html>
<head>
    <title>Image Gallery</title>
    <style>
        body {
            display: grid;
            grid-template-columns: repeat(auto-fill, minmax(200px,
1fr));
            grid-gap: 10px;
            padding: 10px;
            box-sizing: border-box;
        }

        .image {
            width: 100%;
            height: 0;
```

```
            padding-bottom: 100%;
            background-position: center;
            background-repeat: no-repeat;
            background-size: cover;
        }
    </style>
</head>
<body>
    <script>
        for (let i = 0; i < 100; i++) {
            let img = document.createElement('div');
            img.className = 'image';
            img.style.backgroundImage =
'url(https://via.placeholder.com/640x360/' + (200 + i % 10) + '/'
+ (200 + i % 10) + ')';
            document.body.appendChild(img);
        }
    </script>
</body>
</html>
```

31

32

```html
<!DOCTYPE html>
<html>
<head>
    <title>Image Gallery</title>
    <style>
        body {
            display: grid;
            grid-template-columns: repeat(auto-fill, minmax(200px,
1fr));
            grid-gap: 10px;
            padding: 10px;
            box-sizing: border-box;
        }

        .image {
            width: 100%;
```

```
            height: 0;
            padding-bottom: 100%;
            background-position: center;
            background-repeat: no-repeat;
            background-size: cover;
        }
    </style>
</head>
<body>
    <script>
        for (let i = 0; i < 100; i++) {
            let img = document.createElement('div');
            img.className = 'image';
            img.style.backgroundImage =
'url(https://loremflickr.com/' + (200 + i % 10) + '/' + (200 + i %
10) + ')';
            document.body.appendChild(img);
        }
    </script>
</body>
</html>
```

Tip Calculator

Total Bill:

100

Tip Percentage:

20

Calculate Tip

The tip amount is: $20.00

34

```
<!DOCTYPE html>
<html>
<body>

<h2>Tip Calculator</h2>

<form id="tipForm">
  <label for="bill">Total Bill:</label><br>
  <input type="number" id="bill" name="bill" value=""><br>
  <label for="percentage">Tip Percentage:</label><br>
  <input type="number" id="percentage" name="percentage"
value=""><br>
  <input type="button" value="Calculate Tip"
onclick="calculateTip()">
</form>

<p id="result"></p>
```

```
<script>
function calculateTip() {
  let bill = document.getElementById("bill").value;
  let percentage =
document.getElementById("percentage").value;

  let tip = bill * (percentage / 100);

  document.getElementById("result").innerHTML = "The tip
amount is: $" + tip.toFixed(2);
}
</script>

</body>
</html>
```

35

```
<!DOCTYPE html>
<html>

<head>
  <style>
    body {
      display: flex;
      justify-content: center;
      align-items: center;
      height: 100vh;
      background-color: #f2f2f2;
    }

    h2 {
      margin-bottom: 20px;
      background-color: #e26767;
      color: white;
      border-radius: 5px;
      text-align: center;
    }

    #tipForm {
      padding: 20px;
      background-color: #fff;
      border-radius: 10px;
```

36

```css
      box-shadow: 0 2px 5px rgba(0, 0, 0, 0.3);
      width: 300px;
      box-sizing: border-box;
    }

    #tipForm label {
      font-weight: bold;
      color: #333;
    }

    #tipForm input {
      width: 100%;
      padding: 10px;
      margin-bottom: 10px;
      border-radius: 4px;
      border: 1px solid #ccc;
      box-sizing: border-box;
    }

    #tipForm input[type="button"] {
      background-color: #4CAF50;
      color: white;
      border: none;
      cursor: pointer;
    }

    #tipForm input[type="button"]:hover {
      background-color: #2b42c0;
    }

    #result {
      margin-top: 20px;
      font-weight: bold;
    }
  </style>
</head>

<body>
  <div>
    <h2>Tip Calculator</h2>

    <div id="tipForm">
      <label for="bill">Total Bill:</label>
      <input type="number" id="bill" name="bill" value="">
```

37

```
        <label for="percentage">Tip Percentage:</label>
        <input type="number" id="percentage" name="percentage"
value="">
        <input type="button" value="Calculate Tip"
onclick="calculateTip()">
        <p id="result"></p>
      </div>
    </div>
    <script>
      function calculateTip() {
        let bill = document.getElementById("bill").value;
        let percentage =
document.getElementById("percentage").value;

        let tip = bill * (percentage / 100);

        document.getElementById("result").innerHTML = "The tip
amount is: $" + tip.toFixed(2);
      }
    </script>
</body>
</html>
```

38

<!-- This is an upgraded version of your Tip Calculator. I've added
styles using CSS, making use of the various properties such as
'flex', 'margin', 'padding', 'box-shadow', 'color', 'background-
color', 'border-radius', 'width', and 'height'.

In this version, I've added a flex container in the body tag to
center the tip calculator form in the middle of the page. The form
itself has been styled to have a white background with a box
shadow, a specific width, and some padding. The inputs have
been styled to take up the full width of the form, with some
padding and margin for better spacing. The calculate button has
also been given a background color and changes color when
hovered over. The result paragraph has been moved inside the
form for a cleaner look. -->

Registration Form

Name:

Rodrick Rules

Email:

75bc@gmail.com

Password:

••••••••••

Submit

Registration successful!

```
<!DOCTYPE html>
<html>
<body>

<h2>Registration Form</h2>

<form id="registrationForm">
  <label for="name">Name:</label><br>
  <input type="text" id="name" name="name" required><br>
  <label for="email">Email:</label><br>
  <input type="email" id="email" name="email" required><br>
  <label for="password">Password:</label><br>
  <input type="password" id="password" name="password"
required><br>
  <input type="submit" value="Submit">
</form>

<p id="feedback"></p>

<script>
document.getElementById("registrationForm").addEventListener("
submit", function(event){
  event.preventDefault();
```

```
let name = document.getElementById("name").value;
let email = document.getElementById("email").value;
let password = document.getElementById("password").value;

let feedback = document.getElementById("feedback");

if(name == ""){
  feedback.innerHTML = "Name is required.";
  return;
}

if(email == ""){
  feedback.innerHTML = "Email is required.";
  return;
}

if(password == ""){
  feedback.innerHTML = "Password is required.";
  return;
}

if(password.length < 8){
  feedback.innerHTML = "Password must be at least 8
characters.";
  return;
}

feedback.innerHTML = "Registration successful!";
});
</script>

</body>
</html>
```

40

```html
<!DOCTYPE html>
<html>

<head>
  <style>
    body {
      display: flex;
      flex-direction: column;
      align-items: center;
      justify-content: flex-start;
      height: 100vh;
      background-color: #f2f2f2;
      padding: 20px;
      box-sizing: border-box;
    }

    h2 {
      margin-bottom: 20px;
      padding: 10px;
      background-color: #7ea5e0;
      border-radius: 5px;
      color: white;
```

```
    }

    #registrationForm {
      padding: 20px;
      background-color: #fff;
      border-radius: 10px;
      box-shadow: 0 2px 5px rgba(0, 0, 0, 0.3);
      width: 300px;
      box-sizing: border-box;
    }

    #registrationForm label {
      font-weight: bold;
      color: #333;
    }

    #registrationForm input {
      width: 100%;
      padding: 10px;
      margin-bottom: 10px;
      border-radius: 4px;
      border: 1px solid #ccc;
      box-sizing: border-box;
    }

    #registrationForm input[type="button"] {
      background-color: #4CAF50;
      color: white;
      border: none;
      cursor: pointer;
    }

    #registrationForm input[type="button"]:hover {
      background-color: #3217e5;
    }

    #feedback {
      margin-top: 20px;
      font-weight: bold;
    }
  </style>
</head>

<body>
```

```html
<h2>Registration Form</h2>

<div id="registrationForm">
  <label for="name">Name:</label>
  <input type="text" id="name" name="name" required>
  <label for="email">Email:</label>
  <input type="email" id="email" name="email" required>
  <label for="password">Password:</label>
  <input type="password" id="password" name="password"
required>
  <input type="button" value="Submit" id="submitButton">

  <p id="feedback"></p>
</div>
```

```html
<script>
  document.getElementById("submitButton").addEventListener("
click", function (event) {

    let name = document.getElementById("name").value;
    let email = document.getElementById("email").value;
    let password =
document.getElementById("password").value;

    let feedback = document.getElementById("feedback");

    if (name == "") {
      feedback.innerHTML = "Name is required.";
      return;
    }

    if (email == "") {
      feedback.innerHTML = "Email is required.";
      return;
    }

    if (password == "") {
      feedback.innerHTML = "Password is required.";
      return;
    }
```

```
    if (password.length < 8) {
      feedback.innerHTML = "Password must be at least 8
characters.";
      return;
    }

    feedback.innerHTML = "Registration successful!";
  });
  </script>

</body>

</html>
```

<!-- This upgraded version uses CSS to style our registration form.

In this version, we've added a flex container in the body tag to center the registration form in the middle of the page. The form itself has been styled to have a white background with a box shadow, a specific width, and some padding. The inputs have been styled to take up the full width of the form, with some padding and margin for better spacing. The submit button has also been given a background color and changes color when hovered over. The feedback paragraph has been moved inside the form for a cleaner look. -->

44

Custom Countdown Timer

Hours:

`1`

Minutes:

`1`

Seconds:

`0`

Start Countdown

1h 0m 49s

```
<!DOCTYPE html>
<html>
<body>

<h2>Custom Countdown Timer</h2>

<form id="timerForm">
  <label for="hours">Hours:</label><br>
  <input type="number" id="hours" name="hours" min="0"
value="0"><br>
  <label for="minutes">Minutes:</label><br>
  <input type="number" id="minutes" name="minutes" min="0"
max="59" value="0"><br>
  <label for="seconds">Seconds:</label><br>
  <input type="number" id="seconds" name="seconds" min="0"
max="59" value="0"><br>
  <input type="button" value="Start Countdown"
onclick="startCountdown()">
</form>

<p id="countdown"></p>

<script>
let countdownInterval;
```

45

```
function startCountdown() {
  let hours = parseInt(document.getElementById("hours").value);
  let minutes =
parseInt(document.getElementById("minutes").value);
  let seconds =
parseInt(document.getElementById("seconds").value);

  // Convert all to seconds
  let totalSeconds = hours * 3600 + minutes * 60 + seconds;

  // Clear any existing interval
  if(countdownInterval){
    clearInterval(countdownInterval);
  }

  countdownInterval = setInterval(function() {
    if(totalSeconds < 0) {
      clearInterval(countdownInterval);
      document.getElementById("countdown").innerHTML =
"Countdown Finished!";
    } else {
      let hoursRemaining = Math.floor(totalSeconds / 3600);
      let minutesRemaining = Math.floor((totalSeconds % 3600) /
60);
      let secondsRemaining = totalSeconds % 60;
      document.getElementById("countdown").innerHTML =
hoursRemaining + "h " + minutesRemaining + "m " +
secondsRemaining + "s ";
      totalSeconds--;
    }
  }, 1000);
}
</script>

</body>
</html>
```

46

Custom Countdown Timer

Hours:

2

Minutes:

5

Seconds:

0

Start Countdown

2h 4m 42s

47

```
<!DOCTYPE html>
<html>

<head>
  <style>
    body {
      display: flex;
      flex-direction: column;
      align-items: center;
      justify-content: flex-start;
      font-family: Arial, sans-serif;
      background-color: #F5F5F5;
      padding: 20px;
      height: 100vh;
      margin: 0;
    }

    h2 {
      text-align: center;
      font-size: 24px;
      padding: 10px;
```

```css
    font-weight: bold;
    margin-bottom: 30px;
    background-color: #794646;
    color: white;
    border-radius: 5px;
}

#timerForm {
    background-color: #FFFFFF;
    box-shadow: 0px 0px 10px rgba(0, 0, 0, 0.1);
    padding: 20px;
    border-radius: 5px;
    width: 300px;
    display: flex;
    flex-direction: column;
}

#timerForm label {
    margin-bottom: 10px;
    font-weight: bold;
}

#timerForm input {
    margin-bottom: 15px;
    padding: 10px;
    border-radius: 5px;
    border: 1px solid #DDDDDD;
    font-size: 14px;
}

#countdown {
    font-size: 24px;
    font-weight: bold;
    text-align: center;
    margin-top: 20px;
    color: red;
}

#timerForm input[type="button"] {
    background-color: #4CAF50;
    color: white;
    border: none;
    cursor: pointer;
}
```

```css
    #timerForm input[type="button"]:hover {
      background-color: #3217e5;
    }
  </style>
</head>
```

```html
<body>

  <h2>Custom Countdown Timer</h2>

  <div id="timerForm">
    <label for="hours">Hours:</label>
    <input type="number" id="hours" name="hours" min="0"
value="0">
    <label for="minutes">Minutes:</label>
    <input type="number" id="minutes" name="minutes"
min="0" max="59" value="0">
    <label for="seconds">Seconds:</label>
    <input type="number" id="seconds" name="seconds"
min="0" max="59" value="0">
    <input type="button" value="Start Countdown"
onclick="startCountdown()">
  </div>

  <p id="countdown"></p>

  <script>

    let countdownInterval;

    function startCountdown() {
      let hours =
parseInt(document.getElementById("hours").value);
      let minutes =
parseInt(document.getElementById("minutes").value);
      let seconds =
parseInt(document.getElementById("seconds").value);

      // Convert all to seconds
      let totalSeconds = hours * 3600 + minutes * 60 + seconds;

      // Clear any existing interval
      if (countdownInterval) {
```

```
        clearInterval(countdownInterval);
    }

    countdownInterval = setInterval(function () {
      if (totalSeconds < 0) {
        clearInterval(countdownInterval);
        document.getElementById("countdown").innerHTML =
"Countdown Finished!";
      } else {
        let hoursRemaining = Math.floor(totalSeconds / 3600);
        let minutesRemaining = Math.floor((totalSeconds %
3600) / 60);
        let secondsRemaining = totalSeconds % 60;
        document.getElementById("countdown").innerHTML =
hoursRemaining + "h " + minutesRemaining + "m " +
secondsRemaining + "s ";
        totalSeconds--;
      }
    }, 1000);
  }
  </script>

</body>

</html>

<!-- This CSS will center the form in the middle of the page, add
some margin and padding to the elements, round the corners of
the form and input fields, and add a slight shadow to the form.
The fonts are also adjusted, with the countdown timer being
larger and bolder. -->
```

50

Custom Countdown Timer

Hours:

```
0
```

Minutes:

```
3
```

Seconds:

```
0
```

| Start Countdown | Stop Countdown | Reset Countdown |

0h 2m 55s

51

```
<!DOCTYPE html>
<html>

<body>

  <h2>Custom Countdown Timer</h2>

  <form id="timerForm">
    <label for="hours">Hours:</label><br>
    <input type="number" id="hours" name="hours" min="0"
value="0"><br>
    <label for="minutes">Minutes:</label><br>
    <input type="number" id="minutes" name="minutes"
min="0" max="59" value="0"><br>
    <label for="seconds">Seconds:</label><br>
    <input type="number" id="seconds" name="seconds"
min="0" max="59" value="0"><br>
    <input type="button" value="Start Countdown"
onclick="startCountdown()">
    <input type="button" value="Stop Countdown"
onclick="stopCountdown()">
    <input type="button" value="Reset Countdown"
onclick="resetCountdown()">
  </form>
```

```
<p id="countdown"></p>

<script>
  let countdownInterval;
  let totalSeconds;

  function startCountdown() {
    let hours =
parseInt(document.getElementById("hours").value);
    let minutes =
parseInt(document.getElementById("minutes").value);
    let seconds =
parseInt(document.getElementById("seconds").value);

    // Convert all to seconds
    totalSeconds = hours * 3600 + minutes * 60 + seconds;

    // Clear any existing interval
    if (countdownInterval) {
      clearInterval(countdownInterval);
    }

    countdownInterval = setInterval(function () {
      if (totalSeconds < 0) {
        clearInterval(countdownInterval);
        document.getElementById("countdown").innerHTML =
"Countdown Finished!";
      } else {
        let hoursRemaining = Math.floor(totalSeconds / 3600);
        let minutesRemaining = Math.floor((totalSeconds %
3600) / 60);
        let secondsRemaining = totalSeconds % 60;
        document.getElementById("countdown").innerHTML =
hoursRemaining + "h " + minutesRemaining + "m " +
secondsRemaining + "s ";
        totalSeconds--;
      }
    }, 1000);
  }

  function stopCountdown() {
    if (countdownInterval) {
      clearInterval(countdownInterval);
```

```
      }
    }

    function resetCountdown() {
      stopCountdown();
      totalSeconds = 0;
      document.getElementById("countdown").innerHTML = "";
      document.getElementById("hours").value = "0";
      document.getElementById("minutes").value = "0";
      document.getElementById("seconds").value = "0";
    }
  </script>

</body>

</html>
```

012_COUNT TIMER UP2

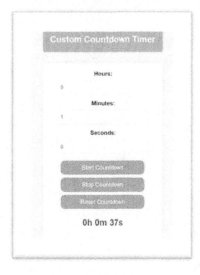

```
<!DOCTYPE html>
<html>

<head>
  <style>
    body {
      font-family: Arial, sans-serif;
      background-color: #F5F5F5;
      padding: 20px;
      display: flex;
      flex-direction: column;
      align-items: center;
      height: 100vh;
      margin: 0;
    }

    h2 {
      text-align: center;
      font-size: 24px;
```

```css
  font-weight: bold;
  margin-bottom: 30px;
  background-color: #e78b8b;
  color: white;
  box-shadow: 0px 0px 10px rgba(0, 0, 0, 0.1);
  padding: 20px;
  border-radius: 5px;
}
#timerForm {
  background-color: #FFFFFF;
  box-shadow: 0px 0px 10px rgba(0, 0, 0, 0.1);
  padding: 20px;
  border-radius: 5px;
  width: 300px;
  display: flex;
  flex-direction: column;
  align-items: center;
}
#timerForm label {
  margin-bottom: 10px;
  font-weight: bold;
}
#timerForm input {
  margin-bottom: 15px;
  padding: 10px;
  border-radius: 5px;
  border: 1px solid #DDDDDD;
  font-size: 14px;
  width: 80%;
}
#timerForm input[type="button"] {
  background-color: #4CAF50;
  /* Green */
  border: none;
```

```
    color: white;
    text-align: center;
    text-decoration: none;
    display: inline-block;
    font-size: 16px;
    margin: 4px 2px;
    cursor: pointer;
    border-radius: 12px;
}

#timerForm input[type="button"]:hover {
    background-color: #07de76;
}
#countdown {
    font-size: 24px;
    font-weight: bold;
    text-align: center;
    margin-top: 20px;
    color: rgba(27, 39, 203)
}
</style>
</head>

<body>

<h2>Custom Countdown Timer</h2>
<div id="timerForm">
    <label for="hours">Hours:</label>
    <input type="number" id="hours" name="hours" min="0"
value="0">
    <label for="minutes">Minutes:</label>
    <input type="number" id="minutes" name="minutes"
min="0" max="59" value="0">
    <label for="seconds">Seconds:</label>
```

```html
    <input type="number" id="seconds" name="seconds"
min="0" max="59" value="0">
    <input type="button" value="Start Countdown"
onclick="startCountdown()">
    <input type="button" value="Stop Countdown"
onclick="stopCountdown()">
    <input type="button" value="Reset Countdown"
onclick="resetCountdown()">

    <p id="countdown"></p>
  </div>

  <script>
    let countdownInterval;
    let totalSeconds;

    function startCountdown() {
      let hours =
parseInt(document.getElementById("hours").value);
      let minutes =
parseInt(document.getElementById("minutes").value);
      let seconds =
parseInt(document.getElementById("seconds").value);

      // Convert all to seconds
      totalSeconds = hours * 3600 + minutes * 60 + seconds;

      // Clear any existing interval
      if (countdownInterval) {
        clearInterval(countdownInterval);
      }

      countdownInterval = setInterval(function () {
        if (totalSeconds < 0) {
```

```
        clearInterval(countdownInterval);
        document.getElementById("countdown").innerHTML =
"Countdown Finished!";
      } else {
        let hoursRemaining = Math.floor(totalSeconds / 3600);
        let minutesRemaining = Math.floor((totalSeconds %
3600) / 60);
        let secondsRemaining = totalSeconds % 60;
        document.getElementById("countdown").innerHTML =
hoursRemaining + "h " + minutesRemaining + "m " +
secondsRemaining + "s ";
        totalSeconds--;
      }
    }, 1000);
  }

  function stopCountdown() {
    if (countdownInterval) {
      clearInterval(countdownInterval);
    }
  }

  function resetCountdown() {
    stopCountdown();
    totalSeconds = 0;
    document.getElementById("countdown").innerHTML = "";
    document.getElementById("hours").value = "0";
    document.getElementById("minutes").value = "0";
    document.getElementById("seconds").value = "0";
  }
  </script>
</body>
</html>
```

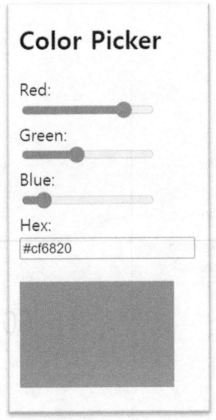

```
<!DOCTYPE html>
<html>
<body>

<h2>Color Picker</h2>

<form>
  <label for="red">Red:</label><br>
  <input type="range" id="red" name="red" min="0" max="255"
value="0" oninput="updateColor()"><br>
  <label for="green">Green:</label><br>
  <input type="range" id="green" name="green" min="0"
max="255" value="0" oninput="updateColor()"><br>
  <label for="blue">Blue:</label><br>
  <input type="range" id="blue" name="blue" min="0"
max="255" value="0" oninput="updateColor()"><br>
```

```
<label for="hex">Hex:</label><br>
<input type="text" id="hex" name="hex"
oninput="hexToRgb()"><br>
</form><br>

<div id="colorDisplay" style="width: 150px; height:
100px;"></div>

<script>
function updateColor() {
  let red = document.getElementById("red").value;
  let green = document.getElementById("green").value;
  let blue = document.getElementById("blue").value;

  let hexColor = "#" + ((1 << 24) + (red << 16) + (green << 8)
+ parseInt(blue)).toString(16).slice(1);
  document.getElementById("colorDisplay").style.backgroundColo
r = hexColor;
  document.getElementById("hex").value = hexColor;
}

function hexToRgb() {
  let hex = document.getElementById("hex").value;

  if (!/^#[0-9A-F]{6}$/i.test(hex)) {
    alert("Please enter a valid hex color.");
    return;
  }

  let bigint = parseInt(hex.slice(1), 16);
  let r = (bigint >> 16) & 255;
  let g = (bigint >> 8) & 255;
  let b = bigint & 255;

  document.getElementById("red").value = r;
  document.getElementById("green").value = g;
  document.getElementById("blue").value = b;

  document.getElementById("colorDisplay").style.backgroundColo
r = hex;
}
</script>

</body>
```

60

</html>

<!-- This is a color picker HTML page where you can create a color by adjusting the red, green, and blue (RGB) values or by entering a hex color code. Here's a breakdown of the code:

HTML Structure: The HTML page structure includes the <!DOCTYPE html>, <html>, and <body> tags. Inside the <body> tag, there are various elements such as <h2>, <form>, and <div>.

Color Picker Form: Inside the <form> tag, there are several <input> elements of type "range" for red, green, and blue colors, each ranging from 0 to 255, and an <input> element of type "text" for the hex color code. The 'oninput' attribute on these elements calls a JavaScript function every time the user changes the input value.

Color Display Area: There's a <div> element with the id "colorDisplay" that shows the color generated from the RGB or Hex input.

JavaScript Functions: Inside the <script> tag, there are two JavaScript functions:

updateColor(): This function is called when the RGB color sliders are moved. It reads the values of the red, green, and blue sliders, converts these values to a hexadecimal color code, and then sets the background color of the "colorDisplay" div to this color. It also sets the hex color code input field to this value.
hexToRgb(): This function is called when the hex color code input field is changed. It converts the hex color code to RGB values, and then sets the RGB color sliders to these values. It also sets the background color of the "colorDisplay" div to the entered hex color. If the entered hex color is not valid, it alerts the user.
The hexadecimal color code is a six-digit, three-byte hexadecimal number: the first two bytes represent the red component, the next two green, and the last two blue. The bytes are each written as two hexadecimal digits and represent a number between 0 and 255. For example, white is represented as #FFFFFF because it is the combination of maximum amounts of red, green, and blue. --
>

Simple Quiz

1. What is the capital of France?

Paris

2. Who wrote "1984"?

3. What is the square root of 81?

9

Submit Quiz

You scored 2 out of 3.

```
<!DOCTYPE html>
<html>
<head>
   <title>Simple Quiz</title>
</head>
<body>
   <h1>Simple Quiz</h1>

   <form id="quiz-form">
      <p>1. What is the capital of France?</p>
      <input type="text" id="q1" name="q1"><br>

      <p>2. Who wrote "1984"?</p>
      <input type="text" id="q2" name="q2"><br>

      <p>3. What is the square root of 81?</p>
      <input type="text" id="q3" name="q3"><br><br>

      <input type="submit" value="Submit Quiz">
   </form>
```

```
    <p id="score"></p>

    <script>
        document.getElementById('quiz-
form').addEventListener('submit', function(event) {
            event.preventDefault();

            let score = 0;

            if
(document.getElementById('q1').value.trim().toLowerCase() ===
'paris') {
                score++;
            }
            if
(document.getElementById('q2').value.trim().toLowerCase() ===
'george orwell') {
                score++;
            }
            if (document.getElementById('q3').value.trim() ===
'9') {
                score++;
            }

            document.getElementById('score').textContent = 'You
scored ' + score + ' out of 3.';
        });
    </script>
</body>
</html>
```

Who is the current president of USA?

Barack Obama

Donald Trump

Joe Biden

Hillary Clinton

Next Question

64

```
<!DOCTYPE html>
<html>

<head>
  <style>
    body {
      display: flex;
      flex-direction: column;
      align-items: center;
      justify-content: center;
      height: 100vh;
      margin: 0;
      background-color: #fafafa;
      font-family: Arial, sans-serif;
    }

    .quiz-container {
      display: flex;
      flex-direction: column;
```

```css
    align-items: center;
    justify-content: center;
    width: 60%;
    padding: 20px;
    border-radius: 10px;
    box-shadow: 0px 0px 10px 2px #888;
    background-color: #fff;
}

.quiz-container h2 {
    font-size: 2em;
    font-weight: 700;
    color: #333;
    text-align: center;
}

.options {
    display: flex;
    flex-direction: column;
    width: 100%;
    margin-top: 20px;
}

.option {
    margin: 10px 0;
    padding: 10px;
    border-radius: 5px;
    box-shadow: 0px 0px 5px 1px #888;
    cursor: pointer;
}

.option:hover {
    background-color: #f0f0f0;
}

button {
    padding: 10px;
    border-radius: 5px;
    box-shadow: 0px 0px 10px 2px #888;
    background-color: #424c8d;
    color: white;
}

button:hover{
```

```
      background-color: blue;
    }
  </style>
</head>

<body>

  <div class="quiz-container" id="quiz-container">
    <h2 id="question"></h2>
    <div class="options" id="option-container">
    </div>
    <button onclick="loadNextQuestion()">Next
Question</button>
  </div>

  <script>
    let questions = [
      {
        question: 'What is the capital of France?',
        options: ['Paris', 'Berlin', 'London', 'Madrid'],
        correctAnswer: 'Paris'
      },
      {
        question: 'Who is the current president of USA?',
        options: ['Barack Obama', 'Donald Trump', 'Joe Biden',
'Hillary Clinton'],
        correctAnswer: 'Joe Biden'
      },
      {
        question: 'What is the process by which plants make their
own food called?',
        options: ['Cellular Respiration', 'Digestion',
'Photosynthesis', 'Osmosis'],
        correctAnswer: 'Photosynthesis'
      },
      {
        question: 'What is the smallest unit of life in all living
organisms called?',
        options: ['Cell', 'Molecule', 'Organ', 'Tissue'],
        correctAnswer: 'Cell'
      },
      {
        question: 'What is the force that pulls objects towards each
other called?',
```

```javascript
        options: ['Friction', 'Magnetic force', 'Electric force',
'Gravity'],
        correctAnswer: 'Gravity'
    },
    {
        question: ' What are the building blocks of proteins?',
        options: ['Nucleotides', 'Amino acids', 'Fatty acids',
'Glucose'],
        correctAnswer: 'Amino acids'
    },
    {
        question: 'What are the four largest planets in our solar
system called?',
        options: ['Earth, Mars, Venus, Mercury', 'Mars, Jupiter,
Saturn, Venus', 'Mercury, Venus, Earth, Mars', 'Jupiter, Saturn,
Uranus, Neptune'],
        correctAnswer: 'Jupiter, Saturn, Uranus, Neptune'
    },
    // add more questions following the same structure
    ];

    let currentQuestion = 0;

    function loadQuestion() {
    let questionContainer =
document.getElementById('question');
    let optionContainer = document.getElementById('option-
container');

    questionContainer.textContent =
questions[currentQuestion].question;
    optionContainer.innerHTML = '';

    for (let i = 0; i < questions[currentQuestion].options.length;
i++) {
        let option = document.createElement('div');
        option.className = 'option';
        option.textContent =
questions[currentQuestion].options[i];
        option.addEventListener('click', function () {
          if (option.textContent ===
questions[currentQuestion].correctAnswer) {
            option.style.backgroundColor = 'lightgreen';
          } else {
```

67

```
          option.style.backgroundColor = 'salmon';
        }
      });
      optionContainer.appendChild(option);
    }
  }

  function loadNextQuestion() {
    currentQuestion++;
    if (currentQuestion < questions.length) {
      loadQuestion();
    } else {
      alert('Quiz finished!');
    }
  }

  loadQuestion();
</script>

</body>

</html>
```

68

```
<!-- This is another simple quiz application using HTML, CSS, and
JavaScript. I've styled the application with some of the properties.
This code only has a few questions for demonstration purposes,
but you can easily extend this to more questions by following the
same structure for each question in the JavaScript array of
objects.
```

```
In this code, when you click an option, it changes color based on
whether it's the correct answer or not. After you have gone
through all questions, an alert will notify you that the quiz is
finished. You can modify this code to add more features as per
your needs. -->
```

Temperature:

47

○ Fahrenheit to Celsius

◉ Celsius to Fahrenheit

Convert

116.60 Fahrenheit

69

```html
<!DOCTYPE html>
<html>

<head>
  <title>Temperature Converter</title>
  <style>
    body {
      font-family: Arial, sans-serif;
    }

    .container {
      margin-top: 50px;
      text-align: center;
    }
  </style>
</head>

<body>

  <div class="container">
    <label for="temp">Temperature:</label><br>
    <input type="text" id="temp" name="temp"><br>
    <input type="radio" id="f_to_c" name="conversion"
value="f_to_c">
    <label for="f_to_c">Fahrenheit to Celsius</label><br>
    <input type="radio" id="c_to_f" name="conversion"
value="c_to_f">
    <label for="c_to_f">Celsius to Fahrenheit</label><br>
```

```
    <button onclick="convertTemperature()">Convert</button>
    <p id="output"></p>
  </div>

  <script>
    function convertTemperature() {
      let temp = document.getElementById('temp').value;
      let output = document.getElementById('output');

      if (document.getElementById('f_to_c').checked) {
        output.innerHTML = ((temp - 32) * 5 / 9).toFixed(2) + '
Celsius';
      } else if (document.getElementById('c_to_f').checked) {
        output.innerHTML = ((temp * 9 / 5) + 32).toFixed(2) + '
Fahrenheit';
      } else {
        output.innerHTML = 'Please select conversion method.';
      }
    }
  </script>

</body>

</html>
```

70

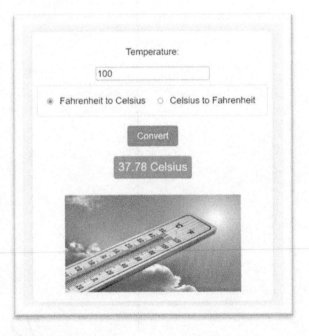

```
<!DOCTYPE html>
<html>

<head>
  <title>Temperature Converter</title>
  <style>
    body {
      font-family: Arial, sans-serif;
      display: flex;
      justify-content: center;
      align-items: center;
      height: 100vh;
      background-color: #f5f5f5;
    }

    .container {
      display: flex;
      flex-direction: column;
      align-items: center;
      padding: 20px;
      border-radius: 10px;
      box-shadow: 0px 0px 15px rgba(0, 0, 0, 0.1);
```

```css
  background-color: #ffffff;
}

label,
input[type="text"] {
  font-size: 1.2em;
  margin: 10px;
}

.radio-container {
  display: flex;
  justify-content: space-around;
  border: 1px solid #cccccc;
  padding: 10px;
  border-radius: 5px;
  width: 100%;
}

.radio-container div {
  display: flex;
  align-items: center;
}

button {
  padding: 10px 20px;
  font-size: 1.2em;
  color: #ffffff;
  background-color: #007bff;
  border: none;
  border-radius: 5px;
  cursor: pointer;
  margin-top: 20px;
}

button:hover {
  background-color: #0056b3;
}

#output {
  padding: 10px;
  border: none;
  border-radius: 5px;
  margin-top: 20px;
  font-size: 1.5em;
```

```
      background-color: #b07c02;
      color: white;
    }

    img {
      width: 80%;
      margin-top: 10px;
    }
  </style>
</head>

<body>

  <div class="container">
    <label for="temp">Temperature:</label>
    <input type="text" id="temp" name="temp">
    <div class="radio-container">
      <div>
        <input type="radio" id="f_to_c" name="conversion"
value="f_to_c">
        <label for="f_to_c">Fahrenheit to Celsius</label>
      </div>
      <div>
        <input type="radio" id="c_to_f" name="conversion"
value="c_to_f">
        <label for="c_to_f">Celsius to Fahrenheit</label>
      </div>
    </div>
    <button onclick="convertTemperature()">Convert</button>
    <p id="output"></p>
    <img id="thermometer" src="thermometer.jpg"
alt="thermometer image" width="300" height="200">
  </div>

  <script>
    function convertTemperature() {
      let temp = document.getElementById('temp').value;
      let output = document.getElementById('output');

      if (document.getElementById('f_to_c').checked) {
        output.innerHTML = ((temp - 32) * 5 / 9).toFixed(2) + '
Celsius';
      } else if (document.getElementById('c_to_f').checked) {
```

73

```
      output.innerHTML = ((temp * 9 / 5) + 32).toFixed(2) + '
Fahrenheit';
    } else {
      output.innerHTML = 'Please select conversion method.';
    }
  }
 </script>

</body>

</html>

<!-- This modification uses flexbox for arranging the radio buttons
and their labels side by side. A border is added around each radio
button and its label using a div element.

In this version, the radio buttons and their labels are grouped
together using div elements, and these div elements are placed
inside a parent container with class .radio-container. This parent
container is styled to provide the border and flexbox layout. -->
```

Roll the Dice (1/6)

2

Roll the Lotto (1/45)

44

```
<!DOCTYPE html>
<html>

<head>
  <title>Dice Roll</title>
  <!-- <link rel="stylesheet" type="text/css" href="styles.css"> --
>
  <style>
    body {
      font-family: Arial, sans-serif;
      text-align: center;
      padding-top: 50px;
    }

    #container {
      width: 300px;
      margin: 0 auto;
    }

    #roll-dice-button, #roll-dice-button2 {
      padding: 10px 20px;
      font-size: 20px;
      margin-bottom: 20px;
    }

    #result, #result2 {
```

```
      font-size: 40px;
    }
  </style>
</head>

<body>
  <div id="container">
    <button id="roll-dice-button">Roll the Dice (1/6)</button>
    <div id="result">0</div>
  </div><hr>

  <div id="container2">
    <button id="roll-dice-button2">Roll the Lotto
(1/45)</button>
    <div id="result2">0</div>
  </div>
  <!-- <script src="script.js"></script> -->
  <script>
    document.getElementById('roll-dice-button').onclick = function
() {
      let result = Math.floor(Math.random() * 6) + 1;
      document.getElementById('result').innerHTML = result;
    };

    document.getElementById('roll-dice-button2').onclick =
function () {
      let result = Math.floor(Math.random() * 45) + 1;
      document.getElementById('result2').innerHTML = result;
    };

  </script>
</body>

</html>
```

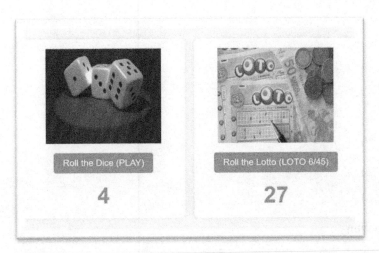

```
<!DOCTYPE html>
<html>

<head>
  <title>Dice Roll</title>
  <style>
    body {
      font-family: Arial, sans-serif;
      display: flex;
      justify-content: center;
      align-items: center;
      height: 100vh;
      background-color: #f5f5f5;
      flex-direction: row;
      gap: 20px;
    }

    .container {
      display: flex;
      flex-direction: column;
      align-items: center;
      padding: 20px;
      border-radius: 10px;
      box-shadow: 0px 0px 15px rgba(0, 0, 0, 0.1);
      background-color: #ffffff;
      width: 80%;
      max-width: 500px;
```

```css
      }
    #result,
    #result2 {
      font-size: 3em;
      font-weight: bold;
      color: #007bff;
      margin-top: 20px;
    }

    button {
      padding: 10px 20px;
      font-size: 1.2em;
      color: #ffffff;
      background-color: #007bff;
      border: none;
      border-radius: 5px;
      cursor: pointer;
      margin-top: 20px;
    }

    button:hover {
      background-color: #0056b3;
    }

    img {
      width: 80%;
      max-width: 300px;
    }
  </style>
</head>

<body>
  <div class="container">
    <img id="dice-image" src="dice.jpg" alt="Dice image"
width="300" height="200">
    <button id="roll-dice-button">Roll the Dice (PLAY)</button>
    <div id="result">0</div>
  </div>

  <div class="container">
    <img id="lotto-image" src="lotto.jpg" alt="Lotto image"
width="300" height="200">
```

```
    <button id="roll-dice-button2">Roll the Lotto (LOTO
6/45)</button>
    <div id="result2">0</div>
  </div>

  <script>
    document.getElementById('roll-dice-button').onclick = function
() {
      let result = Math.floor(Math.random() * 6) + 1;
      document.getElementById('result').innerHTML = result;
    };

    document.getElementById('roll-dice-button2').onclick =
function () {
      let result = Math.floor(Math.random() * 45) + 1;
      document.getElementById('result2').innerHTML = result;
    };
  </script>
</body>

</html>
```

79

```
<!DOCTYPE html>
<html>
<style>
  body {
    margin: 20px;
  }

  #calculator {
    width: 200px;
    margin: auto;
    padding: 20px;
    background: #ddd;
    border-radius: 5px;
  }

  #display {
    width: 100%;
    height: 30px;
    margin-bottom: 10px;
  }

  .button,
```

```css
.operator {
  width: 45px;
  height: 45px;
  margin: 2px;
  cursor: pointer;
  font-size: 18px;
}

#clear,
#equals {
  width: 94px;
  height: 30px;
  margin-top: 10px;
}
</style>
```

```html
<body>
  <div id="calculator">
    <input type="text" id="display" disabled>
    <div id="buttons">
      <button class="button" value="1">1</button>
      <button class="button" value="2">2</button>
      <button class="button" value="3">3</button>
      <button class="button" value="4">4</button>
      <button class="button" value="5">5</button>
      <button class="button" value="6">6</button>
      <button class="button" value="7">7</button>
      <button class="button" value="8">8</button>
      <button class="button" value="9">9</button>
      <button class="button" value="0">0</button>
      <button class="button" value=".">.</button>
      <button class="operator" value="+">+</button>
      <button class="operator" value="-">-</button>
      <button class="operator" value="*">*</button>
      <button class="operator" value="/">/</button>
      <button id="equals" value="=">=</button>
      <button id="clear">C</button>
    </div>
  </div>
  <script>
    let display = document.getElementById('display');
    let buttons =
Array.from(document.getElementsByClassName('button'));
```

```
    let operators =
Array.from(document.getElementsByClassName('operator'));
    let equals = document.getElementById('equals');
    let clear = document.getElementById('clear');

    buttons.map(button => {
      button.addEventListener('click', (e) => {
        display.value += e.target.value;
      })
    });

    operators.map(operator => {
      operator.addEventListener('click', (e) => {
        display.value += e.target.value;
      })
    });

    equals.addEventListener('click', () => {
      try {
        display.value = eval(display.value);
      } catch {
        display.value = "Error";
      }
    });

    clear.addEventListener('click', () => {
      display.value = '';
    });

  </script>
</body>

</html>
```

```
<!DOCTYPE html>
<html>

<head>
  <title>Digital Clock</title>
  <!-- <link rel="stylesheet" type="text/css" href="styles.css"> --
>
  <style>
    body {
      display: flex;
      justify-content: center;
      align-items: center;
      height: 100vh;
      background-color: #333;
      color: white;
      font-family: Arial, sans-serif;
    }

    #clock {
      font-size: 60px;
    }
  </style>
</head>

<body>
```

83

```html
<h1>Digital Clock</h1><pre>    </pre>
<div id="clock"></div>
<!-- <script src="script.js"></script> -->
<script>
  function updateClock() {
    const now = new Date();
    let hours = now.getHours();
    let minutes = now.getMinutes();
    let seconds = now.getSeconds();

    // Pad with a zero if needed
    hours = hours < 10 ? '0' + hours : hours;
    minutes = minutes < 10 ? '0' + minutes : minutes;
    seconds = seconds < 10 ? '0' + seconds : seconds;

    const timeString = `${hours}:${minutes}:${seconds}`;

    document.getElementById('clock').textContent = timeString;
  }

  // Update the clock immediately and then every second
  updateClock();
  setInterval(updateClock, 1000);

</script>
</body>

</html>
```

84

```
<!DOCTYPE html>
<html>

<head>
  <title>Digital Clock</title>
  <style>
    body {
      display: flex;
      flex-direction: column;
      justify-content: center;
      align-items: center;
      height: 100vh;
      background-color: #334;
      color: white;
      font-family: Arial, sans-serif;
      margin: 0;
      padding: 0;
      box-sizing: border-box;
    }

    .clock-container {
      display: flex;
      flex-direction: column;
      justify-content: center;
      align-items: center;
      border: 2px solid white;
```

```
      border-radius: 20px;
      padding: 20px;
      background-color: rgba(0, 0, 0, 0.6);
      box-shadow: 0px 0px 20px 0px rgba(255, 255, 255, 0.75);
    }

    #date {
      font-size: 25px;
      font-weight: bold;
      margin-bottom: 20px;
      text-align: center;
    }

    #clock {
      font-size: 60px;
      font-weight: bold;
      text-align: center;
    }
  </style>
</head>

<body>
  <div class="clock-container">
    <div id="date"></div>
    <div id="clock"></div>
  </div>

  <script>
    function updateClockAndDate() {
      const now = new Date();
      let hours = now.getHours();
      let minutes = now.getMinutes();
      let seconds = now.getSeconds();

      // Format the date
      let year = now.getFullYear();
      let month = now.getMonth() + 1; // January is 0!
      let day = now.getDate();

      // Pad with a zero if needed
      hours = hours < 10 ? '0' + hours : hours;
      minutes = minutes < 10 ? '0' + minutes : minutes;
      seconds = seconds < 10 ? '0' + seconds : seconds;
      month = month < 10 ? '0' + month : month;
```

86

```
    day = day < 10 ? '0' + day : day;

    const timeString = `${hours}:${minutes}:${seconds}`;
    const dateString = `${year}-${month}-${day}`;

    document.getElementById('clock').textContent = timeString;
    document.getElementById('date').textContent = dateString;
  }

    // Update the clock and date immediately and then every
second
    updateClockAndDate();
    setInterval(updateClockAndDate, 1000);
  </script>
</body>

</html>
```

Look again at that dot. That's here. That's home.
That's us. On it everyone you love, everyone you
know, everyone you ever heard of, every human
being who ever was, lived out their lives.

New Quote (Carl Sagan)

88

```html
<!DOCTYPE html>
<html>

<head>
  <title>Random Quote Generator</title>
  <!-- <link rel="stylesheet" type="text/css" href="styles.css"> -->
  <style>
    body {
      font-family: Arial, sans-serif;
      text-align: center;
      padding: 20px;
    }

    #quote-display {
      margin: 20px;
      font-size: 24px;
    }

    button {
      padding: 10px 20px;
      font-size: 20px;
      cursor: pointer;
    }
  </style>
</head>

<body>
  <div id="quote-display">
    <p id="quote"></p>
  </div>
```

```html
    <button id="new-quote-button">New Quote (Carl
Sagan)</button>

    <!-- <script src="script.js"></script> -->

    <script>
    // This array holds the quotes that will be randomly displayed
    let quotes = [
    "Somewhere, something incredible is waiting to be known.",
"We are a way for the cosmos to know itself.",
"Science is a way of thinking much more than it is a body of
knowledge.",
"For small creatures such as we the vastness is bearable only
through love.",
"We're made of star stuff. We are a way for the universe to know
itself.",
"Extraordinary claims require extraordinary evidence.",
"In science it often happens that scientists say, 'You know that's a
really good argument; my position is mistaken,' and then they
would actually change their minds and you never hear that old
view from them again.",
"The cosmos is within us. We are made of star-stuff. We are a
way for the universe to know itself.",
"The beauty of a living thing is not the atoms that go into it, but
the way those atoms are put together.",
"It is far better to grasp the universe as it really is than to persist
in delusion, however satisfying and reassuring.",
"We can judge our progress by the courage of our questions and
the depth of our answers, our willingness to embrace what is true
rather than what feels good.",
"The universe is not required to be in perfect harmony with
human ambition.",
"One of the saddest lessons of history is this: If we've been
bamboozled long enough, we tend to reject any evidence of the
bamboozle. We're no longer interested in finding out the truth.",
"Look again at that dot. That's here. That's home. That's us. On it
everyone you love, everyone you know, everyone you ever heard
of, every human being who ever was, lived out their lives.",
"Imagination will often carry us to worlds that never were, but
without it we go nowhere.",
"The nitrogen in our DNA, the calcium in our teeth, the iron in our
blood, the carbon in our apple pies were made in the interiors of
collapsing stars. We are made of starstuff.",
```

```
"Who are we? We find that we live on an insignificant planet of a
humdrum star lost in a galaxy tucked away in some forgotten
corner of a universe in which there are far more galaxies than
people.",
"Books break the shackles of time – proof that humans can work
magic.",
"It pays to keep an open mind, but not so open your brains fall
out.",
"Our species needs, and deserves, a citizenry with minds wide
awake and a basic understanding of how the world works.",
    // Add as many quotes as you like...
  ];

  // This function selects a random quote from the array
  function getRandomQuote() {
    let randomIndex = Math.floor(Math.random() *
quotes.length);
    return quotes[randomIndex];
  }

  // This function updates the text of the #quote paragraph with
a new random quote
  function displayNewQuote() {
    let quote = getRandomQuote();
    document.getElementById('quote').textContent = quote;
  }

  // This event listener calls the displayNewQuote function each
time the button is clicked
  document.getElementById('new-quote-
button').addEventListener('click', displayNewQuote);

  // This line displays a quote when the page is first loaded
  window.onload = displayNewQuote;

  </script>
</body>

</html>
```

We can judge our progress by the courage of our questions and the depth of our answers, our willingness to embrace what is true rather than what feels good.

New Quote (Carl Sagan)

91

```
<!DOCTYPE html>
<html>

<head>
  <title>Random Quote Generator</title>
  <style>
    body {
      display: flex;
      flex-direction: row;
      justify-content: center;
      align-items: center;
      height: 100vh;
      background-color: #eee;
      color: black;
      font-family: Arial, sans-serif;
      margin: 0;
      padding: 0;
      box-sizing: border-box;
    }

    #image-display {
      width: 40%;
      height: 80vh;
```

```
      background: url('carl_sagan.jpg') no-repeat center
center/cover;
      border-radius: 10px;
      margin-right: 20px;
      box-shadow: 0px 0px 10px 0px rgba(0, 0, 0, 0.75);
    }

    #quote-display {
      width: 40%;
      height: 80vh;
      display: flex;
      flex-direction: column;
      justify-content: center;
      align-items: center;
      border: 2px solid #333;
      border-radius: 10px;
      padding: 20px;
      background-color: rgba(255, 255, 255, 0.9);
      box-shadow: 0px 0px 10px 0px rgba(0, 0, 0, 0.75);
    }

    #quote {
      font-size: 24px;
      font-weight: bold;
      margin-bottom: 20px;
      text-align: center;
    }

    button {
      padding: 10px 20px;
      font-size: 20px;
      cursor: pointer;
      margin-top: 20px;
    }
  </style>
</head>

<body>
  <div id="image-display"></div>
  <div id="quote-display">
    <p id="quote"></p>
    <button id="new-quote-button">New Quote (Carl
Sagan)</button>
  </div>
```

```
<script>
  // This array holds the quotes that will be randomly displayed
  let quotes = [
    "Somewhere, something incredible is waiting to be known.",
    "We are a way for the cosmos to know itself.",
    "Science is a way of thinking much more than it is a body of
knowledge.",
    "For small creatures such as we the vastness is bearable only
through love.",
    "We're made of star stuff. We are a way for the universe to
know itself.",
    "Extraordinary claims require extraordinary evidence.",
    "In science it often happens that scientists say, 'You know
that's a really good argument; my position is mistaken,' and then
they would actually change their minds and you never hear that
old view from them again.",
    "The cosmos is within us. We are made of star-stuff. We are
a way for the universe to know itself.",
    "The beauty of a living thing is not the atoms that go into it,
but the way those atoms are put together.",
    "It is far better to grasp the universe as it really is than to
persist in delusion, however satisfying and reassuring.",
    "We can judge our progress by the courage of our questions
and the depth of our answers, our willingness to embrace what is
true rather than what feels good.",
    "The universe is not required to be in perfect harmony with
human ambition.",
    "One of the saddest lessons of history is this: If we've been
bamboozled long enough, we tend to reject any evidence of the
bamboozle. We're no longer interested in finding out the truth.",
    "Look again at that dot. That's here. That's home. That's us.
On it everyone you love, everyone you know, everyone you ever
heard of, every human being who ever was, lived out their lives.",
    "Imagination will often carry us to worlds that never were,
but without it we go nowhere.",
    "The nitrogen in our DNA, the calcium in our teeth, the iron
in our blood, the carbon in our apple pies were made in the
interiors of collapsing stars. We are made of starstuff.",
    "Who are we? We find that we live on an insignificant planet
of a humdrum star lost in a galaxy tucked away in some forgotten
corner of a universe in which there are far more galaxies than
people.",
```

93

```
        "Books break the shackles of time – proof that humans can
work magic.",
        "It pays to keep an open mind, but not so open your brains
fall out.",
        "Our species needs, and deserves, a citizenry with minds
wide awake and a basic understanding of how the world works.",
        // Add as many quotes as you like...
    ];

    // This function selects a random quote from the array
    function getRandomQuote() {
    let randomIndex = Math.floor(Math.random() *
quotes.length);
        return quotes[randomIndex];
    }
    // This function updates the text of the #quote paragraph with
a new random quote
    function displayNewQuote() {
    let quote = getRandomQuote();
    document.getElementById('quote').textContent = quote;
    }
    // This event listener calls the displayNewQuote function each
time the button is clicked
    document.getElementById('new-quote-
button').addEventListener('click', displayNewQuote);

    // This line displays a quote when the page is first loaded
    window.onload = displayNewQuote;
  </script>
</body>
</html>
<!-- This version of the Random Quote Generator displays an
image of Carl Sagan on the left side and a random quote on the
right side. Both the image and quote containers have a border,
padding, box-shadow, border-radius, width, and height. The quote
is bold and centered. -->
```

The harder the conflict, the more glorious the triumph.

New Quote (Thomas Paine)

```
<!DOCTYPE html>
<html>

<head>
  <title>Random Quote Generator</title>
  <!-- <link rel="stylesheet" type="text/css" href="styles.css"> --
>
  <style>
    body {
      font-family: Arial, sans-serif;
      text-align: center;
      padding: 20px;
    }

    #quote-display {
      margin: 20px;
      font-size: 24px;
    }

    button {
      padding: 10px 20px;
      font-size: 20px;
      cursor: pointer;
    }
  </style>
</head>

<body>
  <div id="quote-display">
    <p id="quote"></p>
  </div>
  <button id="new-quote-button">New Quote (Thomas
Paine)</button>
```

95

```
<!-- <script src="script.js"></script> -->

<script>
  // This array holds the quotes that will be randomly displayed
  let quotes = [
    "These are the times that try men's souls.",
"The harder the conflict, the more glorious the triumph.",
"What we obtain too cheap, we esteem too lightly: it is dearness
only that gives every thing its value.",
"The mind once enlightened cannot again become dark.",
"The world is my country, all mankind are my brethren, and to do
good is my religion.",
"Reason obeys itself; and ignorance submits to whatever is
dictated to it.",
"He that would make his own liberty secure, must guard even his
enemy from oppression; for if he violates this duty, he establishes
a precedent that will reach to himself.",
"It is necessary to the happiness of man that he be mentally
faithful to himself.",
"When we are planning for posterity, we ought to remember that
virtue is not hereditary.",
"Those who expect to reap the blessings of freedom, must, like
men, undergo the fatigue of supporting it.",
"A long habit of not thinking a thing wrong, gives it a superficial
appearance of being right.",
"Tyranny, like hell, is not easily conquered; yet we have this
consolation with us, that the harder the conflict, the more glorious
the triumph.",
"Character is much easier kept than recovered.",
"He who dares not offend cannot be honest.",
"Government, even in its best state, is but a necessary evil; in its
worst state, an intolerable one.",
"My country is the world, and my religion is to do good.",
"The real man smiles in trouble, gathers strength from distress,
and grows brave by reflection.",
"Every science has for its basis a system of principles as fixed and
unalterable as those by which the universe is regulated and
governed.",
"It is the duty of every patriot to protect his country from its
government.",
"Independence is my happiness, and I view things as they are,
without regard to place or person; my country is the world, and
my religion is to do good.",
    // Add as many quotes as you like...
```

```
    ];

    // This function selects a random quote from the array
    function getRandomQuote() {
      let randomIndex = Math.floor(Math.random() *
quotes.length);
      return quotes[randomIndex];
    }

    // This function updates the text of the #quote paragraph with
a new random quote
    function displayNewQuote() {
      let quote = getRandomQuote();
      document.getElementById('quote').textContent = quote;
    }

    // This event listener calls the displayNewQuote function each
time the button is clicked
    document.getElementById('new-quote-
button').addEventListener('click', displayNewQuote);

    // This line displays a quote when the page is first loaded
    window.onload = displayNewQuote;

  </script>
</body>

</html>
```

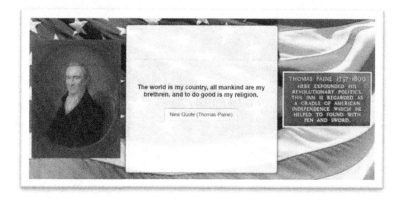

```
<!DOCTYPE html>
<html>
<head>
  <title>Random Quote Generator</title>
  <style>
    body {
      display: flex;
      flex-direction: row;
      justify-content: center;
      align-items: center;
      height: 100vh;
      background: url('thomas_paine3_bg.jpg') no-repeat center
center/cover;
      background-color: rgba(255, 255, 255, 0.3);
      color: black;
      font-family: Arial, sans-serif;
      margin: 0;
      padding: 0;
      box-sizing: border-box;
    }

    #left-image-display,
    #right-image-display {
      width: 25%;
      height: 80vh;
      border-radius: 10px;
      margin: 20px;
      /* box-shadow: 0px 0px 10px 0px rgba(0, 0, 0, 0.75); */
    }
```

```css
    #left-image-display {
      background: url('thomas_paine2.jpg') no-repeat center
center/contain;
    }

    #right-image-display {
      background: url('thomas_paine.jpg') no-repeat center
center/contain;
    }

    #quote-display {
      width: 40%;
      height: 80vh;
      display: flex;
      flex-direction: column;
      justify-content: center;
      align-items: center;
      border: 2px solid #333;
      border-radius: 10px;
      padding: 20px;
      background-color: rgba(255, 255, 255, 0.9);
      box-shadow: 0px 0px 10px 0px rgba(0, 0, 0, 0.75);
    }

    #quote {
      font-size: 24px;
      font-weight: bold;
      margin-bottom: 20px;
      text-align: center;
    }

    button {
      padding: 10px 20px;
      font-size: 20px;
      cursor: pointer;
      margin-top: 20px;
    }
  </style>
</head>
<body>
  <div id="left-image-display"></div>
  <div id="quote-display">
    <p id="quote"></p>
```

```html
    <button id="new-quote-button">New Quote (Thomas
Paine)</button>
  </div>
  <div id="right-image-display"></div>
  <script>
    // This array holds the quotes that will be randomly displayed
    let quotes = [
      "These are the times that try men's souls.",
      "The harder the conflict, the more glorious the triumph.",
      "What we obtain too cheap, we esteem too lightly: it is
dearness only that gives every thing its value.",
      "The mind once enlightened cannot again become dark.",
      "The world is my country, all mankind are my brethren, and
to do good is my religion.",
      "Reason obeys itself; and ignorance submits to whatever is
dictated to it.",
      "He that would make his own liberty secure, must guard
even his enemy from oppression; for if he violates this duty, he
establishes a precedent that will reach to himself.",
      "It is necessary to the happiness of man that he be mentally
faithful to himself.",
      "When we are planning for posterity, we ought to remember
that virtue is not hereditary.",
      "Those who expect to reap the blessings of freedom, must,
like men, undergo the fatigue of supporting it.",
      "A long habit of not thinking a thing wrong, gives it a
superficial appearance of being right.",
      "Tyranny, like hell, is not easily conquered; yet we have this
consolation with us, that the harder the conflict, the more glorious
the triumph.",
      "Character is much easier kept than recovered.",
      "He who dares not offend cannot be honest.",
      "Government, even in its best state, is but a necessary evil;
in its worst state, an intolerable one.",
      "My country is the world, and my religion is to do good.",
      "The real man smiles in trouble, gathers strength from
distress, and grows brave by reflection.",
      "Every science has for its basis a system of principles as
fixed and unalterable as those by which the universe is regulated
and governed.",
      "It is the duty of every patriot to protect his country from its
government.",
```

```
    "Independence is my happiness, and I view things as they
are, without regard to place or person; my country is the world,
and my religion is to do good.",
    // Add as many quotes as you like...
  ];

  // This function selects a random quote from the array
  function getRandomQuote() {
    let randomIndex = Math.floor(Math.random() *
quotes.length);
    return quotes[randomIndex];
  }
  // This function updates the text of the #quote paragraph with
a new random quote
  function displayNewQuote() {
    let quote = getRandomQuote();
    document.getElementById('quote').textContent = quote;
  }
  // This event listener calls the displayNewQuote function each
time the button is clicked
  document.getElementById('new-quote-
button').addEventListener('click', displayNewQuote);

  // This line displays a quote when the page is first loaded
  window.onload = displayNewQuote;
 </script>
</body>
</html>
<!-- This version of the Random Quote Generator displays an
image of Thomas Paine on the left side, another image on the
right side, and a random quote in the center. The background
image is displayed with cover and a transparency of 0.3. The
quote is bold and centered. -->
```

101

```
As a web developer, the three main languages we
use to build websites are HTML, CSS, and
JavaScript. JavaScript is the programming
language, we use HTML to structure the site, and
we use CSS to design and layout the web page.
```

Count Words and Characters

Word count: 41

Character count: 225

```html
<!DOCTYPE html>
<html>

<head>
  <title>Word and Character Counter</title>
  <!-- <link rel="stylesheet" type="text/css" href="styles.css"> -->
  <style>
    body {
      font-family: Arial, sans-serif;
      text-align: center;
      padding: 20px;
    }

    textarea {
      width: 80%;
      height: 150px;
      margin-bottom: 10px;
    }

    button {
      padding: 10px 20px;
      font-size: 20px;
      margin-bottom: 10px;
```

```html
      cursor: pointer;
    }
  </style>
</head>

<body>
  <textarea id="user-input" placeholder="Type
something..."></textarea>
  <button id="count-button">Count Words and
Characters</button>
  <p id="word-count">Word count: 0</p>
  <p id="character-count">Character count: 0</p>

  <!-- <script src="script.js"></script> -->
  <script>
    // This function counts the number of words and characters in
the user's text
    function countWordsAndCharacters() {
      let text = document.getElementById('user-input').value;

      // Count characters
      let characterCount = text.length;
      document.getElementById('character-count').textContent =
'Character count: ' + characterCount;

      // Count words
      let wordCount = text.split(/\s+/).filter(function (word) {
        return word.length > 0;
      }).length;
      document.getElementById('word-count').textContent =
'Word count: ' + wordCount;
    }
    // This event listener calls the countWordsAndCharacters
function each time the button is clicked
    document.getElementById('count-
button').addEventListener('click', countWordsAndCharacters);

  </script>
</body>
</html>
```

103

```
<!DOCTYPE html>
<html>

<head>
  <title>Palindrome Checker</title>
  <!-- <link rel="stylesheet" type="text/css" href="styles.css"> -->

  <style>
    body {
      font-family: Arial, sans-serif;
      text-align: center;
      padding: 20px;
    }

    input {
      margin-bottom: 20px;
      width: 300px;
      font-size: 20px;;
    }

    button {
      padding: 10px 20px;
      font-size: 20px;
      margin-bottom: 10px;
      cursor: pointer;
    }
  </style>
</head>
```

104

```html
<body>
  <input id="user-input" type="text" placeholder="Enter a word
or phrase...">
  <button id="check-button">Check if Palindrome</button>
  <p id="result">result ? !</p>
  <hr>

  <!-- <script src="script.js"></script> -->

  <script>
    function isPalindrome() {
      let text = document.getElementById('user-input').value;
      // Use regex to remove non-alphanumeric characters and
convert to lowercase
      let processedText = text.replace(/[\W_]/g,
'').toLowerCase();
      let reversedText = processedText.split('').reverse().join('');

      if (processedText === reversedText) {
        document.getElementById('result').textContent = '"' + text
+ '" is a palindrome.';
      } else {
        document.getElementById('result').textContent = '"' + text
+ '" is not a palindrome.';
      }
    }

    document.getElementById('check-
button').addEventListener('click', isPalindrome);

  </script>
</body>

</html>

<!-- here's a list of 20 palindromic words and phrases:

"radar",
"level",
"racecar",
"madam",
"rotor",
"civic",
"deed",
```

105

"mom",
"dad",
"pop",
"eye",
"refer",
"reviled did I live", said I, as evil I did deliver",
"Able was I ere I saw Elba" (a famous phrase attributed to
Napoleon Bonaparte),
"A man, a plan, a canal: Panama",
"Madam, in Eden, I'm Adam",
"Never odd or even",
"Don't nod",
"Sir, I demand, I am a maid named Iris",
"Was it a car or a cat I saw?",

Please note that for the phrases, punctuation and spaces are
ignored when checking for palindromicity. This is a common
convention when working with palindromes. -->

<!-- This is Korean palindromes. -->
<!-- 소주 만병만 주소, 스위스, 일대일, 20200202, 토마토, 92829,
오디오, 기러기, 마그마, 부익부, 역곡역, 합집합,
아들딸이 다 컸다 이 딸들아,
다 된 장국 청국장 된다,
다 큰 도라지일지라도 큰다,
여보게 저기 저게 보여, 여보 안경 안 보여, 대한 총기공사 공기총
한대,
나갔다 오나 나오다 갔나, 다시 올 이월이 윤이월이올시다,
생선 사가는 가사선생, 다시 합창합시다, 야 이 달은 밝은 달이야,
짐 사이에 이사짐, 다리 그리고 저고리 그리다,
다시마를 마시다, 다 가져가다,
건조한 조건, 기특한 특기 -->

106

Grocery List Manager

Add an item...   Add Item

bread	Delete	Bought
~~flour~~	Delete	Bought
~~sugar~~	Delete	Bought
fruit	Delete	Bought
onion	Delete	Bought

107

```html
<!DOCTYPE html>
<html>

<head>
  <title>Grocery List Manager</title>
  <!-- <link rel="stylesheet" type="text/css" href="styles.css"> --
>
  <style>
   body {
     font-family: Arial, sans-serif;
     text-align: center;
     padding: 20px;
   }

   input {
     margin-bottom: 10px;
     width: 250px;
     font-size: 20px;
   }

   button {
```

```
      padding: 10px 20px;
      font-size: 20px;
      margin-bottom: 10px;
      cursor: pointer;
    }

    ul {
      list-style: none;
    }

    .bought {
      text-decoration: line-through;
    }

    .item-button {
      margin-left: 20px;
}
  </style>
</head>

<body>
  <h2>Grocery List Manager</h2>
  <input id="item-input" type="text" placeholder="Add an
item...">
  <button id="add-button">Add Item</button>
  <ul id="grocery-list"></ul>

  <!-- <script src="script.js"></script> -->
  <script>
    document.getElementById('add-
button').addEventListener('click', function () {
      let itemInput = document.getElementById('item-input');
      let itemText = itemInput.value;
      itemInput.value = '';

      let listItem = document.createElement('li');
      listItem.textContent = itemText;

      let deleteButton = document.createElement('button');
      deleteButton.textContent = 'Delete';
      deleteButton.classList.add('item-button');
      deleteButton.addEventListener('click', function () {
        listItem.remove();
      });
```

```
    let boughtButton = document.createElement('button');
    boughtButton.textContent = 'Bought';
    boughtButton.classList.add('item-button');
    boughtButton.addEventListener('click', function () {
      listItem.classList.toggle('bought');
    });

    listItem.appendChild(deleteButton);
    listItem.appendChild(boughtButton);
    document.getElementById('grocery-
list').appendChild(listItem);
    });

  </script>
</body>

</html>

<!-- The list disappears when the page is refreshed. -->
```

109

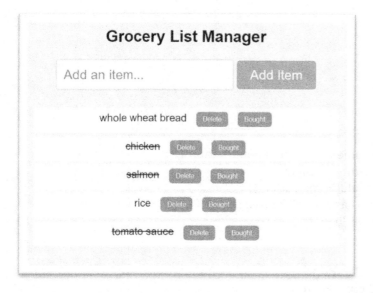

110

```
<!DOCTYPE html>
<html>
<head>
  <title>Grocery List Manager</title>
  <!-- <link rel="stylesheet" type="text/css" href="styles.css"> --
>
  <style>
    body {
      font-family: Arial, sans-serif;
      text-align: center;
      padding: 20px;
      background-color: #f2f2f2;
    }
    input {
      margin-bottom: 10px;
      width: 250px;
      font-size: 20px;
      padding: 10px;
      border-radius: 5px;
      border: 2px solid #ddd;
    }
    button {
      padding: 5px 10px;
      font-size: 10px;
```

```
      margin-bottom: 5px;
      cursor: pointer;
      border-radius: 5px;
      border: none;
      color: white;
    }
    #add-button {
      padding: 10px 20px;
      font-size: 20px;
      background-color: #4CAF50;
    }
    .item-button {
      background-color: #f44336;
      margin-left: 15px;
    }
    ul {
      list-style: none;
      padding-left: 0;
    }
    li {
      background-color: white;
      margin-bottom: 5px;
      padding: 5px;
      border-radius: 5px;
    }
    .bought {
      text-decoration: line-through;
    }
  </style>
</head>

<body>
  <h2>Grocery List Manager</h2>
  <input id="item-input" type="text" placeholder="Add an
item...">
  <button id="add-button">Add Item</button>
  <ul id="grocery-list"></ul>

  <!-- <script src="script.js"></script> -->
  <script>
    document.getElementById('add-
button').addEventListener('click', function () {
      let itemInput = document.getElementById('item-input');
      let itemText = itemInput.value;
```

```
    itemInput.value = '';

    let listItem = document.createElement('li');
    listItem.textContent = itemText;

    let deleteButton = document.createElement('button');
    deleteButton.textContent = 'Delete';
    deleteButton.classList.add('item-button');
    deleteButton.addEventListener('click', function () {
      listItem.remove();
      saveListToLocalStorage();
    });

    let boughtButton = document.createElement('button');
    boughtButton.textContent = 'Bought';
    boughtButton.classList.add('item-button');
    boughtButton.addEventListener('click', function () {
      listItem.classList.toggle('bought');
      saveListToLocalStorage();
    });

    listItem.appendChild(deleteButton);
    listItem.appendChild(boughtButton);
    document.getElementById('grocery-
list').appendChild(listItem);

    saveListToLocalStorage();
  });

  function saveListToLocalStorage() {
    let groceryList =
Array.from(document.getElementById('grocery-
list').children).map(function (listItem) {
      return {
        text: listItem.firstChild.textContent,
        bought: listItem.classList.contains('bought')
      };
    });

    localStorage.setItem('groceryList',
JSON.stringify(groceryList));
  }

  function loadListFromLocalStorage() {
```

```
      let savedList =
JSON.parse(localStorage.getItem('groceryList'));
    if (savedList) {
      let groceryList = document.getElementById('grocery-list');
      groceryList.innerHTML = '';
      for (let item of savedList) {
        let listItem = document.createElement('li');
        listItem.textContent = item.text;

        let deleteButton = document.createElement('button');
        deleteButton.textContent = 'Delete';
        deleteButton.classList.add('item-button');
        deleteButton.addEventListener('click', function () {
          listItem.remove();
          saveListToLocalStorage();
        });

        let boughtButton = document.createElement('button');
        boughtButton.textContent = 'Bought';
        boughtButton.classList.add('item-button');
        boughtButton.addEventListener('click', function () {
          listItem.classList.toggle('bought');
          saveListToLocalStorage();
        });

        listItem.appendChild(deleteButton);
        listItem.appendChild(boughtButton);
        if (item.bought) {
          listItem.classList.add('bought');
        }
        groceryList.appendChild(listItem);
      }
    }
  }
  loadListFromLocalStorage();
 </script>
</body>
</html>
<!-- The list does not disappear even if the page is refreshed. -->
```

113

```
<!DOCTYPE html>
<html>

<head>
  <title>Simple API Fetch</title>
  <style>
    body {
      font-family: Arial, sans-serif;
      text-align: center;
      padding: 20px;
    }

    button {
      padding: 10px 20px;
      font-size: 20px;
      margin-bottom: 10px;
    }

    #image-container {
      width: 100%;
      display: flex;
      justify-content: center;
      align-items: center-10px;
      padding: 20px;
    }
```

```
  #image-container img {
    width: 300px;
    height: auto;
    margin-left: -30px;
  }
  </style>
</head>

<body>
  <button id="fetch-button">Fetch a Dog Image</button>
  <div id="image-container"></div>

  <script>
    document.getElementById('fetch-
button').addEventListener('click', function () {
      fetch('https://api.thedogapi.com/v1/images/search')
      .then(response => response.json())
      .then(data => {
        let imageContainer = document.getElementById('image-
container');
        let img = document.createElement('img');
        img.src = data[0].url;
        imageContainer.innerHTML = '';
        imageContainer.appendChild(img);
      })
      .catch(error => console.error('Error:', error));
    });
  </script>
</body>

</html>
<!-- This code will make the image width 300px and the height
will be set automatically to maintain the aspect ratio of the image.
When each time you click the button, only one image is displayed
at a time.
The image in the #image-container will shift 30 pixels to the left. -
->
```

115

Fetch a Joke

Why are oranges the smartest fruit? Because they are
made to concentrate.

```html
<!DOCTYPE html>
<html>

<head>
    <title>Simple API Fetch</title>
    <!-- <link rel="stylesheet" type="text/css" href="styles.css">
-->
    <style>
        body {
            font-family: Arial, sans-serif;
            text-align: center;
            padding: 20px;
        }

        button {
            padding: 10px 20px;
            font-size: 20px;
            margin-bottom: 10px;
        }

        #joke-container {
            width: 100%;
            display: flex;
            justify-content: center;
            align-items: center;
            padding: 20px;
        }
    </style>
</head>

<body>
```

116

```
    <button id="fetch-button">Fetch a Joke</button>
    <div id="joke-container"></div>

    <!-- <script src="script.js"></script> -->
    <script>
        document.getElementById('fetch-
button').addEventListener('click', function () {
            fetch('https://official-joke-
api.appspot.com/random_joke')
                .then(response => response.json())
                .then(data => {
                    var jokeContainer =
document.getElementById('joke-container');
                    jokeContainer.textContent = data.setup + ' ' +
data.punchline;
                })
                .catch(error => console.error('Error:', error));
        });

    </script>
</body>

</html>
```

117

<!-- [What does a pirate pay for his corn? A buccaneer!]

This is a pun joke, where the humor relies on a word or phrase
that has two meanings or sounds like another word or phrase.

In this case, the joke uses the word "buccaneer." This term has
two relevant meanings here:

1. A buccaneer is a type of pirate, specifically those who operated
in the Caribbean in the 17th and 18th centuries.
"Buccaneer" sounds very similar to "buck an ear," which could
mean "one dollar for each ear of corn."
So, the punchline "a buccaneer" is a pun because it can be
interpreted both as "a pirate" (in line with the question) and "a
buck an ear" (implying that the pirate pays one dollar for each ear
of corn). This play on words creates the humor in the joke. -->

<!-- [How do you tell the difference between a crocodile and an
alligator? You will see one later and one in a while.]

This joke is another example of a pun or play on words, this time involving homophones (words that sound the same but have different meanings). The pun comes from the phrases "see you later, alligator" and "in a while, crocodile," which are often used in a playful context, particularly with children. These phrases rhyme and have a rhythm to them, making them memorable.

Here's the breakdown:

1. The phrase "see you later, alligator" sounds like you are saying you will see the alligator later.
2. The phrase "in a while, crocodile" sounds like you are saying you will see the crocodile in a while.
The joke implies that you can tell the difference between an alligator and a crocodile based on when you will see them ("later" for the alligator and "in a while" for the crocodile), which is, of course, a humorous and absurd way to differentiate between these two reptiles. The humor lies in the unexpected and silly "logic". -->

<!-- [How come the stadium got hot after the game? Because all of the fans left.]

This joke is based on a play on words, specifically the double meaning of the word "fans."

In one sense, "fans" refer to the spectators or supporters who come to watch the game at the stadium.
In another sense, "fans" are devices used to create a breeze and cool down a room or space.
The joke plays on these two meanings. The setup of the joke leads the listener to think of "fans" as spectators at the game. The punchline, however, hinges on interpreting "fans" as cooling devices.

So, the humor comes from the surprise twist in understanding. The stadium got hot not because the cheering supporters (fans) left, but because the cooling devices (fans) left. It's an unexpected and playful interpretation. -->

<!-- [What do you call a sheep with no legs? A cloud.]

This joke relies on the concept of metaphor and the unexpected comparison between two seemingly unrelated things: a sheep and a cloud.

Sheep are often associated with fluffiness due to their wool, much like how clouds in the sky look fluffy. Therefore, if you imagine a sheep without legs, it could resemble a fluffy cloud floating in the sky.

So, when the question is asked, "What do you call a sheep with no legs?" the listener is likely expecting an answer related to mobility or lack thereof. However, the punchline "A cloud" takes an unexpected turn, comparing a legless sheep to a fluffy cloud, which creates the surprise and humor. -->

<!-- [How does a French skeleton say hello? Bone-jour.]

This joke involves a play on words, specifically a pun, which is a form of humor that exploits multiple meanings of a term or of similar-sounding words for an intended humorous effect.

In French, "Bonjour" is a common greeting that means "Good day" or "Hello." The joke replaces the "bon" part of "Bonjour" with "bone," because skeletons are made of bones.

So, the phrase "Bone-jour" sounds very similar to "Bonjour," but changes the meaning to something like "Bone-day," which doesn't make sense in a literal translation but humorously implies that the skeleton is saying "Hello" with a skeleton-themed twist. The humor comes from the surprise and cleverness of this wordplay. ->

Fetch a Trivia Question

Question: What year did "Attack on Titan" first air?

Answer: 2013

```
<!DOCTYPE html>
<html>

<head>
  <title>Simple API Fetch</title>
  <!-- <link rel="stylesheet" type="text/css" href="styles.css"> --
>
  <style>
    body {
      font-family: Arial, sans-serif;
      text-align: center;
      padding: 20px;
    }

    button {
      padding: 10px 20px;
      font-size: 20px;
      margin-bottom: 20px;
    }

    #trivia-container {
      width: 100%;
      height: auto;
      display: flex-wrap;
      justify-content: center;
      align-items: center;
      padding: 20px, 20px;
    }
  </style>
</head>

<body>
```

120

```html
<button id="fetch-button">Fetch a Trivia Question</button>
<div id="trivia-container"></div>

<!-- <script src="script.js"></script> -->
<script>
  document.getElementById('fetch-
button').addEventListener('click', function () {
    fetch('https://opentdb.com/api.php?amount=1')
    .then(response => response.json())
    .then(data => {
      var triviaContainer = document.getElementById('trivia-
container');
      triviaContainer.innerHTML =
`<strong>Question:</strong>
${data.results[0].question}<br><br>
        <strong>Answer:</strong>
${data.results[0].correct_answer}`;
    })
    .catch(error => console.error('Error:', error));
  });

</script>
</body>

</html>
```

121

You are at a crossroads. If you go left, you head towards the mountains. If you go right, you head into the forest.

Go towards the mountains

Go into the forest

122

```
<!DOCTYPE html>
<html>

<head>
    <title>Interactive Story</title>
    <!-- <link rel="stylesheet" type="text/css" href="styles.css">
-->
    <style>
        body {
            font-family: Arial, sans-serif;
            text-align: center;
            padding: 20px;
        }

        #story-container {
            width: 100%;
            display: flex;
            flex-direction: column;
            justify-content: center;
            align-items: center;
            padding: 20px;
        }

        button {
            padding: 10px 20px;
            font-size: 20px;
            margin-bottom: 10px;
        }
    </style>
</head>
```

```html
<body>
    <div id="story-container">
        <p id="story-text"></p>
        <div id="option-buttons"></div>
    </div>

    <!-- <script src="script028.js"></script> -->
    <script>

    const storyText = document.getElementById('story-text')
    const optionButtons = document.getElementById('option-buttons')

    let state = {}

    function startGame() {
        state = {}
        showTextNode(1)
    }

    function showTextNode(textNodeIndex) {
        const textNode = textNodes.find(textNode =>
textNode.id === textNodeIndex)
        storyText.innerText = textNode.text
        while (optionButtons.firstChild) {
            optionButtons.removeChild(optionButtons.firstChild)
        }

        textNode.options.forEach(option => {
            if (showOption(option)) {
                const button = document.createElement('button')
                button.innerText = option.text
                button.classList.add('btn')
                button.addEventListener('click', () =>
selectOption(option))
                optionButtons.appendChild(button)
            }
        })
    }

    function showOption(option) {
        return option.requiredState == null ||
option.requiredState(state)
```

```
        }

    function selectOption(option) {
        const nextTextNodeId = option.nextText
        if (nextTextNodeId <= 0) {
            return startGame()
        }
        state = Object.assign(state, option.setState)
        showTextNode(nextTextNodeId)
    }

    const textNodes = [
        {
            id: 1,
            text: 'You are at a crossroads. If you go left, you
head towards the mountains. If you go right, you head into the
forest.',
            options: [
                {
                    text: 'Go towards the mountains',
                    setState: { mountains: true },
                    nextText: 2
                },
                {
                    text: 'Go into the forest',
                    setState: { forest: true },
                    nextText: 3
                }
            ]
        },
        {
            id: 2,
            text: 'You arrive at the mountains. There is a small
cave nearby.',
            options: [
                {
                    text: 'Enter the cave',
                    requiredState: (currentState) =>
currentState.mountains,
                    setState: { cave: true },
                    nextText: 4
                },
                {
                    text: 'Return to the crossroads',
```

```
                    nextText: 1
                }
            ]
        },
        {
            id: 3,
            text: 'You walk into the forest and find a stream.',
            options: [
                {
                    text: 'Follow the stream',
                    requiredState: (currentState) =>
currentState.forest,
                    setState: { stream: true },
                    nextText: 5
                },
                {
                    text: 'Return to the crossroads',

                    nextText: 1
                }
            ]
        },
        {
            id: 4,
            text: 'You discover a small treasure chest in the
cave!',
            options: [
                {
                    text: 'Return to the crossroads',
                    nextText: 1
                },
                {
                    text: 'End story',
                    nextText: 0
                }
            ]
        },
        {
            id: 5,
            text: 'You follow the stream and discover a waterfall
with a rainbow.',
            options: [
                {
                    text: 'Return to the crossroads',
```

```
                    nextText: 1
            },
            {
                text: 'End story',
                nextText: 0
            }
        ]
    }
]

    startGame()
  </script>
</body>

</html>
```

Interactive Adventure

As a brave adventurer, you find yourself at a crossroads in a mythical land. To the left, the rugged mountains loom. To the right, a dense, mysterious forest whispers with the wind.

Venture towards the mountains   Brave the forest path

```
<!DOCTYPE html>
<html>

<head>
  <title>Interactive Adventure</title>
  <style>
    body {
      font-family: Arial, sans-serif;
      text-align: center;
      padding: 20px;
      background-color: #f2f2f2;
    }

    #story-container {
      width: 80%;
      display: flex;
      flex-direction: column;
      justify-content: center;
      align-items: center;
      padding: 20px;
      margin: auto;
      background-color: #fff;
      border-radius: 5px;
      box-shadow: 0px 10px 20px rgba(0, 0, 0, 0.19), 0px 6px
6px rgba(0, 0, 0, 0.23);
    }

    button {
      padding: 10px 20px;
      font-size: 20px;
      margin: 10px;
```

127

```
      cursor: pointer;
      border-radius: 5px;
      border: none;
      color: white;
      background-color: #4CAF50;
    }
  </style>
</head>

<body>
  <h2>Interactive Adventure</h2>
  <div id="story-container">
    <p id="story-text"></p>
    <div id="option-buttons"></div>
  </div>
  <script src="script028-2.js"></script>
  <!-- <script>

    </script> -->
</body>

</html>

<!-- The expanded story now includes finding a magical crystal in
the mountain, gathering healing flowers in the forest, and
discovering a mystical sword in an ancient temple. The player will
also have the chance to reach the peak of the mountain, offering
them a sense of accomplishment. -->
```

Times Tables Tester

What is 7 x 9?

63

Submit

Correct! Great job.

```html
<!DOCTYPE html>
<html>
<head>
  <title>Times Tables Tester</title>
  <!-- <link rel="stylesheet" type="text/css" href="styles.css"> -->
  <style>
    body {
      font-family: Arial, sans-serif;
      text-align: center;
    }
    #quiz-container {
      margin-top: 100px;
    }
    input,
    button {
      font-size: 20px;
      padding: 10px;
      margin-top: 20px;
      margin-bottom: 20px;
    }
    button {
      cursor: pointer;
    }
  </style>
</head>
<body>
  <div id="quiz-container">
```

```html
    <h1>Times Tables Tester</h1>
    <div id="question">Loading...</div>
    <input id="answer" type="number" min="0" autofocus>
    <button id="submit">Submit</button>
    <div id="feedback">Enter your answer and press
submit</div>
  </div>
  <!-- <script src="script.js"></script> -->
  <script>
    document.getElementById('submit').addEventListener('click',
checkAnswer);

    let num1, num2, correctAnswer;

    function generateQuestion() {
      num1 = Math.floor(Math.random() * 10) + 1;
      num2 = Math.floor(Math.random() * 10) + 1;
      correctAnswer = num1 * num2;
      document.getElementById('question').innerText = `What is
${num1} x ${num2}?`;
    }

    function checkAnswer() {
      let userAnswer = document.getElementById('answer').value;
      if (userAnswer == correctAnswer) {
        document.getElementById('feedback').innerText = 'Correct!
Great job.';
      } else {
        document.getElementById('feedback').innerText = `Sorry,
that's incorrect. The correct answer was ${correctAnswer}.`;
      }
      // Generate a new question
      generateQuestion();
      // Clear the input field
      document.getElementById('answer').value = '';
      // Set focus back to the input field
      document.getElementById('answer').focus();
    }
    // Generate the first question as soon as the page loads
    generateQuestion();
  </script>
</body>
</html>
```

130

Times Tables Tester

What is 72 x 52?

Set Limit: `100` | Set Limit & Start

Sorry, that's incorrect. The correct answer was 6408.

`|` ⌄ | Submit

```
<!DOCTYPE html>
<html>
<head>
  <title>Times Tables Tester</title>
  <!-- <link rel="stylesheet" type="text/css" href="styles.css"> --
>
  <style>
    body {
      font-family: Arial, sans-serif;
      text-align: center;
    }
    #quiz-container {
      margin-top: 100px;
    }
    h1 {
      width: 500px;
      margin: auto;
      padding: 20px;
      border-radius: 10px;
      box-shadow: 0px 0px 15px rgba(33, 33, 34, 0.1);
      background-color: #4638af;
      color: white;
    }
    #question,
    #feedback {
      margin-top: 40px;
      margin-bottom: 0px;
```

```
      font-size: 20px;
    }
    input,
    button {
      font-size: 20px;
      padding: 10px;
      margin-top: 20px;
      margin-bottom: 20px;
    }
    button {
      cursor: pointer;
    }
    hr {
      width: 500px;
      margin: auto;
      /* Optional: this centers the line on the page */
      border: none;
      border-top: 2px solid red;
      /* Change 'red' to any color you want */
    }
  </style>
</head>
<body>
  <div id="quiz-container">
    <h1>Times Tables Tester</h1>
    <div id="question">Set a limit and press <mark>'Set Limit &
Start'</mark> to start</div>
    <label for="limit">Set Limit:</label>
    <input id="limit" type="number" min="10" value="10">
    <button id="set-limit">Set Limit & Start</button>
    <hr>
    <div id="feedback">Enter your answer and press
submit</div>
    <input id="answer" type="number" min="0" autofocus>
    <button id="submit">Submit</button>
  </div>
  <script>
    document.getElementById('submit').addEventListener('click',
checkAnswer);
    document.getElementById('set-limit').addEventListener('click',
generateQuestion);

    let num1, num2, correctAnswer;
```

```
    function generateQuestion() {
      let limit = parseInt(document.getElementById('limit').value);
      num1 = Math.floor(Math.random() * limit) + 1;
      num2 = Math.floor(Math.random() * limit) + 1;
      correctAnswer = num1 * num2;
      document.getElementById('question').innerText = `What is
${num1} x ${num2}?`;
    }

    function checkAnswer() {
      let userAnswer = document.getElementById('answer').value;
      if (userAnswer == correctAnswer) {
        document.getElementById('feedback').innerText = 'Correct!
Great job.';
      } else {
        document.getElementById('feedback').innerText = `Sorry,
that's incorrect. The correct answer was ${correctAnswer}.`;
      }
      // Generate a new question
      generateQuestion();
      // Clear the input field
      document.getElementById('answer').value = '';
      // Set focus back to the input field
      document.getElementById('answer').focus();
    }
  </script>
</body>
</html>

<!-- We can allow the user to choose the upper limit for the times
table. Let's add a new input field and a button so that the user
can set their desired limit. Once the user sets the limit and clicks
the "Set Limit & Start" button, we generate questions based on
that limit.
```

This allows the user to control the difficulty of the times table test by setting the limit to any value, such as 10, 20, 50, 100, or 1000. -->

Guess the Number

Guess a number between 1 and 100

```
59    ⬍    Submit
```
Enter your guess and press submit

```html
<!DOCTYPE html>
<html>
<head>
  <title>Times Tables Tester</title>
  <!-- <link rel="stylesheet" type="text/css" href="styles.css"> -->
  <style>
    body {
      font-family: Arial, sans-serif;
      text-align: center;
    }
    #quiz-container {
      margin-top: 100px;
    }
    h1 {
      width: 500px;
      margin: auto;
      padding: 20px;
      border-radius: 10px;
      box-shadow: 0px 0px 15px rgba(33, 33, 34, 0.1);
      background-color: #4638af;
      color: white;
    }
    #question,
    #feedback {
      margin-top: 40px;
      margin-bottom: 0px;
      font-size: 20px;
```

134

```
    }
    input,
    button {
      font-size: 20px;
      padding: 10px;
      margin-top: 20px;
      margin-bottom: 20px;
    }

    button {
      cursor: pointer;
    }

    hr {
      width: 500px;
      margin: auto;
      /* Optional: this centers the line on the page */
      border: none;
      border-top: 2px solid red;
      /* Change 'red' to any color you want */
    }
  </style>
</head>

<body>
  <div id="quiz-container">
    <h1>Times Tables Tester</h1>
    <div id="question">Set a limit and press <mark>'Set Limit &
Start'</mark> to start</div>
    <label for="limit">Set Limit:</label>
    <input id="limit" type="number" min="10" value="10">
    <button id="set-limit">Set Limit & Start</button>
    <hr>
    <div id="feedback">Enter your answer and press
submit</div>
    <input id="answer" type="number" min="0" autofocus>
    <button id="submit">Submit</button>
  </div>
  <script>
    document.getElementById('submit').addEventListener('click',
checkAnswer);
    document.getElementById('set-limit').addEventListener('click',
generateQuestion);
```

```javascript
    let num1, num2, correctAnswer;

    function generateQuestion() {
      let limit = parseInt(document.getElementById('limit').value);
      num1 = Math.floor(Math.random() * limit) + 1;
      num2 = Math.floor(Math.random() * limit) + 1;
      correctAnswer = num1 * num2;
      document.getElementById('question').innerText = `What is
${num1} x ${num2}?`;
    }

    function checkAnswer() {
      let userAnswer = document.getElementById('answer').value;
      if (userAnswer == correctAnswer) {
        document.getElementById('feedback').innerText = 'Correct!
Great job.';
      } else {
        document.getElementById('feedback').innerText = `Sorry,
that's incorrect. The correct answer was ${correctAnswer}.`;
      }
      // Generate a new question
      generateQuestion();
      // Clear the input field
      document.getElementById('answer').value = '';
      // Set focus back to the input field
      document.getElementById('answer').focus();
    }
  </script>
</body>
</html>
<!-- We can allow the user to choose the upper limit for the times
table. Let's add a new input field and a button so that the user
can set their desired limit. Once the user sets the limit and clicks
the "Set Limit & Start" button, we generate questions based on
that limit.

This allows the user to control the difficulty of the times table test
by setting the limit to any value, such as 10, 20, 50, 100, or
1000. -->
```

```
<!DOCTYPE html>
<html lang="en">
<head>
  <meta charset="UTF-8">
  <meta http-equiv="X-UA-Compatible" content="IE=edge">
  <meta name="viewport" content="width=device-width, initial-
scale=1.0">
  <title>Guess The Number</title>
  <style>
    #container {
      position: absolute;
      top: 50%;
      left: 50%;
      transform: translate(-50%, -50%);
      width: 300px;
      height: 400px;
```

```css
    margin: 0 auto;
    text-align: center;
    border: 10px solid #2c6efe;
    border-radius: 5px;
    outline: 2px dotted #fff;
    outline-offset: -6px;
}
h2 {
    margin-top: 0;
    padding: 15px;
    background-color: #2626ef;
    color: white;
}
form {
    margin-top: 40px;
}
input[type="number"] {
    font-size: 20px;
    font-weight: bold;
    color: blue;
    padding: 10px;
    margin-top: 20px;
    margin-bottom: 20px;
    width: 130px;
    border: 2px solid red;
    border-radius: 10px;
}
.btn {
    width: 50px;
    height: 40px;
    border-radius: 50%;
    padding: 10px 3px;
    border: #ccc 1px solid;
}
.btn-1 {
    background-color: rgb(135, 241, 133);
}
.btn-2 {
    background-color: #fa7c7c;
}
#display {
    font-size: 20px;
    margin-top: 70px;
    color: red;
```

```css
      }
    .output {
      font-size: 20px;
      font-weight: bold;
    }
    #counter {
      position: absolute;
      left: 0;
      bottom: 0;
      width: 100%;
      height: 50px;
    }
    .footer {
      background-color: #4548fb;
      color: white;
      line-height: 50px;
    }
  </style>
</head>
```

```html
<body>
  <div id="container">
    <h2>Guess The Number</h2>
    <p>Guess a number between 1 and 100</p>
    <form action="">
      <input type="number" min="1" max="100" id="try"
autocomplete="off" autofocus>

      <input type="button" value="Check" id="check" class="btn
btn-1" onclick="finding()">
      <input type="button" value="Reset" id="reset" class="btn
btn-2" onclick="window.location.reload()">
    </form>
    <div id="display" class="output"></div>
    <div id="counter" class="footer"></div>
  </div>
  <script>
    var counter = 0;
    var randomNumber = Math.floor(Math.random() * 100) + 1;

    document.getElementById("try").onkeypress = function (e) {
      if (e.keyCode == 13 || e.which == 13) {
        finding();
        return false;
```

```
      }
    }

    function finding() {
      var userNumber = document.getElementById("try").value;

      if (userNumber >= 1 && userNumber <= 100) {
        if (randomNumber > userNumber) {
          document.getElementById("display").innerText = " Too
Low! Try Again!";
        }
        else if (randomNumber < userNumber) {
          document.getElementById("display").innerText = "Too
High! Try Again!";
        }
        else {
          document.getElementById("display").innerHTML =
"<span style='color:blue'>You are correct!</span>";
        }

        document.getElementById("try").value = "";
        counter++;
        document.querySelector("#counter").innerHTML = "Try
Number : " + counter + " time(s)";
      }
      else
        alert("Input a number between 1 and 100.");

      document.getElementById("try").focus();
    }
  </script>
</body>

</html>
<!-- This code references the book by Ms. Ko Kyung-hee. -->
```

140

Sun	Mon	Tue	Wed	Thu	Fri	Sat
						1
2	3	4	5	6	7	8
9	10	11	12	13	14	15
16	17	18	19	20	21	22
23	24	25	26	27	28	29
30	31					

141

```
<!DOCTYPE html>
<html>

<head>
  <title>Calendar</title>
  <!-- <link rel="stylesheet" type="text/css" href="styles.css"> --
>

  <style>
    body {
      font-family: Arial, sans-serif;
      text-align: center;
    }

    #calendar {
      margin: auto;
      margin-top: 50px;
      width: 70%;
    }

    #calendar th {
      padding: 10px;
      background-color: #ccc;
    }
```

```
  #calendar td {
    padding: 10px;
    border: 1px solid #ccc;
  }

  .today {
    background-color: #ff0;
  }
  </style>
</head>

<body>
  <table id="calendar">
    <tr>
      <th>Sun</th>
      <th>Mon</th>
      <th>Tue</th>
      <th>Wed</th>
      <th>Thu</th>
      <th>Fri</th>
      <th>Sat</th>
    </tr>
    <!-- JavaScript will fill this with the days of the month -->
  </table>
  <!-- <script src="script.js"></script> -->

  <script>
    let today = new Date();
    let currentMonth = today.getMonth();
    let currentYear = today.getFullYear();
    let currentDay = today.getDate();

    let daysInMonth = new Date(currentYear, currentMonth + 1,
0).getDate();
    let startDayOfWeek = new Date(currentYear, currentMonth,
1).getDay();
    // "Date" is the date(1,2,3...30,31), and "day" is the day(Sun,
Mon...Sat) of the week.
    let calendar = document.getElementById('calendar');
    let html = '';

    for (let i = 0; i < startDayOfWeek; i++) {
      html += '<td></td>';  // empty days at start
```

142

```
      }

   for (let day = 1; day <= daysInMonth; day++) {
     if (day === currentDay) {
       html += `<td class="today">${day}</td>`;
     } else {
       html += `<td>${day}</td>`;
     }

     if (new Date(currentYear, currentMonth, day).getDay() ===
6) {
         html += '</tr><tr>';  // start a new row at the end of
each week
       }
     }

   calendar.innerHTML += html;

   if (new Date(currentYear, currentMonth,
daysInMonth).getDay() !== 6) {
       calendar.innerHTML += '</tr>';  // end the last row if the
month doesn't end on Saturday
     }
  </script>
</body>
</html>
```

<!-- This example creates a basic calendar for the current month. The JavaScript calculates how many days are in the current month and what day of the week the month starts on, then it generates the HTML for the days of the month, adding a "today" class to the current day which is highlighted with a different background color by the CSS.

This calendar doesn't have navigation buttons for changing the month, it doesn't show the name of the month or the year, and it doesn't handle months that don't start on Sunday very well. But it should give you a starting point to create a more complete and robust calendar if you want to. -->

```
<!DOCTYPE html>
<html>

<head>
   <title>Calendar</title>
   <!-- <link rel="stylesheet" type="text/css" href="styles.css">
-->

   <style>
      body {
         font-family: Arial, sans-serif;
         text-align: center;
      }

      #calendar-header {
         display: flex;
         justify-content: space-evenly;
         margin-bottom: 0px;
         margin-top: 40px;
      }

      #calendar {
```

```
            margin: auto;
            width: 70%;
        }

        #calendar th {
            padding: 10px;
            background-color: #ccc;
        }

        .sunday {
            color: red;
        }

        .saturday {
            color: blue;
        }

        #calendar td {
            padding: 10px;
            border: 1px solid #ccc;
        }

        .today {
            background-color: #ff0;
        }

        button {
            width: 60px;
            height: 40px;
            border-radius: 50%;
            padding: 10px 3px;
            border: #ccc 2px solid;
            cursor: pointer;
        }
    </style>
</head>

<body>
    <div id="calendar-header">
        <button id="prev-month">◀ Prev</button>
        <h2 id="month-year">Month Year</h2>
        <button id="next-month">Next ▶</button>
    </div>
```

```
<table id="calendar">
    <thead>
        <tr>
            <th class="sunday">Sun</th>
            <th>Mon</th>
            <th>Tue</th>
            <th>Wed</th>
            <th>Thu</th>
            <th>Fri</th>
            <th class="saturday">Sat</th>
        </tr>
    </thead>
    <tbody id="calendar-body">
        <!-- JavaScript will fill this with the days of the month -
->
    </tbody>
</table>
<!-- <script src="script.js"></script> -->
<script>
    let today = new Date();
    let currentMonth = today.getMonth();
    let currentYear = today.getFullYear();
    let currentDay = today.getDate();

    let monthNames = ["January", "February", "March", "April",
"May", "June", "July", "August", "September", "October",
"November", "December"];

    document.getElementById('prev-
month').addEventListener('click', () => {
        currentMonth--;
        if (currentMonth < 0) {
            currentMonth = 11;
            currentYear--;
        }
        generateCalendar(currentMonth, currentYear);
    });

    document.getElementById('next-
month').addEventListener('click', () => {
        currentMonth++;
        if (currentMonth > 11) {
            currentMonth = 0;
            currentYear++;
```

```javascript
        }
        generateCalendar(currentMonth, currentYear);
    });

    function generateCalendar(month, year) {
        let daysInMonth = new Date(year, month + 1,
0).getDate();
        let startDayOfWeek = new Date(year, month,
1).getDay();

        let calendarBody =
document.getElementById('calendar-body');
        let html = '<tr>';

        for (let i = 0; i < startDayOfWeek; i++) {
            html += '<td></td>';  // empty days at start
        }

        for (let day = 1; day <= daysInMonth; day++) {
            if (year === today.getFullYear() && month ===
today.getMonth() && day === currentDay) {
                html += `<td class="today">${day}</td>`;
            } else if (new Date(year, month, day).getDay() ===
0) {
                html += `<td class="sunday">${day}</td>`;
            } else if (new Date(year, month, day).getDay() ===
6) {
                html += `<td class="saturday">${day}</td>`;
            } else {
                html += `<td>${day}</td>`;
            }

            if (new Date(year, month, day).getDay() === 6) {
                html += '</tr><tr>';  // start a new row at the
end of each week
            }
        }

        while (new Date(year, month,
daysInMonth).getDay() !== 6) {
            html += '<td></td>';  // fill in empty days at end
            daysInMonth++;
        }
```

147

```
        html += '</tr>';

        calendarBody.innerHTML = html;

        document.getElementById('month-year').innerText =
`${monthNames[month]} ${year}`;
      }

    // Generate the initial calendar as soon as the page loads
    generateCalendar(currentMonth, currentYear);

  </script>
</body>

</html>

<!-- Now we have a more full-fledged calendar that lets you
navigate between months and years, shows the name of the
current month and year, and colors Sundays red and Saturdays
blue. It still has plenty of room for more features, like selecting a
specific date or adding events to dates, but it should serve as a
good starting point. -->
```

```
<!DOCTYPE html>
<html>

<head>
  <title>Calendar</title>
  <link
href="https://stackpath.bootstrapcdn.com/bootstrap/4.5.0/css/bo
otstrap.min.css" rel="stylesheet">

  <style>
  body {
    padding: 50px;
  }

  .sunday {
    color: red;
  }

  .saturday {
    color: blue;
  }
```

```
    .today {
      background-color: #ff0;
    }
  </style>
</head>

<body>
  <div class="container">
    <div class="d-flex justify-content-between my-3">
      <button id="prev-month" class="btn btn-primary">◀
Prev</button>
      <h2 id="month-year">Month Year</h2>
      <button id="next-month" class="btn btn-primary">Next
▶</button>
    </div>
    <table id="calendar" class="table table-bordered">
      <thead>
        <tr>
          <th class="sunday">Sun</th>
          <th>Mon</th>
          <th>Tue</th>
          <th>Wed</th>
          <th>Thu</th>
          <th>Fri</th>
          <th class="saturday">Sat</th>
        </tr>
      </thead>
      <tbody id="calendar-body">
        <!-- JavaScript will fill this with the days of the month -->
      </tbody>
    </table>
  </div>

  <script>
    let today = new Date();
    let currentMonth = today.getMonth();
    let currentYear = today.getFullYear();
    let currentDay = today.getDate();

    let monthNames = ["January", "February", "March", "April",
"May", "June", "July", "August", "September", "October",
"November", "December"];
```

```javascript
    document.getElementById('prev-
month').addEventListener('click', () => {
      currentMonth--;
      if (currentMonth < 0) {
        currentMonth = 11;
        currentYear--;
      }
      generateCalendar(currentMonth, currentYear);
    });

    document.getElementById('next-
month').addEventListener('click', () => {
      currentMonth++;
      if (currentMonth > 11) {
        currentMonth = 0;
        currentYear++;
      }
      generateCalendar(currentMonth, currentYear);
    });

    function generateCalendar(month, year) {
      let daysInMonth = new Date(year, month + 1, 0).getDate();
      let startDayOfWeek = new Date(year, month, 1).getDay();

      let calendarBody = document.getElementById('calendar-
body');
      let html = '<tr>';

      for (let i = 0; i < startDayOfWeek; i++) {
        html += '<td></td>';  // empty days at start
      }

      for (let day = 1; day <= daysInMonth; day++) {
        if (year === today.getFullYear() && month ===
today.getMonth() && day === currentDay) {
          html += `<td class="today">${day}</td>`;
        } else if (new Date(year, month, day).getDay() === 0) {
          html += `<td class="sunday">${day}</td>`;
        } else if (new Date(year, month, day).getDay() === 6) {
          html += `<td class="saturday">${day}</td>`;
        } else {
          html += `<td>${day}</td>`;
        }
```

```javascript
        if (new Date(year, month, day).getDay() === 6) {
            html += '</tr><tr>';  // start a new row at the end of
each week
            }
        }

        while (new Date(year, month, daysInMonth).getDay() !== 6)
{
            html += '<td></td>';  // fill in empty days at end
            daysInMonth++;
        }

        html += '</tr>';

        calendarBody.innerHTML = html;

        document.getElementById('month-year').innerText =
`${monthNames[month]} ${year}`;
        }
        // Generate the initial calendar as soon as the page loads
        generateCalendar(currentMonth, currentYear);
    </script>
</body>
</html>
<!-- In the revised code:
I have included the Bootstrap CSS CDN in the <head> section.
Used Bootstrap classes to enhance the layout of the calendar. The
'd-flex' and 'justify-content-between' classes are used to
horizontally align the elements with space between them.
The table is made more visually appealing and structured with the
'table' and 'table-bordered' classes.
The buttons are made visually appealing with the 'btn' and 'btn-
primary' classes. -->
```

Height Converter

| 170 | | Centimeters ⌄ | to | Feet ⌄ |

| 5.57742782152231 |

```
<!DOCTYPE html>
<html>

<head>
    <title>Height Converter</title>
    <!-- <link rel="stylesheet" type="text/css" href="styles.css">
-->

    <style>
        body {
            font-family: Arial, sans-serif;
            text-align: center;
        }

        #converter {
            margin-top: 50px;
        }

        #converter input,
        #converter select {
            margin: 10px;
            padding: 10px;
        }

        #converter input[readonly] {
            background-color: #eee;
        }
    </style>
</head>
```

```html
<body>
    <h1>Height Converter</h1>
    <form id="converter">
        <input id="inputHeight" type="number"
placeholder="Enter height" required>
        <select id="inputUnit">
            <option value="cm">Centimeters</option>
            <option value="in">Inches</option>
            <option value="ft">Feet</option>
        </select>
        <span> to </span>
        <select id="outputUnit">
            <option value="cm">Centimeters</option>
            <option value="in">Inches</option>
            <option value="ft">Feet</option>
        </select>
        <input id="outputHeight" type="number" readonly>
    </form>
    <!-- <script src="script.js"></script> -->

    <script>
        document.getElementById('inputHeight').addEventListener(
'input', convertHeight);
        document.getElementById('inputUnit').addEventListener('c
hange', convertHeight);
        document.getElementById('outputUnit').addEventListener('
change', convertHeight);

        function convertHeight() {
            let inputHeight =
document.getElementById('inputHeight').value;
            let inputUnit =
document.getElementById('inputUnit').value;
            let outputUnit =
document.getElementById('outputUnit').value;

            let baseHeightInCm;

            switch (inputUnit) {
                case 'cm':
                    baseHeightInCm = inputHeight;
                    break;
                case 'in':
                    baseHeightInCm = inputHeight * 2.54;
```

```javascript
            break;
        case 'ft':
            baseHeightInCm = inputHeight * 30.48;
            break;
    }

    let outputHeight;

    switch (outputUnit) {
        case 'cm':
            outputHeight = baseHeightInCm;
            break;
        case 'in':
            outputHeight = baseHeightInCm / 2.54;
            break;
        case 'ft':
            outputHeight = baseHeightInCm / 30.48;
            break;
    }

    document.getElementById('outputHeight').value =
outputHeight;
    }

  </script>
</body>

</html>
```

155

156

```
<!DOCTYPE html>
<html>

<head>
  <title>Height Converter</title>
  <link
href="https://stackpath.bootstrapcdn.com/bootstrap/4.5.2/css/bo
otstrap.min.css" rel="stylesheet">
  <style>
    .jumbotron {
      background-color: #f8f9fa;
    }

    .container {
      max-width: 500px;
    }

    .form-control {
      margin-bottom: 15px;
    }

    .btn-block {
```

```
      margin-top: 15px;
    }
  </style>
</head>

<body>
  <div class="jumbotron text-center">
    <h1 class="display-4">Height Converter</h1>
  </div>
  <div class="container">
    <form id="converter">
      <input id="inputHeight" class="form-control"
type="number" placeholder="Enter height" required>
      <select id="inputUnit" class="form-control">
        <option value="cm">Centimeters</option>
        <option value="in">Inches</option>
        <option value="ft">Feet</option>
      </select>
      <h5 class="text-center">Convert to</h5>
      <select id="outputUnit" class="form-control">
        <option value="cm">Centimeters</option>
        <option value="in">Inches</option>
        <option value="ft">Feet</option>
      </select>
      <input id="outputHeight" class="form-control"
type="number" readonly>
      <button type="button" id="reset" class="btn btn-secondary
btn-block">Reset</button>
    </form>
  </div>

  <script>
    document.getElementById('inputHeight').addEventListener('inp
ut', convertHeight);
    document.getElementById('inputUnit').addEventListener('chan
ge', convertHeight);
    document.getElementById('outputUnit').addEventListener('cha
nge', convertHeight);
    document.getElementById('reset').addEventListener('click',
resetConverter);

    function convertHeight() {
      let inputHeight =
document.getElementById('inputHeight').value;
```

```javascript
      let inputUnit = document.getElementById('inputUnit').value;
      let outputUnit =
document.getElementById('outputUnit').value;

      let baseHeightInCm;

      switch (inputUnit) {
        case 'cm':
          baseHeightInCm = inputHeight;
          break;
        case 'in':
          baseHeightInCm = inputHeight * 2.54;
          break;
        case 'ft':
          baseHeightInCm = inputHeight * 30.48;
          break;
      }

      let outputHeight;

      switch (outputUnit) {
        case 'cm':
          outputHeight = baseHeightInCm;
          break;
        case 'in':
          outputHeight = baseHeightInCm / 2.54;
          break;
        case 'ft':
          outputHeight = baseHeightInCm / 30.48;
          break;
      }

      document.getElementById('outputHeight').value =
outputHeight;
    }

    function resetConverter() {
      document.getElementById('inputHeight').value = '';
      document.getElementById('outputHeight').value = '';
    }
  </script>
</body>

</html>
```

<!-- We have added some visual styles and functional improvements to our existing HTML document. We've added a Reset button to clear the inputs, and made use of Bootstrap for better styling.
Remember, to see the Bootstrap styles applied, you need to have an active internet connection since the Bootstrap CSS is being loaded from a CDN. You can always download it and reference it locally if you prefer. Also, the layout and colors may be adjusted according to your preferences. -->

<!-- CDN stands for Content Delivery Network. It's a network of servers distributed around the world.

When you host your website or application on a single server, all requests from users are sent to that same server. This can lead to high latency (especially for users far away from the server) and can potentially overload the server, leading to slower response times or even downtime.

A CDN alleviates these issues by caching static content (like images, CSS, and JavaScript) on multiple servers around the world. When a user sends a request, the CDN directs it to the nearest server (also known as an edge server) rather than the original server. This reduces the distance the request has to travel, resulting in faster load times.

The Bootstrap CSS file is hosted on a CDN. This means it's being delivered from a server near the user's location, leading to faster load times. It also takes advantage of the CDN's scalability and availability advantages.

By loading Bootstrap from a CDN, you don't have to host the Bootstrap files on your own server. However, it does require the user to have an internet connection to download the CSS file, which may not be desirable in all situations. -->

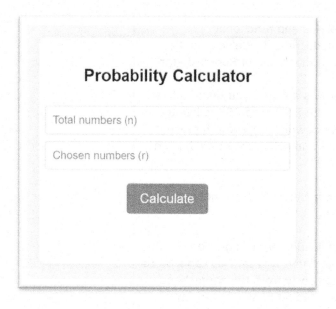

```
<!DOCTYPE html>
<html>

<head>
  <title>Probability Calculator</title>
  <style>
    body {
      font-family: Arial, sans-serif;
      display: flex;
      justify-content: center;
      align-items: center;
      height: 100vh;
      background-color: #f5f5f5;
      flex-direction: column;
      gap: 20px;
    }

    .container {
      display: flex;
      flex-direction: column;
      align-items: center;
      padding: 20px;
      border-radius: 10px;
      box-shadow: 0px 0px 15px rgba(0, 0, 0, 0.1);
```

160

```css
      background-color: #ffffff;
      width: 80%;
      max-width: 500px;
    }

    #result {
      font-size: 2em;
      font-weight: bold;
      color: #007bff;
      margin-top: 20px;
    }

    button {
      padding: 10px 20px;
      font-size: 1.2em;
      color: #ffffff;
      background-color: #007bff;
      border: none;
      border-radius: 5px;
      cursor: pointer;
      margin-top: 20px;
    }

    button:hover {
      background-color: #0056b3;
    }

    input {
      padding: 10px;
      border: 1px solid #cccccc;
      border-radius: 5px;
      font-size: 1em;
      width: 100%;
      margin-top: 10px;
    }
  </style>
</head>

<body>
  <div class="container">
    <h2>Probability Calculator</h2>
    <input id="total-numbers" type="number" min="1"
placeholder="Total numbers (n)" />
```

```html
    <input id="chosen-numbers" type="number" min="1"
placeholder="Chosen numbers (r)" />
    <button onclick="calculateProbability()">Calculate</button>
    <p id="result"></p>
  </div>

  <script>
    function factorial(n) {
      let result = 1;
      for (let i = 2; i <= n; i++) {
        result *= i;
      }
      return result;
    }

    function calculateProbability() {
      const totalNumbers = document.getElementById('total-
numbers').value;
      const chosenNumbers = document.getElementById('chosen-
numbers').value;

      const combinations = factorial(totalNumbers) /
(factorial(chosenNumbers) * factorial(totalNumbers -
chosenNumbers));
      const probability = 1 / combinations;

      document.getElementById('result').innerHTML = 'Probability:
1 in ' + combinations.toLocaleString() + ' (approximately ' +
probability.toFixed(20) + ')';
    }
  </script>
</body>

</html>

<!-- To implement this, I created an HTML form for users to input
their 'n' and 'r' values. We'll then write a JavaScript function to
compute the combination, using the formula C(n, r) = n! / [r!(n-
r)!] which we will call when the button is clicked. -->

<!-- This code takes the user's input for 'n' and 'r', calculates the
combination using the formula, and displays the probability of that
combination. Please note, due to JavaScript's limitation in
```

162

handling large numbers, this calculator may not give accurate results for very large values of 'n' and 'r'. -->

<!-- The probability of winning the lottery where you choose 6 numbers out of 45 (like in many national lotteries) is calculated using combinations, which are ways of choosing items where order doesn't matter.

The formula for combinations is:

$C(n, r) = n! / [r!(n-r)!]$

Where:

n is the total number of options,
r is the number of items to choose,
"!" denotes factorial, which means multiplying all positive integers up to that number. For instance, 5! = 54321 = 120.
Here, n is 45 (because there are 45 numbers to choose from), and r is 6 (because you choose 6 numbers).

So, the total number of possible combinations is:

$C(45, 6) = 45! / [6!(45-6)!] = 8,145,060$

Therefore, the probability of winning is 1 (the successful outcome of getting the winning combination) divided by the total number of combinations:

$P(winning) = 1 / 8,145,060$

So the probability of winning this lottery with one ticket is extremely low, approximately 1 in 8.15 million. -->

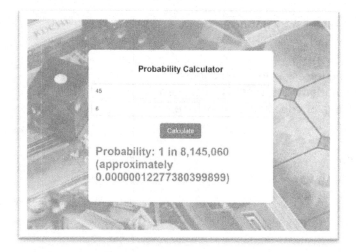

```
<!DOCTYPE html>
<html>

<head>
  <title>Probability Calculator</title>
  <style>
    body:before {
      content: "";
      position: absolute;
      top: 0;
      left: 0;
      width: 100%;
      height: 100%;
      z-index: -1;
      background: url('probability_bg.jpg') no-repeat center center
fixed;
      background-size: cover;
      opacity: 0.5;
    }

    body {
      font-family: Arial, sans-serif;
      display: flex;
      justify-content: center;
      align-items: center;
      height: 100vh;
```

164

```css
    background-color: rgba(245, 245, 245, 0.5);
    flex-direction: column;
    gap: 20px;
    position: relative;
    /* make body positioning context for absolute positioned
pseudo-element */
  }


  .container {
    display: flex;
    flex-direction: column;
    align-items: center;
    padding: 20px;
    border-radius: 10px;
    box-shadow: 0px 0px 15px rgba(0, 0, 0, 0.1);
    background-color: #ffffff;
    width: 80%;
    max-width: 500px;
  }

  #result {
    font-size: 2em;
    font-weight: bold;
    color: #007bff;
    margin-top: 20px;
  }

  button {
    padding: 10px 20px;
    font-size: 1.2em;
    color: #ffffff;
    background-color: #007bff;
    border: none;
    border-radius: 5px;
    cursor: pointer;
    margin-top: 20px;
  }

  button:hover {
    background-color: #0056b3;
  }

  input {
```

```
        padding: 10px;
        border: 1px solid #cccccc;
        border-radius: 5px;
        font-size: 1em;
        width: 100%;
        margin-top: 10px;
      }
    </style>
</head>

<body>
    <div class="container">
      <h2>Probability Calculator</h2>
      <input id="total-numbers" type="number" min="1"
placeholder="Total numbers (n)" />
      <input id="chosen-numbers" type="number" min="1"
placeholder="Chosen numbers (r)" />
      <button onclick="calculateProbability()">Calculate</button>
      <p id="result"></p>
    </div>

    <script>
      function factorial(n) {
        let result = 1;
        for (let i = 2; i <= n; i++) {
          result *= i;
        }
        return result;
      }

      function calculateProbability() {
        const totalNumbers = document.getElementById('total-
numbers').value;
        const chosenNumbers = document.getElementById('chosen-
numbers').value;

        const combinations = factorial(totalNumbers) /
(factorial(chosenNumbers) * factorial(totalNumbers -
chosenNumbers));
        const probability = 1 / combinations;

        document.getElementById('result').innerHTML = 'Probability:
1 in ' + combinations.toLocaleString() + ' (approximately ' +
probability.toFixed(20) + ')';
```

```
    }
  </script>
</body>

</html>
```

<!-- To insert a background image and set its display to 'cover'
and transparency to 0.5, you can modify the CSS as shown above.

This uses the ::before pseudo-element to set the background
image. The pseudo-element is given absolute positioning and set
to cover the whole body element, with its z-index set to -1 so that
it is positioned below the actual content. The image is set to cover
the whole body and not repeat. The opacity is set to 0.5 to make
the image semi-transparent.

The background-color in the body rule is also changed to have 0.5
opacity, to retain the semi-transparent effect. The body is set to
be the positioning context for the ::before pseudo-element by
giving it position: relative.

Please replace 'probability_bg.jpg' with the actual path to your
image. If the image is in the same directory as your HTML file,
you can just keep it as it is. -->

167

168

```
<!DOCTYPE html>
<html>
<head>
    <title>Newsletter Signup Form</title>
    <!-- <link rel="stylesheet" type="text/css" href="styles.css">
-->
    <style>
body {
    font-family: Arial, sans-serif;
    text-align: center;
    padding: 20px;
}

form {
    display: inline-block;
}

label, input {
    margin: 10px 0;
}

input[type="submit"] {
    padding: 10px 20px;
    background-color: blue;
    color: white;
```

```
    border: none;
}

    </style>
</head>
<body>
    <form id="newsletter-form">
        <label for="email">Email:</label><br>
        <input type="email" id="email" name="email"
required><br>
        <input type="submit" value="Subscribe">
    </form>

    <!-- <script src="script.js"></script> -->
    <script>
document.getElementById('newsletter-
form').addEventListener('submit', function(event) {
    // Prevent the form from submitting normally
    event.preventDefault();

    let email = document.getElementById('email').value;

    console.log('Form Submitted! Email:', email);
});

    </script>
</body>
</html>

<!-- In this code:
```

169

The HTML sets up a form with an email input field and a submit
button.
The CSS styles the form, labels, and inputs.
The JavaScript adds an event listener to the form's submit event.
When the form is submitted, it prevents the form from submitting
normally (which would cause the page to refresh), gets the value
of the email input field, and logs it to the console. This simulates
the process of collecting the form data.
To view the form data, you can open the JavaScript console in
your browser's developer tools after clicking the "Subscribe"
button. -->

<!-- Sending emails directly from a client-side JavaScript is not generally possible due to security issues and restrictions imposed by browsers. The common way to send emails in web applications is through a server-side language or using a third-party service.

Here are a few common methods:

1. Using a Server-Side Language: You can use a server-side language like Node.js, PHP, Python, Ruby, etc., to send an email. For example, if you're using Node.js, you could use the nodemailer library to send emails. When the form is submitted, instead of just logging the email to the console, you would send a request to your server with the form data, and your server would send the email.

2. Using a Third-Party Email Service: There are many third-party services that can send emails on your behalf, such as SendGrid, Mailgun, Amazon SES, etc. These services provide APIs that you can use to send emails. In this case, when the form is submitted, you would send a request to the third-party service with the form data, and the service would send the email.

3. Using a Form Submission Service: If you don't want to set up a server or use a third-party email service, you can use a form submission service like Formspree or Getform. These services give you a URL to put in the action attribute of your form. When the form is submitted, the form data is sent to the service, and the service sends you an email with the form data.

Please note that all these options require you to sign up for a service and usually involve some sort of configuration or setup process. Be sure to read the documentation for whichever method you choose to understand how to use it.

Remember that sending emails can sometimes lead to your messages being marked as spam or your email address being blocked if you send a large number of emails, especially if the recipients have not given their consent to receive emails from you. Always make sure you are complying with all relevant laws and regulations when sending emails. -->

<!-- When a user submits their email address via a form on your website, you typically handle that submission with one of the following methods:

170

1. Server-side processing: In this scenario, your website has a backend server (written in a language like Node.js, Python, Django, PHP, etc.). When a user submits the form, a POST request is sent to a specific endpoint on your server with the form data (including the user's email address). The server can then process this data - typically, this would involve saving the email address to a database for later use.

2. Use of a third-party service: If you don't have a backend server, or you prefer not to handle the form submission yourself, you can use a third-party form handling service like Formspree or Netlify forms. These services provide an endpoint that you can use in your form action. When the form is submitted, the data is sent to the third-party service, which can then store the data, send you an email notification, etc.

3. Use of a mailing list or newsletter service: Services like Mailchimp, Sendinblue, or Constant Contact provide form handling specifically designed for newsletter signups. These services provide you with a form or an endpoint to use in your form action, and when the form is submitted, they automatically add the submitted email address to your mailing list.

In any of these methods, the email address is typically stored in a database or list so you can use it to send the newsletter. It's important to remember that when you are collecting and storing people's email addresses, you must comply with all relevant laws and regulations, such as obtaining the user's consent and providing a way for them to unsubscribe. -->

172

```
<!DOCTYPE html>
<html>
<head>
    <title>Newsletter Signup Form</title>
    <!-- <link rel="stylesheet" type="text/css" href="styles.css">
-->
    <style>
body {
    font-family: Arial, sans-serif;
    text-align: center;
    padding: 20px;
}

form {
    display: inline-block;
}

label, input {
    margin: 10px 0;
}

input[type="submit"] {
```

```
    padding: 10px 20px;
    background-color: blue;
    color: white;
    border: none;
}

    </style>
</head>
<body>
    <form id="newsletter-form">
        <label for="email">Email:</label><br>
        <input type="email" id="email" name="email"
required><br>
        <input type="submit" value="Subscribe">
    </form>

    <!-- <script src="script.js"></script> -->
    <script>
document.getElementById('newsletter-
form').addEventListener('submit', function(event) {
    // Prevent the form from submitting normally
    event.preventDefault();

    let email = document.getElementById('email').value;

    console.log('Form Submitted! Email:', email);
});

    </script>
</body>
</html>

<!-- In this code:
```

The HTML sets up a form with an email input field and a submit button.
The CSS styles the form, labels, and inputs.
The JavaScript adds an event listener to the form's submit event. When the form is submitted, it prevents the form from submitting normally (which would cause the page to refresh), gets the value of the email input field, and logs it to the console. This simulates the process of collecting the form data.

To view the form data, you can open the JavaScript console in your browser's developer tools after clicking the "Subscribe" button. -->

<!-- Sending emails directly from a client-side JavaScript is not generally possible due to security issues and restrictions imposed by browsers. The common way to send emails in web applications is through a server-side language or using a third-party service.

Here are a few common methods:

1. Using a Server-Side Language: You can use a server-side language like Node.js, PHP, Python, Ruby, etc., to send an email. For example, if you're using Node.js, you could use the nodemailer library to send emails. When the form is submitted, instead of just logging the email to the console, you would send a request to your server with the form data, and your server would send the email.

2. Using a Third-Party Email Service: There are many third-party services that can send emails on your behalf, such as SendGrid, Mailgun, Amazon SES, etc. These services provide APIs that you can use to send emails. In this case, when the form is submitted, you would send a request to the third-party service with the form data, and the service would send the email.

3. Using a Form Submission Service: If you don't want to set up a server or use a third-party email service, you can use a form submission service like Formspree or Getform. These services give you a URL to put in the action attribute of your form. When the form is submitted, the form data is sent to the service, and the service sends you an email with the form data.

Please note that all these options require you to sign up for a service and usually involve some sort of configuration or setup process. Be sure to read the documentation for whichever method you choose to understand how to use it.

Remember that sending emails can sometimes lead to your messages being marked as spam or your email address being blocked if you send a large number of emails, especially if the recipients have not given their consent to receive emails from you. Always make sure you are complying with all relevant laws and regulations when sending emails. -->

<!-- When a user submits their email address via a form on your website, you typically handle that submission with one of the following methods:

1. Server-side processing: In this scenario, your website has a backend server (written in a language like Node.js, Python, Django, PHP, etc.). When a user submits the form, a POST request is sent to a specific endpoint on your server with the form data (including the user's email address). The server can then process this data - typically, this would involve saving the email address to a database for later use.

2. Use of a third-party service: If you don't have a backend server, or you prefer not to handle the form submission yourself, you can use a third-party form handling service like Formspree or Netlify forms. These services provide an endpoint that you can use in your form action. When the form is submitted, the data is sent to the third-party service, which can then store the data, send you an email notification, etc.

3. Use of a mailing list or newsletter service: Services like Mailchimp, Sendinblue, or Constant Contact provide form handling specifically designed for newsletter signups. These services provide you with a form or an endpoint to use in your form action, and when the form is submitted, they automatically add the submitted email address to your mailing list.

In any of these methods, the email address is typically stored in a database or list so you can use it to send the newsletter. It's important to remember that when you are collecting and storing people's email addresses, you must comply with all relevant laws and regulations, such as obtaining the user's consent and providing a way for them to unsubscribe. -->

Generate Username

ShinyKnight

176

```
<!DOCTYPE html>
<html>
<head>
  <title>Random Username Generator</title>
  <!-- <link rel="stylesheet" type="text/css" href="styles.css"> -->
  <style>
    body {
      font-family: Arial, sans-serif;
      text-align: center;
      padding: 20px;
    }
    #generate-button {
      padding: 10px 20px;
      background-color: blue;
      color: white;
      border: none;
      cursor: pointer;
      letter-spacing: 2px;
    }
    #username-display {
      margin-top: 20px;
      font-size: 24px;
      letter-spacing: 1.5px;
    }
  </style>
</head>
<body>
  <button id="generate-button">Generate Username</button>
  <p id="username-display"></p>
```

```html
<!-- <script src="script.js"></script> -->
<script>
  const adjectives = ['Awesome', 'Shiny', 'Fast', 'Clever',
'Brave'];
  const nouns = ['Unicorn', 'Turtle', 'Rocket', 'Knight', 'Coder'];

  function getRandomElement(array) {
    const randomIndex = Math.floor(Math.random() *
array.length);
    return array[randomIndex];
  }

  function generateUsername() {
    const randomAdjective = getRandomElement(adjectives);
    const randomNoun = getRandomElement(nouns);
    return randomAdjective + randomNoun;
  }

  document.getElementById('generate-
button').addEventListener('click', function () {
    const username = generateUsername();
    document.getElementById('username-display').textContent
= username;
  });
</script>
</body>
</html>
<!-- In this code:
The HTML sets up a button for generating usernames and a
paragraph for displaying the generated username.
The CSS styles the button and the username display.
The JavaScript does the following:
Defines two arrays of adjectives and nouns.
Defines a function getRandomElement for getting a random
element from an array.
Defines a function generateUsername for generating a random
username by concatenating a random adjective and a random
noun.
Adds an event listener to the generate button that generates a
random username and displays it in the username display when
the button is clicked. -->
```

177

Generate Username

Trustworthy Hudson

```
<!DOCTYPE html>
<html>

<head>
  <title>Random Username Generator</title>
  <!-- <link rel="stylesheet" type="text/css" href="styles.css"> -->
  <style>
    body {
      font-family: Arial, sans-serif;
      text-align: center;
      padding: 20px;
    }

    #generate-button {
      padding: 10px 20px;
      background-color: blue;
      color: white;
      border: none;
      cursor: pointer;
      letter-spacing: 2px;
    }

    #username-display {
      margin-top: 20px;
      font-size: 24px;
      letter-spacing: 1.5px;
    }
  </style>
</head>

<body>
```

```html
<button id="generate-button">Generate Username</button>
<p id="username-display"></p>

<!-- <script src="script.js"></script> -->
<script>
  const generateUsername = () => {
    const adjectives = ["Adept", "Brave", "Cautious", "Daring",
"Efficient", "Fearless", "Gracious", "Humble", "Imaginative",
"Joyful", "Keen", "Loyal", "Meticulous", "Noble", "Optimistic",
"Patient", "Quick", "Reliable", "Sincere", "Trustworthy"];
    const nouns = ["Liam", "Noah", "Oliver", "James", "Elijah",
"Henry", "William", "Lucas", "Benjamin", "Theodore", "Olivia",
"Emma", "Amelia", "Charlotte", "Ava", "Sophia", "Luca", "Waylon",
"Kai", "Hudson"];

    const adjective = adjectives[Math.floor(Math.random() *
adjectives.length)];
    const noun = nouns[Math.floor(Math.random() *
nouns.length)];

    return `${adjective} ${noun}`;
  }

  document.getElementById("generate-
button").addEventListener("click", () => {
    document.getElementById("username-display").textContent
= generateUsername();
  });
</script>
</body>
</html>
<!-- I have so far collected the following most popular baby
names in the USA for 2023. There are more names that need to
be collected to meet your request of having 20 names. -->
<!-- This will ensure that there is a space between the adjective
and the noun, creating usernames like "Shiny Turtle" instead of
"ShinyTurtle". The key change here is in the return statement of
the generateUsername function, where a space character (" ") is
inserted between the ${adjective} and ${noun} placeholders. -->
```

Age Calculator

Enter your birthdate: | 1997 – 05 – 05 | 📅 | | Calculate Age |

You are 26 years old.

```html
<!DOCTYPE html>
<html>
<head>
    <title>Age Calculator</title>
    <!-- <link rel="stylesheet" type="text/css" href="styles.css">
-->
    <style>
body {
    font-family: Arial, sans-serif;
    margin: 0;
    padding: 0;
    display: flex;
    flex-direction: column;
    align-items: center;
    justify-content: center;
    height: 100vh;
    background-color: #f0f0f0;
}

form {
    margin-bottom: 1em;
}

button {
    margin-left: 1em;
}

    </style>
</head>
<body>
    <h1>Age Calculator</h1>
```

180

```html
    <form id="age-calculator-form">
        <label for="birthdate">Enter your birthdate:</label>
        <input type="date" id="birthdate">
        <button type="submit">Calculate Age</button>
    </form>
    <p id="result"></p>
<!-- <script src="script.js"></script> -->
<script>
document.getElementById("age-calculator-
form").addEventListener("submit", function(e) {
    e.preventDefault();

    const birthdate = new
Date(document.getElementById("birthdate").value);
    const today = new Date();

    let age = today.getFullYear() - birthdate.getFullYear();
    const month = today.getMonth() - birthdate.getMonth();

    if (month < 0 || (month === 0 && today.getDate() <
birthdate.getDate())) {
        age--;
    }

    document.getElementById("result").textContent = "You are "
+ age + " years old.";
});
</script>
</body>
</html>
<!-- The HTML code creates a simple form where users can enter
their birthdate. The CSS provides some basic styling. The
JavaScript code handles the form submission event, calculates the
user's age based on their birthdate and the current date, and
displays the result on the page.
Please note that the date input field may not work correctly in all
browsers. This is a limitation of HTML5 date input, which is not
fully supported in all browsers (such as Firefox). If you need to
support all browsers, you may need to use a JavaScript date
picker library. -->
```

181

```
<!DOCTYPE html>
<html>
<head>
  <title>Simple Drawing App</title>
  <!-- <link rel="stylesheet" type="text/css" href="styles.css"> --
>
  <style>
    body {
      display: flex;
      justify-content: center;
      align-items: center;
      height: 100vh;
      background-color: #f0f0f0;
      margin: 0;
      padding: 0;
    }
    #drawing-area {
      border: 1px solid black;
    }
  </style>
</head>
<body>
  <canvas id="drawing-area" width="800"
height="600"></canvas>
  <!-- <script src="script.js"></script> -->
  <script>
    const canvas = document.getElementById('drawing-area');
    const ctx = canvas.getContext('2d');
```

```javascript
    let drawing = false;

    canvas.addEventListener('mousedown', e => {
      drawing = true;
      draw(e);
    });

    canvas.addEventListener('mousemove', draw);
    canvas.addEventListener('mouseup', () => {
      drawing = false;
      ctx.beginPath();
    });

    function draw(e) {
      if (!drawing) return;
      ctx.lineWidth = 5;
      ctx.lineCap = 'round';
      ctx.strokeStyle = 'black';

      ctx.lineTo(e.clientX - canvas.offsetLeft, e.clientY -
canvas.offsetTop);
      ctx.stroke();
      ctx.beginPath();
      ctx.moveTo(e.clientX - canvas.offsetLeft, e.clientY -
canvas.offsetTop);
    }
  </script>
</body>
</html>
```

183

```html
<!-- This code creates a simple drawing app where users can
draw lines with their mouse. The HTML sets up a canvas for the
user to draw on. The CSS centers the canvas on the page and
adds a border around it. The JavaScript handles the mouse events
for starting a line (mousedown), drawing a line (mousemove), and
ending a line (mouseup). The draw function draws a line from the
previous mouse position to the current mouse position.
You can further enhance this application by adding features like
changing the color and width of the lines, erasing, and saving
drawings. -->
```

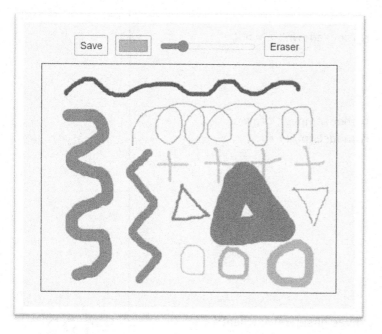

184

```
<!DOCTYPE html>
<html>

<head>
  <title>Enhanced Drawing App</title>
  <!-- <link rel="stylesheet" type="text/css" href="styles.css"> --
>
  <style>
    body {
      display: flex;
      justify-content: center;
      align-items: center;
      flex-direction: column;
      height: 100vh;
      background-color: #f0f0f0;
      margin: 0;
      padding: 0;
    }

    #drawing-area {
      border: 1px solid black;
      margin-top: 10px;
```

```
    }

  div {
    display: flex;
    justify-content: center;
    gap: 10px;
  }
  </style>
</head>

<body>
  <div>
    <button id="save-btn">Save</button>
    <input type="color" id="color-picker">
    <input type="range" id="brush-size" min="1" max="50">
    <button id="eraser-btn">Eraser</button>
  </div>
  <canvas id="drawing-area" width="400"
height="300"></canvas>
  <!-- <script src="script.js"></script> -->
  <script>
    const canvas = document.getElementById('drawing-area');
    const ctx = canvas.getContext('2d');
    const colorPicker = document.getElementById('color-picker');
    const brushSize = document.getElementById('brush-size');
    const saveBtn = document.getElementById('save-btn');
    const eraserBtn = document.getElementById('eraser-btn');

    let drawing = false;
    let erasing = false;

    canvas.addEventListener('mousedown', e => {
      drawing = true;
      draw(e);
    });

    canvas.addEventListener('mousemove', draw);

    canvas.addEventListener('mouseup', () => {
      drawing = false;
      ctx.beginPath();
    });

    colorPicker.addEventListener('change', () => {
```

```
      ctx.strokeStyle = colorPicker.value;
    });

    brushSize.addEventListener('change', () => {
      ctx.lineWidth = brushSize.value;
    });

    eraserBtn.addEventListener('click', () => {
      erasing = !erasing;
      if (erasing) {
        ctx.globalCompositeOperation = 'destination-out';
      } else {
        ctx.globalCompositeOperation = 'source-over';
      }
    });

    saveBtn.addEventListener('click', () => {
      const dataUrl = canvas.toDataURL('image/png');
      const newTab = window.open('about:blank', 'image');
      newTab.document.write("<img src='" + dataUrl + "'
alt='Canvas Image'/>");
    });

    function draw(e) {
      if (!drawing) return;
      ctx.lineCap = 'round';

      ctx.lineTo(e.clientX - canvas.offsetLeft, e.clientY -
canvas.offsetTop);
      ctx.stroke();
      ctx.beginPath();
      ctx.moveTo(e.clientX - canvas.offsetLeft, e.clientY -
canvas.offsetTop);
    }

  </script>
</body>

</html>

<!-- Here's an extended version of the previous code that adds
the following features:

1. The ability to change the color of the lines.
```

186

2. The ability to change the width of the lines.
3. An eraser tool.
4. A button to save the drawing as an image.

This version of the code adds a color picker input, a range input to control the brush size, an eraser button, and a save button. The JavaScript code has been updated to handle these new elements and their events. The eraser button toggles the globalCompositeOperation between source-over (normal drawing) and destination-out (which "erases" pixels by making them transparent). The save button opens the current state of the canvas in a new tab as an image. -->

```
<!DOCTYPE html>
<html>

<head>
  <title>BMI Calculator</title>
  <!-- <link rel="stylesheet" type="text/css" href="styles.css"> --
>
  <style>
   body {
     display: flex;
     justify-content: center;
     align-items: center;
     height: 100vh;
     background-color: #f0f0f0;
     margin: 0;
     padding: 0;
   }

   #calculator {
     text-align: center;
     background-color: #fff;
     padding: 20px;
     border-radius: 10px;
```

```
      box-shadow: 0px 0px 10px 0px rgba(0, 0, 0, 0.15);
    }

    input {
      margin-bottom: 10px;
    }
  </style>
</head>

<body>
  <div id="calculator">
    <h1>BMI Calculator</h1>
    <label for="weight">Weight in Kilograms:</label><br>
    <input type="number" id="weight" required><br>
    <label for="height">Height in Centimeters:</label><br>
    <input type="number" id="height" step="1" required><br>
    <button id="calculate">Calculate</button>
    <p id="result"></p>
    <!-- When setting the unit of height to meters, change
'Centimeters' to 'Meters' and 'step 1' to '0.01'. Additionally,
remove '10000' from the calculation formula in JavaScript. -->
  </div>

  <!-- <script src="script.js"></script> -->
  <script>
    document.getElementById('calculate').addEventListener('click',
function () {
      var weight = document.getElementById('weight').value;
      var height = document.getElementById('height').value;
      var result = document.getElementById('result');

      if (height === "" || isNaN(height)) {
        result.textContent = "Please provide valid height!";
      } else if (weight === "" || isNaN(weight)) {
        result.textContent = "Please provide valid weight!";
      } else {
        var bmi = (weight / (height * height / 10000)).toFixed(2);
        result.textContent = "Your BMI is " + bmi;
      }
    });

  </script>
</body>
```

189

```
</html>

<!-- In this code, the HTML file creates the structure of the BMI
calculator, including the input fields for weight and height, and the
button to calculate the BMI. The CSS file styles the calculator to
center it on the page and gives it a basic design. The JavaScript
file adds functionality to the calculator. When the calculate button
is clicked, it retrieves the values entered for weight and height,
calculates the BMI (weight divided by height squared), and
displays the result. If the weight or height input is missing or not
a number, it displays an error message. -->
```

BMI Calculator

BMI, or Body Mass Index, is a measure used to determine whether a person has a healthy body weight for a given height. It is defined as the individual's body mass divided by the square of their height. The unit of BMI is kg/m².

The BMI categories for adults according to the World Health Organization (WHO) are:
- Below 18.5: Underweight
- 18.5–24.9: Normal weight
- 25–29.9: Overweight
- 30 or above: Obesity

Please note that while BMI is a useful screening tool, it does not directly measure body fat. It's always a good idea to speak with a healthcare professional for a full understanding of your health.

Height (cm):

`169`

Weight (kg):

`61`

`Calculate BMI`

Your BMI is 21.36. This is considered normal weight.

```
<!DOCTYPE html>
<html>

<head>
  <title>BMI Calculator</title>
  <style>
    body {
      font-family: Arial, sans-serif;
    }

    .container {
      max-width: 600px;
      margin: auto;
      padding: 20px;
    }

    .input-group {
      margin-bottom: 10px;
    }

    .input-group label {
      display: block;
```

```
        }

    .result {
      margin-top: 20px;
    }
  </style>
</head>

<body>
  <div class="container">
    <h1>BMI Calculator</h1>
    <p>
      BMI, or Body Mass Index, is a measure used to determine
whether a person has a healthy body weight for a given
      height.
      It is defined as the individual's body mass divided by the
square of their height. The unit of BMI is kg/m².
      <br><br>
      The BMI categories for adults according to the World Health
Organization (WHO) are:<br>
        - Below 18.5: Underweight<br>
        - 18.5-24.9: Normal weight<br>
        - 25-29.9: Overweight<br>
        - 30 or above: Obesity<br><br>
      Please note that while BMI is a useful screening tool, it does
not directly measure body fat.
      It's always a good idea to speak with a healthcare
professional for a full understanding of your health.
    </p>
    <div class="input-group">
      <label for="height">Height (cm):</label>
      <input type="number" id="height">
    </div>
    <div class="input-group">
      <label for="weight">Weight (kg):</label>
      <input type="number" id="weight">
    </div>

    <!-- Examine the difference in JavaScript code when using 'id'
on a button versus using 'onclick'. -->
    <button onclick="calculateBMI()">Calculate BMI</button>
    <hr>
    <div class="result" id="result"></div>
    <hr>
```

```
  </div>
  <!-- <script src="script.js"></script> -->
  <script>
    function calculateBMI() {
      let height = document.getElementById('height').value;
      let weight = document.getElementById('weight').value;

      // convert height from cm to m
      height = height / 100;

      let bmi = weight / (height * height);

      let result = document.getElementById('result');

      if (bmi < 18.5) {
        result.innerHTML = "Your BMI is " + bmi.toFixed(2) + ".
This is considered underweight.";
      } else if (bmi >= 18.5 && bmi < 24.9) {
        result.innerHTML = "Your BMI is " + bmi.toFixed(2) + ".
This is considered normal weight.";
      } else if (bmi >= 25 && bmi < 29.9) {
        result.innerHTML = "Your BMI is " + bmi.toFixed(2) + ".
This is considered overweight.";
      } else {
        result.innerHTML = "Your BMI is " + bmi.toFixed(2) + ".
This is considered obese.";
      }
    }

  </script>
</body>

</html>
```

<!-- This script gets the height and weight values from the input fields, then calculates the BMI. The toFixed(2) function is used to round the BMI to two decimal places. The result is then displayed in the "result" element.

You can save this code in a file named "script.js" in the same directory as your "index.html" file.

Remember, this is a very basic version of a BMI calculator and doesn't take into account factors like age, gender, or muscle

mass, which can influence the BMI. Always consult with a
healthcare professional for accurate health information. -->

BMI Calculator

BMI, or Body Mass Index, is a measure used to determine whether a person has a healthy body weight for a given height. It is defined as the individual's body mass divided by the square of their height. The unit of BMI is kg/m².

The BMI categories for adults according to the World Health Organization (WHO) are:
- Below 18.5: Underweight
- 18.5–24.9: Normal weight
- 25–29.9: Overweight
- 30 or above: Obesity

Please note that while BMI is a useful screening tool, it does not directly measure body fat. It's always a good idea to speak with a healthcare professional for a full understanding of your health.

Height (cm):

180

Weight (kg):

70

Calculate BMI

Your BMI is 21.60. This is considered normal weight.

```
<!DOCTYPE html>
<html>

<head>
  <title>BMI Calculator</title>
  <style>
    body {
      font-family: Arial, sans-serif;
    }

    .container {
      max-width: 600px;
      margin: auto;
```

```css
      /* padding: 20px; */
      border: 1px solid #ccc;
      border-radius: 5px;
      box-shadow: 0 0 10px rgba(0, 0, 0, 0.1);
      background-color: #f8f8f8;
    }
    .content {
      padding: 20px;
    }
    p {
      font-size: 0.9em;
      /* Reduce font size */
      background-color: #e0e0e0;
      /* Background color for paragraph */
      padding: 10px;
      border-radius: 5px;
    }
    .input-group {
      max-width: 400px;
      margin-bottom: 10px;
    }
    .input-group label {
      display: block;
    }
    .input-group input {
      width: 100%;
      padding: 10px;
      border: 2px solid #333;
      /* Border for input fields */
      border-radius: 5px;
      color: #333;
    }
    button {
      padding: 10px 20px;
      background-color: #009688;
      /* Background color for button */
      color: white;
      border: none;
      border-radius: 5px;
      cursor: pointer;
    }
    .result {
      margin-top: 20px;
    }
```

```
  .result-display {
    display: flex;
    justify-content: space-between;
    align-items: center;
  }
  img {
    width: 300px;
    height: 200px;
    border-radius: 5px;
    box-shadow: 0 0 10px rgba(0, 0, 0, 0.1);
  }
 </style>
</head>
<body>
 <div class="container">
   <div class="content">
     <h1>BMI Calculator</h1>
     <p>
       BMI, or Body Mass Index, is a measure used to determine
whether a person has a healthy body weight for a given
       height.
       It is defined as the individual's body mass divided by the
square of their height. The unit of BMI is kg/m².
       <br><br>
       The BMI categories for adults according to the World Health
Organization (WHO) are:<br>
       - Below 18.5: Underweight<br>
       - 18.5–24.9: Normal weight<br>
       - 25–29.9: Overweight<br>
       - 30 or above: Obesity<br><br>
       Please note that while BMI is a useful screening tool, it
does not directly measure body fat.
       It's always a good idea to speak with a healthcare
professional for a full understanding of your health.
     </p>
     <div class="input-group">
       <label for="height">Height (cm):</label>
       <input type="number" id="height">
     </div>
     <div class="input-group">
       <label for="weight">Weight (kg):</label>
       <input type="number" id="weight">
     </div>
     <button onclick="calculateBMI()">Calculate BMI</button>
```

```html
      <div class="result-display">
        <div class="result" id="result"></div>
        <img src="bmi_calculate.jpg" alt="BMI Calculation">
      </div>
    </div>
  </div>
  <script>
    function calculateBMI() {
      let height = document.getElementById('height').value;
      let weight = document.getElementById('weight').value;

      // convert height from cm to m
      height = height / 100;

      let bmi = weight / (height * height);

      let result = document.getElementById('result');

      if (bmi < 18.5) {
        result.innerHTML = "Your BMI is " + bmi.toFixed(2) + ".
This is considered underweight.";
      } else if (bmi >= 18.5 && bmi < 24.9) {
        result.innerHTML = "Your BMI is " + bmi.toFixed(2) + ".
This is considered normal weight.";
      } else if (bmi >= 25 && bmi < 29.9) {
        result.innerHTML = "Your BMI is " + bmi.toFixed(2) + ".
This is considered overweight.";
      } else {
        result.innerHTML = "Your BMI is " + bmi.toFixed(2) + ".
This is considered obese.";
      }
    }
  </script>
</body>
</html>
```

BMI Calculator

BMI, or Body Mass Index, is a measure used to determine whether a person has a healthy body weight for a given height.

Height (cm):

174

Weight (kg):

68

Calculate BMI

Your BMI is 22.46. This is considered normal weight.

```
<!DOCTYPE html>
<html>

<head>
  <title>BMI Calculator</title>
  <!-- Include Bootstrap CSS -->
  <link
href="https://stackpath.bootstrapcdn.com/bootstrap/4.3.1/css/bo
otstrap.min.css" rel="stylesheet">
</head>

<body>
  <div class="container mt-5">
    <div class="card">
      <div class="card-body">
        <h1 class="card-title text-center">BMI Calculator</h1>
        <p class="card-text text-center">
          <i>BMI, or Body Mass Index, is a measure used to
determine whether a person has a healthy body weight for a
          given height.</i>
        </p>
        <form>
```

```html
        <div class="form-group">
          <label for="height">Height (cm):</label>
          <input type="number" id="height" class="form-
control">
        </div>
        <div class="form-group">
          <label for="weight">Weight (kg):</label>
          <input type="number" id="weight" class="form-
control">
        </div>
        <button type="button" onclick="calculateBMI()"
class="btn btn-primary btn-block">Calculate BMI</button>
      </form>
      <div class="mt-3" id="result"></div>
    </div>
  </div>
</div>
<script>
  function calculateBMI() {
    let height = document.getElementById('height').value;
    let weight = document.getElementById('weight').value;

    // convert height from cm to m
    height = height / 100;

    let bmi = weight / (height * height);

    let result = document.getElementById('result');

    if (bmi < 18.5) {
      result.innerHTML = "Your BMI is " + bmi.toFixed(2) + ".
This is considered underweight.";
    } else if (bmi >= 18.5 && bmi < 24.9) {
      result.innerHTML = "Your BMI is " + bmi.toFixed(2) + ".
This is considered normal weight.";
    } else if (bmi >= 25 && bmi < 29.9) {
      result.innerHTML = "Your BMI is " + bmi.toFixed(2) + ".
This is considered overweight.";
    } else {
      result.innerHTML = "Your BMI is " + bmi.toFixed(2) + ".
This is considered obese.";
    }
  }
</script>
```

```
</body>

</html>

<!-- We enhanced our existing code by incorporating Bootstrap to
make the UI better. We added Bootstrap classes to our existing
HTML elements for better styling and layout.

This code uses Bootstrap's card and form elements to create a
clean layout for our BMI Calculator. The mt-5 class adds some
margin at the top of the container to move it away from the edge
of the viewport. The button now utilizes Bootstrap's button classes
for a more appealing look.

Remember to add the link to the Bootstrap CSS at the top of our
HTML file for these styles to take effect.

The colors and other styles can be customized further by adding
more Bootstrap classes or your own custom styles. -->
```

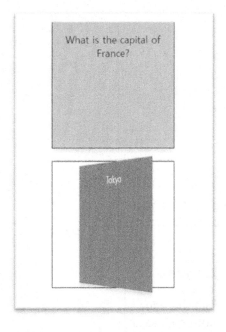

```
<!DOCTYPE html>
<html>

<head>
  <title>Flashcards</title>
  <!-- <link rel="stylesheet" type="text/css" href="styles.css"> --
>
  <style>
    .card {
      perspective: 1000px;
      width: 200px;
      height: 200px;
      position: relative;
      margin: 0 auto 20px;
      border: 1px solid #000;
      cursor: pointer;
    }

    .card-inner {
      position: relative;
      width: 100%;
      height: 100%;
```

```
      text-align: center;
      transition: transform 0.6s;
      transform-style: preserve-3d;
      box-shadow: 0 4px 8px 0 rgba(0, 0, 0, 0.2);
    }

    .card:hover .card-inner {
      transform: rotateY(180deg);
    }

    .card-front,
    .card-back {
      position: absolute;
      width: 100%;
      height: 100%;
      backface-visibility: hidden;
    }

    .card-front {
      background-color: #bbb;
      color: black;
    }

    .card-back {
      background-color: #2980b9;
      color: white;
      transform: rotateY(180deg);
    }
  </style>
</head>

<body>
  <div class="card" onclick="flipCard(this)">
    <div class="card-inner">
      <div class="card-front">
        <p>What is the capital of France?</p>
      </div>
      <div class="card-back">
        <p>Paris</p>
      </div>
    </div>
  </div>
  <div class="card" onclick="flipCard(this)">
    <div class="card-inner">
```

```
      <div class="card-front">
        <p>What is the capital of Japan?</p>
      </div>
      <div class="card-back">
        <p>Tokyo</p>
      </div>
    </div>
  </div>
  <!-- <script src="script.js"></script> -->
  <script>
    function flipCard(card) {
      card.querySelector('.card-inner').classList.toggle('is-flipped');
    }

  </script>
</body>

</html>

<!-- In this example, each flashcard is a div with the class "card".
Inside the card, there is another div with the class "card-inner"
that contains the front and back of the card. The front of the card
shows the question, and the back shows the answer.

The CSS adds a flip effect to the card when it's hovered over. The
"perspective" property gives the flip a 3D effect, and the
"backface-visibility" property hides the back of the card until it's
flipped over.

The JavaScript code toggles the "is-flipped" class when a card is
clicked. The "is-flipped" class changes the transform property of
the card to rotate it 180 degrees, flipping it over to show the
back. -->
```

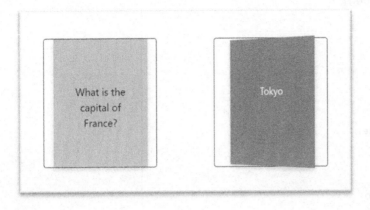

```
<!DOCTYPE html>
<html>

<head>
  <title>Flashcards</title>
  <link
href="https://stackpath.bootstrapcdn.com/bootstrap/4.3.1/css/bo
otstrap.min.css" rel="stylesheet">

  <style>
    .card {
      perspective: 1000px;
      width: 200px;
      height: 200px;
      margin: 20px auto;
      border: 1px solid #000;
      cursor: pointer;
    }

    .card-inner {
      position: relative;
      width: 100%;
      height: 100%;
      text-align: center;
      transition: transform 0.6s;
      transform-style: preserve-3d;
      box-shadow: 0 4px 8px 0 rgba(0, 0, 0, 0.2);
    }
```

```css
    .card:hover .card-inner {
      transform: rotateY(180deg);
    }

    .card-front,
    .card-back {
      position: absolute;
      width: 100%;
      height: 100%;
      backface-visibility: hidden;
    }

    .card-front {
      background-color: #bbb;
      color: black;
      padding: 70px 20px;
    }

    .card-back {
      background-color: #2980b9;
      color: white;
      transform: rotateY(180deg);
      padding: 70px 20px;
    }
  </style>
</head>

<body>
  <div class="container my-5">
    <div class="row justify-content-center">
      <div class="card col-sm-4" onclick="flipCard(this)">
        <div class="card-inner">
          <div class="card-front">
            <p>What is the capital of France?</p>
          </div>
          <div class="card-back">
            <p>Paris</p>
          </div>
        </div>
      </div>
      <div class="card col-sm-4" onclick="flipCard(this)">
        <div class="card-inner">
          <div class="card-front">
            <p>What is the capital of Japan?</p>
```

```
          </div>
          <div class="card-back">
            <p>Tokyo</p>
          </div>
        </div>
      </div>
    </div>
  </div>
  <script>
    function flipCard(card) {
      card.querySelector('.card-inner').classList.toggle('is-flipped');
    }
  </script>
</body>

</html>

<!-- We enhance our existing code by incorporating Bootstrap for
a more user-friendly design and responsive layout.

In the above code:

Bootstrap's CDN has been added in the <head> tag to use
Bootstrap classes.
A Bootstrap container class has been added for center alignment
and responsive padding.
Each card is wrapped within a row and col-sm-4 to make them
responsive and to allow them to stack vertically on smaller
screens.
A my-5 class has been added for vertical spacing.
Please remember to load the Bootstrap CSS file to apply these
styles correctly. -->
```

207

Password Strength Checker

```
........|
```

Strong

```
<!DOCTYPE html>
<html>

<head>
  <title>Password Strength Checker</title>
  <!-- <link rel="stylesheet" type="text/css" href="styles.css"> -->
  <style>
    body {
      font-family: Arial, sans-serif;
    }

    input {
      margin: 20px 0;
      padding: 10px;
      width: 200px;
    }
  </style>
</head>

<body>
  <h2>Password Strength Checker</h2>
  <input id="password" type="password"
oninput="checkPasswordStrength(this.value)" placeholder="Enter
password" />
  <p id="passwordStrength"></p>
  <!-- <script src="script.js"></script> -->
  <script>
    function checkPasswordStrength(password) {
```

```javascript
    var strength = 0;

    // Check length
    if (password.length >= 8) {
      strength++;
    }

    // Check for lowercase letters
    if (/[a-z]/.test(password)) {
      strength++;
    }

    // Check for uppercase letters
    if (/[A-Z]/.test(password)) {
      strength++;
    }

    // Check for numbers
    if (/[0-9]/.test(password)) {
      strength++;
    }

    // Check for special characters
    if (/[^a-zA-Z0-9]/.test(password)) {
      strength++;
    }

    var passwordStrength =
document.getElementById('passwordStrength');

    switch (strength) {
      case 0:
        passwordStrength.textContent = '';
        break;
      case 1:
        passwordStrength.textContent = 'Very weak';
        break;
      case 2:
        passwordStrength.textContent = 'Weak';
        break;
      case 3:
        passwordStrength.textContent = 'Medium';
        break;
      case 4:
```

```
            passwordStrength.textContent = 'Strong';
            break;
        case 5:
            passwordStrength.textContent = 'Very strong';
            break;
        }
    }

  </script>
</body>

</html>

<!-- The JavaScript code tests the password against several
regular expressions to determine its strength. Each condition it
meets (such as containing a lowercase letter) increases its
strength by one. The strength is then displayed on the page. Note
that this is a very basic password strength checker and might not
meet all your needs. It could be expanded to include other checks,
such as checking against a list of common passwords. -->
```

Password Strength Checker

This tool checks the strength of a password
based on length, types of characters used,
and comparison to a list of common passwords.

············|

Extremely strong

Estimated break time: Decades

```html
<!DOCTYPE html>
<html>

<head>
  <title>Password Strength Checker</title>
  <!-- <link rel="stylesheet" type="text/css" href="styles.css"> --
>
  <style>
  body {
    font-family: Arial, sans-serif;
    display: flex;
    justify-content: center;
    align-items: center;
    height: 100vh;
    margin: 0;
    background-color: #f0f0f0;
  }

  .center {
    text-align: center;
  }

  input {
    margin: 20px 0;
    padding: 10px;
    width: 200px;
  }
```

211

```html
    </style>
  </head>

  <body>
    <div class="center">
      <h1>Password Strength Checker</h1>
      <p>This tool checks the strength of a password<br> based on
length, types of characters used,<br>
        and comparison to a list
        of common passwords.</p>
      <input id="password" type="password"
oninput="checkPasswordStrength(this.value)" placeholder="Enter
password" />
      <p id="passwordStrength"></p>
      <p id="breakTime"></p>
    </div>
    <!-- <script src="script.js"></script> -->
    <script>
    var commonPasswords = ['123456', 'password', '12345678',
'qwerty', 'abc123'];

    function checkPasswordStrength(password) {
      var strength = 0;

      // Check length
      if (password.length >= 8) {
        strength++;
      }

      // Check for lowercase letters
      if (/[a-z]/.test(password)) {
        strength++;
      }

      // Check for uppercase letters
      if (/[A-Z]/.test(password)) {
        strength++;
      }

      // Check for numbers
      if (/[0-9]/.test(password)) {
        strength++;
      }
```

```
      // Check for special characters
      if (/[^a-zA-Z0-9]/.test(password)) {
        strength++;
      }

      // Check against list of common passwords
      if (!commonPasswords.includes(password)) {
        strength++;
      }

      var passwordStrength =
document.getElementById('passwordStrength');
      var breakTime = document.getElementById('breakTime');

      switch (strength) {
        case 0:
          passwordStrength.textContent = '';
          breakTime.textContent = '';
          break;
        case 1:
          passwordStrength.textContent = 'Very weak';
          breakTime.textContent = 'Estimated break time: Instant';
          break;
        case 2:
          passwordStrength.textContent = 'Weak';
          breakTime.textContent = 'Estimated break time:
Seconds';
          break;
        case 3:
          passwordStrength.textContent = 'Medium';
          breakTime.textContent = 'Estimated break time: Hours';
          break;
        case 4:
          passwordStrength.textContent = 'Strong';
          breakTime.textContent = 'Estimated break time: Days';
          break;
        case 5:
          passwordStrength.textContent = 'Very strong';
          breakTime.textContent = 'Estimated break time: Years';
          break;
        case 6:
          passwordStrength.textContent = 'Extremely strong';
          breakTime.textContent = 'Estimated break time:
Decades';
```

```
      break;
    }
  }

  </script>
</body>

</html>

<!-- We first center the display and add a title and description.
And we add the common passwords check and estimated
password-breaking time to the JavaScript file. For simplicity, we'll
use a small list of common passwords and a very rough estimate
for the breaking time. This is a very basic and rough estimate of
the password. -->
```

```
<!DOCTYPE html>
<html>

<head>
  <title>Password Strength Checker</title>
  <!-- Include Bootstrap CSS -->
  <link
href="https://stackpath.bootstrapcdn.com/bootstrap/4.3.1/css/bo
otstrap.min.css" rel="stylesheet">
</head>

<body>
  <div class="container">
    <div class="row justify-content-center">
      <div class="col-12 col-md-8 col-lg-6">
        <div class="card my-5">
          <div class="card-body">
            <h1 class="card-title text-center">Password Strength
Checker</h1>
            <p class="card-text text-center">This tool checks the
strength of a password based on length, types of
            characters used, and comparison to a list of common
passwords.</p>
            <input class="form-control" id="password"
type="password" oninput="checkPasswordStrength(this.value)"
            placeholder="Enter password">
            <div id="passwordStrength" class="progress my-4">
```

```
        <div id="passwordStrengthBar" class="progress-bar"
role="progressbar" style="width: 0%;" aria-valuenow="0"
            aria-valuemin="0" aria-valuemax="100"></div>
      </div>
      <p id="breakTime" class="card-text text-center"></p>
    </div>
  </div>
  </div>
  </div>

<script>
  var commonPasswords = ['123456', 'password', '12345678',
'qwerty', 'abc123'];

  function checkPasswordStrength(password) {
    var strength = 0;

    if (password.length >= 8) { strength++; }
    if (/[a-z]/.test(password)) { strength++; }
    if (/[A-Z]/.test(password)) { strength++; }
    if (/[0-9]/.test(password)) { strength++; }
    if (/[^a-zA-Z0-9]/.test(password)) { strength++; }
    if (!commonPasswords.includes(password)) { strength++; }

    var passwordStrengthBar =
document.getElementById('passwordStrengthBar');
    var breakTime = document.getElementById('breakTime');

    passwordStrengthBar.style.width = strength * 16.667 + '%';

    switch (strength) {
      case 0:
        breakTime.textContent = '';
        break;
      case 1:
        breakTime.textContent = 'Estimated break time: Instant';
        break;
      case 2:
        breakTime.textContent = 'Estimated break time:
Seconds';
        break;
      case 3:
        breakTime.textContent = 'Estimated break time: Hours';
```

```
          break;
      case 4:
          breakTime.textContent = 'Estimated break time: Days';
          break;
      case 5:
          breakTime.textContent = 'Estimated break time: Years';
          break;
      case 6:
          breakTime.textContent = 'Estimated break time:
Decades';
          break;
      }
    }
  </script>
</body>
</html>

<!-- We can enhance the layout and functionality of your existing
code by incorporating Bootstrap. Bootstrap provides a
powerful, responsive grid system along with many components
that can help enhance the UI/UX.
This introduces a progress bar to visually represent the password
strength. Additionally, the code also utilizes the
card component for better styling and layout.
This code will create a responsive card with a title and description
centered in the middle. As you type the password, the progress
bar will fill up and the estimated break time will update according
to the password strength.

Remember to add the link to the Bootstrap CSS at the top of your
HTML file for these styles to take effect.
The colors of the progress bar can also be updated with the
Bootstrap classes "bg-success", "bg-info", "bg-warning", and "bg-
danger" depending on the strength of the password. For example,
you can add passwordStrengthBar.classList.add('bg-success');
when the strength is 5 or 6. Similarly, add 'bg-warning' when the
strength is 3 or 4, and 'bg-danger' when the strength is 1 or 2. --
>
```

217

Fibonacci Sequence Generator

Enter a number and generate the Fibonacci sequence up to that number.

| 500 | | Generate |

Fibonacci Sequence: 0, 1, 1, 2, 3, 5, 8, 13, 21, 34, 55, 89, 144, 233, 377

218

```
<!DOCTYPE html>
<html>

<head>
  <title>Fibonacci Sequence Generator</title>
  <!-- <link rel="stylesheet" type="text/css" href="styles.css"> -->
  <style>
    body {
      font-family: Arial, sans-serif;
      display: flex;
      justify-content: center;
      align-items: center;
      height: 100vh;
      margin: 0;
      background-color: #f0f0f0;
    }

    .center {
      text-align: center;
    }

    input,
```

```
    button {
      margin: 20px 0;
      padding: 10px;
    }
  </style>
</head>

<body>
  <div class="center">
    <h1>Fibonacci Sequence Generator</h1>
    <p>Enter a number and generate the Fibonacci sequence up
to that number.</p>
    <input id="num" type="number" placeholder="Enter a
number" />
    <button onclick="generateFibonacci()">Generate</button>
    <p id="sequence"></p>
  </div>
  <!-- <script src="script.js"></script> -->
  <script>
    function generateFibonacci() {
      var num = document.getElementById('num').value;
      var sequence = [0, 1];

      while ((sequence[sequence.length - 1] +
sequence[sequence.length - 2]) <= num) {
        sequence.push(sequence[sequence.length - 1] +
sequence[sequence.length - 2]);
      }

      document.getElementById('sequence').innerText = 'Fibonacci
Sequence: ' + sequence.join(', ');
    }

  </script>
```

```html
</body>

</html>

<!-- This program will generate the Fibonacci sequence up to the
number that the user enters in the input field. When the user
clicks the "Generate" button, the generateFibonacci function is
called, which generates the Fibonacci sequence and displays it on
the webpage. -->

<!-- The Fibonacci sequence is a series of numbers in which each
number is the sum of the two preceding ones, usually starting
with 0 and 1.

So, the sequence goes: 0, 1, 1, 2, 3, 5, 8, 13, 21, 34, and so
forth.

As you can see, each number in the sequence is obtained by
adding the two numbers directly before it. The Fibonacci sequence
is named after Italian mathematician Leonardo of Pisa, who was
also known as Fibonacci. The sequence was introduced to the
western world in his 1202 book Liber Abaci, but the sequence had
been previously stated in Indian mathematics. -->
```

Fibonacci Sequence Generator

Enter a number and generate the Fibonacci sequence up to that number.

| 100 | Generate |

Fibonacci Sequence: 0, 1, 1, 2, 3, 5, 8, 13, 21, 34, 55, 89

221

```html
<!DOCTYPE html>
<html>

<head>
  <title>Fibonacci Sequence Generator</title>
  <link
href="https://stackpath.bootstrapcdn.com/bootstrap/4.5.0/css/bo
otstrap.min.css" rel="stylesheet">
</head>

<body>
  <div class="container">
    <div class="row justify-content-center align-items-center vh-
100">
      <div class="col-6">
        <h1 class="text-center">Fibonacci Sequence
Generator</h1>
        <p class="text-center">Enter a number and generate the
Fibonacci sequence up to that number.</p>
        <div class="input-group mb-3">
          <input id="num" type="number" class="form-control"
placeholder="Enter a number" />
          <div class="input-group-append">
            <button onclick="generateFibonacci()" class="btn btn-
outline-secondary">Generate</button>
          </div>
        </div>
```

```
      <p id="sequence"></p>
    </div>
  </div>
</div>

<script>
  function generateFibonacci() {
    var num = document.getElementById('num').value;
    var sequence = [0, 1];

    while ((sequence[sequence.length - 1] +
sequence[sequence.length - 2]) <= num) {
      sequence.push(sequence[sequence.length - 1] +
sequence[sequence.length - 2]);
    }

    document.getElementById('sequence').innerText = 'Fibonacci
Sequence: ' + sequence.join(', ');
  }
</script>
</body>

</html>

<!-- In the revised code:
```

I've included the Bootstrap CSS CDN in the <head> section.
Added Bootstrap's grid system classes such as container, row, col-
6, justify-content-center, and align-items-center to center align
the Fibonacci generator form in the middle of the page.
Wrapped the input field and button within Bootstrap's input-group
class to group them together and applied the Bootstrap class
form-control to the input field for better styling.
The button is styled using Bootstrap's btn and btn-outline-
secondary classes. -->

Loan Calculator

Loan Amount:

1000

Interest Rate (%):

5

Loan Term (years):

3

Calculate

Monthly Payment: $29.97

223

```
<!DOCTYPE html>
<html>

<head>
  <style>
    body {
      font-family: Arial, sans-serif;
    }

    .container {
      width: 300px;
      padding: 16px;
      background-color: #f1f1f1;
      margin: 0 auto;
      margin-top: 100px;
      border-radius: 4px;
    }

    label {
      width: 100%;
      display: block;
      margin-top: 20px;
```

```
      }

    input[type="number"],
    input[type="range"] {
      width: 100%;
      padding: 4px;
      box-sizing: border-box;
    }

    button {
      margin-top: 10px;
    }

    #output {
      margin-top: 16px;
    }
  </style>
</head>

<body>
  <div class="container">
    <h2>Loan Calculator</h2>
    <label for="loanAmount">Loan Amount:</label>
    <input type="number" id="loanAmount" min="1" value="">

    <label for="interestRate">Interest Rate (%):</label>
    <input type="number" id="interestRate" min="1" max="100"
value="">

    <label for="loanTerm">Loan Term (years):</label>
    <input type="number" id="loanTerm" min="1" value="">

    <button onclick="calculateLoan()">Calculate</button>

    <p id="output"></p>
  </div>

  <script>
    function calculateLoan() {
      var loanAmount =
document.getElementById("loanAmount").value;
      var interestRate =
document.getElementById("interestRate").value / 100 / 12;
```

```
    var loanTerm =
document.getElementById("loanTerm").value * 12;

    var x = Math.pow(1 + interestRate, loanTerm);
    var monthlyPayment = (loanAmount * x * interestRate) / (x
- 1);

    document.getElementById("output").innerHTML = "Monthly
Payment: $" + monthlyPayment.toFixed(2);
    }
  </script>
</body>

</html>

<!-- Here's how this works:
```

The HTML sets up a simple form where the user can input the loan
amount, interest rate, and loan term. These values are read by
the JavaScript when the "Calculate" button is clicked.
The JavaScript function calculateLoan() is triggered when the
"Calculate" button is clicked. This function grabs the values from
the HTML form, performs the loan calculation, and then updates a
paragraph element with id "output" with the result.
The loan calculation uses the formula for calculating the monthly
payment on a loan, given the principal amount, interest rate, and
number of payment periods.
The CSS just provides some basic styling to center the form on
the page and space out the elements.
You can copy this code into an HTML file and open it in your web
browser to see the loan calculator in action. Note that this is a
very basic example and you might want to add more functionality
and error checking for a real-world application. -->

225

Loan Calculator

Loan Amount($):

```
10000
```

Interest Rate (%):

```
7
```

Loan Term (years):

```
5
```

Grace Period (years):

```
Deferment period?
```

Repayment Period (years):

```
Repayment period?
```

Calculate

Monthly Payment	Total Payment	Total Interest
$198.01	$11880.72	$1880.72

226

```
<!DOCTYPE html>
<html>

<head>
  <style>
    body {
      font-family: Arial, sans-serif;
      line-height: 1.5;
    }

    .container {
      width: 400px;
      padding: 16px;
      background-color: #f1f1f1;
      margin: 0 auto;
      margin-top: 30px;
      border-radius: 4px;
```

```
    }

    h1 {
      color: blue;
      text-align: center;
    }

    label {
      width: 100%;
      display: block;
      margin-bottom: 3px;
    }

    input[type="number"],
    select {
      width: 100%;
      padding: 4px;
      box-sizing: border-box;
    }

    input {
      margin-bottom: 15px;
    }

    #output {
      margin-top: 16px;
    }
  </style>
</head>

<body>
  <div class="container">
    <h1>Loan Calculator</h1>

    <label for="loanAmount">Loan Amount($):</label>
    <input type="number" id="loanAmount" min="1" value=""
placeholder="What is my loan amount?" autofocus>

    <label for="interestRate">Interest Rate (%):</label>
    <input type="number" id="interestRate" min="1" max="100"
value="" placeholder="What is the annual interest rate?">

    <label for="loanTerm">Loan Term (years):</label>
```

```
    <input type="number" id="loanTerm" min="1" value=""
placeholder="What is the loan period?">

    <!-- The deferment period and repayment period do not
actually function, there's only a form. -->
    <label for="gracePeriod">Grace Period (years):</label>
    <input type="number" id="gracePeriod" min="0" value=""
placeholder="Deferment period?">

    <label for="repaymentPeriod">Repayment Period
(years):</label>
    <input type="number" id="repaymentPeriod" min="1"
value="" placeholder="Repayment period?">

    <button onclick="calculateLoan()">Calculate</button>

    <div id="output"></div>
  </div>

  <script>

  function calculateLoan() {
    var loanAmount =
parseFloat(document.getElementById("loanAmount").value);
    var interestRate =
parseFloat(document.getElementById("interestRate").value) / 100
/ 12;
    var loanTerm =
parseFloat(document.getElementById("loanTerm").value) * 12;
    var gracePeriod =
parseFloat(document.getElementById("gracePeriod").value);
    var repaymentPeriod =
parseFloat(document.getElementById("repaymentPeriod").value);

    var x = Math.pow(1 + interestRate, loanTerm);
    var monthlyPayment = (loanAmount * x * interestRate) / (x
- 1);
    var totalPayment = monthlyPayment * loanTerm;
    var totalInterest = totalPayment - loanAmount;

    var output = `
      <table border="1">
        <tr>
          <th>Monthly Payment</th>
```

```
        <th>Total Payment</th>
        <th>Total Interest</th>
      </tr>
      <tr>
        <td>$${monthlyPayment.toFixed(2)}</td>
        <td>$${totalPayment.toFixed(2)}</td>
        <td>$${totalInterest.toFixed(2)}</td>
      </tr>
    </table>
    `;

    document.getElementById("output").innerHTML = output;
  }
</script>
</body>

</html>
```

<!-- Please note that this is a basic upgrade and does not include loan calculations for grace periods or different repayment periods. Those elements are present in the form but do not affect the calculation. The grace period and repayment period could affect the loan calculation significantly, depending on how you want to interpret those values. If you need more complex loan calculations, you may need to adjust the calculateLoan function.

Also, the new layout may need to be refined further according to your specific design preferences. -->

230

```
<!DOCTYPE html>
<html>

<head>
  <title>Loan Calculator</title>
  <link rel="stylesheet"
href="https://stackpath.bootstrapcdn.com/bootstrap/4.3.1/css/bo
otstrap.min.css">
</head>

<body>
  <div class="container mt-5">
    <h1 class="text-center text-primary">Loan Calculator</h1>
    <div class="row justify-content-center">
      <div class="col-md-6">
        <div class="form-group">
          <label for="loanAmount">Loan Amount($):</label>
```

```html
        <input type="number" id="loanAmount" min="1"
class="form-control" placeholder="What is my loan amount?"
        autofocus>
    </div>

    <div class="form-group">
      <label for="interestRate">Interest Rate (%):</label>
      <input type="number" id="interestRate" min="1"
max="100" class="form-control"
        placeholder="What is the annual interest rate?">
    </div>

    <div class="form-group">
      <label for="gracePeriod">Grace Period (years):</label>
      <input type="number" id="gracePeriod" min="0"
class="form-control" placeholder="Deferment period?">
    </div>

    <div class="form-group">
      <label for="repaymentPeriod">Repayment Period
(years):</label>
      <input type="number" id="repaymentPeriod" min="1"
class="form-control" placeholder="Repayment period?">
    </div>

    <button onclick="calculateLoan()" class="btn btn-primary
btn-block">Calculate</button>

    <div id="output" class="mt-3"></div>
   </div>
  </div>
 </div>

 <script>
  function calculateLoan() {
    var loanAmount =
parseFloat(document.getElementById("loanAmount").value);
```

```
    var interestRate =
parseFloat(document.getElementById("interestRate").value) / 100
/ 12;
    var gracePeriod =
parseFloat(document.getElementById("gracePeriod").value) * 12;
    var repaymentPeriod =
parseFloat(document.getElementById("repaymentPeriod").value)
* 12;

    var x = Math.pow(1 + interestRate, repaymentPeriod);
    var monthlyPayment = (loanAmount * x * interestRate) / (x
- 1);
    var totalPayment = monthlyPayment * (gracePeriod +
repaymentPeriod);
    var totalInterest = totalPayment - loanAmount;

    var output = `
      <table class="table table-bordered">
        <tr>
          <th>Monthly Payment</th>
          <th>Total Payment</th>
          <th>Total Interest</th>
        </tr>
        <tr>
          <td>$${monthlyPayment.toFixed(2)}</td>
          <td>$${totalPayment.toFixed(2)}</td>
          <td>$${totalInterest.toFixed(2)}</td>
        </tr>
      </table>
    `;

    document.getElementById("output").innerHTML = output;
  }
  </script>

  <!-- Importing the Bootstrap JavaScript library -->
  <script
src="https://stackpath.bootstrapcdn.com/bootstrap/4.3.1/js/boot
strap.min.js"></script>
```

```
</body>

</html>

<!-- Calculating loan repayments with grace periods and different
repayment periods can be complex, as it depends on the terms of
the loan and how interest is calculated during the grace period. A
common assumption is that interest does not accrue during the
grace period.

This is a simplified version where the calculation for the
repayment period begins only after the grace period. During the
grace period, the loan does not accumulate any interest.

Please note that this is a simplified loan calculator and may not
reflect the exact terms of a real-world loan. In a real loan, interest
may still accrue during the grace period, even if payments are not
required, and there may be other factors to consider, such as fees
and penalties. Always consult with a financial advisor or loan
officer for accurate calculations. -->
```

234

```
<!DOCTYPE html>
<html>

<head>
  <title>Weather App</title>
  <style>
    body {
      font-family: Arial, sans-serif;
    }

    #app {
      width: 500px;
      margin: 0 auto;
      text-align: center;
    }

    #city {
      width: 200px;
      padding: 10px;
      margin: 20px 0;
    }
  </style>
</head>

<body>
  <div id="app">
    <h1>Weather App</h1>
```

```html
    <input type="text" id="city" placeholder="Enter a city
name">
    <button onclick="getWeather()">Get Weather</button>
    <div id="weather"></div>
  </div>
  <!-- We'll be using the OpenWeatherMap API. It's a free API, but
you will need to sign up to get your own API key. -->
  <script>
    async function getWeather() {
      const city = document.getElementById('city').value;
      const response = await
fetch(`http://api.openweathermap.org/data/2.5/weather?q=${cit
y}&appid=7608ff1b560bc531e31**e640daee61b&units=metric`);
      const data = await response.json();
    // This is my key. After signing up, you should also verify your
email. The processing time can take about 10 minutes. Do not
include brackets when inputting.
{7608ff1b560bc531e31**e640daee61b}
      if (response.ok) {
        const weatherDiv = document.getElementById('weather');
        weatherDiv.innerHTML = `
          <h2>Weather in ${data.name}</h2>
          <p><strong>Temperature:</strong>
${data.main.temp} °C</p>
          <p><strong>Weather:</strong>
${data.weather[0].description}</p>
        `;
      } else {
        alert(data.message);
      }
    }
  </script>
</body>
</html>
<!-- In the JavaScript code, replace YOUR_API_KEY with the
```

235

In the JavaScript code, replace YOUR_API_KEY with the
actual API key that you get from OpenWeatherMap. The function
getWeather is called when the "Get Weather" button is clicked. It
sends a request to the OpenWeatherMap API with the city name
that the user has entered, and then it displays the temperature
and weather description in the weather div.

Please note that the fetch API used in the JavaScript is not
supported in Internet Explorer. Also, you should serve your HTML
from a server (like a local development server) because modern

browsers do not allow requests to APIs directly from local files due to CORS policy. -->

<!-- CORS stands for Cross-Origin Resource Sharing. It's a security feature that browsers implement to prevent a web page from making requests to a different domain than the one the web page came from, unless the server on the other domain explicitly allows it.

A 'domain' in this context includes the protocol (http or https), the hostname, and the port. If any of these components are different between two URLs, they're considered to be on different 'origins'.

Here's a simple example of where CORS comes into play: Suppose you visit a webpage at http://example.com. This webpage includes JavaScript that tries to make an AJAX request (a way to fetch data from the server without refreshing the page) to http://api.example.com. Even though both URLs contain 'example.com', they're on different origins because their subdomains ('www' vs 'api') are different.

Browsers' same-origin policy would normally block the webpage at http://example.com from receiving the response to the AJAX request to http://api.example.com. However, if the server at api.example.com includes the appropriate CORS headers in its response, then the browser will allow the webpage to receive the response.

The CORS mechanism supports secure cross-origin requests and data transfers between browsers and servers. Modern browsers use CORS in an API container - such as XMLHttpRequest or Fetch - to mitigate risks of cross-origin HTTP requests.

To be specific, for security reasons, browsers prohibit web pages from making requests to a different domain than the one the web page came from, unless the other domain gives explicit permission using CORS headers.

This is a simplified explanation. The actual implementation of CORS and same-origin policy can get quite complex, because it needs to handle various edge cases and security considerations. -->

236

Weather in Seoul

Get Weather

Current Weather

Temperature: 25.21 °C

Weather: moderate rain

```
<!DOCTYPE html>
<html>

<head>
  <title>Weather App</title>
  <style>
    body {
      font-family: Arial, sans-serif;
    }

    #app {
      width: 500px;
      margin: 0 auto;
      text-align: center;
    }
  </style>
</head>

<body>
  <div id="app">
    <h1>Weather in Seoul</h1>
    <button onclick="getWeather()">Get Weather</button>
    <div id="weather"></div>
  </div>
  <script>
    async function getWeather() {
```

```
        const response = await
fetch(`http://api.openweathermap.org/data/2.5/weather?q=Seoul
&appid=7608ff1b560bc531e31**e640daee61b&units=metric`);
        const data = await response.json();
        // This is my key. After signing up, you should also verify
your email. The processing time can take about 10 minutes. Do
not include brackets when inputting.
{7608ff1b560bc531e31**e640daee61b}
        if (response.ok) {
            const weatherDiv = document.getElementById('weather');
            weatherDiv.innerHTML = `
                <h2>Current Weather</h2>
                <p><strong>Temperature:</strong>
${data.main.temp} °C</p>
                <p><strong>Weather:</strong>
${data.weather[0].description}</p>
                `;
        } else {
            alert(data.message);
        }
    }

    </script>
</body>

</html>

<!-- Just like before, replace YOUR_API_KEY with the actual API
key that you get from OpenWeatherMap. When you click the "Get
Weather" button, the app fetches and displays the current
temperature and weather in Seoul.

Remember that the fetch API used in the JavaScript code is not
supported in Internet Explorer. Also, you should serve your HTML
from a server (like a local development server) because modern
browsers do not allow requests to APIs directly from local files due
to CORS policy. -->
```

Weather App

New York   Get Weather

Weather in New York

Temperature: 25.91 °C

Weather: scattered clouds

239

```html
<!DOCTYPE html>
<html>

<head>
  <title>Weather App</title>
  <link rel="stylesheet"
href="https://stackpath.bootstrapcdn.com/bootstrap/5.1.1/css/bo
otstrap.min.css">
</head>

<body>
  <div class="container">
    <div class="row justify-content-center">
      <div class="col-md-6 text-center">
        <h1 class="my-5">Weather App</h1>
        <input type="text" id="city" class="form-control"
placeholder="Enter a city name">
        <button onclick="getWeather()" class="btn btn-primary
mt-3">Get Weather</button>
        <div id="weather" class="mt-3"></div>
      </div>
    </div>
  </div>

  <script
src="https://cdn.jsdelivr.net/npm/axios@0.24.0/dist/axios.min.js"
></script>
  <script>
    async function getWeather() {
      const city = document.getElementById('city').value;
```

```
        try {
            const response = await
axios.get(`http://api.openweathermap.org/data/2.5/weather?q=$
{city}&appid=7608ff1b560bc531e31##e640daee61b&units=metr
ic`);
            // Replace YOUR_API_KEY with the actual API key that you
get from OpenWeatherMap.
            const data = response.data;
            const weatherDiv = document.getElementById('weather');
            weatherDiv.innerHTML = `
                <h2 class="fw-bold">Weather in
${data.name}</h2>
                <p><strong>Temperature:</strong>
${data.main.temp} °C</p>
                <p><strong>Weather:</strong>
${data.weather[0].description}</p>
            `;
        } catch (error) {
            if (error.response) {
                alert(error.response.data.message);
            } else if (error.request) {
                alert('The request was made but no response was
received');
            } else {
                alert('Error', error.message);
            }
        }
    }
  </script>
</body>

</html>
```

240

```
<!-- Here is your enhanced code using Bootstrap 5. In addition to
the Bootstrap CSS and JS files, I also incorporated the axios
library for making HTTP requests in JavaScript because it
simplifies error handling. It also works well in the browser and
with Node.js.

Please note that you should switch to https for fetching data from
the API, as many browsers will block http requests for security
reasons. However, the OpenWeatherMap's free tier does not
support https, so you may want to use another weather API if
you're experiencing issues.

Also, make sure you replace the API key with your own. And
remember to keep it confidential, as it's generally a bad practice
to expose API keys in public/production code. -->
```

ToDo List

Enter a new task

Add Task

- ☐ Submit the design proposal [Delete]
- ☑ ~~Practice Spanish for 20 minutes~~ [Delete]
- ☐ Call parents [Delete]
- ☑ ~~Grocery shopping~~ [Delete]
- ☐ Buy new indoor plants [Delete]

241

```
<!DOCTYPE html>
<html>
<head>
    <title>ToDo List</title>
    <style>
body {
    font-family: Arial, sans-serif;
}

#app {
    width: 400px;
    margin: 0 auto;
    text-align: center;
}

#new-task {
    width: 100%;
    padding: 10px;
```

```css
    margin: 20px 0;
}

.task {
    text-align: left;
}

.completed {
    text-decoration: line-through;
}

    </style>
</head>
<body>
    <div id="app">
        <h1>ToDo List</h1>
        <input type="text" id="new-task" placeholder="Enter a
new task">
        <button onclick="addTask()">Add Task</button>
        <ul id="task-list"></ul>
    </div>
    <script>
let tasks = [];

function addTask() {
    const taskInput = document.getElementById('new-task');
    const newTask = taskInput.value;
    if (newTask) {
        tasks.push({
            text: newTask,
            completed: false,
        });
        taskInput.value = '';
        renderTasks();
```

```
        }
    }


    function renderTasks() {
        const taskList = document.getElementById('task-list');
        taskList.innerHTML = '';
        tasks.forEach((task, index) => {
            const li = document.createElement('li');
            li.className = 'task' + (task.completed ? ' completed' : '');
            li.innerHTML = `
                <input type="checkbox"
onchange="toggleTask(${index})" ${task.completed ? 'checked' :
''}>
                ${task.text}
                <button
onclick="deleteTask(${index})">Delete</button>
            `;
            taskList.appendChild(li);
        });
    }

    function toggleTask(index) {
        tasks[index].completed = !tasks[index].completed;
        renderTasks();
    }

    function deleteTask(index) {
        tasks.splice(index, 1);
        renderTasks();
    }

    </script>
</body>
</html>
```

243

<!-- Here's how it works:

The addTask function gets called when the "Add Task" button is clicked. It reads the user's input, creates a new task object, and pushes it into the tasks array. Then it clears the input field and updates the task list.

The renderTasks function clears the task list and recreates it based on the tasks array. Each task is an li element, which includes a checkbox, the task text, and a "Delete" button. The onclick attribute of the checkbox and the "Delete" button are set to call toggleTask and deleteTask respectively, with the index of the task as an argument.

The toggleTask function toggles the completed attribute of the specified task and updates the task list.

The deleteTask function removes the specified task from the tasks array and updates the task list.

Remember to serve this HTML file from a server, because modern browsers may not allow it to work as expected when it's opened directly from the file system. -->

<!-- Here are ten examples of to-do list items:

Morning Routine:
Wake up at 6:30 am
20 minutes of meditation
Breakfast: Oatmeal and fruits
Workout for 30 minutes

Work:

Check and reply to emails

Finish the quarterly report

Attend project strategy meeting at 2 pm

Submit the design proposal

Learning:

Spend 1 hour learning Python from online course

Read for 30 minutes (Currently reading: "Sapiens: A Brief History of Humankind")

Practice Spanish on Duolingo for 15 minutes

Health:

Make an appointment for the annual health check-up

Buy vitamins and supplements

Cook a healthy dinner (Try a new salad recipe)

Personal:

Call parents

Pay the electricity bill

Organize the wardrobe

Write in the personal journal

Weekend:

Plan a hiking trip

Grocery shopping

Visit the new art exhibition downtown

Movie night: Watch "The Godfather"

Home Improvement:

Fix the leaking faucet in the bathroom

Paint the living room wall

Buy new indoor plants

Install the new light fixture

Social:

Schedule a coffee date with friends

Write a thank you note to Jane

Plan the details for the upcoming birthday party

Volunteer at the local food bank

Fitness:

Run for 3 miles in the morning

Attend yoga class in the evening

Plan next week's workout routine

Research healthy meal prep recipes

Financial:

Review monthly budget

Save 10% of income in a savings account

Invest in stocks

Meet with financial advisor to discuss investment portfolio

These are just examples and you can modify them according to your preferences and needs. -->

246

```
<!DOCTYPE html>
<html>

<head>
  <title>ToDo List</title>
  <link rel="stylesheet"
href="https://stackpath.bootstrapcdn.com/bootstrap/4.5.0/css/bo
otstrap.min.css">
</head>

<body>
  <div id="app" class="container mt-5">
    <h1 class="text-center mb-4">ToDo List</h1>
    <div class="input-group mb-3">
      <input type="text" id="new-task" class="form-control"
placeholder="Enter a new task">
      <div class="input-group-append">
        <button class="btn btn-outline-secondary" type="button"
onclick="addTask()">Add Task</button>
      </div>
```

```
    </div>
    <ul id="task-list" class="list-group"></ul>
  </div>
  <script>
    let tasks = [];

    function addTask() {
      const taskInput = document.getElementById('new-task');
      const newTask = taskInput.value;
      if (newTask) {
        tasks.push({
          text: newTask,
          completed: false,
        });
        taskInput.value = '';
        renderTasks();
      }
    }

    function renderTasks() {
      const taskList = document.getElementById('task-list');
      taskList.innerHTML = '';
      tasks.forEach((task, index) => {
        const li = document.createElement('li');
        li.className = 'list-group-item d-flex justify-content-
between align-items-center' + (task.completed ? ' list-group-item-
success' : '');
        li.innerHTML = `
                  <div class="form-check">
                    <input class="form-check-input"
type="checkbox" onchange="toggleTask(${index})"
${task.completed ? 'checked' : ''}>
                    <label class="form-check-label
${task.completed ? 'text-decoration-line-through' : ''}">
```

248

```
                    ${task.text}
                </label>
            </div>
            <button class="btn btn-danger btn-sm"
onclick="deleteTask(${index})">Delete</button>
                `;

    taskList.appendChild(li);
  });
}


function toggleTask(index) {
  tasks[index].completed = !tasks[index].completed;
  renderTasks();
}


function deleteTask(index) {
  tasks.splice(index, 1);
  renderTasks();
}
  </script>
</body>

</html>


<!-- This updated version of your code incorporates Bootstrap
styles to make your ToDo list app more aesthetically pleasing and
user-friendly. The Bootstrap styles added include the "container"
class to center the content, the "input-group" class to group the
input field and button, and the "list-group" class to style the list of
tasks. -->
```

Tax Calculator

10000

15

Calculate Tax

Tax: $1500.00

Total: $11500.00

250

```
<!DOCTYPE html>
<html>

<head>
  <title>Tax Calculator</title>
  <style>
    body {
      font-family: Arial, sans-serif;
    }

    #app {
      width: 300px;
      margin: 0 auto;
      text-align: center;
    }

    #cost,
    #tax-rate {
      width: 100%;
      padding: 10px;
      margin: 20px 0;
    }
  </style>
</head>
```

```
<body>
  <div id="app">
    <h1>Tax Calculator</h1>
    <input type="number" id="cost" min="0" step="0.01"
placeholder="Item Cost">
    <input type="number" id="tax-rate" min="0" max="100"
step="0.01" placeholder="Tax Rate (%)">
    <button onclick="calculateTax()">Calculate Tax</button>
    <div id="output"></div>
  </div>
  <script>
    function calculateTax() {
      const cost =
parseFloat(document.getElementById('cost').value);
      const taxRate = parseFloat(document.getElementById('tax-
rate').value) / 100;
      const tax = cost * taxRate;
      const total = cost + tax;
      const output = document.getElementById('output');
      output.innerHTML = `
        <p><strong>Tax:</strong> $${tax.toFixed(2)}</p>
        <p><strong>Total:</strong> $${total.toFixed(2)}</p>
      `;
    }
  </script>
</body>

</html>

<!-- Here's how it works:
```

251

The calculateTax function gets called when the "Calculate Tax"
button is clicked. It reads the cost and the tax rate from the user's
input, calculates the tax and the total cost, and then displays
these values in the output div.
Please make sure to validate the user input in a real-world
application. This simple example assumes that the user always
enters valid numbers. -->

Tax Calculator

10000

15.5

Calculate Tax

Tax: $1550.00

Total: $11550.00

```html
<!DOCTYPE html>
<html>

<head>
  <title>Tax Calculator</title>
  <link rel="stylesheet"
href="https://stackpath.bootstrapcdn.com/bootstrap/4.5.0/css/bo
otstrap.min.css">
</head>

<body>
  <div class="container mt-5">
    <div class="row">
      <div class="col-md-4 offset-md-4">
        <h1 class="text-center mb-4">Tax Calculator</h1>
        <div class="form-group">
          <input type="number" id="cost" min="0" step="0.01"
placeholder="Item Cost" class="form-control">
        </div>
        <div class="form-group">
          <input type="number" id="tax-rate" min="0" max="100"
step="0.01" placeholder="Tax Rate (%)"
          class="form-control">
        </div>
```

```
      <button onclick="calculateTax()" class="btn btn-primary
btn-block">Calculate Tax</button>
      <div id="output" class="mt-3"></div>
    </div>
   </div>
 </div>
 <script>
  function calculateTax() {
    const cost =
parseFloat(document.getElementById('cost').value);
    const taxRate = parseFloat(document.getElementById('tax-
rate').value) / 100;
    const tax = cost * taxRate;
    const total = cost + tax;
    const output = document.getElementById('output');
    output.innerHTML = `
      <p><strong>Tax:</strong> $${tax.toFixed(2)}</p>
      <p><strong>Total:</strong> $${total.toFixed(2)}</p>
    `;
  }
 </script>
</body>

</html>
```

253

**Blog Title
(What is the blog topic?)**

This is the blog content.
(Record your writings or photos.)

Comments

This is the start of my blog.

I deeply appreciate you doing this.

My grandfather was a coal miner.

```
Write a comment
```

```
Post Comment
```

254

```
<!DOCTYPE html>
<html>
<head>
    <title>Simple Blog</title>
    <style>
body {
    font-family: Arial, sans-serif;
}

#app {
    width: 400px;
    margin: 0 auto;
}

h2 {
  margin-top: 50px;
}

#comment-input {
    width: 100%;
    padding: 10px;
```

```css
    margin: 20px 0;
}

.comment {
    border-top: 1px solid #ccc;
    padding: 10px 0;
}

    </style>
</head>
```
```html
<body>
    <div id="app">
        <h3>Blog Title <br>(What is the blog topic?)</h3>
        <p>This is the blog content. <br>(Record your writings or
photos.)</p>
        <h2>Comments</h2>
        <div id="comments"></div>
        <input type="text" id="comment-input"
placeholder="Write a comment">
        <button onclick="addComment()">Post
Comment</button>
    </div>
    <script>
let comments = [];

function addComment() {
    const commentInput = document.getElementById('comment-
input');
    const newComment = commentInput.value;
    if (newComment) {
        comments.push(newComment);
        commentInput.value = '';
        renderComments();
    }
}

function renderComments() {
    const commentsDiv = document.getElementById('comments');
    commentsDiv.innerHTML = '';
    comments.forEach(comment => {
        const div = document.createElement('div');
        div.className = 'comment';
        div.textContent = comment;
        commentsDiv.appendChild(div);
```

```
    });
}

    </script>
</body>
</html>

<!-- In this simple example, comments are not stored anywhere,
so they will be lost when the page is reloaded.

Here's how it works:

The addComment function gets called when the "Post Comment"
button is clicked. It reads the user's input, pushes it into the
comments array, clears the input field, and then updates the
comments section.

The renderComments function clears the comments section and
recreates it based on the comments array. Each comment is a div
element with the comment class.

This simple blog does not interact with a server, so it does not
support features such as storing comments permanently, user
authentication, or serving different blog posts. For a real-world
blog, you would typically use a backend server and a database. --
>
```

Blog Title
(What is the blog topic?)

This is the blog content.
(Record your writings or photos.)

Comments

Such an interesting film

Seeing the nice people from communities

It's a shame that most people moves out.

| Write a comment | Post Comment |

257

```
<!DOCTYPE html>
<html>
<head>
  <title>Simple Blog</title>
  <!-- Include Bootstrap CSS -->
  <link
href="https://stackpath.bootstrapcdn.com/bootstrap/4.3.1/css/bo
otstrap.min.css" rel="stylesheet" />
  <!-- Additional Custom Styles -->
  <style>
    body {
      padding: 20px;
    }

    .comment {
      border-top: 1px solid #ccc;
      padding: 10px 0;
    }
  </style>
</head>
<body>
  <div id="app">
```

```html
    <h3 class="mb-4">Blog Title <br>(What is the blog
topic?)</h3>
    <p>This is the blog content. <br>(Record your writings or
photos.)</p>
    <h2 class="mt-5 mb-3">Comments</h2>
    <div id="comments"></div>
    <div class="input-group mt-3">
      <input type="text" id="comment-input" class="form-control"
placeholder="Write a comment">
      <div class="input-group-append">
        <button onclick="addComment()" class="btn btn-outline-
secondary">Post Comment</button>
      </div>
    </div>
  </div>
  <script>
    let comments = [];

    function addComment() {
      const commentInput =
document.getElementById('comment-input');
      const newComment = commentInput.value;
      if (newComment) {
        comments.push(newComment);
        commentInput.value = '';
        renderComments();
      }
    }
    function renderComments() {
      const commentsDiv =
document.getElementById('comments');
      commentsDiv.innerHTML = '';
      comments.forEach(comment => {
        const div = document.createElement('div');
        div.className = 'comment';
        div.textContent = comment;
        commentsDiv.appendChild(div);
      });
    }
  </script>
</body>
</html>
```

259

```
<!DOCTYPE html>
<html>

<head>
  <title>Currency Converter</title>
  <style>
    body {
      font-family: Arial, sans-serif;
    }

    #app {
      width: 300px;
      margin: 0 auto;
      text-align: center;
    }

    #amount,
    #from-currency,
    #to-currency {
      width: 100%;
      padding: 10px;
      margin: 20px 0;
    }
  </style>
```

```
</head>

<body>
  <div id="app">
    <h2>Currency Converter</h2>
    <input type="number" id="amount" min="0" step="0.01"
placeholder="Amount">
    <input type="text" id="from-currency" placeholder="From
Currency (e.g., USD)">
    <input type="text" id="to-currency" placeholder="To Currency
(e.g., EUR)">
    <button onclick="convertCurrency()">Convert</button>
    <div id="output"></div>
  </div>
  <script>
    async function convertCurrency() {
      const amount =
parseFloat(document.getElementById('amount').value);
      const fromCurrency = document.getElementById('from-
currency').value.toUpperCase();
      const toCurrency = document.getElementById('to-
currency').value.toUpperCase();

      // https://v6.exchangerate-
api.com/v6/YOUR_API_KEY/latest/USD      Create their own key
number.

      const response = await fetch(`https://v6.exchangerate-
api.com/v6/aaf53da1eba53d98819909**/latest/${fromCurrency}
`);
      const data = await response.json();
      if (data && data.conversion_rates) {
        const rate = data.conversion_rates[toCurrency];
        const convertedAmount = amount * rate;
        document.getElementById('output').innerHTML =
`${amount} ${fromCurrency} = ${convertedAmount.toFixed(2)}
${toCurrency}`;
      } else {
        document.getElementById('output').innerHTML = 'An error
occurred while fetching the exchange rates.';
      }
    }

  </script>
```

```
</body>

</html>
```

<!-- Here's a list of 20 more commonly used currencies and their corresponding countries:

GBP (Great Britain Pound) - United Kingdom
JPY (Japanese Yen) - Japan
AUD (Australian Dollar) - Australia
CAD (Canadian Dollar) - Canada
CHF (Swiss Franc) - Switzerland
CNY (Chinese Yuan) - China
SEK (Swedish Krona) - Sweden
NZD (New Zealand Dollar) - New Zealand
MXN (Mexican Peso) - Mexico
SGD (Singapore Dollar) - Singapore
HKD (Hong Kong Dollar) - Hong Kong
NOK (Norwegian Krone) - Norway
KRW (South Korean Won) - South Korea
TRY (Turkish Lira) - Turkey
INR (Indian Rupee) - India
RUB (Russian Ruble) - Russia
BRL (Brazilian Real) - Brazil
ZAR (South African Rand) - South Africa
SAR (Saudi Riyal) - Saudi Arabia
AED (United Arab Emirates Dirham) - United Arab Emirates
Users can enter these currency codes in the "From Currency" and "To Currency" fields of the currency converter.

Please note that availability of exchange rate data may depend on the specifics of the API you're using. The ExchangeRate-API mentioned in the previous response supports over 160 currency codes. -->

<!-- You can use the ExchangeRate-API to fetch current exchange rates and calculate converted amounts. You'll need to sign up for a free API key on their website.

Here's how it works:

The convertCurrency function gets called when the "Convert" button is clicked. It reads the amount and the currencies from the user's input, sends a request to the ExchangeRate-API, calculates

the converted amount based on the received exchange rate, and displays the result in the output div.
Replace YOUR_API_KEY with your actual API key from ExchangeRate-API.

Please make sure to handle errors and validate user input in a real-world application. This simple example assumes that the user always enters valid input and that the API always returns valid data.

It's also important to note that free API keys often have limitations, such as a limited number of requests per month. You may need to upgrade to a paid plan or find another API if you need to make more requests.

Finally, it's recommended to serve this HTML from a server, because some features may not work as expected when the HTML is opened directly from the file system. -->

Currency Converter

```
10000
```

```
USD - United States Dollar          ⌄
```

to

```
JPY - Japanese Yen                   ⌄
```

Convert

10000 USD = 1,387,104.00 JPY

263

```html
<!DOCTYPE html>
<html>

<head>
  <title>Currency Converter</title>
  <style>
   body {
     font-family: Arial, sans-serif;
   }

   #app {
     width: 300px;
     margin: 0 auto;
     text-align: center;
   }

   #amount,
   #from-currency,
   #to-currency {
     width: 100%;
     padding: 10px;
```

```
      margin: 20px 0;
    }

    button {
      margin: 20px;
    }
  </style>
</head>

<body>
  <div id="app">
    <h2>Currency Converter</h2>
    <input type="number" id="amount" min="0" step="0.01"
placeholder="Amount">

    <select id="from-currency">
      <option value="KRW">KRW - South Korean Won</option>
      <option value="USD">USD - United States Dollar</option>
      <option value="EUR">EUR - Euro</option>
      <option value="GBP">GBP - Great Britain Pound</option>
      <option value="JPY">JPY - Japanese Yen</option>
      <option value="AUD">AUD - Australian Dollar</option>
      <option value="CAD">CAD - Canadian Dollar</option>
      <option value="CHF">CHF - Swiss Franc</option>
      <option value="CNY">CNY - Chinese Yuan</option>
      <option value="SEK">SEK - Swedish Krona</option>
      <option value="NZD">NZD - New Zealand Dollar</option>
      <option value="MXN">MXN - Mexican Peso</option>
      <option value="SGD">SGD - Singapore Dollar</option>
      <option value="HKD">HKD - Hong Kong Dollar</option>
      <option value="NOK">NOK - Norwegian Krone</option>
      <option value="TRY">TRY - Turkish Lira</option>
      <option value="INR">INR - Indian Rupee</option>
      <option value="RUB">RUB - Russian Ruble</option>
      <option value="BRL">BRL - Brazilian Real</option>
      <option value="ZAR">ZAR - South African Rand</option>
      <option value="SAR">SAR - Saudi Riyal</option>
      <option value="AED">AED - United Arab Emirates
Dirham</option>
    </select>
    <p>to</p>
    <select id="to-currency">
      <option value="USD">USD - United States Dollar</option>
      <option value="EUR">EUR - Euro</option>
```

```html
      <option value="GBP">GBP - Great Britain Pound</option>
      <option value="JPY">JPY - Japanese Yen</option>
      <option value="AUD">AUD - Australian Dollar</option>
      <option value="CAD">CAD - Canadian Dollar</option>
      <option value="CHF">CHF - Swiss Franc</option>
      <option value="CNY">CNY - Chinese Yuan</option>
      <option value="SEK">SEK - Swedish Krona</option>
      <option value="NZD">NZD - New Zealand Dollar</option>
      <option value="MXN">MXN - Mexican Peso</option>
      <option value="SGD">SGD - Singapore Dollar</option>
      <option value="HKD">HKD - Hong Kong Dollar</option>
      <option value="NOK">NOK - Norwegian Krone</option>
      <option value="KRW">KRW - South Korean Won</option>
      <option value="TRY">TRY - Turkish Lira</option>
      <option value="INR">INR - Indian Rupee</option>
      <option value="RUB">RUB - Russian Ruble</option>
      <option value="BRL">BRL - Brazilian Real</option>
      <option value="ZAR">ZAR - South African Rand</option>
      <option value="SAR">SAR - Saudi Riyal</option>
      <option value="AED">AED - United Arab Emirates
Dirham</option>
    </select>
```

```html
    <button onclick="convertCurrency()">Convert</button>
    <div id="output"></div>
  </div>
  <script>
    async function convertCurrency() {
      const amount =
parseFloat(document.getElementById('amount').value);
      const fromCurrency = document.getElementById('from-
currency').value;
      const toCurrency = document.getElementById('to-
currency').value;

      const response = await fetch(`https://v6.exchangerate-
api.com/v6/aaf53da1eba53d98819909**/latest/${fromCurrency}
`);
      const data = await response.json();
      if (data && data.conversion_rates) {
        const rate = data.conversion_rates[toCurrency];
        const convertedAmount = amount * rate;
        const formattedAmount = new Intl.NumberFormat('en-US',
{ minimumFractionDigits: 2 }).format(convertedAmount);
```

```
      document.getElementById('output').innerHTML =
`${amount} ${fromCurrency} = ${formattedAmount}
${toCurrency}`;
    } else {
      document.getElementById('output').innerHTML = 'An error
occurred while fetching the exchange rates.';
    }
  }


  </script>
</body>

</html>

<!-- We can modify the JavaScript code to format the converted
amount with commas as thousands separators.

Here's what's new:

Intl.NumberFormat('en-US', { minimumFractionDigits:
2 }).format(convertedAmount): This line creates a new
Intl.NumberFormat object, which is used to format numbers
according to specific locale settings. 'en-US' is the locale, which
formats numbers with commas as thousands separators and dots
as decimal separators. { minimumFractionDigits: 2 } is an options
object, which specifies that at least 2 fraction digits should be
used.
Replace YOUR_API_KEY with your actual API key from
ExchangeRate-API.

This modification will make the converted amount easier to read
for users. -->
```

Currency Converter

| 1,000 |

| EUR - Euro | ⌄ |

to

| USD - United States Dollar | ⌄ |

Convert

1,000 EUR = 1,123.40 USD

```
<!DOCTYPE html>
<html>

<head>
  <title>Currency Converter</title>
  <style>
    body {
      font-family: Arial, sans-serif;
    }

    #app {
      width: 300px;
      margin: 0 auto;
      text-align: center;
    }

    #amount,
    #from-currency,
    #to-currency {
      width: 100%;
      padding: 10px;
      margin: 20px 0;
```

```
    }

    button {
      margin: 20px;
    }
  </style>
</head>

<body>
  <div id="app">
    <h2>Currency Converter</h2>
    <!-- <input type="number" id="amount" min="0" step="0.01"
placeholder="Amount"> (Change the code below to insert a
thousand unit comma separator.)-->

    <input type="text" id="amount" oninput="formatInput(this)"
placeholder="Amount">


    <select id="from-currency">
      <option value="KRW">KRW - South Korean Won</option>
      <option value="USD">USD - United States Dollar</option>
      <option value="EUR">EUR - Euro</option>
      <option value="GBP">GBP - Great Britain Pound</option>
      <option value="JPY">JPY - Japanese Yen</option>
      <option value="AUD">AUD - Australian Dollar</option>
      <option value="CAD">CAD - Canadian Dollar</option>
      <option value="CHF">CHF - Swiss Franc</option>
      <option value="CNY">CNY - Chinese Yuan</option>
      <option value="SEK">SEK - Swedish Krona</option>
      <option value="NZD">NZD - New Zealand Dollar</option>
      <option value="MXN">MXN - Mexican Peso</option>
      <option value="SGD">SGD - Singapore Dollar</option>
      <option value="HKD">HKD - Hong Kong Dollar</option>
      <option value="NOK">NOK - Norwegian Krone</option>
      <option value="TRY">TRY - Turkish Lira</option>
      <option value="INR">INR - Indian Rupee</option>
      <option value="RUB">RUB - Russian Ruble</option>
      <option value="BRL">BRL - Brazilian Real</option>
      <option value="ZAR">ZAR - South African Rand</option>
      <option value="SAR">SAR - Saudi Riyal</option>
      <option value="AED">AED - United Arab Emirates
Dirham</option>
    </select>
```

```html
    <p>to</p>
    <select id="to-currency">
     <option value="USD">USD - United States Dollar</option>
     <option value="EUR">EUR - Euro</option>
     <option value="GBP">GBP - Great Britain Pound</option>
     <option value="JPY">JPY - Japanese Yen</option>
     <option value="AUD">AUD - Australian Dollar</option>
     <option value="CAD">CAD - Canadian Dollar</option>
     <option value="CHF">CHF - Swiss Franc</option>
     <option value="CNY">CNY - Chinese Yuan</option>
     <option value="SEK">SEK - Swedish Krona</option>
     <option value="NZD">NZD - New Zealand Dollar</option>
     <option value="MXN">MXN - Mexican Peso</option>
     <option value="SGD">SGD - Singapore Dollar</option>
     <option value="HKD">HKD - Hong Kong Dollar</option>
     <option value="NOK">NOK - Norwegian Krone</option>
     <option value="KRW">KRW - South Korean Won</option>
     <option value="TRY">TRY - Turkish Lira</option>
     <option value="INR">INR - Indian Rupee</option>
     <option value="RUB">RUB - Russian Ruble</option>
     <option value="BRL">BRL - Brazilian Real</option>
     <option value="ZAR">ZAR - South African Rand</option>
     <option value="SAR">SAR - Saudi Riyal</option>
     <option value="AED">AED - United Arab Emirates
Dirham</option>
    </select>

    <button onclick="convertCurrency()">Convert</button>
    <div id="output"></div>
  </div>

  <script>

    // New function created to insert a thousand unit comma
separator.
    function formatInput(input) {
      // Remove previous formatting
      let value = input.value.replace(/,/g, '');
      // Format the new value
      input.value = parseFloat(value).toLocaleString('en-US',
{ maximumFractionDigits: 2 });
    }

    async function convertCurrency() {
```

```
      // The formatted amount with comma separators is first
stored separately before the format is removed.
    let textamount = document.getElementById('amount').value;
    // const amount =
parseFloat(document.getElementById('amount').value); (The code
has been modified as below to remove the previous formatting (to
convert it back to a number).)
    const amount =
parseFloat(document.getElementById('amount').value.replace(/,/
g, ''));

    const fromCurrency = document.getElementById('from-
currency').value;
    const toCurrency = document.getElementById('to-
currency').value;

    const response = await fetch(`https://v6.exchangerate-
api.com/v6/aaf53da1eba53d98819909**/latest/${fromCurrency}
`);
    const data = await response.json();
    if (data && data.conversion_rates) {
      const rate = data.conversion_rates[toCurrency];
      const convertedAmount = amount * rate;
      const formattedAmount = new Intl.NumberFormat('en-US',
{ minimumFractionDigits: 2 }).format(convertedAmount);
      document.getElementById('output').innerHTML =
`${textamount} ${fromCurrency} = ${formattedAmount}
${toCurrency}`;
    } else {
      document.getElementById('output').innerHTML = 'An error
occurred while fetching the exchange rates.';
    }
  }
  </script>
</body>

</html>

<!-- Unfortunately, the input element of type "number" does not
support formatting the input with comma as thousands separators
because the browser treats the input as a number and numbers
do not support the concept of thousands separators.
```

270

However, there is a workaround to this. We can use an input of type "text", and write a JavaScript function that formats the user's input as they type.

Here's how it works:

oninput="formatInput(this)": This calls the formatInput function every time the user changes the input.
input.value.replace(/,/g, ''): This removes all commas from the input value.
parseFloat(value).toLocaleString('en-US', { maximumFractionDigits: 2 }): This converts the value to a float (since toLocaleString formats integers without decimal places), formats it as a US English string, and sets the formatted value as the input's new value.
document.getElementById('amount').value.replace(/,/g, ''): This removes all commas from the input value before parsing it as a float. We need to do this because parseFloat stops parsing when it encounters a comma.
Please note that this method has a few downsides:

It may cause confusion if users are allowed to enter values manually, since they might not expect the input to change as they type.
It might not handle invalid input correctly. For example, if a user enters a value that's not a number, parseFloat will return NaN, and toLocaleString will convert it to the string "NaN". You might want to add additional input validation to handle these cases.
Browsers handle the oninput event differently. In most modern browsers, the event is fired for every change to the input's value. However, in Internet Explorer 9 and earlier, the event is only fired when the input loses focus. -->

Currency Converter

10,000

USD - United States Dollar

EUR - Euro

Convert

10,000 USD = 8,901.00 EUR

```
<!DOCTYPE html>
<html>

<head>
  <!-- Including Bootstrap 4 -->
  <link rel="stylesheet"
href="https://maxcdn.bootstrapcdn.com/bootstrap/4.0.0/css/boot
strap.min.css">

  <title>Currency Converter</title>
</head>

<body>
  <div id="app" class="container mt-5 text-center">
    <h2 class="mb-4">Currency Converter</h2>

    <div class="row">
      <div class="col-md-6 mb-3">
        <input type="text" id="amount"
oninput="formatInput(this)" class="form-control"
placeholder="Amount">
      </div>
      <div class="col-md-3 mb-3">
        <select id="from-currency" class="form-control">
        <option value="KRW">KRW - South Korean
Won</option>
        <option value="USD">USD - United States
Dollar</option>
```

```
        <option value="EUR">EUR - Euro</option>
        <option value="GBP">GBP - Great Britain
Pound</option>
        <option value="JPY">JPY - Japanese Yen</option>
        <option value="AUD">AUD - Australian Dollar</option>
        <option value="CAD">CAD - Canadian Dollar</option>
        <option value="CHF">CHF - Swiss Franc</option>
        <option value="CNY">CNY - Chinese Yuan</option>
        <option value="SEK">SEK - Swedish Krona</option>
        <option value="NZD">NZD - New Zealand
Dollar</option>
        <option value="MXN">MXN - Mexican Peso</option>
        <option value="SGD">SGD - Singapore Dollar</option>
        <option value="HKD">HKD - Hong Kong Dollar</option>
        <option value="NOK">NOK - Norwegian Krone</option>
        <option value="TRY">TRY - Turkish Lira</option>
        <option value="INR">INR - Indian Rupee</option>
        <option value="RUB">RUB - Russian Ruble</option>
        <option value="BRL">BRL - Brazilian Real</option>
        <option value="ZAR">ZAR - South African
Rand</option>
        <option value="SAR">SAR - Saudi Riyal</option>
        <option value="AED">AED - United Arab Emirates
Dirham</option>
      </select>
    </div>
    <div class="col-md-3 mb-3">
      <select id="to-currency" class="form-control">
        <option value="USD">USD - United States
Dollar</option>
        <option value="EUR">EUR - Euro</option>
        <option value="GBP">GBP - Great Britain
Pound</option>
        <option value="JPY">JPY - Japanese Yen</option>
        <option value="AUD">AUD - Australian Dollar</option>
        <option value="CAD">CAD - Canadian Dollar</option>
        <option value="CHF">CHF - Swiss Franc</option>
        <option value="CNY">CNY - Chinese Yuan</option>
        <option value="SEK">SEK - Swedish Krona</option>
        <option value="NZD">NZD - New Zealand
Dollar</option>
        <option value="MXN">MXN - Mexican Peso</option>
        <option value="SGD">SGD - Singapore Dollar</option>
        <option value="HKD">HKD - Hong Kong Dollar</option>
```

```html
        <option value="NOK">NOK - Norwegian Krone</option>
        <option value="KRW">KRW - South Korean
Won</option>
        <option value="TRY">TRY - Turkish Lira</option>
        <option value="INR">INR - Indian Rupee</option>
        <option value="RUB">RUB - Russian Ruble</option>
        <option value="BRL">BRL - Brazilian Real</option>
        <option value="ZAR">ZAR - South African
Rand</option>
        <option value="SAR">SAR - Saudi Riyal</option>
        <option value="AED">AED - United Arab Emirates
Dirham</option>
      </select>
    </div>
  </div>

  <button onclick="convertCurrency()" class="btn btn-primary
mb-3">Convert</button>
  <div id="output"></div>
</div>

<script>
  function formatInput(input) {

    let value = input.value.replace(/,/g, '');

    input.value = parseFloat(value).toLocaleString('en-US',
{ maximumFractionDigits: 2 });
  }

  async function convertCurrency() {

    let textamount = document.getElementById('amount').value;

    const amount =
parseFloat(document.getElementById('amount').value.replace(/,/
g, ''));

    const fromCurrency = document.getElementById('from-
currency').value;
    const toCurrency = document.getElementById('to-
currency').value;
```

274

```
      const response = await fetch(`https://v6.exchangerate-
api.com/v6/aaf53da1eba53d98819909**/latest/${fromCurrency}
`);
      const data = await response.json();
      if (data && data.conversion_rates) {
        const rate = data.conversion_rates[toCurrency];
        const convertedAmount = amount * rate;
        const formattedAmount = new Intl.NumberFormat('en-US',
{ minimumFractionDigits: 2 }).format(convertedAmount);
        document.getElementById('output').innerHTML =
`${textamount} ${fromCurrency} = ${formattedAmount}
${toCurrency}`;
      } else {
        document.getElementById('output').innerHTML = 'An error
occurred while fetching the exchange rates.';
      }
    }
  </script>
</body>

</html>
```

```
<!-- We have added the Bootstrap 4 CSS file at the top of your
HTML file in a <link> tag. We have also added Bootstrap classes
to our existing HTML elements to style them:

`container` to center the content and give it a max-width.
`row` and `col-md-*` to create a responsive grid layout.
`form-control` to style your inputs and selects.
`btn` and `btn-primary` to style your button.
`mt-*` and `mb-*` classes to add margin to the top and bottom
of various elements. -->
```

Speed Typing Game

dolor

Start typing...

33

11

```html
<!DOCTYPE html>
<html>

<head>
  <title>Speed Typing Game</title>
  <style>
    body {
      font-family: Arial, sans-serif;
      text-align: center;
    }

    #word-display {
      font-size: 36px;
    }

    #word-input {
      font-size: 24px;
      width: 300px;
    }

    #timer {
      color: rgb(250, 4, 4);
    }

    #score {
```

276

```
      color: blue;
    }
  </style>
</head>

<body>
  <h1>Speed Typing Game</h1>
  <p id="word-display"></p>
  <input id="word-input" type="text" placeholder="Start
typing...">
  <h3 id="timer">60</h3>
  <h2 id="score">0</h2>

  <script>
    const words = ['lorem', 'ipsum', 'dolor', 'sit', 'amet',
'consectetur', 'adipiscing', 'elit'];

    let score = 0;
    let time = 60;
    let isPlaying;

    // Select elements
    const wordInput = document.getElementById('word-input');
    const wordDisplay = document.getElementById('word-
display');
    const scoreDisplay = document.getElementById('score');
    const timeDisplay = document.getElementById('timer');

    // Game loop
    const gameLoop = setInterval(() => {
      if (time > 0 && isPlaying) {
        time--;
      } else if (time === 0) {
        isPlaying = false;
      }

      timeDisplay.innerHTML = time;
    }, 1000);

    // Event listeners
    wordInput.addEventListener('input', startMatch);

    function startMatch() {
      if (wordInput.value === wordDisplay.innerHTML) {
```

```
      isPlaying = true;
      wordInput.value = '';
      score++;
      scoreDisplay.innerHTML = score;
      showWord(words);
    }
  }

  // Show random word
  function showWord(words) {
    const randIndex = Math.floor(Math.random() *
words.length);
    wordDisplay.innerHTML = words[randIndex];
  }

  showWord(words);

 </script>
</body>

</html>

<!-- This is a simple version of a speed typing game. The game
will display a random word from the array words. The player
needs to type the word in the input box. If the typed word
matches the displayed word, the score increases by one. If the
timer reaches 0, the game ends. The player's score is displayed
and updated in real time.

This is a very basic implementation and there's a lot of room for
improvements. For instance, you could add a "Game Over"
screen, improve the UI, and increase the difficulty over time by
decreasing the timer or using longer words. -->
```

Speed Typing Game

curabitur

Start typing...

0

12

Game Over

Your final score is 12.

Try Again

```
<!DOCTYPE html>
<html>

<head>
  <title>Speed Typing Game</title>
  <style>
    body {
      font-family: Arial, sans-serif;
      text-align: center;
    }

    #word-display {
      font-size: 36px;
    }

    #word-input {
      font-size: 24px;
      width: 300px;
      transition: width 0.5s;
    }

    /* There are countless ways to improve the UI. Here's an
example of a very simple improvement. Add a title and
```

```
instructions, and make the input box larger when the game is
active: */
    #word-input.active {
      width: 100%;
    }

    #timer {
      color: rgb(250, 4, 4);
    }

    #score {
      color: blue;
    }
  </style>
</head>

<body>
  <h1>Speed Typing Game</h1>
  <p id="word-display"></p>
  <input id="word-input" type="text" placeholder="Start
typing...">
  <h3 id="timer">60</h3>
  <h2 id="score">0</h2>

  <div id="game-over" style="display: none;">
    <h1>Game Over</h1>
    <p>Your final score is <span id="final-score"></span>.</p>
    <button onclick="restartGame()">Try Again</button>
  </div>

  <script>
    // You can add as many words as you want. Here's an example
with 20 words:
    const words = ['lorem', 'ipsum', 'dolor', 'sit', 'amet',
'consectetur', 'adipiscing', 'elit', 'morbi', 'vulputate', 'massa', 'quis',
'sem', 'curabitur', 'aenean', 'ligula', 'pellentesque', 'mollis',
'praesent', 'porttitor'];


    let score = 0;
    let time = 60;
    let isPlaying = false;

    // Select elements
```

```javascript
    const wordInput = document.getElementById('word-input');
    const wordDisplay = document.getElementById('word-
display');
   const scoreDisplay = document.getElementById('score');
   const timeDisplay = document.getElementById('timer');

   // Game loop
   const gameLoop = setInterval(() => {
     if (time > 0 && isPlaying) {
       time--;
     } else if (time === 0) {
       isPlaying = false;
       wordInput.classList.remove('active');
       document.getElementById('game-over').style.display =
'block';
       document.getElementById('final-score').innerText = score;
     }

     timeDisplay.innerHTML = time;
   }, 1000);

   // Event listeners
   wordInput.addEventListener('input', startMatch);

   // Add 'active' class when the game starts
   function startMatch() {
     if (wordInput.value === wordDisplay.innerHTML) {
       wordInput.classList.add('active');
       isPlaying = true;
       wordInput.value = '';
       score++;
       scoreDisplay.innerHTML = score;
       showWord(words);

       // subtract one second from the timer every time the score
reaches a multiple of 5: Increasing difficulty over time:
       if (score % 5 === 0) {
         time--;
       }
     }
   }

   // Show random word
   function showWord(words) {
```

```
    const randIndex = Math.floor(Math.random() *
words.length);
    wordDisplay.innerHTML = words[randIndex];
  }

  showWord(words);

  function restartGame() {
    score = 0;
    time = 60;
    isPlaying = true;
    wordInput.classList.add('active');
    document.getElementById('game-over').style.display =
'none';
    scoreDisplay.innerHTML = score;
    showWord(words);
  }


  </script>
</body>

</html>

<!-- The timer will start when you type the first correct word, and
the "Game Over" screen will appear when the timer reaches 0. If
you want the game to start immediately when the page loads, you
can set isPlaying to true at the beginning and add the 'active'
class to the wordInput element. -->

<!-- Remember, these are just examples. Feel free to modify
them as needed or come up with your own ideas! -->
```

282

Speed Typing Game

mollis

moli

0

19

Game Over

Your final score is 19.

Try Again

```
<!DOCTYPE html>
<html>
<head>
  <link rel="stylesheet"
href="https://maxcdn.bootstrapcdn.com/bootstrap/4.0.0/css/boot
strap.min.css">
  <title>Speed Typing Game</title>
</head>

<body class="bg-light">
  <div class="container text-center py-5">
    <h1 class="mb-5">Speed Typing Game</h1>
    <h2 id="word-display" class="display-4 mb-5"></h2>
    <input id="word-input" type="text" placeholder="Start
typing..." class="form-control form-control-lg mb-4">
    <h3 id="timer" class="text-danger mb-4">60</h3>
    <h2 id="score" class="text-primary mb-5">0</h2>

    <div id="game-over" style="display: none;">
```

283

```
    <h1 class="mb-4">Game Over</h1>
    <p class="mb-4">Your final score is <span id="final-
score"></span>.</p>
    <button onclick="restartGame()" class="btn btn-
primary">Try Again</button>
  </div>
 </div>

 <script>
   const words = ['lorem', 'ipsum', 'dolor', 'sit', 'amet',
'consectetur', 'adipiscing', 'elit', 'morbi', 'vulputate', 'massa', 'quis',
'sem', 'curabitur', 'aenean', 'ligula', 'pellentesque', 'mollis',
'praesent', 'porttitor'];


   let score = 0;
   let time = 60;
   let isPlaying = false;


   const wordInput = document.getElementById('word-input');
   const wordDisplay = document.getElementById('word-
display');
   const scoreDisplay = document.getElementById('score');
   const timeDisplay = document.getElementById('timer');

   const gameLoop = setInterval(() => {
     if (time > 0 && isPlaying) {
       time--;
     } else if (time === 0) {
       isPlaying = false;
       wordInput.classList.remove('active');
       document.getElementById('game-over').style.display =
'block';
       document.getElementById('final-score').innerText = score;
```

```
      }

    timeDisplay.innerHTML = time;
  }, 1000);

  wordInput.addEventListener('input', startMatch);

  function startMatch() {
    if (wordInput.value === wordDisplay.innerHTML) {
      wordInput.classList.add('active');
      isPlaying = true;
      wordInput.value = '';
      score++;
      scoreDisplay.innerHTML = score;
      showWord(words);

      if (score % 5 === 0) {
        time--;
      }
    }
  }

  function showWord(words) {
    const randIndex = Math.floor(Math.random() *
words.length);
    wordDisplay.innerHTML = words[randIndex];
  }

  showWord(words);

  function restartGame() {
    score = 0;
    time = 60;
    isPlaying = true;
```

```
    wordInput.classList.add('active');
    document.getElementById('game-over').style.display =
'none';
    scoreDisplay.innerHTML = score;
    showWord(words);
    }
  </script>
</body>

</html>
```

<!-- In the enhanced version:

I have included Bootstrap CDN link in the `<head>` tag to use
Bootstrap classes.

I have used `container`, `text-center`, `py-5` classes for the
parent `div`. `container` provides a responsive fixed width
container, `text-center` centers the text, and `py-5` provides
vertical padding.

I have used the `form-control` and `form-control-lg` classes to
style the input field.

The `mb-*` classes are used to provide margin at the bottom of
elements.

I've also used `text-primary` and `text-danger` to color the
timer and score elements.
For the Game Over message and button, I've included the `btn`
and `btn-primary` classes for the button, and `mb-4` to space
out the elements. -->

Mad Libs Game

dog	sleep
nice	hard

Generate Story

Your Mad Libs Story

Once upon a time, there was a very nice dog. The dog was always sleep hard in the forest.

```
<!DOCTYPE html>
<html>

<head>
  <title>Mad Libs Game</title>
  <style>
    body {
      font-family: Arial, sans-serif;
      text-align: center;
    }

    .form-container {
      margin-top: 50px;
    }

    .madlib-story {
      display: none;
      margin-top: 50px;
    }

    button {
      margin-top: 20px;
    }
  </style>
</head>
```

287

```
<body>
  <h1>Mad Libs Game</h1>
  <div class="form-container">
    <input id="noun" type="text" placeholder="Enter a noun...">
    <input id="verb" type="text" placeholder="Enter a verb...">
    <input id="adjective" type="text" placeholder="Enter an
adjective...">
    <input id="adverb" type="text" placeholder="Enter an
adverb...">
    <button onclick="generateStory()">Generate Story</button>
  </div>

  <div id="madlib-story" class="madlib-story">
    <h2>Your Mad Libs Story</h2>
    <p id="story"></p>
  </div>

  <script>
    function generateStory() {
      var noun = document.getElementById("noun").value;
      var verb = document.getElementById("verb").value;
      var adjective =
document.getElementById("adjective").value;
      var adverb = document.getElementById("adverb").value;

      var story = `Once upon a time, there was a very
${adjective} ${noun}. The ${noun} was always ${verb}
${adverb} in the forest.`;

      document.getElementById("story").innerHTML = story;

      document.getElementById("madlib-story").style.display =
'block';
    }
  </script>
</body>

</html>

<!-- In this game, the user will provide a noun, verb, adjective,
and adverb. When they press the "Generate Story" button, a short
story is generated using these words and displayed on the page. -
->
```

<!-- Mad Libs is a phrasal template word game where one player prompts others for a list of words to substitute for blanks in a story before reading the often comical or nonsensical story aloud. The game is frequently played as a party game or as a pastime.

The game was invented in the United States, and more than 110 million copies of Mad Libs books have been sold since the series was first published in 1958.

In the context of a coding project, creating a digital version of a Mad Libs game could involve:

1. Defining a story template with blanks for words such as nouns, verbs, adjectives, etc.
2. Prompting the user to input a word for each blank.
3. Inserting the user's words into the correct places in the story.
4. Displaying the completed story to the user. -->

<!-- The name "Mad Libs" is essentially a play on words. The term "ad lib" is short for the Latin phrase "ad libitum," which means "at one's pleasure" or "as you desire." In the context of performances, "ad lib" refers to the spontaneous, on-the-spot improvisation of lines that are not in the script.

The game's creators, Leonard Stern and Roger Price, invented it at a New York City restaurant in 1953. As the story goes, they overheard an argument about the correct adverb to use in a certain context. That incident inspired them to develop a game about filling in the blanks with different parts of speech.

The "mad" part of the name was added for fun and to suggest a sense of zaniness, as the results of the game are often nonsensical and humorous.

So, "Mad Libs" is a pun on "ad lib," with a touch of madness thrown in. It's a fitting name for a game that's all about spontaneous creativity and humor! -->

```
<!DOCTYPE html>
<html>

<head>
  <title>Mad Libs Game</title>
  <style>
    body {
      font-family: Arial, sans-serif;
      display: flex;
      flex-direction: column;
      align-items: center;
      justify-content: center;
      margin: 0;
      padding: 0;
      background-color: #f5f5f5;
      color: #333;
    }

    .form-container {
      display: flex;
      flex-direction: column;
      width: 300px;
      margin: 10px auto;
      padding: 20px;
```

```css
  border: 2px solid #888;
  border-radius: 5px;
  box-shadow: 0px 0px 10px 0px rgba(0, 0, 0, 0.1);
  background-color: #fff;
}

select {
  margin: 10px 0;
  padding: 10px;
  font-size: 1em;
  border: 2px solid #333;
  border-radius: 5px;
  background-color: #fafafa;
  width: 100%;
  box-sizing: border-box;
}

button {
  margin: 20px 0;
  padding: 10px;
  border: none;
  border-radius: 5px;
  background-color: #333;
  color: #fff;
  cursor: pointer;
  font-weight: bold;
}

button:hover {
  background-color: #888;
}

.madlib-story {
  display: none;
  margin: 10px auto;
  padding: 10px;
  width: 50%;
  border: 2px solid #888;
  border-radius: 5px;
  box-shadow: 0px 0px 10px 0px rgba(0, 0, 0, 0.3);
  background-color: #b7ebb2;
  font-size: 1.5em;
}
```

```
    h1 {
      color: #333;
      text-align: center;
      font-size: 2em;
    }

    h2 {
      color: #333;
      text-align: center;
      font-size: 1.2em;
    }

    p {
      text-align: justify;
    }

    option {
      color: rgb(48, 16, 205);
    }

    .noun {
      color: red;
    }

    .verb {
      color: rgb(88, 13, 13);
    }

    .adjective {
      color: brown;
    }

    .adverb {
      color: rgb(35, 16, 156);
    }
  </style>
</head>
</style>
</head>

<body>
  <h1>Mad Libs Game</h1>
  <div class="form-container">
    <select id="noun">
```

```html
    <option value="" selected disabled>Select a noun</option>
    <option value="cat">desk</option>
    <option value="dog">bread</option>
    <option value="mouse">camping</option>
    <option value="tree">tree</option>
    <option value="book">book</option>
    <option value="house">house</option>
    <option value="car">car</option>
    <option value="bird">regrigerator</option>
    <option value="computer">computer</option>
    <option value="phone">phone</option>
  </select>
  <select id="verb">
    <option value="" selected disabled>Select a verb</option>
    <option value="run">Run</option>
    <option value="jump">Jump</option>
    <option value="play">Play</option>
    <option value="laugh">Laugh</option>
    <option value="sing">Sing</option>
    <option value="dance">Dance</option>
    <option value="read">Read</option>
    <option value="write">Write</option>
    <option value="eat">Eat</option>
    <option value="sleep">Sleep</option>
  </select>
  <select id="adjective">
    <option value="" selected disabled>Select an
adjective</option>
    <option value="happy">Happy</option>
    <option value="sad">Sad</option>
    <option value="big">Big</option>
    <option value="small">Small</option>
    <option value="fast">Fast</option>
    <option value="slow">Slow</option>
    <option value="hot">Hot</option>
    <option value="cold">Cold</option>
    <option value="bright">Bright</option>
    <option value="dark">Dark</option>
  </select>
  <select id="adverb">
    <option value="" selected disabled>Select an
adverb</option>
    <option value="quickly">Quickly</option>
    <option value="slowly">Slowly</option>
```

```html
    <option value="happily">Happily</option>
    <option value="sadly">Sadly</option>
    <option value="silently">Silently</option>
    <option value="loudly">Loudly</option>
    <option value="easily">Easily</option>
    <option value="hardly">Hardly</option>
    <option value="carefully">Carefully</option>
    <option value="recklessly">Recklessly</option>
  </select>
  <button onclick="generateStory()">Generate Story</button>
</div>

<div id="madlib-story" class="madlib-story">
  <h2>Your Mad Libs Story</h2>
  <p id="story"></p>
</div>
<script>
  var stories = [
    "A lazy {{noun}} named Whiskers lived in a small village. He
loved {{verb}} the world go by from his {{adjective}} cushion.
One day, he saw a {{noun}} scurrying across the floor.
{{adverb}}, Whiskers chased the {{noun}}, enjoying a thrilling
game of chase. To his surprise, Whiskers discovered he loved the
excitement. From that day, he decided to be an {{adjective}}
{{noun}}.",
    "In a bustling city, a lonely {{noun}} named Percy lived atop
a tall building. Percy watched children {{verb}} in the park,
wishing he had a friend. One day, he gathered courage and
{{verb}} down, introducing himself to a little {{noun}}. She
named him 'Buddy', and they became {{adjective}} friends,
sharing sandwiches and giggles {{adverb}}.",
    "{{noun}}, a curious {{noun}}, lived in a small tank. She
often wondered about life beyond her glass walls. One day, her
owner left the lid open. {{adverb}}, {{noun}} jumped out,
landing in a bigger tank. She was scared but {{adverb}}. She
realized a bigger world waited for her, full of {{adjective}}
wonders.",
    "Benny, a brave {{noun}}, lived in a peaceful countryside
farm. He spent his days {{verb}} sheep and guarding the
{{noun}}. One chilly night, he heard a whimpering sound from
the woods. Benny found a lost {{noun}}, shivering and scared.
He guided the {{noun}} home, and they became {{adjective}}.
Benny realized he was not just a guard {{noun}}, but a
{{adjective}} protector.",
```

"Oliver, an owl, loved the tranquility of night. He adored the twinkling stars and the rustling leaves. However, he felt alone, as everyone else slept. One night, he met Luna, a {{noun}}. She also loved the night and its {{adjective}} beauty. Together, they {{verb}} the night, sharing stories. Oliver finally found his companion {{adverb}} under the {{adjective}} starlight."
    ];


```
    function generateStory() {
      var noun = document.getElementById("noun").value;
      var verb = document.getElementById("verb").value;
      var adjective =
document.getElementById("adjective").value;
      var adverb = document.getElementById("adverb").value;
      // Choose a random story
      var storyTemplate = stories[Math.floor(Math.random() *
stories.length)];
      // Replace placeholders in the story
      var story = storyTemplate.replace(/{{noun}}/g, `<span
class='noun'>${noun}</span>`)
        .replace(/{{verb}}/g, `<span
class='verb'>${verb}</span>`)
        .replace(/{{adjective}}/g, `<span
class='adjective'>${adjective}</span>`)
        .replace(/{{adverb}}/g, `<span
class='adverb'>${adverb}</span>`);

      document.getElementById("story").innerHTML = story;

      document.getElementById("madlib-story").style.display =
'block';
    }
  </script>
</body>
</html>
```

```html
<!DOCTYPE html>
<html>

<head>
  <link rel="stylesheet"
href="https://maxcdn.bootstrapcdn.com/bootstrap/4.0.0/css/bootstrap.min.css">
  <title>Mad Libs Game</title>
</head>

<body class="bg-light">
  <div class="container py-5">
    <h1 class="text-center mb-5">Mad Libs Game</h1>
    <div class="form-container card p-5">
      <select id="noun" class="form-control mb-3">
        <option value="" selected disabled>Select a
noun</option>
        <option value="cat">desk</option>
```

```html
      <option value="dog">bread</option>
      <option value="mouse">camping</option>
      <option value="tree">tree</option>
      <option value="book">book</option>
      <option value="house">house</option>
      <option value="car">car</option>
      <option value="bird">regrigerator</option>
      <option value="computer">computer</option>
      <option value="phone">phone</option>
    </select>
    <select id="verb" class="form-control mb-3">
      <option value="" selected disabled>Select a
verb</option>
      <option value="run">Run</option>
      <option value="jump">Jump</option>
      <option value="play">Play</option>
      <option value="laugh">Laugh</option>
      <option value="sing">Sing</option>
      <option value="dance">Dance</option>
      <option value="read">Read</option>
      <option value="write">Write</option>
      <option value="eat">Eat</option>
      <option value="sleep">Sleep</option>
    </select>
    <select id="adjective" class="form-control mb-3">
      <option value="" selected disabled>Select an
adjective</option>
      <option value="happy">Happy</option>
      <option value="sad">Sad</option>
      <option value="big">Big</option>
      <option value="small">Small</option>
      <option value="fast">Fast</option>
      <option value="slow">Slow</option>
      <option value="hot">Hot</option>
      <option value="cold">Cold</option>
      <option value="bright">Bright</option>
      <option value="dark">Dark</option>
    </select>
    <select id="adverb" class="form-control mb-3">
      <option value="" selected disabled>Select an
adverb</option>
      <option value="quickly">Quickly</option>
      <option value="slowly">Slowly</option>
      <option value="happily">Happily</option>
```

297

```html
        <option value="sadly">Sadly</option>
        <option value="silently">Silently</option>
        <option value="loudly">Loudly</option>
        <option value="easily">Easily</option>
        <option value="hardly">Hardly</option>
        <option value="carefully">Carefully</option>
        <option value="recklessly">Recklessly</option>
      </select>
      <button onclick="generateStory()" class="btn btn-primary
btn-block">Generate Story</button>
    </div>

    <div id="madlib-story" class="madlib-story card mt-5 p-5"
style="display: none;">
      <h2 class="text-center">Your Mad Libs Story</h2>
      <p id="story" class="mt-4"></p>
    </div>
  </div>

  <script>
    var stories = [
      "A lazy {{noun}} named Whiskers lived in a small village. He
loved {{verb}} the world go by from his {{adjective}} cushion.
One day, he saw a {{noun}} scurrying across the floor.
{{adverb}}, Whiskers chased the {{noun}}, enjoying a thrilling
game of chase. To his surprise, Whiskers discovered he loved the
excitement. From that day, he decided to be an {{adjective}}
{{noun}}.",
      "In a bustling city, a lonely {{noun}} named Percy lived atop
a tall building. Percy watched children {{verb}} in the park,
wishing he had a friend. One day, he gathered courage and
{{verb}} down, introducing himself to a little {{noun}}. She
named him 'Buddy', and they became {{adjective}} friends,
sharing sandwiches and giggles {{adverb}}.",
      "{{noun}}, a curious {{noun}}, lived in a small tank. She
often wondered about life beyond her glass walls. One day, her
owner left the lid open. {{adverb}}, {{noun}} jumped out,
landing in a bigger tank. She was scared but {{adverb}}. She
realized a bigger world waited for her, full of {{adjective}}
wonders.",
      "Benny, a brave {{noun}}, lived in a peaceful countryside
farm. He spent his days {{verb}} sheep and guarding the
{{noun}}. One chilly night, he heard a whimpering sound from
the woods. Benny found a lost {{noun}}, shivering and scared.
```

He guided the {{noun}} home, and they became {{adjective}}. Benny realized he was not just a guard {{noun}}, but a {{adjective}} protector.",

"Oliver, an owl, loved the tranquility of night. He adored the twinkling stars and the rustling leaves. However, he felt alone, as everyone else slept. One night, he met Luna, a {{noun}}. She also loved the night and its {{adjective}} beauty. Together, they {{verb}} the night, sharing stories. Oliver finally found his companion {{adverb}} under the {{adjective}} starlight."
        ];

```
    function generateStory() {
      var noun = document.getElementById("noun").value;
      var verb = document.getElementById("verb").value;
      var adjective =
document.getElementById("adjective").value;
      var adverb = document.getElementById("adverb").value;

      // Choose a random story
      var storyTemplate = stories[Math.floor(Math.random() *
stories.length)];

      // Replace placeholders in the story
      var story = storyTemplate.replace(/{{noun}}/g, `<span
class='noun'>${noun}</span>`)
        .replace(/{{verb}}/g, `<span
class='verb'>${verb}</span>`)
        .replace(/{{adjective}}/g, `<span
class='adjective'>${adjective}</span>`)
        .replace(/{{adverb}}/g, `<span
class='adverb'>${adverb}</span>`);

      document.getElementById("story").innerHTML = story;

      document.getElementById("madlib-story").style.display =
'block';
    }
  </script>
</body>

</html>
```

Virtual Dice Roll

Roll the Dice

5

300

```
<!DOCTYPE html>
<html>

<head>
    <title>Virtual Dice Roll</title>
    <style>
        body {
            font-family: Arial, sans-serif;
            text-align: center;
        }

        #dice {
            font-size: 56px;
            color: #ff0000;
            margin-top: 20px;
        }

        button {
```

```
            margin-top: 20px;
            padding: 10px 20px;
            font-size: 20px;
        }
    </style>
</head>

<body>
    <h1>Virtual Dice Roll</h1>
    <button onclick="rollDice()">Roll the Dice</button>
    <p id="dice">?</p>

    <script>
        function rollDice() {
            var dice = Math.floor(Math.random() * 6) + 1;
            document.getElementById("dice").innerHTML = dice;
        }
    </script>
</body>

</html>
```

```
<!-- In this program, when the "Roll the Dice" button is clicked, a
random number between 1 and 6 is generated and displayed on
the page, simulating the roll of a dice. -->

<!-- Similar to coding number 016. The location of onclick is
different. -->
```

302

```
<!DOCTYPE html>
<html>

<head>
  <title>Virtual Dice Roll</title>
  <style>
    body {
      font-family: Arial, sans-serif;
      text-align: center;
      background-image: linear-gradient(rgba(255, 255, 255, 0.5),
rgba(255, 255, 255, 0.9)), url('dice_6pcs.jpg');
      background-size: cover;
      background-image: 0.2;
      display: flex;
      flex-direction: column;
      align-items: center;
      justify-content: center;
      height: 100vh;
      margin: 0;
```

```css
  color: #333;
  background-color: #f8f8f8;
}

h1 {
  color: balck;
  background-color: white;
}

#dice-container {
  display: flex;
  justify-content: center;
  align-items: center;
  width: 400px;
  height: 300px;
  border: 2px solid #333;
  border-radius: 10px;
  padding: 20px;
  margin: 20px;
  box-shadow: 0px 10px 20px rgba(0, 0, 0, 0.19), 0px 6px
6px rgba(0, 0, 0, 0.23);
}

#dice {
  font-size: 56px;
  font-weight: bold;
  width: 100%;
  height: 100%;
  text-align: center;
}

button {
  padding: 10px 20px;
  font-size: 20px;
```

```
      font-weight: bold;
      color: rgb(254, 252, 252);
      background-color: #0303fd;
      border: none;
      border-radius: 5px;
      cursor: pointer;
      margin-top: 20px;
    }

    button:hover {
      background-color: #f70505;
    }
  </style>
</head>

<body>
  <h1>Virtual Dice Roll</h1>
  <button onclick="rollDice()">Roll the Dice</button>
  <div id="dice-container">
    <img id="dice" src="dice_6pcs.jpg" />
  </div>

  <script>
    function rollDice() {
      var dice = Math.floor(Math.random() * 6) + 1;
      document.getElementById("dice").src = 'dice_no' + dice +
'.jpg';
    }
  </script>
</body>

</html>
```

```
<!DOCTYPE html>
<html>

<head>
  <title>Virtual Dice Roll</title>
  <link rel="stylesheet"
href="https://stackpath.bootstrapcdn.com/bootstrap/4.3.1/css/bo
otstrap.min.css">
  <style>
    body {
      font-family: Arial, sans-serif;
      background-image: linear-gradient(rgba(255, 255, 255, 0.5),
rgba(255, 255, 255, 0.9)), url('dice_6pcs.jpg');
      background-size: cover;
      background-image: 0.2;
      height: 100vh;
      margin: 0;
      color: #333;
```

```
      display: flex;
      flex-direction: column;
      align-items: center;
      justify-content: center;
    }

    #dice-container {
      display: flex;
      justify-content: center;
      align-items: center;
      width: 400px;
      height: 300px;
      border: 2px solid #333;
      border-radius: 10px;
      padding: 20px;
      margin: 20px;
      box-shadow: 0px 10px 20px rgba(0, 0, 0, 0.19), 0px 6px
6px rgba(0, 0, 0, 0.23);
    }

    .btn-primary {
      font-size: 20px;
      font-weight: bold;
      margin-top: 20px;
    }

    #history {
      margin-top: 50px;
      max-width: 500px;
    }

    .history-entry {
      background-color: #f8f9fa;
      padding: 10px;
      margin-bottom: 10px;
      border-radius: 5px;
    }
  </style>
</head>
<body>
  <div class="container text-center">
    <h1 class="my-4">Virtual Dice Roll</h1>
    <button id="roll-button" class="btn btn-primary">Roll the
Dice</button>
```

```
    <div id="dice-container" class="my-4">
      <img id="dice" src="dice_no6.jpg" class="img-fluid" />
    </div>

    <div id="history">
      <h2>Roll History</h2>
      <!-- History entries will be added here -->
    </div>
  </div>
  <script src="https://code.jquery.com/jquery-
3.3.1.slim.min.js"></script>
  <script
src="https://stackpath.bootstrapcdn.com/bootstrap/4.3.1/js/boot
strap.min.js"></script>
  <script>
    $(document).ready(function () {
      $('#roll-button').click(function () {
        var dice = Math.floor(Math.random() * 6) + 1;
        $("#dice").attr("src", 'dice_no' + dice + '.jpg');

        // Add roll result to history
        var entry = $('<div>').addClass('history-entry').text('You
rolled a ' + dice);
        $('#history').append(entry);
      });
    });
  </script>
</body>
</html>
<!-- In this revised code, I have added roll history functionality
using jQuery. Each time a roll is made, the result is added to this
history section, allowing you to see previous results.
Please replace 'dice_no' + dice + '.jpg' with your own image file
paths.
Please note that you need to host your images somewhere
accessible to your HTML file, and replace the URLs in the code
with the URLs of your images. -->
```

307

308

```
<!DOCTYPE html>
<html>

<head>
    <title>Image Carousel</title>
    <style>
        .carousel {
            position: relative;
            width: 300px;
            height: 200px;
            margin: auto;
            overflow: hidden;
        }

        .carousel img {
            width: 100%;
            height: 100%;
```

```
        position: absolute;
        transition: opacity 1s;
        opacity: 0;
      }

      .carousel img.active {
        opacity: 1;
      }

      .buttons {
        text-align: center;
        margin-top: 10px;
      }
    </style>
</head>

<body>
    <div class="carousel">
        <!-- It is possible to check the operation with the
background color even without images. -->
        <img src="image1.jpg" class="active" style="background-
color: red;">
        <img src="image2.jpg" style="background-color:
yellow;">
        <img src="image3.jpg" style="background-color: green;">
        <img src="image4.png" style="background-color: gray;">
        <img src="image5.jpg" style="background-color: blue;">
        <img src="image6.jpg" style="background-color:
orange;">
        <img src="image7.jpg" style="background-color:
orangered;">
    </div>
    <div class="buttons">
        <button onclick="changeImage(-1)">Prev</button>
```

```
      <button onclick="changeImage(1)">Next</button>
   </div>

   <script>
      let images =
Array.from(document.querySelectorAll('.carousel img'));
      let currentImageIndex = 0;

      function changeImage(direction) {
         images[currentImageIndex].classList.remove('active');
         currentImageIndex = (currentImageIndex + direction +
images.length) % images.length;
         images[currentImageIndex].classList.add('active');
      }
   </script>
</body>

</html>
<!-- Remember to replace image1.jpg, image2.jpg,  image3.jpg,
and so on with the actual paths to your images.

The changeImage function switches the active image. It first
removes the 'active' class from the current image, then changes
currentImageIndex by adding the direction (1 for next, -1 for
previous). The images.length is added to handle negative indices,
and the modulus operator % is used to wrap around to the
beginning of the array when the end is reached. Finally, the
'active' class is added to the new current image, causing it to
appear. -->
```

```
00:15:87   [ Start ]   [ Stop ]   [ Reset ]
```

```
<!DOCTYPE html>
<html>

<head>
  <!-- <link rel="stylesheet" type="text/css" href="styles.css"> --
>
  <style>
    body {
      display: flex;
      justify-content: center;
      align-items: center;
      height: 100vh;
      font-family: Arial, sans-serif;
      background-color: #f0f0f0;
    }

    #stopwatch {
      font-size: 50px;
      margin-bottom: 20px;
    }

    button {
      margin: 5px;
      padding: 10px 20px;
      font-size: 20px;
    }
```

311

```html
  </style>
</head>

<body>
  <div id="stopwatch">
    <span id="minutes">00</span>:<span
id="seconds">00</span>:<span id="hundredths">00</span>
  </div>
  <button id="start-btn">Start</button>
  <button id="stop-btn">Stop</button>
  <button id="reset-btn">Reset</button>

  <!-- <script src="stopwatch.js"></script> -->
  <script>
    let minutes = 0, seconds = 0, hundredths = 0, t;

    function add() {
      hundredths++;
      if (hundredths >= 100) {
        hundredths = 0;
        seconds++;
        if (seconds >= 60) {
          seconds = 0;
          minutes++;
        }
      }

    document.getElementById('minutes').textContent = (minutes
> 9 ? "" : "0") + minutes;
    document.getElementById('seconds').textContent = (seconds
> 9 ? "" : "0") + seconds;
    document.getElementById('hundredths').textContent =
(hundredths > 9 ? "" : "0") + hundredths;
```

312

```
        startTimer();
    }

    function startTimer() {
        t = setTimeout(add, 10); // 10 will   run it every 100th of a
second
    }

    document.getElementById('start-btn').addEventListener('click',
function () {
        if (!t) startTimer();
    });

    document.getElementById('stop-btn').addEventListener('click',
function () {
        clearTimeout(t);
        t = false;
    });

    document.getElementById('reset-
btn').addEventListener('click', function () {
        clearTimeout(t);
        t = false;
        minutes = 0; seconds = 0; hundredths = 0;
        document.getElementById('minutes').textContent = "00";
        document.getElementById('seconds').textContent = "00";
        document.getElementById('hundredths').textContent = "00";
    });

  </script>
</body>
</html>
```

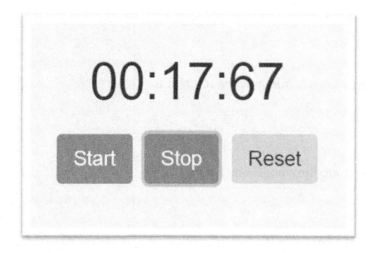

314

```
<!DOCTYPE html>
<html>

<head>
  <!-- Bootstrap CSS -->
  <link
href="https://stackpath.bootstrapcdn.com/bootstrap/4.3.1/css/bo
otstrap.min.css" rel="stylesheet">
  <!-- jQuery -->
  <script src="https://code.jquery.com/jquery-
3.4.1.min.js"></script>
  <style>
    body {
      display: flex;
      justify-content: center;
      align-items: center;
      height: 100vh;
      font-family: Arial, sans-serif;
      background-color: #f0f0f0;
    }

    #stopwatch {
      font-size: 50px;
      margin-bottom: 20px;
    }
  </style>
</head>
```

```
<body>
  <div class="text-center">
    <div id="stopwatch" class="display-2">
      <span id="minutes">00</span>:<span
id="seconds">00</span>:<span id="hundredths">00</span>
    </div>
    <button id="start-btn" class="btn btn-primary btn-lg mr-
2">Start</button>
    <button id="stop-btn" class="btn btn-danger btn-lg mr-
2">Stop</button>
    <button id="reset-btn" class="btn btn-warning btn-
lg">Reset</button>
  </div>
  <script>
    let minutes = 0, seconds = 0, hundredths = 0, t;

    function add() {
      hundredths++;
      if (hundredths >= 100) {
        hundredths = 0;
        seconds++;
        if (seconds >= 60) {
          seconds = 0;
          minutes++;
        }
      }

    $('#minutes').text((minutes > 9 ? "" : "0") + minutes);
    $('#seconds').text((seconds > 9 ? "" : "0") + seconds);
    $('#hundredths').text((hundredths > 9 ? "" : "0") +
hundredths);

    startTimer();
  }

  function startTimer() {
    t = setTimeout(add, 10); // 10 will  run it every 100th of a
second
  }

  $('#start-btn').click(function () {
    if (!t) startTimer();
  });
```

315

```
$('#stop-btn').click(function () {
  clearTimeout(t);
  t = false;
});

$('#reset-btn').click(function () {
  clearTimeout(t);
  t = false;
  minutes = 0; seconds = 0; hundredths = 0;
  $('#minutes').text("00");
  $('#seconds').text("00");
  $('#hundredths').text("00");
});

  </script>
</body>

</html>

<!-- In this updated version, I have used Bootstrap's button
classes to style the buttons, and jQuery's click function to handle
button clicks instead of inline onclick attributes. Note that you
must replace document.getElementById('element') with the
jQuery equivalent $('#element'). -->
```

```
<!DOCTYPE html>
<html>

<head>
  <title>Countdown Timer</title>
  <!-- <link rel="stylesheet" type="text/css" href="styles.css"> -->
  <style>
    body {
      display: flex;
      justify-content: center;
      align-items: center;
      height: 100vh;
      font-family: Arial, sans-serif;
      background-color: #f0f0f0;
      flex-direction: column;
    }

    #countdown {
      font-size: 50px;
```

```
      margin-top: 20px;
    }

    button {
      margin: 5px;
      padding: 10px 20px;
      font-size: 20px;
    }
  </style>
</head>
<h1>Countdown Timer</h1>
<body>
  <input id="time-input" type="number" placeholder="Enter time
in seconds">
  <button id="start-countdown">Start</button>
  <div id="countdown">
    <span id="timer">00</span>
  </div>

  <!-- <script src="countdown.js"></script> -->
  <script>
    let countdown; // variable to hold setInterval

    document.getElementById('start-
countdown').addEventListener('click', function () {
      let timeInput = document.getElementById('time-
input').value; // Get user input
      if (!timeInput) return; // Return if input is empty

      timeInput = parseInt(timeInput);
      if (isNaN(timeInput) || timeInput < 0) return; // Return if
input is not a positive number
```

```
      if (countdown) clearInterval(countdown); // If a countdown
is already active, clear it

     countdown = setInterval(function () {
       if (timeInput <= 0) { // If the countdown should be over
         clearInterval(countdown); // Clear the countdown
         document.getElementById('timer').textContent = "00"; //
Reset the displayed countdown
       } else {
         timeInput--; // Subtract one second
         document.getElementById('timer').textContent =
(timeInput > 9 ? "" : "0") + timeInput; // Display the new time
       }
     }, 1000); // Run the function every second
   });

  </script>
</body>

</html>

<!-- This countdown timer will count down every second from the
user input until it reaches zero. You can create styles.css and
countdown.js files in the same directory as your HTML file and
copy the respective code into these files. When you open your
HTML file in a web browser, you will see a simple countdown
timer. -->
```

319

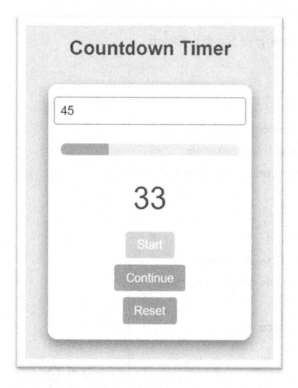

320

```
<!DOCTYPE html>
<html>
<head>
  <title>Countdown Timer</title>
  <style>
    body {
      font-family: Arial, sans-serif;
      background-color: #6bfc74;
      display: flex;
      flex-direction: column;
      align-items: center;
      justify-content: center;
      height: 100vh;
      margin: 0;
      color: #333;
    }

    #timer-container {
      display: flex;
```

```css
  flex-direction: column;
  align-items: center;
  justify-content: center;
  background-color: #fff;
  border-radius: 15px;
  box-shadow: 0px 10px 20px rgba(0, 0, 0, 0.5);
  padding: 20px;
  margin-top: 20px;
  width: 300px;
}

#timer {
  font-size: 50px;
  margin: 20px;
}

#progress-bar {
  width: 100%;
  background-color: #dce97d;
  border-radius: 15px;
  overflow: hidden;
  margin-top: 20px;
  margin-bottom: 20px;
}

#progress-bar div {
  height: 20px;
  background-color: #4caf50;
}

button {
  padding: 10px 20px;
  border: none;
  background-color: #4caf50;
  color: #fff;
  border-radius: 5px;
  font-size: 20px;
  cursor: pointer;
  margin: 5px;
}

button:disabled {
  background-color: #ccc;
}
```

```css
    #time-input {
      width: 100%;
      padding: 10px;
      font-size: 20px;
      margin-bottom: 10px;
      border: 1px solid #333;
      border-radius: 5px;
    }
  </style>
</head>
```
```html
<body>
  <h1>Countdown Timer</h1>
  <div id="timer-container">
    <input id="time-input" type="number" placeholder="Enter
time in seconds">
    <div id="progress-bar">
      <div></div>
    </div>
    <span id="timer">00</span>
    <button id="start-countdown">Start</button>
    <button id="pause-countdown" disabled>Pause</button>
    <button id="reset-countdown" disabled>Reset</button>
  </div>
  <script>
    let countdown; // variable to hold setInterval
    let originalTime;
    let isPaused = false;

    function setProgress(time) {
      const progress = document.querySelector('#progress-bar
div');
      progress.style.width = ((originalTime - time) / originalTime)
* 100 + '%';
    }

    document.getElementById('start-
countdown').addEventListener('click', function () {
      let timeInput = document.getElementById('time-
input').value; // Get user input
      if (!timeInput) return; // Return if input is empty

      timeInput = parseInt(timeInput);
```

```javascript
    if (isNaN(timeInput) || timeInput <= 0) return; // Return if
input is not a positive number

    originalTime = timeInput;

    if (countdown) clearInterval(countdown); // If a countdown
is already active, clear it

    document.getElementById('start-countdown').disabled =
true;
    document.getElementById('pause-countdown').disabled =
false;
    document.getElementById('reset-countdown').disabled =
false;

    countdown = setInterval(function () {
      if (timeInput <= 0) { // If the countdown should be over
        clearInterval(countdown); // Clear the countdown
        document.getElementById('timer').textContent = "00"; //
Reset the displayed countdown
      } else {
        timeInput--; // Subtract one second
        document.getElementById('timer').textContent =
(timeInput > 9 ? "" : "0") + timeInput; // Display the new time
        setProgress(timeInput);
      }
    }, 1000); // Run the function every second
  });

  document.getElementById('pause-
countdown').addEventListener('click', function () {
    if (isPaused) {
      document.getElementById('pause-countdown').textContent
= 'Pause';
      countdown = setInterval(function () {
        let timeInput =
parseInt(document.getElementById('timer').textContent);
        if (timeInput <= 0) {
          clearInterval(countdown);
          document.getElementById('timer').textContent = "00";
        } else {
          timeInput--;
          document.getElementById('timer').textContent =
(timeInput > 9 ? "" : "0") + timeInput;
```

323

```
            setProgress(timeInput);
          }
      }, 1000);
    } else {
      clearInterval(countdown);
      document.getElementById('pause-countdown').textContent
= 'Continue';
    }
    isPaused = !isPaused;
  });

  document.getElementById('reset-
countdown').addEventListener('click', function () {
    clearInterval(countdown);
    document.getElementById('timer').textContent = "00";
    document.getElementById('time-input').value = '';
    document.querySelector('#progress-bar div').style.width =
'0%';
    document.getElementById('start-countdown').disabled =
false;
    document.getElementById('pause-countdown').disabled =
true;
    document.getElementById('pause-countdown').textContent
= 'Pause';
    document.getElementById('reset-countdown').disabled =
true;
    isPaused = false;
  });
  </script>
</body>
</html>
<!--
The "Stop" button is now renamed to "Pause" and acts as a
pause/resume button that toggles between states when clicked.

This version of the code adds a pause/resume functionality. If the
"Pause" button is clicked during the countdown, it pauses the
countdown and changes the button text to "Continue". When the
"Continue" button is clicked, the countdown resumes from where
it was paused. -->
```

324

```
<!DOCTYPE html>
<html>

<head>
  <!-- Bootstrap CSS -->
  <link
href="https://stackpath.bootstrapcdn.com/bootstrap/4.3.1/css/bo
otstrap.min.css" rel="stylesheet">
  <!-- jQuery -->
  <script src="https://code.jquery.com/jquery-
3.4.1.min.js"></script>
  <style>
    body {
      font-family: Arial, sans-serif;
      background-color: #6bfc74;
      display: flex;
      flex-direction: column;
      align-items: center;
      justify-content: center;
```

```
      height: 100vh;
      margin: 0;
      color: #333;
    }

    #timer-container {
      display: flex;
      flex-direction: column;
      align-items: center;
      justify-content: center;
      background-color: #fff;
      border-radius: 15px;
      box-shadow: 0px 10px 20px rgba(0, 0, 0, 0.5);
      padding: 20px;
      margin-top: 20px;
      width: 300px;
    }

    #timer {
      font-size: 50px;
      margin: 20px;
    }

    #progress-bar {
      width: 100%;
      background-color: #dce97d;
      border-radius: 15px;
      overflow: hidden;
      margin-top: 20px;
      margin-bottom: 20px;
    }

    #progress-bar div {
      height: 20px;
      background-color: #4caf50;
    }
  </style>
</head>

<body>
  <h1 class="text-center">Countdown Timer</h1>
```

```html
<div id="timer-container" class="text-center">
    <input id="time-input" class="form-control" type="number"
placeholder="Enter time in seconds">
    <div id="progress-bar" class="mt-4">
      <div></div>
    </div>
    <span id="timer" class="display-4">00</span>
    <button id="start-countdown" class="btn btn-success btn-lg
mt-2">Start</button>
    <button id="pause-countdown" class="btn btn-warning btn-lg
mt-2" disabled>Pause</button>
    <button id="reset-countdown" class="btn btn-danger btn-lg
mt-2" disabled>Reset</button>
  </div>

  <script>
    let countdown; // variable to hold setInterval
    let originalTime;
    let isPaused = false;

    function setProgress(time) {
      $('#progress-bar div').width((((originalTime - time) /
originalTime) * 100 + '%');
    }

    $('#start-countdown').click(function () {
      let timeInput = $('#time-input').val(); // Get user input
      if (!timeInput) return; // Return if input is empty

      timeInput = parseInt(timeInput);
      if (isNaN(timeInput) || timeInput <= 0) return; // Return if
input is not a positive number

      originalTime = timeInput;

      if (countdown) clearInterval(countdown); // If a countdown
is already active, clear it

      $('#start-countdown').prop('disabled', true);
      $('#pause-countdown').prop('disabled', false);
      $('#reset-countdown').prop('disabled', false);
```

```
        countdown = setInterval(function () {
          if (timeInput <= 0) { // If the countdown should be over
            clearInterval(countdown); // Clear the countdown
            $('#timer').text("00"); // Reset the displayed countdown
          } else {
            timeInput--; // Subtract one second
            $('#timer').text((timeInput > 9 ? "" : "0") + timeInput);
// Display the new time
            setProgress(timeInput);
          }
        }, 1000); // Run the function every second
      });

      $('#pause-countdown').click(function () {
        if (isPaused) {
          $('#pause-countdown').text('Pause');
          countdown = setInterval(function () {
            let timeInput = parseInt($('#timer').text());
            if (timeInput <= 0) {
              clearInterval(countdown);
              $('#timer').text("00");
            } else {
              timeInput--;
              $('#timer').text((timeInput > 9 ? "" : "0") +
timeInput);
              setProgress(timeInput);
            }
          }, 1000);
        } else {
          clearInterval(countdown);
          $('#pause-countdown').text('Continue');
        }
        isPaused = !isPaused;
      });

      $('#reset-countdown').click(function () {
        clearInterval(countdown);
        $('#timer').text("00");
        $('#time-input').val('');
        $('#progress-bar div').width('0%');
```

328

```
    $('#start-countdown').prop('disabled', false);
    $('#pause-countdown').prop('disabled', true);
    $('#pause-countdown').text('Pause');
    $('#reset-countdown').prop('disabled', true);
    isPaused = false;
  });
 </script>
</body>

</html>

<!-- The code now makes use of Bootstrap's form and button
classes to enhance the design. The jQuery has been updated to
handle the button clicks and manipulations of the HTML elements.
-->
```

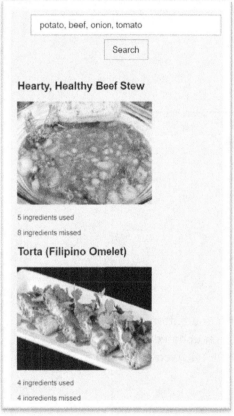

330

```
<!DOCTYPE html>
<html>

<head>
  <title>Recipe founder</title>
  <!-- <link rel="stylesheet" type="text/css" href="styles.css"> --
>
  <style>
   body {
     display: flex;
     justify-content: center;
```

```
    align-items: center;
    height: auto;
    font-family: Arial, sans-serif;
    background-color: #f0f0f0;
    flex-direction: column;
  }

  #ingredient-input {
    width: 400px;
    margin: 5px;
    padding: 10px 20px;
    font-size: 20px;
    margin-top: 20px;
  }

  button {
    margin: 5px;
    padding: 10px 20px;
    font-size: 20px;
  }

  #recipes {
    width: 80%;
    margin-top: 20px;
  }
 </style>
</head>

<body>
  <input id="ingredient-input" type="text" placeholder="Enter
ingredients separated by comma">
  <button id="search-recipes">Search</button>
  <div id="recipes"></div>
```

331

```
<!-- <script src="recipe_finder.js"></script> -->
<script>
  document.getElementById('search-
recipes').addEventListener('click', function () {
    let ingredientInput = document.getElementById('ingredient-
input').value;
    if (!ingredientInput) return;

    const ingredients = ingredientInput.split(',').map(ingredient
=> ingredient.trim());

    fetch(`https://api.spoonacular.com/recipes/findByIngredient
s?ingredients=${ingredients.join(',')}&apiKey=e10bd3da8db9481
98e44192d5e24a7**`)
      .then(response => response.json())
      .then(data => {
        const recipesElement =
document.getElementById('recipes');
        recipesElement.innerHTML = ''; // Clear previous results

        data.forEach(recipe => {
          const recipeElement = document.createElement('div');
          recipeElement.innerHTML = `
            <h2>${recipe.title}</h2>
            <img src="${recipe.image}" alt="${recipe.title}">
            <p>${recipe.usedIngredientCount} ingredients
used</p>
            <p>${recipe.missedIngredientCount} ingredients
missed</p>
          `;

          recipesElement.appendChild(recipeElement);
        });
      })
```

```
      .catch(error => console.error('Error:', error));
   });


   </script>
</body>


</html>
```

<!-- To build a recipe finder using HTML, CSS, and JavaScript, we need a public API that provides recipe data based on ingredients. A popular choice is the "Spoonacular" API. You can create an account on their website and get a free API key. Keep in mind that there are limits on the number of requests you can make with a free account. For now, I'll provide a structure for the application, and you can replace 'YOUR_API_KEY' with your actual key.

```
${ingredients.join(',')}&apiKey=YOUR_API_KEY`)
${ingredients.join(',')}&apiKey=e10bd3da8db948198e44192d5e2
4a7**`)
```


https://spoonacular.com/food-api

This JavaScript code will take the user's input (assumed to be a list of ingredients separated by commas), make a request to the Spoonacular API with those ingredients, and then display the resulting recipes in the #recipes element. Note that the API request URL includes 'YOUR_API_KEY', which should be replaced with your actual Spoonacular API key.

Remember to handle and display errors in a user-friendly way in a production environment. The above catch block logs errors to the console, but these won't be visible to users. -->

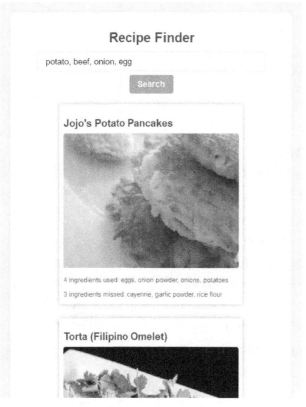

334

```
<!DOCTYPE html>
<html>

<head>
  <title>Recipe Finder</title>
  <style>
    body {
      display: flex;
      justify-content: center;
      align-items: center;
      height: auto;
      font-family: Arial, sans-serif;
      background-color: #f0f0f0;
      flex-direction: column;
      color: #333;
    }
```

```css
#recipe-finder {
  display: flex;
  flex-direction: column;
  align-items: center;
  width: 80%;
  background-color: #fff;
  padding: 20px;
  border-radius: 10px;
  box-shadow: 0px 0px 10px rgba(0, 0, 0, 0.1);
  margin-top: 20px;
}

#recipe-finder h1 {
  font-size: 2em;
  margin-bottom: 10px;
}

#ingredient-input {
  width: 80%;
  margin: 5px;
  padding: 10px 20px;
  font-size: 20px;
  border-radius: 5px;
  border: 1px solid #ddd;
}

button {
  margin: 5px;
  padding: 10px 20px;
  font-size: 20px;
  border-radius: 5px;
  border: none;
  background-color: #ff6347;
  color: white;
  cursor: pointer;
  font-weight: bold;
}

button:hover {
  background-color: #ff7f50;
}

#recipes {
  width: 70%;
```

```css
    margin-top: 20px;
    display: flex;
    flex-direction: column;
    gap: 10px;
  }

  .recipe {
    border: 1px solid #ddd;
    border-radius: 5px;
    padding: 10px;
    box-shadow: 0px 0px 10px rgba(0, 0, 0, 0.3);
    margin-bottom: 20px;
  }

  .recipe h2 {
    font-size: 1.5em;
    margin-bottom: 10px;
  }

  .recipe p {
    margin-bottom: 5px;
  }

  .recipe img {
    width: 100%;
    height: auto;
    border-radius: 5px;
  }
  </style>
</head>

<body>
  <div id="recipe-finder">
    <h1>Recipe Finder</h1>
    <input id="ingredient-input" type="text" placeholder="Enter
ingredients separated by comma">
    <button id="search-recipes">Search</button>
    <div id="recipes"></div>
  </div>

  <script>
    document.getElementById('search-
recipes').addEventListener('click', function () {
```

```
    let ingredientInput = document.getElementById('ingredient-
input').value;
    if (!ingredientInput) return;

    const ingredients = ingredientInput.split(',').map(ingredient
=> ingredient.trim());

    fetch(`https://api.spoonacular.com/recipes/findByIngredient
s?ingredients=${ingredients.join(',')}&apiKey=e10bd3da8db9481
98e44192d5e24a7**`)
      .then(response => response.json())
      .then(data => {
        const recipesElement =
document.getElementById('recipes');
        recipesElement.innerHTML = ''; // Clear previous results

        data.forEach(recipe => {
          const recipeElement = document.createElement('div');
          recipeElement.classList.add('recipe'); // Add class for
styling
          recipeElement.innerHTML = `
            <h2>${recipe.title}</h2>
            <img src="${recipe.image}" alt="${recipe.title}">
            <p>${recipe.usedIngredientCount} ingredients
used: ${recipe.usedIngredients.map(i => i.name).join(", ")}</p>
            <p>${recipe.missedIngredientCount} ingredients
missed: ${recipe.missedIngredients.map(i => i.name).join(",
")}</p>
          `;
          recipesElement.appendChild(recipeElement);
        });
      })
      .catch(error => console.error('Error:', error));
  });

  </script>
</body>

</html>

<!-- In order to display the actual ingredients used and missed,
we need to extract this information from the API response.
Luckily, the Spoonacular API provides this information in its
response data.
```

337

To get the names of the used and missed ingredients, we modified the script.

In this version of the script, recipe.usedIngredients.map(i => i.name).join(", ") and recipe.missedIngredients.map(i => i.name).join(", ") are used to extract the names of the used and missed ingredients from the API response, and to join them into a single string separated by commas.

Remember to replace the API key with your own. -->

339

```html
<!DOCTYPE html>
<html>

<head>
  <!-- Bootstrap CSS -->
  <link
href="https://stackpath.bootstrapcdn.com/bootstrap/4.3.1/css/bo
otstrap.min.css" rel="stylesheet">
  <!-- jQuery -->
  <script src="https://code.jquery.com/jquery-
3.4.1.min.js"></script>
  <!-- Bootstrap JS -->
  <script
src="https://stackpath.bootstrapcdn.com/bootstrap/4.3.1/js/boot
strap.min.js"></script>
</head>

<body>
```

```
<div id="recipe-finder" class="container my-4">
  <h1 class="text-center">Recipe Finder</h1>
  <input id="ingredient-input" class="form-control my-3" type="text"
    placeholder="Enter ingredients separated by comma">
  <button id="search-recipes" class="btn btn-danger btn-block">Search</button>
  <div id="recipes" class="row mt-4"></div>
</div>

<script>
  $('#search-recipes').click(function () {
    let ingredientInput = $('#ingredient-input').val();
    if (!ingredientInput) return;

    const ingredients = ingredientInput.split(',').map(ingredient => ingredient.trim());

    $.get(`https://api.spoonacular.com/recipes/findByIngredients?ingredients=${ingredients.join(',')}&apiKey=e10bd3da8db948198e44192d5e24a7**`, function (data) {
      const recipesElement = $('#recipes');
      recipesElement.empty(); // Clear previous results

      data.forEach(recipe => {
        const recipeElement = $(`
          <div class="col-12 col-md-6 col-lg-4 col-xl-3 mb-4">
            <div class="card">
              <img src="${recipe.image}" alt="${recipe.title}" class="card-img-top">
              <div class="card-body">
                <h5 class="card-title">${recipe.title}</h5>
```

```
                <p class="card-
text">${recipe.usedIngredientCount} ingredients used:
${recipe.usedIngredients.map(i => i.name).join(", ")}</p>
                <p class="card-
text">${recipe.missedIngredientCount} ingredients missed:
${recipe.missedIngredients.map(i => i.name).join(", ")}</p>
            </div>
          </div>
        </div>
      `);
      recipesElement.append(recipeElement);
    });
  }).catch(error => console.error('Error:', error));
});
</script>
</body>

</html>


<!-- The updated HTML now uses Bootstrap's grid classes to
create responsive recipe cards. The recipe cards will now adjust
their width based on the width of the viewport. The JavaScript
part now uses jQuery's $.get method for fetching data and
jQuery's .empty() and .append() methods for manipulating the
HTML elements. -->


<!-- Remember to replace the API key with your own. -->
```

341

Bill Splitter

amount: `321`

tip%: `15`

number: `4`

Calculate

Total bill with tip: $369.15
Each person should pay: $92.29

```
<!DOCTYPE html>
<html>
<head>
  <title>Bill Splitter</title>
  <!-- <link rel="stylesheet" type="text/css" href="styles.css"> --
>
  <style>
    body {
      display: flex;
      justify-content: center;
      align-items: center;
      height: 100vh;
      font-family: Arial, sans-serif;
      background-color: #f0f0f0;
      flex-direction: column;
    }

    .input-container {
      display: flex;
      align-items: center;
      justify-content: space-between;
      width: 200px;
      margin-bottom: 10px;
    }

    label {
      margin-right: 10px;
    }
```

342

```css
    button {
      margin: 5px;
      padding: 10px 20px;
      font-size: 20px;
    }

    #result {
      font-size: 20px;
      margin-top: 20px;
      white-space: pre-line;
      /* This will interpret the newline character correctly */
    }
  </style>
</head>
<body>
  <h2>Bill Splitter</h2>
  <div class="input-container">
    <label for="bill-input">amount: </label>
    <input id="bill-input" type="number" placeholder="Enter bill amount" min="0">
  </div>
  <div class="input-container">
    <label for="tip-input">tip%: </label>
    <input id="tip-input" type="number" placeholder="Enter tip percentage" min="0">
  </div>
  <div class="input-container">
    <label for="people-input">number: </label>
    <input id="people-input" type="number" placeholder="Enter number of people" min="1">
  </div>
  <button id="calculate-tip">Calculate</button>
  <div id="result"></div>

  <!-- <script src="bill_splitter.js"></script> -->
  <script>
    document.getElementById('calculate-tip').addEventListener('click', function () {
      const bill = parseFloat(document.getElementById('bill-input').value);
      const tipPercentage = parseFloat(document.getElementById('tip-input').value);
      const people = parseInt(document.getElementById('people-input').value);
```

343

```javascript
    if (isNaN(bill) || isNaN(tipPercentage) || isNaN(people) || bill
< 0 || tipPercentage < 0 || people < 1) {
        document.getElementById('result').textContent = "Please
enter valid inputs!";
        return;
    }

    const tipAmount = bill * (tipPercentage / 100);
    const totalAmount = bill + tipAmount;
    const splitAmount = totalAmount / people;

    document.getElementById('result').textContent = `Total bill
with tip: $${totalAmount.toFixed(2)}\nEach person should pay:
$${splitAmount.toFixed(2)}`;
    });
  </script>
</body>
</html>
```

<!-- In this JavaScript code, we get the bill, tip percentage, and
number of people from the inputs, calculate the total bill amount
including tip, then divide this total by the number of people. The
results are then displayed. If the user doesn't enter valid inputs, a
message is displayed asking for valid inputs. You can create
styles.css and bill_splitter.js files in the same directory as your
HTML file and copy the respective code into these files. When you
open your HTML file in a web browser, you will see the extended
bill splitter. -->

<!-- In order to introduce a line break in the output text, we can
use the newline character \n within the template literal. This
would need to be styled with CSS as white-space: pre-line; or
white-space: pre-wrap; to allow the browser to interpret the
newline character correctly.

The white-space: pre-line; rule will cause the browser to respect
newline characters in the text content, so \n will produce a line
break. -->

344

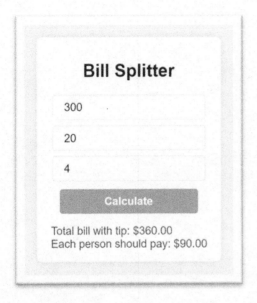

```
<!DOCTYPE html>
<html>

<head>
  <title>Bill Splitter</title>
  <style>
    body {
      display: flex;
      justify-content: center;
      align-items: center;
      height: 100vh;
      font-family: Arial, sans-serif;
      background-color: #f0f0f0;
      flex-direction: column;
    }

    #bill-splitter {
      display: flex;
```

```css
    flex-direction: column;
    align-items: center;
    background-color: #fff;
    padding: 20px;
    border-radius: 10px;
    box-shadow: 0px 0px 10px rgba(0, 0, 0, 0.1);
}

#bill-splitter h1 {
    font-size: 2em;
    margin-bottom: 20px;
}

input {
    width: 80%;
    padding: 10px 20px;
    margin: 5px;
    font-size: 20px;
    border-radius: 5px;
    border: 1px solid #ddd;
}

button {
    width: 85%;
    padding: 10px;
    font-size: 20px;
    border-radius: 5px;
    border: none;
    margin-top: 10px;
    background-color: #ff6347;
    color: white;
    cursor: pointer;
    font-weight: bold;
}
```

```css
  button:hover {
    background-color: #ff7f50;
  }

  #result {
    font-size: 20px;
    color: #333;
    margin-top: 20px;
    white-space: pre-line;
    /* This will interpret the newline character correctly */
  }
</style>
</head>
```

```html
<body>
  <div id="bill-splitter">
    <h1>Bill Splitter</h1>
    <input id="bill-input" type="number" placeholder="Enter bill amount" min="0">
    <input id="tip-input" type="number" placeholder="Enter tip percentage" min="0">
    <input id="people-input" type="number" placeholder="Enter number of people" min="1">
    <button id="calculate-tip">Calculate</button>
    <div id="result"></div>
  </div>

  <script>
    document.getElementById('calculate-tip').addEventListener('click', function () {
      const bill = parseFloat(document.getElementById('bill-input').value);
```

```
    const tipPercentage =
parseFloat(document.getElementById('tip-input').value);
    const people = parseInt(document.getElementById('people-
input').value);

    if (isNaN(bill) || isNaN(tipPercentage) || isNaN(people) || bill
< 0 || tipPercentage < 0 || people < 1) {
      document.getElementById('result').textContent = "Please
enter valid inputs!";
      return;
    }

    const tipAmount = bill * (tipPercentage / 100);
    const totalAmount = bill + tipAmount;
    const splitAmount = totalAmount / people;

    document.getElementById('result').textContent = `Total bill
with tip: $${totalAmount.toFixed(2)}\nEach person should pay:
$${splitAmount.toFixed(2)}`;
    });
  </script>
</body>

</html>

<!-- This version of the code creates a more visually pleasing and
user-friendly interface for the bill splitter application. It features a
rounded and shadowed box that contains all elements of the app,
a hover effect on the button, more space around the inputs, and a
larger title. The inputs and button have also been widened, and
their text size has been increased for better readability. -->
```

Bill Splitter

200

20

2

Calculate

Total bill with tip: $240.00
Each person should pay: $120.00

349

```
<!DOCTYPE html>
<html>

<head>
  <title>Bill Splitter</title>
  <link rel="stylesheet"
href="https://maxcdn.bootstrapcdn.com/bootstrap/4.0.0/css/boot
strap.min.css">
  <script
src="https://ajax.googleapis.com/ajax/libs/jquery/3.5.1/jquery.m
in.js"></script>
  <script
src="https://maxcdn.bootstrapcdn.com/bootstrap/4.0.0/js/bootstr
ap.min.js"></script>
```

```html
  <style>
   #result {
     white-space: pre-line;
   }
  </style>
</head>

<body>
  <div class="container d-flex align-items-center justify-content-
center" style="height: 100vh;">
    <div id="bill-splitter" class="card p-4">
      <h1 class="mb-4">Bill Splitter</h1>
      <div class="form-group">
        <input id="bill-input" type="number" class="form-control"
placeholder="Enter bill amount" min="0">
      </div>
      <div class="form-group">
        <input id="tip-input" type="number" class="form-control"
placeholder="Enter tip percentage" min="0">
      </div>
      <div class="form-group">
        <input id="people-input" type="number" class="form-
control" placeholder="Enter number of people" min="1">
      </div>
      <button id="calculate-tip" class="btn btn-danger btn-
block">Calculate</button>
      <div id="result" class="mt-3"></div>
    </div>
  </div>

  <script>
    $('#calculate-tip').click(function () {
      const bill = parseFloat($('#bill-input').val());
```

```javascript
    const tipPercentage = parseFloat($('#tip-input').val());
    const people = parseInt($('#people-input').val());

    if (isNaN(bill) || isNaN(tipPercentage) || isNaN(people) || bill
< 0 || tipPercentage < 0 || people < 1) {
      $('#result').text("Please enter valid inputs!");
      return;
    }

    const tipAmount = bill * (tipPercentage / 100);
    const totalAmount = bill + tipAmount;
    const splitAmount = totalAmount / people;

    $('#result').text(`Total bill with tip:
$${totalAmount.toFixed(2)}\nEach person should pay:
$${splitAmount.toFixed(2)}`);
  });
  </script>
</body>

</html>
```

<!-- Here is an enhanced version of our code using Bootstrap and jQuery. In this update, We've utilized Bootstrap's form and button classes to style our inputs and buttons. Also, a few Bootstrap classes have been used to handle the layout and centering of elements. We've used jQuery for handling click events which helps simplify your JavaScript code.

Ensure that you have the Bootstrap and jQuery CDN links included in the head section of your HTML. -->

352

```
<!DOCTYPE html>
<html>

<head>
  <!-- <link rel="stylesheet" type="text/css" href="styles.css"> --
>
  <style>
    body {
      display: flex;
      justify-content: center;
      align-items: center;
      height: 100vh;
      font-family: Arial, sans-serif;
      background-color: #f0f0f0;
      flex-direction: column;
    }

    button {
      margin: 5px;
      padding: 10px 20px;
      font-size: 20px;
```

```
      }
    textarea {
      width: 80%;
      height: 100px;
      margin: 10px 0;
      padding: 10px;
      font-size: 18px;
    }
  </style>
</head>

<body>
  <h2>Morse Code Translator</h2>
  <textarea id="input-text" placeholder="Enter text
here"></textarea>
  <button id="to-morse">Translate to Morse Code</button>
  <textarea id="input-morse" placeholder="Enter Morse code
here"></textarea>
  <button id="to-text">Translate to Text</button>

  <!-- <script src="morse_translator.js"></script> -->
  <script>
    const MorseCode = {
      'a': '.-', 'b': '-...', 'c': '-.-.', 'd': '-..', 'e': '.', 'f': '..-.', 'g': '--.',
'h': '....',
      'i': '..', 'j': '.---', 'k': '-.-', 'l': '.-..', 'm': '--', 'n': '-.', 'o': '---',
'p': '.--.',
      'q': '--.-', 'r': '.-.', 's': '...', 't': '-', 'u': '..-', 'v': '...-', 'w': '.--',
'x': '-..-',
      'y': '-.--', 'z': '--..', '1': '.----', '2': '..---', '3': '...--', '4': '....-',
'5': '.....', '6': '-....',
      '7': '--...', '8': '---..', '9': '----.', '0': '-----', ' ': '/'
    };

    const inverseMorseCode = {};
    for (const key in MorseCode) {
      inverseMorseCode[MorseCode[key]] = key;
    }

    document.getElementById('to-morse').addEventListener('click',
function () {
      const inputText = document.getElementById('input-
text').value.toLowerCase();
```

353

```
      let outputMorse = '';
      for (let i = 0; i < inputText.length; i++) {
        if (MorseCode[inputText[i]]) {
          outputMorse += MorseCode[inputText[i]] + ' ';
        } else {
          outputMorse += '? ';
        }
      }
      document.getElementById('input-morse').value =
outputMorse;
    });

    document.getElementById('to-text').addEventListener('click',
function () {
      const inputMorse = document.getElementById('input-
morse').value.split(' ');
      let outputText = '';
      for (let i = 0; i < inputMorse.length; i++) {
        if (inverseMorseCode[inputMorse[i]]) {
          outputText += inverseMorseCode[inputMorse[i]];
        } else {
          outputText += '?';
        }
      }
      document.getElementById('input-text').value = outputText;
    });
  </script>
</body>
</html>
<!-- Here, we create two lookup tables: MorseCode for text to
Morse code translation, and inverseMorseCode for Morse code to
text translation. The `to-morse button` translates the text in the
input-text textarea to Morse code and outputs it in the input-
morse textarea. The `to-text button` does the opposite.
In this code, when a character in the text input does not exist in
the MorseCode lookup table, a question mark followed by a space
will be appended to the output Morse code. Similarly, when a
Morse code in the Morse code input does not exist in the
inverseMorseCode lookup table, a question mark will be appended
to the output text. This gives a visual indication of the characters
that couldn't be translated. -->
```

354

```
<!DOCTYPE html>
<html>

<head>
  <title>Morse Code Translator</title>
  <link rel="stylesheet"
href="https://maxcdn.bootstrapcdn.com/bootstrap/4.0.0/css/boot
strap.min.css">
</head>

<body class="d-flex justify-content-center align-items-center"
style="height: 100vh; background-color: #f0f0f0;">
  <div class="card p-5">
    <h2 class="text-center mb-5">Morse Code Translator</h2>
    <div class="form-group">
      <label for="input-text">Enter Text:</label>
```

```html
    <textarea id="input-text" class="form-control"
rows="3"></textarea>
    </div>
    <div class="form-group">
      <button id="to-morse" class="btn btn-primary w-
100">Translate to Morse Code</button>
    </div>
    <div class="form-group">
      <label for="input-morse">Enter Morse Code:</label>
      <textarea id="input-morse" class="form-control"
rows="3"></textarea>
    </div>
    <div class="form-group">
      <button id="to-text" class="btn btn-primary w-
100">Translate to Text</button>
    </div>
  </div>

  <script src="https://code.jquery.com/jquery-
3.6.0.min.js"></script>
  <script>
    const MorseCode = {
      'a': '.-', 'b': '-...', 'c': '-.-.', 'd': '-..', 'e': '.', 'f': '..-.', 'g': '--.',
'h': '....',
      'i': '..', 'j': '.---', 'k': '-.-', 'l': '.-..', 'm': '--', 'n': '-.', 'o': '---',
'p': '.--.',
      'q': '--.-', 'r': '.-.', 's': '...', 't': '-', 'u': '..-', 'v': '...-', 'w': '.--',
'x': '-..-',
      'y': '-.--', 'z': '--..', '1': '.----', '2': '..---', '3': '...--', '4': '....-',
'5': '.....', '6': '-....',
      '7': '--...', '8': '---..', '9': '----.', '0': '-----', ' ': '/'
    };

    const inverseMorseCode = {};
    for (const key in MorseCode) {
      inverseMorseCode[MorseCode[key]] = key;
    }

    $('#to-morse').click(function () {
      const inputText = $('#input-text').val().toLowerCase();
      let outputMorse = '';
      for (let i = 0; i < inputText.length; i++) {
        if (MorseCode[inputText[i]]) {
          outputMorse += MorseCode[inputText[i]] + ' ';
```

356

```
      } else {
        outputMorse += '? ';
      }
    }
    $('#input-morse').val(outputMorse);
  });

  $('#to-text').click(function () {
    const inputMorse = $('#input-morse').val().split(' ');
    let outputText = '';
    for (let i = 0; i < inputMorse.length; i++) {
      if (inverseMorseCode[inputMorse[i]]) {
        outputText += inverseMorseCode[inputMorse[i]];
      } else {
        outputText += '?';
      }
    }
    $('#input-text').val(outputText);
  });
 </script>
</body>

</html>

<!-- In this code, I used the Bootstrap classes to create a
responsive and user-friendly layout. jQuery is used to select
elements and handle click events more concisely and intuitively. --
>
```

357

358

```
<!DOCTYPE html>
<html>

<head>
  <!-- <link rel="stylesheet" type="text/css" href="styles.css"> --
>
  <style>
    body {
      display: flex;
      justify-content: center;
      align-items: center;
      height: 100vh;
      font-family: Arial, sans-serif;
      background-color: #f0f0f0;
      flex-direction: column;
    }
```

```css
  button {
    margin: 5px;
    padding: 10px 20px;
    font-size: 20px;
  }

  textarea {
    width: 80%;
    height: 100px;
    margin: 10px 0;
    padding: 10px;
    font-size: 18px;
  }
  </style>
</head>
```

```html
<body>
  <h2>New Language Cipher</h2>
  <textarea id="input-english" placeholder="Enter English text
here"></textarea>
  <button id="to-new-language">Translate to New
Language</button>
  <textarea id="input-new-language" placeholder="Enter New
Language text here"></textarea>
  <button id="to-english">Translate to English</button>

  <!-- <script src="new_language_translator.js"></script> -->
  <script>
   const NewLanguage = {
     'a': '!', 'b': '@', 'c': '#', 'd': '$', 'e': '%', 'f': '^', 'g': '&', 'h': '*',
'i': '(', 'j': ')',
     'k': '-', 'l': '=', 'm': '+', 'n': '[', 'o': ']', 'p': '{', 'q': '}', 'r': ';',
's': ':', 't': ',',
```

```
    'u': '.', 'v': '<', 'w': '>', 'x': '/', 'y': ':', 'z': '|', ' ': '~', '!': 'x'
  };

  const inverseNewLanguage = {};
  for (const key in NewLanguage) {
    inverseNewLanguage[NewLanguage[key]] = key;
  }

  document.getElementById('to-new-
language').addEventListener('click', function () {
    const inputEnglish = document.getElementById('input-
english').value.toLowerCase();
    let outputNewLanguage = '';
    for (let i = 0; i < inputEnglish.length; i++) {
      if (NewLanguage[inputEnglish[i]]) {
        outputNewLanguage += NewLanguage[inputEnglish[i]] +
'';
      } else {
        outputNewLanguage += '?';
      }
    }
    document.getElementById('input-new-language').value =
outputNewLanguage;
  });

  document.getElementById('to-
english').addEventListener('click', function () {
    const inputNewLanguage =
document.getElementById('input-new-language').value;
    let outputEnglish = '';
    for (let i = 0; i < inputNewLanguage.length; i++) {
      if (inverseNewLanguage[inputNewLanguage[i]]) {
        outputEnglish +=
inverseNewLanguage[inputNewLanguage[i]];
```

```
      } else {
        outputEnglish += '?';
      }
    }
    document.getElementById('input-english').value =
outputEnglish;
    });
  </script>
</body>
</html>
```
<!-- Creating a new language is quite a broad task, but to keep things simple, let's create a basic substitution cipher, where each English letter is replaced with a unique symbol.

Similar to the Morse Code Translator, we'll need text areas for English and the new language, and buttons to execute the translations.

Similar to the Morse code example, we will create two translation functions, but this time for English to the new language and vice versa.

In this example, the new language is just English with all the letters and the space character replaced with different symbols. The 'to-new-language' button translates the text in the 'input-english' textarea to the new language and outputs it in the 'input-new-language' textarea. The 'to-english' button does the opposite.

In this coding, when a character in the text input does not exist in the lookup table, a question mark followed by a space will be appended to the output text. This gives a visual indication of the characters that couldn't be translated. -->

```
<!DOCTYPE html>
<html>

<head>
  <title>New Language Cipher</title>
  <link rel="stylesheet"
href="https://maxcdn.bootstrapcdn.com/bootstrap/4.0.0/css/boot
strap.min.css">
</head>

<body class="d-flex justify-content-center align-items-center"
style="height: 100vh; background-color: #f0f0f0;">
  <div class="card p-5">
    <h2 class="text-center mb-5">New Language Cipher</h2>
    <div class="form-group">
      <label for="input-english">Enter English Text:</label>
      <textarea id="input-english" class="form-control"
rows="3"></textarea>
    </div>
```

```html
    <div class="form-group">
      <button id="to-new-language" class="btn btn-primary w-
100">Translate to New Language</button>
    </div>
    <div class="form-group">
      <label for="input-new-language">Enter New Language
Text:</label>
      <textarea id="input-new-language" class="form-control"
rows="3"></textarea>
    </div>
    <div class="form-group">
      <button id="to-english" class="btn btn-primary w-
100">Translate to English</button>
    </div>
  </div>

  <script src="https://code.jquery.com/jquery-
3.6.0.min.js"></script>
  <script>
  const NewLanguage = {
    'a': '!', 'b': '@', 'c': '#', 'd': '$', 'e': '%', 'f': '^', 'g': '&', 'h': '*',
'i': '(', 'j': ')',
    'k': '-', 'l': '=', 'm': '+', 'n': '[', 'o': ']', 'p': '{', 'q': '}', 'r': ';',
's': ':', 't': ',',
    'u': '.', 'v': '<', 'w': '>', 'x': '/', 'y': ':', 'z': '|', ' ': '~', '!': 'x'
  };

  const inverseNewLanguage = {};
  for (const key in NewLanguage) {
    inverseNewLanguage[NewLanguage[key]] = key;
  }

  $('#to-new-language').click(function () {
    const inputEnglish = $('#input-english').val().toLowerCase();
    let outputNewLanguage = '';
    for (let i = 0; i < inputEnglish.length; i++) {
      if (NewLanguage[inputEnglish[i]]) {
        outputNewLanguage += NewLanguage[inputEnglish[i]];
      } else {
        outputNewLanguage += '?';
      }
    }
    $('#input-new-language').val(outputNewLanguage);
  });
```

```
    $('#to-english').click(function () {
      const inputNewLanguage = $('#Input-new-language').val();
      let outputEnglish = '';
      for (let i = 0; i < inputNewLanguage.length; i++) {
        if (inverseNewLanguage[inputNewLanguage[i]]) {
          outputEnglish +=
inverseNewLanguage[inputNewLanguage[i]];
        } else {
          outputEnglish += '?';
        }
      }
      $('#input-english').val(outputEnglish);
    });
  </script>
</body>

</html>

<!-- This updated code uses Bootstrap classes to style the layout
and jQuery for handling button click events and for manipulating
the textarea values. The Bootstrap card is used to contain all of
the elements and center them in the viewport, and the form and
button Bootstrap classes are used to style the inputs and buttons.
jQuery is used to simplify the event handling and manipulation of
the textarea values, making the JavaScript code easier to read
and write. -->
```

058_MEMORY GAME1

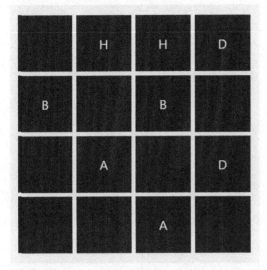

```
<!DOCTYPE html>
<html>

<head>
  <style>
    body {
      display: flex;
      justify-content: center;
      align-items: center;
      height: 100vh;
      background-color: #f0f0f0;
    }

    #game-board {
      width: 600px;
      height: 600px;
      display: grid;
      grid-template-columns: repeat(4, 1fr);
      grid-gap: 10px;
    }

    .card {
      width: 100%;
      height: 0;
      padding-bottom: 100%;
      background-color: #000;
```

```css
      position: relative;
      cursor: pointer;
    }

    .card div {
      color: #fff;
      position: absolute;
      top: 50%;
      left: 50%;
      transform: translate(-50%, -50%);
      font-size: 2em;
      display: none;
    }
  </style>
</head>

<body>
  <div id="game-board"></div>

  <script>
    let cards = ['A', 'B', 'C', 'D', 'E', 'F', 'G', 'H', 'A', 'B', 'C', 'D', 'E',
'F', 'G', 'H'];
    cards.sort(() => 0.5 - Math.random());

    let firstCard = null;
    let secondCard = null;

    const gameBoard = document.getElementById('game-board');

    for (let i = 0; i < cards.length; i++) {
      const cardElement = document.createElement('div');
      cardElement.classList.add('card');

      const innerDiv = document.createElement('div');
      innerDiv.textContent = cards[i];
      cardElement.appendChild(innerDiv);

      gameBoard.appendChild(cardElement);

      cardElement.addEventListener('click', function () {
        if (firstCard === null) {
          firstCard = cardElement;
          innerDiv.style.display = 'block';
        } else if (secondCard === null) {
```

```
            secondCard = cardElement;
            innerDiv.style.display = 'block';

            if (firstCard.textContent === secondCard.textContent) {
              firstCard = null;
              secondCard = null;
            } else {
              setTimeout(function () {
                firstCard.children[0].style.display = 'none';
                secondCard.children[0].style.display = 'none';
                firstCard = null;
                secondCard = null;
              }, 1000);
            }
          }
        });
      }
  </script>
</body>

</html>
```

<!-- In the above code, I've added an extra div inside each card to contain the card's text. This inner div is absolutely positioned and translated to the center of the card.

Initially, display of the inner div is set to none. On click event, it is set to block to reveal the card, and if the cards don't match, it is set back to none to hide the card again. -->

367

```
<!DOCTYPE html>
<html>

<head>
  <style>
    body {
      display: flex;
      justify-content: center;
      align-items: center;
      height: 100vh;
      background-color: #f0f0f0;
      flex-direction: column;
    }

    #reset-button {
      margin-bottom: 20px;
      padding: 10px;
      background-color: #ff0000;
      color: #ffffff;
      cursor: pointer;
    }

    #game-board {
      width: 600px;
```

368

```
      height: 600px;
      display: grid;
      grid-template-columns: repeat(4, 1fr);
      grid-gap: 10px;
    }

    .card {
      width: 100%;
      height: 0;
      padding-bottom: 100%;
      background-color: #000;
      position: relative;
      cursor: pointer;
    }

    .card div {
      color: #fff;
      position: absolute;
      top: 50%;
      left: 50%;
      transform: translate(-50%, -50%);
      font-size: 2em;
      display: none;
    }
  </style>
</head>

<body>
  <button id="reset-button">Reset Memory-Game</button>
  <div id="game-board"></div>

  <script>
    let cards = ['Lion', 'Tiger', 'Bear', 'Elephant', 'pig', 'cat', 'dog',
'cow', 'Lion', 'Tiger', 'Bear', 'Elephant', 'pig', 'cat', 'dog', 'cow'];
    let firstCard = null;
    let secondCard = null;
    let pairsFound = 0;

    const gameBoard = document.getElementById('game-board');
    const resetButton = document.getElementById('reset-button');

    function shuffleAndDealCards() {
      cards.sort(() => 0.5 - Math.random());
      gameBoard.innerHTML = '';
```

```
for (let i = 0; i < cards.length; i++) {
  const cardElement = document.createElement('div');
  cardElement.classList.add('card');

  const innerDiv = document.createElement('div');
  innerDiv.textContent = cards[i];
  cardElement.appendChild(innerDiv);

  gameBoard.appendChild(cardElement);

  cardElement.addEventListener('click', function () {
    if (firstCard === null) {
      firstCard = cardElement;
      innerDiv.style.display = 'block';
    } else if (secondCard === null) {
      secondCard = cardElement;
      innerDiv.style.display = 'block';

      if (firstCard.textContent === secondCard.textContent)
{

        firstCard = null;
        secondCard = null;
        pairsFound++;

        if (pairsFound === cards.length / 2) {
          alert('Congratulations! You found all pairs.');
        }
      } else {
        setTimeout(function () {
          firstCard.children[0].style.display = 'none';
          secondCard.children[0].style.display = 'none';
          firstCard = null;
          secondCard = null;
        }, 1000);
      }
    }
  });
  }
}

resetButton.addEventListener('click', function () {
  pairsFound = 0;
```

370

```
    shuffleAndDealCards();
  });

    shuffleAndDealCards(); // Call this function at the start to deal
the cards
  </script>
</body>

</html>

<!-- To implement a victory condition, we'll need a counter to
track how many pairs have been found. When this counter equals
the total number of pairs, the player wins.

We'll also add a reset button that, when clicked, will shuffle the
cards and reset the game.

Finally, I'll replace the letters with some animal names. For
simplicity, I'll just use 8 different animals.

In this code, the shuffleAndDealCards function takes care of
shuffling the cards, emptying the game board, and dealing the
shuffled cards onto the game board. This function is called when
the reset button is clicked and also once at the start to deal the
cards initially.

The pairsFound variable tracks the number of pairs that have
been found. Every time a pair is found, this number is
incremented. If the number of pairs found equals the total number
of pairs (cards.length / 2), an alert is shown to congratulate the
player for finding all pairs. -->
```

371

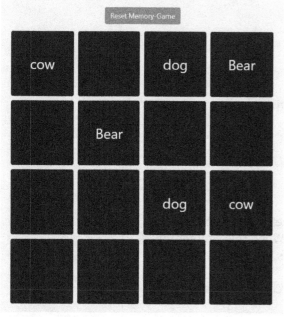

372

```
<!DOCTYPE html>
<html>

<head>
  <link
href="https://maxcdn.bootstrapcdn.com/bootstrap/4.0.0/css/boot
strap.min.css" rel="stylesheet">
  <style>
    body {
      height: 100vh;
      background-color: #f0f0f0;
      display: flex;
      flex-direction: column;
      align-items: center;
      justify-content: center;
    }

    #game-board {
      width: 600px;
      height: 600px;
      display: grid;
      grid-template-columns: repeat(4, 1fr);
```

```
    grid-gap: 10px;
  }

  .card {
    width: 100%;
    height: 0;
    padding-bottom: 100%;
    background-color: #000;
    position: relative;
    cursor: pointer;
  }

  .card div {
    color: #fff;
    position: absolute;
    top: 50%;
    left: 50%;
    transform: translate(-50%, -50%);
    font-size: 2em;
    display: none;
  }
  </style>
</head>

<body>
  <button id="reset-button" class="btn btn-danger mb-3">Reset
Memory-Game</button>
  <div id="game-board"></div>

  <script src="https://code.jquery.com/jquery-
3.5.1.min.js"></script>
  <script>
  let cards = ['Lion', 'Tiger', 'Bear', 'Elephant', 'pig', 'cat', 'dog',
'cow', 'Lion', 'Tiger', 'Bear', 'Elephant', 'pig', 'cat', 'dog', 'cow'];
  let firstCard = null;
  let secondCard = null;
  let pairsFound = 0;

  function shuffleAndDealCards() {
    cards.sort(() => 0.5 - Math.random());
    $('#game-board').empty();

    $.each(cards, (i, cardText) => {
```

```javascript
      let cardElement = $(`<div
class="card"><div>${cardText}</div></div>`);
      $('#game-board').append(cardElement);

      cardElement.on('click', function () {
        if (!firstCard) {
          firstCard = cardElement;
          firstCard.children().show();
        } else if (!secondCard) {
          secondCard = cardElement;
          secondCard.children().show();

          if (firstCard.text() === secondCard.text()) {
            firstCard = secondCard = null;
            pairsFound++;
            if (pairsFound === cards.length / 2) {
              alert('Congratulations! You found all pairs.');
            }
          } else {
            setTimeout(function () {
              firstCard.children().hide();
              secondCard.children().hide();
              firstCard = secondCard = null;
            }, 1000);
          }
        }
      });
    });
  }

  $('#reset-button').on('click', function () {
    pairsFound = 0;
    shuffleAndDealCards();
  });

  shuffleAndDealCards();
 </script>
</body>

</html>

<!-- The changes in the JavaScript code mostly involve using
jQuery methods instead of native JavaScript ones, for instance:
```

374

`` `$('#game-board').empty();` `` replaces `` `gameBoard.innerHTML = '';` ``

The loop `` `$.each(cards, (i, cardText) => {...}` `` replaces the `` `for` `` loop for creating the cards.

`` `cardElement.on('click', function() {...})` `` replaces `` `cardElement.addEventListener('click', function() {...})` ``

`` `$('#reset-button').on('click', function () {...})` `` replaces `` `resetButton.addEventListener('click', function () {...})` ``

Also, I've added a reference to the Bootstrap CSS in the head of your HTML, and a reference to the jQuery library before the script tag in your body. This enables the use of Bootstrap styles and jQuery respectively. -->

375

```
<!DOCTYPE html>
<html>
<head>
  <title>Tic Tac Toe</title>
  <!-- <link rel="stylesheet" type="text/css" href="style.css"> --
>
  <style>
    body {
      display: flex;
      flex-direction: column;
      align-items: center;
      justify-content: center;
      height: 100vh;
    }

    #board {
      display: grid;
      grid-template-columns: repeat(3, 100px);
      grid-template-rows: repeat(3, 100px);
      gap: 10px;
    }
```

```css
    #board div {
      width: 100%;
      height: 100%;
      display: flex;
      align-items: center;
      justify-content: center;
      border: 1px solid;
      font-size: 2em;
    }

    button {
      display: block;
      width: 100px;
      margin-bottom: 20px;
    }
  </style>
</head>
<body>
  <h2>Tic-Tac-Toe Game</h2>
  <button onclick="resetBoard()">Reset Game</button>
  <div id="board"></div>
  <!-- <script src="script.js"></script> -->
  <script>
    let board = [
      ['', '', ''],
      ['', '', ''],
      ['', '', '']
    ];

    let currentPlayer = 'X';

    function resetBoard() {
      board = [
        ['', '', ''],
        ['', '', ''],
        ['', '', '']
      ];
      currentPlayer = 'X';
      drawBoard();
    }

    function drawBoard() {
      document.getElementById('board').innerHTML = '';
```

```
    for (let i = 0; i < 3; i++) {
      for (let j = 0; j < 3; j++) {
        document.getElementById('board').innerHTML += `<div
onclick="makeMove(${i}, ${j})">${board[i][j]}</div>`;
      }
    }
  }

  function makeMove(i, j) {
    if (board[i][j] !== '') return;
    board[i][j] = currentPlayer;
    if (checkWin(currentPlayer)) {
      setTimeout(() => {
        alert(`Player ${currentPlayer} wins!`);
        resetBoard();
      }, 100);
      return;
    }
    currentPlayer = currentPlayer === 'X' ? 'O' : 'X';
    drawBoard();
  }

  function checkWin(player) {
    for (let i = 0; i < 3; i++) {
      if (board[i][0] === player && board[i][1] === player &&
board[i][2] === player) return true;
      if (board[0][i] === player && board[1][i] === player &&
board[2][i] === player) return true;
    }
    if (board[0][0] === player && board[1][1] === player &&
board[2][2] === player) return true;
    if (board[0][2] === player && board[1][1] === player &&
board[2][0] === player) return true;
    return false;
  }
  drawBoard();
  </script>
</body>
</html>
```

378

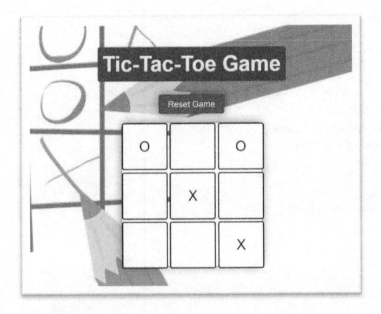

```
<!DOCTYPE html>
<html>

<head>
  <title>Tic Tac Toe</title>
  <style>
    body {
      display: flex;
      flex-direction: column;
      align-items: center;
      justify-content: center;
      height: 100vh;
      /* background-color: #f0f0f0; */
      font-family: Arial, sans-serif;
      background: url('tic-tac-toe.png') no-repeat center center
fixed;
      background-size: cover;
    }

    h1 {
      margin-bottom: 30px;
      text-align: center;
      color: #f8f806;
      font-size: 3em;
```

```css
      padding: 10px;
      border: 1px solid #333;
      border-radius: 5px;
      background-color: #333;
    }

    #board {
      display: grid;
      grid-template-columns: repeat(3, 100px);
      grid-template-rows: repeat(3, 100px);
      gap: 10px;
      border: 1px solid #333;
      border-radius: 10px;
      box-shadow: 0px 0px 20px rgba(0, 0, 0, 0.6);
    }

    #board div {
      width: 100%;
      height: 100%;
      display: flex;
      align-items: center;
      justify-content: center;
      border: 3px solid;
      font-size: 2em;
      background-color: #fff;
      border-radius: 5px;
    }

    button {
      display: block;
      width: 150px;
      padding: 10px;
      margin-bottom: 20px;
      border: none;
      border-radius: 5px;
      background-color: #2409f4;
      color: #fff;
      font-size: 1.2em;
      cursor: pointer;
      box-shadow: 0px 0px 20px rgba(0, 0, 0, 0.6);
    }
  </style>
</head>
```

```
<body>
  <h1>Tic-Tac-Toe Game</h1>
  <button onclick="resetBoard()">Reset Game</button>
  <div id="board"></div>

  <script>
    let board = [
      ['', '', ''],
      ['', '', ''],
      ['', '', '']
    ];

    let currentPlayer = 'X';

    function resetBoard() {
      board = [
        ['', '', ''],
        ['', '', ''],
        ['', '', '']
      ];
      currentPlayer = 'X';
      drawBoard();
    }

    function drawBoard() {
      document.getElementById('board').innerHTML = '';
      for (let i = 0; i < 3; i++) {
        for (let j = 0; j < 3; j++) {
          document.getElementById('board').innerHTML += `<div
onclick="makeMove(${i}, ${j})">${board[i][j]}</div>`;
        }
      }
    }

    function makeMove(i, j) {
      if (board[i][j] !== '') return;
      board[i][j] = currentPlayer;
      if (checkWin(currentPlayer)) {
        setTimeout(() => {
          alert(`Player ${currentPlayer} wins!`);
          resetBoard();
        }, 100);
        return;
      }
```

```
      currentPlayer = currentPlayer === 'X' ? 'O' : 'X';
      drawBoard();
    }

    function checkWin(player) {
      for (let i = 0; i < 3; i++) {
        if (board[i][0] === player && board[i][1] === player &&
board[i][2] === player) return true;
        if (board[0][i] === player && board[1][i] === player &&
board[2][i] === player) return true;
      }
      if (board[0][0] === player && board[1][1] === player &&
board[2][2] === player) return true;
      if (board[0][2] === player && board[1][1] === player &&
board[2][0] === player) return true;
      return false;
    }

    drawBoard();

  </script>
</body>

</html>

<!-- This is a simple upgrade of a tic-tac-toe game with the use of
CSS styles and a background image. -->

<!-- This version of the code includes a big title and improved
styling for the board, its cells and the reset button. The board and
the cells now have a shadow and rounded corners, the
background color of the cells is white, and the reset button is
larger, has rounded corners, a shadow, a hover effect, and its text
is white on a dark background.  -->
```

Hangman Game

j q _ e _ y

a	b	c	d	e	f	g	h	i	j	k	l	m

n	o	p	q	r	s	t	u	v	w	x	y	z

Reset Game

383

```html
<!DOCTYPE html>
<html>

<head>
  <title>Hangman Game</title>
  <!-- <link rel="stylesheet" type="text/css" href="style.css"> -->
  <style>
    body {
      display: flex;
      flex-direction: column;
      align-items: center;
      justify-content: center;
      height: 100vh;
    }

    #word-container {
      font-size: 2em;
      margin-bottom: 20px;
    }
```

```css
   #keyboard div {
     display: inline-block;
     width: 30px;
     height: 30px;
     border: 1px solid;
     margin: 2px;
     text-align: center;
     line-height: 30px;
     cursor: pointer;
   }

   #reset-button {
     margin-top: 20px;
   }
 </style>
</head>
```

```html
<body>
 <h1>Hangman Game</h1>
 <div id="word-container"></div>
 <div id="keyboard"></div>
 <button id="reset-button" onclick="resetGame()">Reset
Game</button>

 <!-- <script src="script.js"></script> -->
 <script>
   let words = ["script", "style", "html", "css", "coding", "jquery",
"bootstrap", "beginner"];
   let word = "";
   let answerArray = [];
   let remainingLetters = 0;

   function resetGame() {
     word = words[Math.floor(Math.random() * words.length)];
```

```
    answerArray = [];
    for (let i = 0; i < word.length; i++) {
      answerArray[i] = "_";
    }
    remainingLetters = word.length;
    document.getElementById('word-container').innerText =
answerArray.join(" ");
    drawKeyboard();
  }


  function drawKeyboard() {
    let keyboard = document.getElementById('keyboard');
    keyboard.innerHTML = "";
    for (let i = 65; i <= 90; i++) {
      let letter = String.fromCharCode(i).toLowerCase();
      let letterElement = document.createElement('div');
      letterElement.innerText = letter;
      letterElement.onclick = function () {
        makeGuess(letter);
      };
      keyboard.appendChild(letterElement);
    }
  }


  function makeGuess(letter) {
    let isCorrectGuess = false;
    for (let j = 0; j < word.length; j++) {
      if (word[j] === letter && answerArray[j] === "_") {
        answerArray[j] = letter;
        remainingLetters--;
        isCorrectGuess = true;
      }
    }
```

```
    if (isCorrectGuess) {
      document.getElementById('word-container').innerText =
answerArray.join(" ");
    }

    if (remainingLetters === 0) {
      setTimeout(() => {
        alert('Congratulations! The word was ' + word);
        resetGame();
      }, 100);
    }
  }

  resetGame();
  </script>
</body>
</html>
<!-- In this simple Hangman game:
1. The word to guess is randomly selected from a predefined array
of words.
2. The resetGame function is used to start a new game. It picks a
new word, initializes the answer array with underscores (_), and
displays the new puzzle to the user.
3. The drawKeyboard function generates clickable elements for
each letter of the alphabet.
4. When a letter is clicked, the makeGuess function checks if the
letter is in the word. If it is, the underscore in the corresponding
position of the answerArray is replaced with the correct letter, and
the display is updated.
5. If all the letters in the word have been guessed (i.e., there are
no more underscores left in the answer array), the user is
congratulated and a new game starts. -->
```

<!-- Hangman is a popular word guessing game. The game is usually played with two or more players. Here's how it works:

1. One player, the "host," thinks of a word or phrase and draws a blank line for each letter in the word(s). If there are multiple words in the phrase, spaces are left between the words.

2. The other players then guess one letter at a time. The guessing player's goal is to guess the word or phrase before the hangman is completely drawn.

3. If a guessed letter appears in the word, the host writes it in all its correct positions. If the letter does not appear in the word, the host begins drawing the hangman—a simple stick figure—on a gallows.

387

4. The players continue guessing letters. With each incorrect guess, a new part of the hangman is added. The order of the hangman parts can vary, but a common order is: head, body, left arm, right arm, left leg, right leg.

5. If the hangman is completed (all six parts are drawn) before the word is guessed, the host wins. If the word is guessed before the hangman is completed, the guessing player wins.

In a digital version of the game, you might select a random word from a predetermined list and automatically fill in the blanks, update the hangman drawing, and check for a win or loss after each guess.

The game can be a good project for beginners to practice working with strings, arrays, and conditional logic in a fun and interactive way. -->

```
<!DOCTYPE html>
<html>

<head>
  <title>Hangman Game</title>
  <style>
    body {
      display: flex;
      justify-content: center;
      align-items: center;
      height: 100vh;
      font-family: Arial, sans-serif;
      background-color: #f0f0f0;
      margin: 40px;
    }

    #game-area {
      display: flex;
      flex-direction: row;
      align-items: center;
      border: 1px solid #333;
```

```css
  padding: 20px;
  box-shadow: 0px 0px 10px rgba(0, 0, 0, 0.1);
  border-radius: 10px;
  background-color: #fff;
}

#game-area img {
  height: 200px;
  width: auto;
  margin-right: 20px;
}

#game-content {
  display: flex;
  flex-direction: column;
  align-items: center;
}

h1 {
  margin-bottom: 20px;
}

#word-container {
  font-size: 2em;
  margin-bottom: 20px;
}

#keyboard div {
  display: inline-block;
  width: 30px;
  height: 30px;
  border: 1px solid;
  margin: 2px;
  text-align: center;
  line-height: 30px;
  cursor: pointer;
}

#reset-button {
  margin-top: 20px;
}

select {
  margin-bottom: 20px;
```

```
    }
  </style>
</head>

<body>
  <div id="game-area">
    <img src="hangman_rope.png" alt="Hangman Game">
    <div id="game-content">
      <h1>Hangman Game</h1>
      <select id="category-selector" onchange="resetGame()">
        <option value="animal">Animal</option>
        <option value="food">Food</option>
        <option value="nation">Nation</option>
      </select>
      <div id="word-container"></div>
      <div id="keyboard"></div>
      <button id="reset-button" onclick="resetGame()">Reset
Game</button>
    </div>
  </div>

  <script>
    let categories = {
      "animal": ["elephant", "giraffe", "kangaroo", "dog", "cat",
"cow"],
      "food": ["hamburger", "spaghetti", "sandwich", "bread",
"ramen", "kimchi"],
      "nation": ["australia", "brazil", "canada", "korea", "japan",
"china"]
    };
    let word = "";
    let answerArray = [];
    let remainingLetters = 0;

    function resetGame() {
      let category = document.getElementById('category-
selector').value;
      let words = categories[category];
      word = words[Math.floor(Math.random() * words.length)];
      answerArray = [];
      for (let i = 0; i < word.length; i++) {
        answerArray[i] = "_";
      }
      remainingLetters = word.length;
```

```
        document.getElementById('word-container').innerText =
answerArray.join(" ");
        drawKeyboard();
    }

    function drawKeyboard() {
      let keyboard = document.getElementById('keyboard');
      keyboard.innerHTML = "";
      for (let i = 65; i <= 90; i++) {
        let letter = String.fromCharCode(i).toLowerCase();
        let letterElement = document.createElement('div');
        letterElement.innerText = letter;
        letterElement.onclick = function () {
          makeGuess(letter);
        };
        keyboard.appendChild(letterElement);
      }
    }

    function makeGuess(letter) {
      let isCorrectGuess = false;
      for (let j = 0; j < word.length; j++) {
        if (word[j] === letter && answerArray[j] === "_") {
          answerArray[j] = letter;
          remainingLetters--;
          isCorrectGuess = true;
        }
      }

      if (isCorrectGuess) {
        document.getElementById('word-container').innerText =
answerArray.join(" ");
      }

      if (remainingLetters === 0) {
        setTimeout(() => {
          alert('Congratulations! The word was ' + word);
          resetGame();
        }, 100);
      }
    }

    resetGame();
  </script>
```

391

```
</body>

</html>

<!-- This version of the code contains a category selector.
Depending on the selected category, the game selects a random
word from that category to start the game. The game area is now
divided into two parts - the hangman image on the left, and the
game content on the right. The entire game area, including the
image, is centered on the page. -->
```

```
<!DOCTYPE html>
<html>
<head>
  <title>Hangman Game</title>
  <link rel="stylesheet"
href="https://maxcdn.bootstrapcdn.com/bootstrap/4.0.0/css/boot
strap.min.css">
  <style>
    body {
      padding: 40px;
      background-color: #fafafa;
    }

    #game-area {
      background-color: #ff6347;
      border: 3px solid #ffa500;
      box-shadow: 10px 10px 5px grey;
```

```
      padding: 20px;
    }

    .keyboard-letter {
      padding: 5px;
      border: 1px solid #000;
      cursor: pointer;
      display: flex;
      justify-content: center;
      align-items: center;
    }

    #keyboard {
      display: grid;
      grid-template-columns: repeat(6, 1fr);
      gap: 10px;
    }

    #message {
      height: 30px;
    }

    #reset-button {
      margin-top: 20px;
    }
  </style>
</head>
<body>
  <div id="game-area" class="container d-flex align-items-
center">
    <img class="mr-4" src="hangman_rope.png" alt="Hangman
Game" height="300">
    <div id="game-content">
      <h1 class="mb-4">Hangman Game</h1>
      <div id="message" class="mb-4"></div>
      <select id="category-selector" class="form-control mb-
4"></select>
      <div id="word-container" class="mb-4"></div>
      <div id="keyboard" class="mb-4"></div>
      <button id="reset-button" class="btn btn-dark">Reset
Game</button>
    </div>
  </div>
```

```html
<script src="https://code.jquery.com/jquery-
3.5.1.min.js"></script>
  <script>
    let categories = {
      "animal": ["elephant", "giraffe", "kangaroo", "dog", "cat",
"cow"],
      "food": ["hamburger", "spaghetti", "sandwich", "bread",
"ramen", "kimchi"],
      "nation": ["australia", "brazil", "canada", "korea", "japan",
"china"]
    };
    let word = "";
    let answerArray = [];
    let remainingLetters = 0;

    function resetGame() {
      let category = $("#category-selector").val();
      let words = categories[category];
      word = words[Math.floor(Math.random() * words.length)];
      answerArray = [];
      for (let i = 0; i < word.length; i++) {
        answerArray[i] = "_";
      }
      remainingLetters = word.length;
      $("#word-container").text(answerArray.join(" "));
      $("#message").text("");
      drawKeyboard();
    }

    function drawKeyboard() {
      let keyboard = $("#keyboard");
      keyboard.empty();
      for (let i = 65; i <= 90; i++) {
        let letter = String.fromCharCode(i).toLowerCase();
        let letterElement =
$('<div>').text(letter).addClass('keyboard-letter');
        letterElement.on('click', function () {
          makeGuess(letter);
        });
        keyboard.append(letterElement);
      }
    }

    function makeGuess(letter) {
```

395

```javascript
      let isCorrectGuess = false;
      for (let j = 0; j < word.length; j++) {
        if (word[j] === letter && answerArray[j] === "_") {
          answerArray[j] = letter;
          remainingLetters--;
          isCorrectGuess = true;
        }
      }

      if (isCorrectGuess) {
        $("#word-container").text(answerArray.join(" "));
      }

      if (remainingLetters === 0) {
        $("#message").text('Congratulations! The word was ' +
word);
        setTimeout(resetGame, 2000);
      }
    }

    $.each(categories, function (key, value) {
      $('#category-
selector').append($('<option>').text(key).attr('value', key));
    });

    $('#reset-button').on('click', function () {
      resetGame();
    });

    resetGame();
  </script>
</body>
</html>
```

<!-- In this updated code:
1. I've added margin to the body and button, so there will be more spacing around these elements.
2. I've added flexbox CSS to `.keyboard-letter` to center the letters in the keys.
3. I've moved the `resetGame()` call inside the conditional check for a correct guess, ensuring the game resets after the success message is displayed.
4 I've added a 2-second delay before the game resets, allowing players to see the success message before the game resets. -->

Daily Planner

00:00		Delete
01:00		Delete
02:00		Delete
03:00		Delete
04:00		Delete
05:00		Delete
06:00		Delete
07:00		Delete

```
<!DOCTYPE html>
<html>

<head>
  <title>Daily Planner</title>
  <!-- <link rel="stylesheet" type="text/css" href="style.css"> --
>
  <style>
    body {
      display: flex;
      flex-direction: column;
      align-items: center;
      justify-content: center;
      font-family: Arial, sans-serif;
    }

    #planner {
      width: 400px;
    }

    .hour-block {
      display: flex;
      justify-content: space-between;
```

```
      border: 1px solid;
      padding: 10px;
      margin-bottom: 5px;
    }

    .hour-block input {
      flex-grow: 1;
      margin-left: 10px;
      margin-right: 10px;
    }

    .hour-block button {
      margin-left: auto;
    }
  </style>
</head>

<body>
  <h1>Daily Planner</h1>
  <div id="planner"></div>

  <!-- <script src="script.js"></script> -->
  <script>
    let planner = new Array(24).fill('');

    function drawPlanner() {
      let plannerElement = document.getElementById('planner');
      plannerElement.innerHTML = '';
      for (let i = 0; i < 24; i++) {
        let hourBlock = document.createElement('div');
        hourBlock.classList.add('hour-block');
        let timeElement = document.createElement('span');
        timeElement.innerText = i < 10 ? `0${i}:00` : `${i}:00`;
        let inputElement = document.createElement('input');
        inputElement.value = planner[i];
        inputElement.onchange = function (event) {
          planner[i] = event.target.value;
        };
        let deleteButton = document.createElement('button');
        deleteButton.innerText = 'Delete';
        deleteButton.onclick = function () {
          planner[i] = '';
          drawPlanner();
        };
```

```
    hourBlock.appendChild(timeElement);
    hourBlock.appendChild(inputElement);
    hourBlock.appendChild(deleteButton);
    plannerElement.appendChild(hourBlock);
  }
}

drawPlanner();

  </script>
</body>

</html>

<!-- In this simple daily planner:

1. The day is divided into 24 hour-blocks, each represented by a
div with a span to show the hour, an input to add/edit the event,
and a button to delete the event.
2. The drawPlanner function is used to display the planner. It
loops over the 24 hours of the day, and for each hour, it creates a
new div for the hour-block and appends it to the planner.
3. The inputElement's onchange event updates the event in the
planner when the user edits the event.
4. The deleteButton's onclick event deletes the event from the
planner and redraws the planner.

Please note, this is a simple version and does not persist the data.
If you refresh the page, all the data will be lost. To persist the
data, you could use something like localStorage to save the
planner array and load it when the page loads. -->
```

399

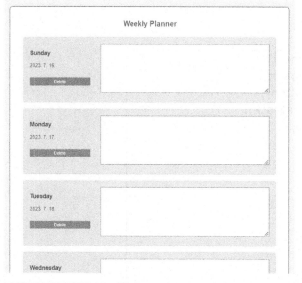

400

```
<!DOCTYPE html>
<html>

<head>
  <title>Weekly Planner</title>
  <style>
    body {
      display: flex;
      justify-content: center;
      align-items: center;
      font-family: Arial, sans-serif;
      background-color: #f0f0f0;
      padding: 20px;
    }

    #planner {
      display: flex;
      flex-direction: column;
      align-items: center;
      border: 1px solid #333;
      padding: 20px;
      box-shadow: 0px 0px 10px rgba(0, 0, 0, 0.1);
      border-radius: 10px;
      background-color: #fff;
      width: 90%;
```

```css
}

#planner h2 {
  text-align: center;
  color: #4a47a3;
}

.day-block {
  display: flex;
  justify-content: space-between;
  border: 1px solid #ccc;
  padding: 20px;
  margin: 10px;
  border-radius: 5px;
  background-color: #ade8f4;
  width: 90%;
  box-shadow: 0px 0px 10px rgba(0, 0, 0, 0.05);
}

.day-info {
  display: flex;
  flex-direction: column;
  width: 25%;
  color: #183d5d;
}

.day-block h3 {
  color: #03396c;
  margin-bottom: 20px;
}

.day-block span {
  font-size: 1.0em;
  margin-bottom: 10px;
}

.day-block textarea {
  width: 70%;
  height: 150px;
  margin-bottom: 10px;
}

.day-block button {
  background-color: #dc3545;
```

```
      color: #fff;
      border: none;
      padding: 5px 10px;
      margin-top: 20px;
      cursor: pointer;
    }
  </style>
</head>

<body>
  <div id="planner">
    <h2>Weekly Planner</h2>
  </div>

  <script>
    let days = ["Sunday", "Monday", "Tuesday", "Wednesday",
"Thursday", "Friday", "Saturday"];
    let today = new Date();
    let startOfWeek = today.getDate() - today.getDay();
    let planner = document.getElementById('planner');

    function drawPlanner() {
      for (let i = 0; i < 7; i++) {
        let dayDate = new Date(today.setDate(startOfWeek + i));
        let dayBlock = document.createElement('div');
        dayBlock.classList.add('day-block');

        let dayInfo = document.createElement('div');
        dayInfo.classList.add('day-info');

        let dayTitle = document.createElement('h3');
        dayTitle.innerText = days[i];

        let dayDateElement = document.createElement('span');
        dayDateElement.innerText =
dayDate.toLocaleDateString();

        let deleteButton = document.createElement('button');
        deleteButton.innerText = "Delete";
        deleteButton.onclick = function () {
          textarea.value = "";
          localStorage.removeItem(`plans-
${dayDate.toLocaleDateString()}`);
        };
```

402

```
        dayInfo.appendChild(dayTitle);
        dayInfo.appendChild(dayDateElement);
        dayInfo.appendChild(deleteButton);

        let textarea = document.createElement('textarea');
        textarea.value = localStorage.getItem(`plans-
${dayDate.toLocaleDateString()}`) || "";
        textarea.onchange = function (event) {
          localStorage.setItem(`plans-
${dayDate.toLocaleDateString()}`, event.target.value);
        };

        dayBlock.appendChild(dayInfo);
        dayBlock.appendChild(textarea);
        planner.appendChild(dayBlock);
      }
    }

    drawPlanner();
  </script>
</body>

</html>

<!-- This version of the weekly planner has a more colorful design
with blue shades for the day blocks and red for the delete button.
Each day block also has a shadow for a slight 3D effect. The
layout is modified to have the day, date, and delete button on the
left side, and a larger text area on the right side. The planner uses
local storage to save the tasks of each day, and the delete button
deletes the tasks for the corresponding day. -->
```

403

```
<!DOCTYPE html>
<html>

<head>
  <title>Planners</title>
  <style>
    body {
      display: flex;
      justify-content: center;
      align-items: flex-start;
      font-family: Arial, sans-serif;

      padding: 20px;
      height: auto;
      box-sizing: border-box;
      overflow-y: auto;
      background-color: #e8f6f3;
    }

    #weekly-planner,
    #daily-planner {
      display: flex;
```

```css
  flex-direction: column;
  align-items: center;

  padding: 20px;
  box-shadow: 0px 0px 10px rgba(0, 0, 0, 0.1);
  border-radius: 10px;

  width: 45%;
  margin-right: 10px;
  border: 1px solid #7cdbd5;
  background-color: #c8ffff;
}

.planner-container h2 {
  text-align: center;
  color: #005792;
}

/* Styles for weekly planner */
.day-block {
  display: flex;
  justify-content: space-between;
  border: 1px solid #ccc;
  padding: 10px;
  margin: 10px;
  border-radius: 5px;

  width: 90%;
  box-shadow: 0px 0px 10px rgba(0, 0, 0, 0.05);
  background-color: #ffe66d;
}

.day-info {
  display: flex;
  flex-direction: column;
  width: 30%;
  color: #193549;
}

.day-block h4 {
  color: #005792;
  margin-bottom: 5px;
}
```

```css
.day-block span {
  font-size: 1.0em;
  margin-bottom: 5px;
}

.day-block textarea {
  width: 65%;
  height: 100px;
  margin-bottom: 5px;
}

.day-block button {
  background-color: #ff6b6b;
  color: #fff;
  border: none;
  padding: 5px 5px;
  margin-top: 5px;
  cursor: pointer;
}

/* Styles for daily planner */
.hour-block {
  display: flex;
  justify-content: space-between;
  border: 1px solid #ffe66d;
  padding: 10px;
  margin-bottom: 5px;
  width: 90%;
}

.hour-block span {
  width: 20%;
}

.hour-block input {
  flex-grow: 1;
  margin-left: 10px;
  margin-right: 10px;
}

.hour-block button {
  margin-left: auto;
  background-color: #ff6b6b;
}
```

```
    /* Change the width of the 'weekly-planner-blocks' and 'daily-
planner-blocks' */
    .weekly-blocks {
      width: 90%;
      /* Change as per your requirement */
    }

    .daily-blocks {
      width: 90%;
      /* Change as per your requirement */
    }
  </style>
</head>

<body>
  <div id="weekly-planner" class="planner-container">
    <h2>Weekly Planner</h2>
    <div id="weekly-planner-blocks" class="weekly-
blocks"></div>
  </div>

  <div id="daily-planner" class="planner-container">
    <h2>Daily Planner</h2>
    <div id="daily-planner-blocks" class="daily-blocks"></div>
  </div>

  <script>
    let days = ["Sunday", "Monday", "Tuesday", "Wednesday",
"Thursday", "Friday", "Saturday"];
    let today = new Date();
    let startOfWeek = today.getDate() - today.getDay();

    /* Weekly Planner */
    function drawWeeklyPlanner() {
      let planner = document.getElementById('weekly-planner-
blocks');
      planner.innerHTML = '';

      for (let i = 0; i < 7; i++) {
        let dayBlock = document.createElement('div');
        dayBlock.classList.add('day-block');
```

```
        let dayDate = new Date(today.getFullYear(),
today.getMonth(), startOfWeek + i);

        let dayInfo = document.createElement('div');
        dayInfo.classList.add('day-info');

        let dayNameElement = document.createElement('h4');
        dayNameElement.innerText = days[dayDate.getDay()];

        let dayDateElement = document.createElement('span');
        dayDateElement.innerText =
dayDate.toLocaleDateString();

        let deleteButton = document.createElement('button');
        deleteButton.innerText = 'Delete';
        deleteButton.onclick = function () {
          localStorage.removeItem(`plans-
${dayDate.toLocaleDateString()}`);
          drawWeeklyPlanner();
        };

        dayInfo.appendChild(dayNameElement);
        dayInfo.appendChild(dayDateElement);
        dayInfo.appendChild(deleteButton);

        let textarea = document.createElement('textarea');
        textarea.value = localStorage.getItem(`plans-
${dayDate.toLocaleDateString()}`) || "";
        textarea.onchange = function (event) {
          localStorage.setItem(`plans-
${dayDate.toLocaleDateString()}`, event.target.value);
        };

        dayBlock.appendChild(dayInfo);
        dayBlock.appendChild(textarea);
        planner.appendChild(dayBlock);
    }
  }

  /* Daily Planner */
  let plannerDay = new Array(24).fill('');

  function drawDailyPlanner() {
```

408

```
    let plannerElement = document.getElementById('daily-
planner-blocks');
    plannerElement.innerHTML = '';
    for (let i = 0; i < 24; i++) {
      let hourBlock = document.createElement('div');
      hourBlock.classList.add('hour-block');
      let timeElement = document.createElement('span');
      timeElement.innerText = i < 10 ? `0${i}:00` : `${i}:00`;
      let inputElement = document.createElement('input');
      inputElement.value = plannerDay[i];
      inputElement.onchange = function (event) {
        plannerDay[i] = event.target.value;
      };
      let deleteButton = document.createElement('button');
      deleteButton.innerText = 'Delete';
      deleteButton.onclick = function () {
        plannerDay[i] = '';
        drawDailyPlanner();
      };
      hourBlock.appendChild(timeElement);
      hourBlock.appendChild(inputElement);
      hourBlock.appendChild(deleteButton);
      plannerElement.appendChild(hourBlock);
    }
  }

  drawWeeklyPlanner();
  drawDailyPlanner();

  </script>
</body>

</html>
```

409

410

```
<!DOCTYPE html>
<html>
<head>
  <title>Planners</title>
  <!-- Bootstrap CSS -->
  <link
href="https://stackpath.bootstrapcdn.com/bootstrap/4.3.1/css/bo
otstrap.min.css" rel="stylesheet">
  <style>
   body {
     padding: 20px;
     height: auto;
     font-family: Arial, sans-serif;
     box-sizing: border-box;
     overflow-y: auto;
     background-color: #e8f6f3;
     display: flex;
     justify-content: space-around;
   }

   .planner-container {
```

```css
  display: flex;
  flex-direction: column;
  padding: 20px;
  box-shadow: 0px 0px 10px rgba(0, 0, 0, 0.1);
  border-radius: 10px;
  border: 1px solid #7cdbd5;
  background-color: #c8ffff;
  width: 45%;
}

.planner-container h2 {
  text-align: center;
  color: #005792;
}

/* Styles for weekly planner */
.day-block {
  border: 1px solid #ccc;
  padding: 10px;
  margin: 10px;
  border-radius: 5px;
  background-color: #ffe66d;
}

.day-block h4 {
  color: #005792;
  margin-bottom: 5px;
}

.day-block textarea {
  width: 70%;
  height: 100px;
  margin-bottom: 5px;
}

.day-block button {
  background-color: #ff6b6b;
  color: #fff;
  border: none;
  padding: 5px 5px;
  cursor: pointer;
}

/* Styles for daily planner */
```

411

```
    .hour-block {
      border: 1px solid #ffe66d;
      padding: 10px;
      margin-bottom: 5px;
    }

    .hour-block span {
      width: 20%;
    }

    .hour-block input {
      flex-grow: 1;
      margin-left: 10px;
      margin-right: 10px;
    }

    .hour-block button {
      margin-left: auto;
      background-color: #ff6b6b;
      color: #fff;
      border: none;
      padding: 5px 5px;
      cursor: pointer;
    }
  </style>
</head>
<body>
  <div id="weekly-planner" class="planner-container">
    <h2>Weekly Planner</h2>
    <div id="weekly-planner-blocks" class="weekly-
blocks"></div>
  </div>
  <div id="daily-planner" class="planner-container">
    <h2>Daily Planner</h2>
    <div id="daily-planner-blocks" class="daily-blocks"></div>
  </div>
  <!-- jQuery and Bootstrap Bundle (includes Popper) -->
  <script src="https://code.jquery.com/jquery-
3.3.1.slim.min.js"></script>
  <script
src="https://stackpath.bootstrapcdn.com/bootstrap/4.3.1/js/boot
strap.bundle.min.js"></script>
  <script>
    $(document).ready(function () {
```

```
    let days = ["Sunday", "Monday", "Tuesday", "Wednesday",
"Thursday", "Friday", "Saturday"];
    let today = new Date();
    let startOfWeek = today.getDate() - today.getDay();
    /* Weekly Planner */
    function drawWeeklyPlanner() {
      let planner = $('#weekly-planner-blocks');
      planner.empty();

      for (let i = 0; i < 7; i++) {
        let dayBlock = $('<div>').addClass('day-block d-flex
justify-content-between');
        let dayDate = new Date(today.getFullYear(),
today.getMonth(), startOfWeek + i);

        let dayInfo = $('<div>').addClass('day-info');
        let dayNameElement =
$('<h4>').text(days[dayDate.getDay()]);
        let dayDateElement =
$('<span>').text(dayDate.toLocaleDateString());
        let deleteButton = $('<button>').addClass('btn btn-
danger').text('Delete');
        deleteButton.on('click', function () {
          localStorage.removeItem(`plans-
${dayDate.toLocaleDateString()}`);
          drawWeeklyPlanner();
        });

        dayInfo.append(dayNameElement, dayDateElement,
deleteButton);

        let textarea = $('<textarea>').addClass('form-
control').val(localStorage.getItem(`plans-
${dayDate.toLocaleDateString()}`) || "");
        textarea.on('change', function () {
          localStorage.setItem(`plans-
${dayDate.toLocaleDateString()}`, $(this).val());
        });

        dayBlock.append(dayInfo, textarea);
        planner.append(dayBlock);
      }
    }
    /* Daily Planner */
```

413

```
    let plannerDay = new Array(24).fill('');

    function drawDailyPlanner() {
      let plannerElement = $('#daily-planner-blocks');
      plannerElement.empty();
      for (let i = 0; i < 24; i++) {
        let hourBlock = $('<div>').addClass('hour-block d-flex
justify-content-between');
        let timeElement = $('<span>').text(i < 10 ? `0${i}:00` :
`${i}:00`);
        let inputElement = $('<input>').addClass('form-
control').val(plannerDay[i]);
        inputElement.on('change', function () {
          plannerDay[i] = $(this).val();
        });
        let deleteButton = $('<button>').addClass('btn btn-
danger').text('Delete');
        deleteButton.on('click', function () {
          plannerDay[i] = '';
          drawDailyPlanner();
        });
        hourBlock.append(timeElement, inputElement,
deleteButton);
        plannerElement.append(hourBlock);
      }
    }
    drawWeeklyPlanner();
    drawDailyPlanner();
  });
  </script>
</body>
</html>
```

414

415

```
<!DOCTYPE html>
<html>

<head>
  <title>Note Taking App</title>
  <style>
    body {
      font-family: Arial, sans-serif;
      display: flex;
      flex-direction: column;
      justify-content: center;
      margin: 0 auto;
      max-width: 800px;
      padding: 0 20px;
      box-sizing: border-box;
    }

    #note-form {
      margin-bottom: 20px;
    }
```

```
  #note-title,
  #note-text {
    margin-bottom: 10px;
    width: 100%;
    box-sizing: border-box;
  }

  .note {
    border: 2px solid #f80606;
    padding: 10px;
    margin-bottom: 10px;
    white-space: pre-wrap;
    /* This will handle line breaks */
    overflow-wrap: break-word;
    /* This will prevent long words from extending beyond the
note width */
  }

  .note h2 {
    margin: 0;
    padding: 0;
    line-height: 0;
    /* Adjust as needed */
  }

  .note p {
    margin: 0;
    padding: 0;
    line-height: 1.2;
    /* Adjust as needed */
  }

  .note button {
    display: block;
    margin-bottom: 0px;
  }
  </style>
</head>

<body>
  <h1>Note Taking App</h1>
  <form id="note-form">
    <input type="text" id="note-title" placeholder="Note Title"
required>
```

```html
    <textarea id="note-text" rows='5' cols='100'
placeholder="Your Note Here" required></textarea>
    <button type="submit">Add Note</button>
  </form>
  <form id="take-form">
    <div id="notes"></div>
  </form>

  <!-- <script src="script.js"></script> -->
  <script>
    // Initialize notes from localStorage if available
    let notes = JSON.parse(localStorage.getItem('notes')) || [];

    // Select DOM elements
    const noteForm = document.getElementById('note-form');
    const noteTitle = document.getElementById('note-title');
    const noteText = document.getElementById('note-text');
    const noteContainer = document.getElementById('notes');

    // Form submission event listener
    noteForm.addEventListener('submit', function (e) {
      e.preventDefault();

      notes.push({ title: noteTitle.value, text: noteText.value });
      noteTitle.value = '';
      noteText.value = '';

      localStorage.setItem('notes', JSON.stringify(notes));
      displayNotes();
    });

    // Function to display notes
    function displayNotes() {
      const notesHTML = notes.map((note, i) => `
    <div class="note">
      <h2>${note.title}</h2>
      <p>${note.text}</p>
      <button onclick="deleteNote(${i})">Delete</button>
    </div>
    `).join('');

      noteContainer.innerHTML = notesHTML;
    }
```

417

```
    // Function to delete a note
    function deleteNote(i) {
      notes.splice(i, 1);
      localStorage.setItem('notes', JSON.stringify(notes));
      displayNotes();
    }

    // Display notes on load
    displayNotes();

  </script>
</body>

</html>
```

419

```
<!DOCTYPE html>
<html>

<head>
  <title>Note Taking App</title>
  <style>
    body {
      display: flex;
      flex-direction: column;
      justify-content: center;
      align-items: center;
      font-family: 'Arial', sans-serif;
      background-color: #f0f0f0;
      height: auto;
      margin: 0;
      padding: 20px;
      box-sizing: border-box;
    }

    h1 {
      color: #4a47a3;
      font-size: 2.5em;
```

```css
    margin-bottom: 20px;
}

#note-form {
  display: flex;
  flex-direction: column;
  width: 100%;
  max-width: 600px;
  margin-bottom: 40px;
}

#note-title,
#note-text {
  padding: 10px;
  border-radius: 5px;
  border: none;
  margin-bottom: 10px;
  font-size: 1.2em;
  box-shadow: 2px 2px 8px rgba(0, 0, 0, 0.1);
}

#note-form button {
  background-color: #4a47a3;
  color: #fff;
  border: none;
  border-radius: 5px;
  padding: 10px;
  font-size: 1.2em;
  cursor: pointer;
  transition: background-color 0.3s ease;
}

#note-form button:hover {
  background-color: #6755a8;
}

.note {
  border: 1px solid #ccc;
  border-radius: 5px;
  padding: 0px 20px;
  margin-bottom: 20px;
  width: 100%;
  max-width: 600px;
  box-shadow: 2px 2px 8px rgba(0, 0, 0, 0.1);
```

```
      background-color: #fff;
      white-space: pre-wrap;
    }

    .note h2 {
      color: #4a47a3;
      line-height: 0px;
      margin: 0px;
    }

    .note p {
      margin: 0px;
    }

    .note button {
      background-color: #dc3545;
      color: #fff;
      border: none;
      border-radius: 5px;
      padding: 5px 10px;
      cursor: pointer;
      transition: background-color 0.3s ease;
      float: right;
    }

    .note button:hover {
      background-color: #e35b70;
    }

  </style>
</head>

<body>
  <h1>Note Taking App</h1>
  <form id="note-form">
    <input type="text" id="note-title" placeholder="Note Title"
required>
    <textarea id="note-text" placeholder="Your Note Here"
required></textarea>
    <button type="submit">Add Note</button>
  </form>
  <div id="notes"></div>

  <!-- <script src="script.js"></script> -->
```

421

```
<script>
  // Initialize notes from localStorage if available
  let notes = JSON.parse(localStorage.getItem('notes')) || [];

  // Select DOM elements
  const noteForm = document.getElementById('note-form');
  const noteTitle = document.getElementById('note-title');
  const noteText = document.getElementById('note-text');
  const noteContainer = document.getElementById('notes');

  // Form submission event listener
  noteForm.addEventListener('submit', function (e) {
    e.preventDefault();

    notes.push({ title: noteTitle.value, text: noteText.value });
    noteTitle.value = '';
    noteText.value = '';

    localStorage.setItem('notes', JSON.stringify(notes));
    displayNotes();
  });

  // Function to display notes
  function displayNotes() {
    const notesHTML = notes.map((note, i) => `
<div class="note">
  <h2>${note.title}</h2>
  <p>${note.text}</p>
  <button onclick="deleteNote(${i})">Delete</button>
</div>
`).join('');

    noteContainer.innerHTML = notesHTML;
  }

  // Function to delete a note
  function deleteNote(i) {
    notes.splice(i, 1);
    localStorage.setItem('notes', JSON.stringify(notes));
    displayNotes();
  }

  // Display notes on load
  displayNotes();
```

```
  </script>
</body>

</html>

<!-- This code provides the following changes:

1. A centralized layout using flexbox and centering the contents
on the screen.
2. Added more padding and margin spacing.
3. Incorporated colorful buttons with a hover effect to improve
user experience.
4. Box shadows are applied to inputs, buttons, and notes to give a
bit of depth.
5. Border radius is used to round corners for a modern look.
6. Inputs are widened and their font sizes are increased for better
readability.
7. The delete button in each note is floated to the right side for a
neat appearance.

This will give you a colorful and modern look for your note-taking
app. You can further modify the colors and styles as per your
requirements. -->
```

424

```
<!DOCTYPE html>
<html>

<head>
  <title>Note Taking App</title>
  <link rel="stylesheet"
href="https://stackpath.bootstrapcdn.com/bootstrap/4.5.0/css/bo
otstrap.min.css">
  <script src="https://code.jquery.com/jquery-
3.5.1.min.js"></script>
  <script
src="https://stackpath.bootstrapcdn.com/bootstrap/4.5.0/js/boot
strap.min.js"></script>

  <style>
    body {
      background-color: #f0f0f0;
      padding: 20px;
    }

    #note-form button:hover {
      background-color: #6755a8;
    }
```

```css
.note {
  white-space: pre-wrap;
}

.note button {
  float: right;
}

.note button:hover {
  background-color: #e35b70;
}
  </style>
</head>

<body>
  <h1 class="text-center text-primary mb-4">Note Taking
App</h1>
  <form id="note-form" class="mb-5">
    <div class="form-group">
      <input type="text" class="form-control mb-3" id="note-title"
placeholder="Note Title" required>
      <textarea class="form-control mb-3" id="note-text"
placeholder="Your Note Here" required></textarea>
      <button type="submit" class="btn btn-primary btn-
block">Add Note</button>
    </div>
  </form>
  <div id="notes"></div>

  <script>
    // Initialize notes from localStorage if available
    let notes = JSON.parse(localStorage.getItem('notes')) || [];

    // Form submission event listener
    $('#note-form').on('submit', function (e) {
      e.preventDefault();

      notes.push({ title: $('#note-title').val(), text: $('#note-
text').val() });
      $('#note-title').val('');
      $('#note-text').val('');

      localStorage.setItem('notes', JSON.stringify(notes));
```

425

```
    displayNotes();
  });

  // Function to display notes
  function displayNotes() {
    const notesHTML = notes.map((note, i) => `
  <div class="note card p-3 mb-3">
    <h2 class="text-primary">${note.title}</h2>
    <p>${note.text}</p>
    <button class="btn btn-danger"
onclick="deleteNote(${i})">Delete</button>
  </div>
 `).join('');

    $('#notes').html(notesHTML);
  }

  // Function to delete a note
  function deleteNote(i) {
    notes.splice(i, 1);
    localStorage.setItem('notes', JSON.stringify(notes));
    displayNotes();
  }

  // Display notes on load
  displayNotes();
 </script>
</body>
</html>
<!-- This code incorporates Bootstrap's CSS and JavaScript
libraries, as well as jQuery. The styling rules have been
significantly simplified thanks to Bootstrap's utility classes, and
jQuery is used to handle the form submission and delete note
events.

Make sure to replace the `src` attributes of the `link` and
`script` tags with the URLs of the actual Bootstrap and jQuery
versions you're using. Also, please be aware that using Bootstrap
and jQuery could make your page load slower, particularly on
slower connections, because the user's browser needs to
download the additional files. -->
```

426

My Portfolio

About Me

Welcome to my portfolio! I am a web developer skilled in HTML, CSS, and JavaScript.

Projects

Project 1

Description of Project 1

Project 2

Description of Project 2

Contact Me

You can reach me at my-email@example.com

427

```
<!DOCTYPE html>
<html>

<head>
  <title>My Portfolio</title>
  <!-- <link rel="stylesheet" href="styles.css"> -->
  <style>
    body {
      font-family: Arial, sans-serif;
      margin: 0;
      padding: 0;
      box-sizing: border-box;
    }

    header {
      background-color: #f8f9fa;
      padding: 20px;
      text-align: center;
    }
```

```
    section {
      padding: 20px;
      margin-bottom: 20px;
    }

    .project {
      background-color: #f8f9fa;
      padding: 10px;
      margin: 10px 0;
    }
  </style>
</head>

<body>
  <header>
    <h1>My Portfolio</h1>
  </header>

  <section id="about-me">
    <h2>About Me</h2>
    <p>Welcome to my portfolio! I am a web developer skilled in
HTML, CSS, and JavaScript.</p>
  </section>

  <section id="projects">
    <h2>Projects</h2>
    <div class="project">
      <h3>Project 1</h3>
      <p>Description of Project 1</p>
    </div>
    <div class="project">
      <h3>Project 2</h3>
      <p>Description of Project 2</p>
    </div>
  </section>

  <section id="contact">
    <h2>Contact Me</h2>
    <p>You can reach me at my-email@example.com</p>
  </section>
</body>

</html>
```

```
<!-- A personal portfolio website is a great way to showcase your
skills, projects, and experience. Here's a very basic example of a
portfolio website. Keep in mind that you'd usually want to spend
more time on design and content to make it stand out.

In this HTML, there are three main sections: an "About Me"
section, a "Projects" section, and a "Contact Me" section. Each
project is represented by a div with a class of "project", which
includes the title and a brief description of the project.

The CSS is very simple, just adding some padding and margins to
make the layout more clear. The "project" class has a different
background color to help each project stand out.

You would replace the placeholder text with your own information,
and likely add more sections, more detailed project descriptions,
and links to live versions and/or source code of your projects. You
might also want to add a navigation bar, and more advanced
styling and animations using CSS and JavaScript. -->
```

```
<!DOCTYPE html>
<html lang="en">

<head>
  <meta charset="UTF-8">
  <meta name="viewport" content="width=device-width, initial-
scale=1.0">
  <title>My Profile</title>
  <script src="https://kit.fontawesome.com/2257b35322.js"
crossorigin="anonymous"></script>

  <style>
    /* CSS initialization  */
    * {
      margin: 0px;
      padding: 0px;
```

```css
  box-sizing: border-box;
}

ul,
ol {
  list-style: none;
}

a {
  text-decoration: none;
}

/*  profile box */

section {
  width: 350px;
  padding: 25px;
  background-color: #eef8ed;
  margin: 50px auto;
  box-shadow: 10px 10px 30px rgba(0, 0, 0, 0.3);
  border-radius: 10px;
}

/* top button */
section nav.menu {
  width: 100%;
}

section nav.menu::after {
  content: "";
  display: block;
  clear: both;
}

section nav.menu a {
  font-size: 20px;
  color: #666;
}

section nav.menu a:nth-of-type(1) {
  float: right;
}

section nav.menu a:nth-of-type(2) {
```

431

```css
    float: left;
}

/* profile area */
section article.profile {
  width: 100%;
  text-align: center;
}

section article.profile img {
  width: 200px;
  height: 200px;
  border-radius: 50%;
  margin-bottom: 20px;
}

section article.profile h1 {
  font-weight: bold;
  font-size: 22px;
  font-family: "arial";
  line-height: 1;
  color: #4118e5;
  margin-bottom: 5px;
}

section article.profile h2 {
  font-weight: normal;
  font-size: 14px;
  font-family: "arial";
  color: #8b8888;
  margin-bottom: 30px;
}

section a.btnView {
  display: block;
  width: 180px;
  height: 35px;
  margin: 0px auto 15px;
  background-color: #444;
  border-radius: 16px;
  font-weight: bold;
  font-size: 14px;
  font-family: "arial";
  color: #fff;
```

432

```css
    line-height: 32px;
    text-align: center;
    background: linear-gradient(45deg, #4affff, #05dcf9);
    box-shadow: 5px, 10px, 20px rgba(1, 81, 81, 0.493);
}

/* contact list */
section ul.contact {
    margin-bottom: 25px;
}

section ul.contact li {
    width: 100%;
    padding: 10px 0px;
    border-bottom: 1px solid #a3a1a1;
}

section ul.contact li:last-child {
    border-bottom: none;
}

section ul.contact li i {
    width: 20%;
    text-align: center;
    color: #555;
    font-size: 15px;
    text-shadow: 2px 2px 2px #ddd;
}

section ul.contact li span {
    font-weight: normal;
    font-size: 11px;
    font-family: "orbitron";
    color: #555;
    letter-spacing: 1px;
    cursor: pointer;
}

section ul.contact {
    display: none;
    /* Rest of your CSS */
}

/* CSS to style the popup */
```

```css
.popup {
  display: none;
  position: fixed;
  width: 300px;
  height: 200px;
  top: 50%;
  left: 50%;
  transform: translate(-50%, -50%);
  background-color: #f4f4f4;
  border: 1px solid #8008f8;
  border-radius: 5px;
  padding: 10px;
  box-shadow: 0px 0px 10px rgba(0, 0, 0, 0.3);
}

.popup textarea {
  width: 100%;
  height: 80%;
}

.popup button {
  width: 100%;
  height: 20%;
  background-color: #039191;
  border: none;
  color: white;
  cursor: pointer;
}

/* CSS to hide a new section */
section article.more-info {
  display: none;
  text-align: left;
  font-family: "arial";
  color: #666;
  margin-top: 20px;
}

section article.more-info h3 {
  font-size: 18px;
  font-weight: bold;
  margin-bottom: 10px;
}
```

```
    section article.more-info p {
      font-size: 14px;
    }
  </style>
</head>

<body>
  <section>
    <nav class="menu">
      <a id="menu-icon" href="#"><i class="fas fa-
bars"></i></a>
      <a id="note-icon" href="#"><i class="far fa-sticky-
note"></i></a>
    </nav>

    <div id="note-popup" class="popup">
      <textarea id="note-text" placeholder="Write a
note..."></textarea>
      <button id="note-save">Save Note</button>
    </div>

    <article class="profile">
      <img src="profile-girl.jpg" alt="my profile image">

      <h1>FUNCODING</h1>
      <h2>PLANET ECO DEVELOPER</h2>

      <a href="#" id="btnView" class="btnView">FIND
MORE</a>
    </article>

    <article class="more-info">
      <h3>About FUNCODING</h3>
      <p>FUNCODING is a planet eco developer, passionate about
creating solutions that are friendly to our planet. They
      have been involved in various eco projects across the
globe, creating sustainable tech solutions.</p>
    </article>

    <ul id="contact-list" class="contact">
      <li>
        <i class="fas fa-envelope "></i>
        <span>funcoding@naver.com</span>
```

435

```html
      </li>
      <li>
        <i class="fab fa-facebook-f"></i>
        <span>Welcome to My Facebook</span>
      </li>
    </ul>
  </section>
  <script>
    // Define initial states for elements
    var contactList = document.getElementById("contact-list");
    contactList.style.display = "none";

    var notePopup = document.getElementById("note-popup");
    notePopup.style.display = "none";

    var moreInfo = document.querySelector(".more-info");
    moreInfo.style.display = "none";

    document.getElementById("menu-
icon").addEventListener("click", function (event) {
      event.preventDefault();
      if (contactList.style.display === "none") {
        contactList.style.display = "block";
      } else {
        contactList.style.display = "none";
      }
    });

    document.getElementById("note-
icon").addEventListener("click", function (event) {
      event.preventDefault();
      if (notePopup.style.display === "none") {
        notePopup.style.display = "block";
      } else {
        notePopup.style.display = "none";
      }
    });

    document.getElementById("note-
save").addEventListener("click", function () {
      var noteText = document.getElementById("note-
text").value;
      localStorage.setItem("note", noteText);
      notePopup.style.display = "none";
```

436

```
    });

  window.onload = function () {
   var savedNote = localStorage.getItem("note");
   if (savedNote) {
     document.getElementById("note-text").value = savedNote;
   }
  };

  document.getElementById("btnView").addEventListener("click"
, function (event) {
   event.preventDefault();
   if (moreInfo.style.display === "none") {
     moreInfo.style.display = "block";
   } else {
     moreInfo.style.display = "none";
   }
  });

 </script>

</body>

</html>
```

437

438

```
<!DOCTYPE html>
<html lang="en">

<head>
  <meta charset="UTF-8">
  <meta name="viewport" content="width=device-width, initial-
scale=1.0">
  <title>My Profile</title>
  <script src="https://kit.fontawesome.com/2257b35322.js"
crossorigin="anonymous"></script>
  <link
href="https://stackpath.bootstrapcdn.com/bootstrap/4.3.1/css/bo
otstrap.min.css" rel="stylesheet">
  <script src="https://code.jquery.com/jquery-
3.4.1.slim.min.js"></script>
```

```
    <script
src="https://stackpath.bootstrapcdn.com/bootstrap/4.3.1/js/boot
strap.min.js"></script>

    <!-- Add your styles here -->

</head>

<body>
    <section class="p-3 m-5 bg-light rounded shadow-lg">
        <nav class="menu d-flex justify-content-between">
            <a id="menu-icon" href="#"><i class="fas fa-
bars"></i></a>
            <a id="note-icon" href="#"><i class="far fa-sticky-
note"></i></a>
        </nav>

        <div id="note-popup" class="popup bg-light border rounded
p-2 shadow position-absolute"
            style="width: 300px; height: 200px; top: 50%; left: 50%;
transform: translate(-50%, -50%); display: none;">
            <textarea id="note-text" class="w-100 h-75"
placeholder="Write a note..."></textarea>
            <button id="note-save" class="btn btn-primary w-100 h-
25">Save Note</button>
        </div>

        <article class="profile text-center">
            <img src="profile-girl.jpg" alt="my profile image"
class="rounded-circle mb-2"
                style="width: 200px; height: 200px;">

            <h1 class="font-weight-bold text-primary mb-
1">FUNCODING</h1>
```

```
    <h2 class="text-secondary mb-3">PLANET ECO
DEVELOPER</h2>

    <a href="#" id="btnView" class="btnView btn btn-block btn-
primary w-50 mx-auto">FIND MORE</a>
    </article>

    <article class="more-info text-left text-secondary mt-2"
style="display: none;">
    <h3 class="font-weight-bold mb-1">About
FUNCODING</h3>
    <p>FUNCODING is a planet eco developer, passionate about
creating solutions that are friendly to our planet. They
    have been involved in various eco projects across the
globe, creating sustainable tech solutions.</p>
    </article>

    <ul id="contact-list" class="contact list-unstyled mb-3"
style="display: none;">
    <li class="d-flex align-items-center mb-1">
    <i class="fas fa-envelope mr-2 text-secondary"></i>
    <span class="text-
secondary">funcoding@naver.com</span>
    </li>
    <li class="d-flex align-items-center">
    <i class="fab fa-facebook-f mr-2 text-secondary"></i>
    <span class="text-secondary">Welcome to My
Facebook</span>
    </li>
    </ul>
  </section>
  <script>
    // jQuery for interactivity
```

440

```
$(document).ready(function () {
  $("#menu-icon").click(function (e) {
    e.preventDefault();
    $("#contact-list").toggle();
  });

  $("#note-icon").click(function (e) {
    e.preventDefault();
    $("#note-popup").toggle();
  });

  $("#note-save").click(function () {
    var noteText = $("#note-text").val();
    localStorage.setItem("note", noteText);
    $("#note-popup").hide();
  });

  $(window).on('load', function () {
    var savedNote = localStorage.getItem("note");
    if (savedNote) {
      $("#note-text").val(savedNote);
    }
  });

  $("#btnView").click(function (e) {
    e.preventDefault();
    $(".more-info").toggle();
  });
});
</script>
</body>
</html>
```

441

Task Tracker

| New task | 연도 - 월 - 일 🗓 | Add Task |

supper - Thu Jun 29 2023 [Delete]
swimming poll making - Sun Jul 02 2023 [Delete]
Welcome to My Portfolio - Sat Jul 08 2023 [Delete]
homework - Wed Jul 19 2023 [Delete]

442

```html
<!DOCTYPE html>
<html>

<head>
  <title>Task Tracker</title>
  <!-- <link rel="stylesheet" href="style.css"> -->
  <style>
    body {
      margin: 20px;
    }
  </style>
</head>

<body>
  <h2>Task Tracker</h2>
  <form id="task-form">
    <input type="text" id="task-input" placeholder="New task"
required>
    <input type="date" id="due-date-input" required>
    <input type="submit" value="Add Task">
  </form>

  <div id="task-list">
    <!-- Tasks will be displayed here -->
  </div>

  <!-- <script src="app.js"></script> -->
  <script>
    // Array to hold tasks
    let tasks = JSON.parse(localStorage.getItem('tasks')) || [];
```

```javascript
    tasks = tasks.map(task => {
      return {
        ...task,
        dueDate: new Date(task.dueDate)
      };
    });

    document.getElementById('task-
form').addEventListener('submit', addTask);

    function addTask(event) {
      event.preventDefault();

      const taskInput = document.getElementById('task-input');
      const dueDateInput = document.getElementById('due-date-
input');

      // Create task object and add it to tasks array
      const task = {
        name: taskInput.value,
        dueDate: new Date(dueDateInput.value)
      };
      tasks.push(task);

      // Persist tasks in local storage
      localStorage.setItem('tasks', JSON.stringify(tasks));

      // Update the task display
      updateTaskDisplay();

      // Clear input fields
      taskInput.value = '';
      dueDateInput.value = '';
    }

    function updateTaskDisplay() {
      const taskList = document.getElementById('task-list');

      // Clear the task list
      taskList.innerHTML = '';

      // Create a new list item for each task and append it to the
task list
      for (let i = 0; i < tasks.length; i++) {
```

443

```javascript
      const listItem = document.createElement('div');
      // Check if the date is valid before displaying it
      if (isNaN(tasks[i].dueDate.getTime())) {
        listItem.textContent = `${tasks[i].name} - No Due
Date`;
      } else {
        listItem.textContent = `${tasks[i].name} -
${tasks[i].dueDate.toDateString()}`;
      }

      // Create delete button
      const deleteButton = document.createElement('button');
      deleteButton.textContent = "Delete";
      deleteButton.addEventListener('click', function () {
        tasks = tasks.filter(task => task !== tasks[i]); // remove
the task from the tasks array
        localStorage.setItem('tasks', JSON.stringify(tasks)); //
update tasks in localStorage
        updateTaskDisplay(); // re-display the tasks
      });

      listItem.appendChild(deleteButton); // add the delete
button to the task
      taskList.appendChild(listItem);
    }
  }
  updateTaskDisplay();

  </script>
</body>
</html>
<!-- In this code, I added a delete button to each task. The button
has an event listener that, when clicked, removes the associated
task from the tasks array, updates the tasks in localStorage, and
then calls updateTaskDisplay to refresh the displayed task list. -->
```

444

Task Tracker

New task	연도-월-일	□	Add Task

Sort by date (asc) Sort by date (desc)

Task	Date	Complete	Delete
supper	Thu Jun 29 2023	☑	Delete
swimming poll making	Sun Jul 02 2023	☐	Delete
Welcome to My Portfolio	Sat Jul 08 2023	☑	Delete
homework	Wed Jul 19 2023	☐	Delete
call parents	Sat Aug 05 2023	☐	Delete

445

```html
<!DOCTYPE html>
<html>

<head>
  <title>Task Tracker</title>
  <style>
    body {
      font-family: Arial, sans-serif;
      background-color: #e9ecef;
      padding: 10px;
    }

    #app {
      width: 600px;
      margin: 0 auto;
    }

    #task-form {
      display: flex;
      justify-content: space-between;
      margin-bottom: 20px;
      background-color: #f8d7da;
      padding: 10px;
      border-radius: 10px;
      box-shadow: 5px 5px 15px rgba(0, 0, 0, 0.1);
```

```
}

#task-form input[type="text"],
#task-form input[type="date"] {
  flex: 1;
  margin-right: 10px;
  padding: 5px;
  border: 1px solid #ced4da;
  border-radius: 5px;
}

#task-form input[type="submit"] {
  padding: 5px 10px;
  color: white;
  border: none;
  border-radius: 5px;
  cursor: pointer;
  font-weight: bold;
  background-color: #17a2b8;
}

#task-form input[type="submit"]:hover {
  background-color: #138496;
}

#task-list {
  border: 1px solid #000;
  margin: 0px;
  padding: 10px;
  box-sizing: border-box;
  table-layout: fixed;
  border-collapse: collapse;
  width: 100%;
}

#task-list button {
  background-color: #dc3545;
}

#task-list button:hover {
  background-color: #c82333;
}

table#task-list th,
```

```css
    table#task-list td {
      border: 1px solid #000;
      padding: 10px;
      text-align: center;
      overflow: hidden;
      text-overflow: ellipsis;
    }

    #sort {
      display: flex;
      justify-content: center;
      margin-bottom: 10px;
    }

    #sort button {
      margin-right: 5px;
    }

    h1 {
      text-align: center;
    }
  </style>
</head>

<body>
  <h1>Task Tracker</h1>
  <div id="app">
    <form id="task-form">
      <input type="text" id="task-input" placeholder="New task"
required>
      <input type="date" id="due-date-input" required>
      <input type="submit" value="Add Task">
    </form>

    <div id="sort">
      <button id="sort-asc">Sort by date (asc)</button>
      <button id="sort-desc">Sort by date (desc)</button>
    </div>

    <table id="task-list">
      <thead>
        <tr>
          <th style="width:220px;">Task</th>
          <th style="width:120px;">Date</th>
```

```
        <th style="width:70px;">Complete</th>
        <th style="width:80px;">Delete</th>
      </tr>
    </thead>
    <tbody>
      <!-- Tasks will be displayed here -->
    </tbody>
  </table>
</div>
<script>
  // Array to hold tasks
  let tasks = JSON.parse(localStorage.getItem('tasks')) || [];
  tasks = tasks.map(task => {
    return {
      ...task,
      dueDate: new Date(task.dueDate),
      completed: task.completed || false,  // Add completed
property
    };
  });

  document.getElementById('task-
form').addEventListener('submit', addTask);

  function addTask(event) {
    event.preventDefault();

    const taskInput = document.getElementById('task-input');
    const dueDateInput = document.getElementById('due-date-
input');

    // Create task object and add it to tasks array
    const task = {
      name: taskInput.value,
      dueDate: new Date(dueDateInput.value),
      completed: false,  // New tasks are not completed
    };
    tasks.push(task);

    // Persist tasks in local storage
    localStorage.setItem('tasks', JSON.stringify(tasks));

    // Update the task display
    updateTaskDisplay();
```

448

```
    // Clear input fields
    taskInput.value = '';
    dueDateInput.value = '';
}


// Add event listeners for sort buttons
document.getElementById('sort-asc').addEventListener('click',
function () {
    tasks.sort((a, b) => a.dueDate - b.dueDate);
    updateTaskDisplay();
});

document.getElementById('sort-
desc').addEventListener('click', function () {
    tasks.sort((a, b) => b.dueDate - a.dueDate);
    updateTaskDisplay();
});

function updateTaskDisplay() {
    const taskList = document.getElementById('task-
list').querySelector('tbody');
    taskList.innerHTML = '';

    for (let i = 0; i < tasks.length; i++) {
      const row = document.createElement('tr');

      const taskCell = document.createElement('td');
      taskCell.textContent = tasks[i].name;
      taskCell.style.width = '220px';
      row.appendChild(taskCell);

      const dateCell = document.createElement('td');
      dateCell.textContent = isNaN(tasks[i].dueDate.getTime()) ?
'No Due Date' : tasks[i].dueDate.toDateString();
      dateCell.style.width = '120px';
      row.appendChild(dateCell);

      const completeCell = document.createElement('td');
      completeCell.style.width = '70px';
      const completeCheckbox =
document.createElement('input');
      completeCheckbox.type = 'checkbox';
      completeCheckbox.checked = tasks[i].completed;
```

```
        completeCheckbox.addEventListener('change', function () {
          tasks[i].completed = completeCheckbox.checked;
          localStorage.setItem('tasks', JSON.stringify(tasks)); //
update tasks in localStorage
          updateTaskDisplay();
        });
        completeCell.appendChild(completeCheckbox);
        row.appendChild(completeCell);

        const deleteCell = document.createElement('td');
        deleteCell.style.width = '80px';
        const deleteButton = document.createElement('button');
        deleteButton.textContent = "Delete";
        deleteButton.addEventListener('click', function () {
          tasks.splice(i, 1); // remove the task from the tasks array
          localStorage.setItem('tasks', JSON.stringify(tasks)); //
update tasks in localStorage
          updateTaskDisplay(); // re-display the tasks
        });
        deleteCell.appendChild(deleteButton);
        row.appendChild(deleteCell);

        taskList.appendChild(row);
      }
    }

    updateTaskDisplay();  // call this function immediately after
defining it to load tasks on page load
  </script>
</body>
</html>
```

```
<!DOCTYPE html>
<html>

<head>
  <title>Task Tracker</title>
  <link rel="stylesheet"
href="https://stackpath.bootstrapcdn.com/bootstrap/4.3.1/css/bo
otstrap.min.css">
  <script src="https://code.jquery.com/jquery-
3.4.1.min.js"></script>
</head>

<body>
  <div class="container mt-5">
    <h1 class="text-center">Task Tracker</h1>
    <form id="task-form" class="mt-5">
      <div class="form-group">
        <input type="text" id="task-input" class="form-control"
placeholder="New task" required>
      </div>
      <div class="form-group">
```

```
        <input type="date" id="due-date-input" class="form-
control" required>
      </div>
      <input type="submit" class="btn btn-primary" value="Add
Task">
    </form>
    <div id="sort" class="mt-3">
      <button id="sort-asc" class="btn btn-outline-
secondary">Sort by date (asc)</button>
      <button id="sort-desc" class="btn btn-outline-
secondary">Sort by date (desc)</button>
    </div>
    <table id="task-list" class="table table-bordered mt-3">
      <thead>
        <tr>
          <th style="width:220px;">Task</th>
          <th style="width:120px;">Date</th>
          <th style="width:70px;">Complete</th>
          <th style="width:80px;">Delete</th>
        </tr>
      </thead>
      <tbody>
        <!-- Tasks will be displayed here -->
      </tbody>
    </table>
  </div>
  <script>
    $(document).ready(function () {
      let tasks = JSON.parse(localStorage.getItem('tasks')) || [];
      tasks = tasks.map(task => {
        return {
          ...task,
          dueDate: new Date(task.dueDate),
          completed: task.completed || false,
        };
      });

      $('#task-form').on('submit', function (event) {
        event.preventDefault();
        const taskInput = $('#task-input');
        const dueDateInput = $('#due-date-input');

        const task = {
          name: taskInput.val(),
```

```javascript
      dueDate: new Date(dueDateInput.val()),
      completed: false,
    };
    tasks.push(task);

    localStorage.setItem('tasks', JSON.stringify(tasks));

    updateTaskDisplay();
    taskInput.val('');
    dueDateInput.val('');
  });

  $('#sort-asc').on('click', function () {
    tasks.sort((a, b) => a.dueDate - b.dueDate);
    updateTaskDisplay();
  });

  $('#sort-desc').on('click', function () {
    tasks.sort((a, b) => b.dueDate - a.dueDate);
    updateTaskDisplay();
  });

  function updateTaskDisplay() {
    const taskList = $('#task-list tbody');
    taskList.html('');

    tasks.forEach((task, i) => {
      const row = $('<tr>');
      const taskCell = $('<td>').text(task.name).css('width',
'220px');
      const dateCell =
$('<td>').text(isNaN(task.dueDate.getTime()) ? 'No Due Date' :
task.dueDate.toDateString()).css('width', '120px');
      const completeCell = $('<td>').css('width', '70px');
      const completeCheckbox = $('<input>').attr('type',
'checkbox').prop('checked', task.completed).on('change', function
() {
        tasks[i].completed = this.checked;
        localStorage.setItem('tasks', JSON.stringify(tasks));
        updateTaskDisplay();
      });
      completeCell.append(completeCheckbox);
      const deleteCell = $('<td>').css('width', '80px');
```

453

```
        const deleteButton = $('<button>').addClass('btn btn-
danger').text("Delete").on('click', function () {
            tasks.splice(i, 1);
            localStorage.setItem('tasks', JSON.stringify(tasks));
            updateTaskDisplay();
        });
        deleteCell.append(deleteButton);
        row.append(taskCell, dateCell, completeCell, deleteCell);
        taskList.append(row);
      });
    }

    updateTaskDisplay();
  });
  </script>
</body>

</html>
```

Budget Tracker

Balance: $250

| Enter description | Enter amount | Add Transaction |

Income

May Pay: $200
Jun Pay: $200

Expenses

Grocery: $100
Cloth: $50

```
<!DOCTYPE html>
<html>

<head>
  <title>Budget Tracker</title>
  <!-- <link rel="stylesheet" type="text/css" href="styles.css"> --
>
  <style>
    body {
      font-family: Arial, sans-serif;
      margin: 30px;
    }

    #balance {
      font-size: 2em;
      color: blue;
    }

    form {
      margin-bottom: 2em;
    }

    ul {
      list-style-type: none;
```

```
    }
  </style>
</head>

<body>
  <h1>Budget Tracker</h1>
  <div id="balance">Balance: $0</div>
  <br>
  <form id="money-form">
    <input type="text" id="desc" placeholder="Enter
description">
    <input type="number" id="amount" placeholder="Enter
amount">
    <button type="submit">Add Transaction</button>
  </form>

  <!-- "When entering an amount, if it is greater than 0, it is
recorded as income. If it's a negative number less than 0, it's
recorded as an expense." -->
  <h2>Income</h2>
  <ul id="income-list"></ul>

  <h2>Expenses</h2>
  <ul id="expenses-list"></ul>

  <!-- <script src="script.js"></script> -->
  <script>
    let balance = 0;
    let income = [];
    let expenses = [];

    document.getElementById('money-
form').addEventListener('submit', function (e) {
      e.preventDefault();

      let desc = document.getElementById('desc').value;
      let amount =
Number(document.getElementById('amount').value);

      if (amount >= 0) {
        income.push({ desc: desc, amount: amount });
        addToIncomeList(desc, amount);
      } else {
        expenses.push({ desc: desc, amount: amount });
```

456

```
    addToExpensesList(desc, amount);
  }

  balance += amount;
  document.getElementById('balance').innerText = 'Balance:
$' + balance;

  document.getElementById('desc').value = '';
  document.getElementById('amount').value = '';
});

function addToIncomeList(desc, amount) {
  let listItem = document.createElement('li');
  listItem.innerText = desc + ': $' + amount;
  document.getElementById('income-
list').appendChild(listItem);
}

function addToExpensesList(desc, amount) {
  let listItem = document.createElement('li');
  listItem.innerText = desc + ': $' + Math.abs(amount);
  document.getElementById('expenses-
list').appendChild(listItem);
}

  </script>
</body>

</html>
```

<!-- We build a budget tracker application using HTML, CSS, and JavaScript! Let's break this down into several key steps. Please note, this will be a simplified version to get you started. For more complex features, you might need to explore more advanced topics or libraries.

1. Design the layout: Before we start coding, we need to have a clear idea of how our application will look. For this application, we'll need input fields for income and expenses, a submit button, a list to display the income and expenses, and a field to display the balance.

2. Create the HTML structure: Based on our design, we'll create the HTML structure for our application.

457

3. Style the application with CSS: After we've created our HTML structure, we'll style it using CSS to make it look appealing.

4. Add functionality with JavaScript: Finally, we'll use JavaScript to add functionality to our application. This will include adding income and expenses, calculating the balance, and updating the display.

This is a very simple example that doesn't include any error checking, data persistence, or visualizations. As you learn more about JavaScript and web development, you can add these features and more to your application.   -->

458

459

```
<!DOCTYPE html>
<html>

<head>
  <title>Budget Tracker</title>
  <style>
    body {
      font-family: Arial, sans-serif;
      background-color: #e9ecef;
      display: flex;
      flex-direction: column;
      align-items: center;
    }

    #app {
      width: 900px;
      display: flex;
      justify-content: space-around;
      background-color: #f8f9fa;
      padding: 20px;
      border-radius: 10px;
      margin-top: 20px;
    }

    #income,
    #expenses {
      width: 40%;
    }

    #balance {
      font-size: 2em;
```

```css
    color: #17a2b8;
    margin-top: 20px;
  }

  form {
    display: flex;
    justify-content: space-around;
    margin-bottom: 2em;
  }

  ul {
    list-style-type: none;
    padding: 0;
  }

  li {
    line-height: 25px;
  }

  h2 {
    color: #17a2b8;
  }

  #income h2,
  #income ul {
    color: #28a745;
  }

  #expenses h2,
  #expenses ul {
    color: #dc3545;
  }

  #subtotal {
    font-weight: bold;
    margin-top: 1em;
  }
  </style>
</head>

<body>
  <h1>Budget Tracker</h1>

  <div id="app">
```

```html
    <div id="income">
      <h2>Income</h2>
      <form id="income-form">
        <input type="text" id="income-desc" placeholder="Enter
income description" required>
        <input type="number" id="income-amount"
placeholder="Enter amount" min="0" required>
        <button type="submit">Add Income</button>
      </form>
      <ul id="income-list"></ul>
      <div id="income-total"></div>
    </div>

    <div id="expenses">
      <h2>Expenses</h2>
      <form id="expenses-form">
        <input type="text" id="expenses-desc" placeholder="Enter
expense description" required>
        <input type="number" id="expenses-amount"
placeholder="Enter amount" min="0" required>
        <button type="submit">Add Expense</button>
      </form>
      <ul id="expenses-list"></ul>
      <div id="expenses-total"></div>
    </div>
  </div>

  <div id="balance">Balance: $0</div>

  <script>
    let balance = 0;
    let income = JSON.parse(localStorage.getItem("income")) ||
[];
    let expenses = JSON.parse(localStorage.getItem("expenses"))
|| [];

    window.onload = function () {
      income.forEach(item => addToIncomeList(item.desc,
item.amount));
      expenses.forEach(item => addToExpensesList(item.desc,
item.amount));
      updateIncomeTotal();
      updateExpensesTotal();
      updateBalance();
```

461

```
    }

    document.getElementById('income-
form').addEventListener('submit', function (e) {
        e.preventDefault();

        let desc = document.getElementById('income-desc').value;
        let amount = Number(document.getElementById('income-
amount').value);

        income.push({ desc: desc, amount: amount });
        addToIncomeList(desc, amount);

        localStorage.setItem("income", JSON.stringify(income));

        updateIncomeTotal();
        updateBalance();

        document.getElementById('income-desc').value = '';
        document.getElementById('income-amount').value = '';
    });

    document.getElementById('expenses-
form').addEventListener('submit', function (e) {
        e.preventDefault();

        let desc = document.getElementById('expenses-desc').value;
        let amount = Number(document.getElementById('expenses-
amount').value);

        expenses.push({ desc: desc, amount: amount });
        addToExpensesList(desc, amount);

        localStorage.setItem("expenses", JSON.stringify(expenses));

        updateExpensesTotal();
        updateBalance();

        document.getElementById('expenses-desc').value = '';
        document.getElementById('expenses-amount').value = '';
    });

    function addToIncomeList(desc, amount) {
        let listItem = document.createElement('li');
```

```javascript
    listItem.innerHTML = `
    <span>${desc}: $${amount.toLocaleString()}</span>
    <button class="edit">Edit</button>
    <button class="delete">Delete</button>
  `;
    listItem.querySelector(".edit").addEventListener("click",
function () {
      let newDesc = prompt("Enter new description:", desc);
      let newAmount = prompt("Enter new amount:", amount);
      if (newDesc && newAmount) {
        let index = income.findIndex(item => item.desc ===
desc && item.amount === amount);
        income[index] = { desc: newDesc, amount:
parseFloat(newAmount) };
        localStorage.setItem("income", JSON.stringify(income));
        listItem.querySelector("span").innerText =
`${newDesc}: $${parseFloat(newAmount).toLocaleString()}`;
        updateIncomeTotal();
        updateExpensesTotal();
        updateBalance();
      }
    });
    listItem.querySelector(".delete").addEventListener("click",
function () {
      let index = income.findIndex(item => item.desc === desc
&& item.amount === amount);
      income.splice(index, 1);
      localStorage.setItem("income", JSON.stringify(income));
      listItem.remove();
      updateIncomeTotal();
      updateExpensesTotal();
      updateBalance();
    });
    document.getElementById('income-
list').appendChild(listItem);
  }

  function addToExpensesList(desc, amount) {
    let listItem = document.createElement('li');
    listItem.innerHTML = `
    <span>${desc}: $${amount.toLocaleString()}</span>
    <button class="edit">Edit</button>
    <button class="delete">Delete</button>
  `;
```

```javascript
        listItem.querySelector(".edit").addEventListener("click",
function () {
        let newDesc = prompt("Enter new description:", desc);
        let newAmount = prompt("Enter new amount:", amount);
        if (newDesc && newAmount) {
          let index = expenses.findIndex(item => item.desc ===
desc && item.amount === amount);
          expenses[index] = { desc: newDesc, amount:
parseFloat(newAmount) };
          localStorage.setItem("expenses",
JSON.stringify(expenses));
          listItem.querySelector("span").innerText =
`${newDesc}: $${parseFloat(newAmount).toLocaleString()}`;
          updateIncomeTotal();
          updateExpensesTotal();
          updateBalance();
        }
      });
      listItem.querySelector(".delete").addEventListener("click",
function () {
        let index = expenses.findIndex(item => item.desc ===
desc && item.amount === amount);
        expenses.splice(index, 1);
        localStorage.setItem("expenses",
JSON.stringify(expenses));
        listItem.remove();
        updateIncomeTotal();
        updateExpensesTotal();
        updateBalance();
      });
      document.getElementById('expenses-
list').appendChild(listItem);
    }

   function updateIncomeTotal() {
     let totalIncome = income.reduce((sum, item) => sum +
item.amount, 0);
     document.getElementById('income-total').innerText =
'Income Total: $' + totalIncome.toLocaleString();
   }

   function updateExpensesTotal() {
     let totalExpenses = expenses.reduce((sum, item) => sum +
item.amount, 0);
```

```
        document.getElementById('expenses-total').innerText =
'Expenses Total: $' + Math.abs(totalExpenses).toLocaleString();
    }

    function updateBalance() {
        let totalIncome = income.reduce((sum, item) => sum +
item.amount, 0);
        let totalExpenses = expenses.reduce((sum, item) => sum +
item.amount, 0);
        let balance = totalIncome - totalExpenses;
        document.getElementById('balance').innerText = 'Balance:
$' + balance.toLocaleString();
    }

  </script>
</body>
</html>
<!-- The addToIncomeList and addToExpensesList functions are
updated to add an "Edit" and a "Delete" button to each list item.
The "Edit" button triggers a prompt to enter a new description and
amount, and updates the list item and Local Storage data
accordingly. The "Delete" button removes the item from the list
and from the Local Storage data.

The subtotals and balance update immediately whenever an item
is edited or deleted. -->
```

465

Budget Tracker

Income

Enter income description

Enter amount

Add Income

May Payment: $100   Edit Delete

April payment: $400   Edit Delete

Income Total: $500

Expenses

Enter expense description

Enter amount

Add Expense

Food: $50   Edit Delete

Cloth: $100   Edit Delete

Expenses Total: $150

Balance: $350

466

```
<!DOCTYPE html>
<html>

<head>
  <title>Budget Tracker</title>
  <link rel="stylesheet"
href="https://stackpath.bootstrapcdn.com/bootstrap/4.3.1/css/bo
otstrap.min.css">
  <script src="https://code.jquery.com/jquery-
3.4.1.min.js"></script>
  <style>
  #balance {
    margin-bottom: 50px;
  }
```

```
  hr {
    border-top: 2px solid #037ef8;
  }
  </style>
</head>

<body>
  <div class="container mt-5">
    <h1 class="text-center">Budget Tracker</h1>

    <div id="app" class="mt-5">
      <div id="income" class="mb-4">
        <h2 class="text-success">Income</h2>
        <form id="income-form">
          <div class="form-group">
            <input type="text" id="income-desc" class="form-control" placeholder="Enter income description" required>
          </div>
          <div class="form-group">
            <input type="number" id="income-amount" class="form-control" placeholder="Enter amount" min="0" required>
          </div>
          <button type="submit" class="btn btn-success">Add Income</button>
        </form>
        <ul id="income-list" class="list-group mt-3"></ul>
        <div id="income-total" class="font-weight-bold mt-3"></div>
      </div>
      <hr>
      <div id="expenses" class="mb-4">
        <h2 class="text-danger">Expenses</h2>
        <form id="expenses-form">
          <div class="form-group">
            <input type="text" id="expenses-desc" class="form-control" placeholder="Enter expense description" required>
          </div>
          <div class="form-group">
            <input type="number" id="expenses-amount" class="form-control" placeholder="Enter amount" min="0" required>
          </div>
```

```
      <button type="submit" class="btn btn-danger">Add
Expense</button>
      </form>
      <ul id="expenses-list" class="list-group mt-3"></ul>
      <div id="expenses-total" class="font-weight-bold mt-
3"></div>
    </div>
  </div>
  <hr>
  <div id="balance" class="font-weight-bold text-info mt-
7">Balance: $0</div>

</div>

<script>
  $(document).ready(function () {
    let balance = 0;
    let income = JSON.parse(localStorage.getItem("income")) ||
[];
    let expenses =
JSON.parse(localStorage.getItem("expenses")) || [];

    function loadItems() {
      $('#income-list').empty();
      $('#expenses-list').empty();
      income.forEach(item => addToIncomeList(item.desc,
item.amount));
      expenses.forEach(item => addToExpensesList(item.desc,
item.amount));
      updateIncomeTotal();
      updateExpensesTotal();
      updateBalance();
    }

    loadItems();

    $('#income-form').on('submit', function (e) {
      e.preventDefault();

      let desc = $('#income-desc').val();
      let amount = Number($('#income-amount').val());

      income.push({ desc: desc, amount: amount });
      localStorage.setItem("income", JSON.stringify(income));
```

```javascript
    loadItems();

    $('#income-desc').val('');
    $('#income-amount').val('');
  });

  $('#expenses-form').on('submit', function (e) {
    e.preventDefault();

    let desc = $('#expenses-desc').val();
    let amount = Number($('#expenses-amount').val());

    expenses.push({ desc: desc, amount: amount });
    localStorage.setItem("expenses",
JSON.stringify(expenses));

    loadItems();

    $('#expenses-desc').val('');
    $('#expenses-amount').val('');
  });

  function addToIncomeList(desc, amount) {
    const item = $('<li>').addClass('list-group-item d-flex
justify-content-between align-items-center').html(`${desc}:
$${amount}<span><button class="btn btn-success btn-sm mr-2
edit">Edit</button><button class="btn btn-danger btn-sm
delete">Delete</button></span>`);
    item.find('.edit').on('click', function () {
      editItem(desc, amount, true);
    });
    item.find('.delete').on('click', function () {
      deleteItem(desc, amount, true);
    });
    $('#income-list').append(item);
  }

  function addToExpensesList(desc, amount) {
    const item = $('<li>').addClass('list-group-item d-flex
justify-content-between align-items-center').html(`${desc}:
$${amount}<span><button class="btn btn-success btn-sm mr-2
edit">Edit</button><button class="btn btn-danger btn-sm
delete">Delete</button></span>`);
```

469

```
    item.find('.edit').on('click', function () {
      editItem(desc, amount, false);
    });
    item.find('.delete').on('click', function () {
      deleteItem(desc, amount, false);
    });
    $('#expenses-list').append(item);
  }

  function updateIncomeTotal() {
    let totalIncome = income.reduce((sum, item) => sum +
item.amount, 0);
    $('#income-total').text('Income Total: $' +
totalIncome.toLocaleString());
  }

  function updateExpensesTotal() {
    let totalExpenses = expenses.reduce((sum, item) => sum
+ item.amount, 0);
    $('#expenses-total').text('Expenses Total: $' +
totalExpenses.toLocaleString());
  }

  function updateBalance() {
    let totalIncome = income.reduce((sum, item) => sum +
item.amount, 0);
    let totalExpenses = expenses.reduce((sum, item) => sum
+ item.amount, 0);
    let balance = totalIncome - totalExpenses;
    $('#balance').text('Balance: $' + balance.toLocaleString());
  }

  function editItem(desc, amount, isIncome) {
    const newDesc = prompt("Enter new description:", desc);
    const newAmount = Number(prompt("Enter new amount:",
amount));

    if (newDesc !== null && newAmount !== null) {
      if (isIncome) {
        const index = income.findIndex(item => item.desc
=== desc && item.amount === amount);
        income[index] = { desc: newDesc, amount:
newAmount };
```

470

```
        localStorage.setItem("income",
JSON.stringify(income));
      } else {
        const index = expenses.findIndex(item => item.desc
=== desc && item.amount === amount);
        expenses[index] = { desc: newDesc, amount:
newAmount };
        localStorage.setItem("expenses",
JSON.stringify(expenses));
      }

      loadItems();
    }
   }

   function deleteItem(desc, amount, isIncome) {
     if (isIncome) {
       const index = income.findIndex(item => item.desc ===
desc && item.amount === amount);
       income.splice(index, 1);
       localStorage.setItem("income", JSON.stringify(income));
     } else {
       const index = expenses.findIndex(item => item.desc
=== desc && item.amount === amount);
       expenses.splice(index, 1);
       localStorage.setItem("expenses",
JSON.stringify(expenses));
     }

     loadItems();
   }
  });
 </script>

</body>

</html>
```

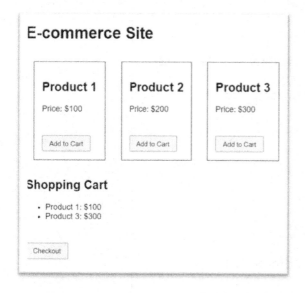

```
<!DOCTYPE html>
<html>

<head>
  <title>E-commerce Site</title>
  <!-- <link rel="stylesheet" type="text/css" href="styles.css"> --
>
  <style>
    body {
      font-family: Arial, sans-serif;
    }

    #products {
      display: flex;
      flex-wrap: wrap;
    }

    .product {
      margin: 1em;
      padding: 1em;
      border: 1px solid #000;
    }

    button {
```

```
      margin-top: 2em;
      padding: 0.5em 1em;
    }
  </style>
</head>

<body>
  <h1>E-commerce Site</h1>

  <div id="products">
    <!-- Products will be added here by JavaScript -->
  </div>

  <h2>Shopping Cart</h2>
  <ul id="cart">
    <!-- Cart items will be added here by JavaScript -->
  </ul>

  <button id="checkout">Checkout</button>

  <!-- <script src="script.js"></script> -->

  <script>
    let products = [
      { id: 1, name: 'Product 1', price: 100 },
      { id: 2, name: 'Product 2', price: 200 },
      { id: 3, name: 'Product 3', price: 300 },
    ];

    let cart = [];

    // Display products
    products.forEach(product => {
      let productElement = document.createElement('div');
      productElement.className = 'product';

      let nameElement = document.createElement('h2');
      nameElement.innerText = product.name;
      productElement.appendChild(nameElement);

      let priceElement = document.createElement('p');
      priceElement.innerText = 'Price: $' + product.price;
      productElement.appendChild(priceElement);
```

```
    let buttonElement = document.createElement('button');
    buttonElement.innerText = 'Add to Cart';
    buttonElement.addEventListener('click', function () {
      addToCart(product);
    });
    productElement.appendChild(buttonElement);

    document.getElementById('products').appendChild(productEl
ement);
  });

  // Add to cart function
  function addToCart(product) {
    cart.push(product);

    let cartItemElement = document.createElement('li');
    cartItemElement.innerText = product.name + ': $' +
product.price;
    document.getElementById('cart').appendChild(cartItemElem
ent);
  }

  // Checkout function
  document.getElementById('checkout').addEventListener('click',
function () {
    if (cart.length > 0) {
      alert('Purchase made! Total cost: $' + cart.reduce((total,
product) => total + product.price, 0));
      cart = [];
      document.getElementById('cart').innerHTML = '';
    } else {
      alert('Your cart is empty!');
    }
  });

</script>
</body>

</html>

<!-- Creating a simplified e-commerce site with HTML, CSS, and
JavaScript is a great way to practice your web development skills!
Let's start with a basic version. Here's an outline of what we'll do:
```

474

Design the layout: This involves planning how the website will look. We'll need a list of products, a shopping cart, and a checkout button.

Create the HTML structure: Based on our design, we'll create the HTML structure.

Style the application with CSS: We'll then style our website to make it look good.

Add functionality with JavaScript: Finally, we'll add functionality. This includes adding products to the cart and simulating the purchase process. -->

<!-- This is a very basic example and doesn't include features like quantity selection, product images, categories, product descriptions, and so on. It also doesn't persist the cart contents if the page is refreshed, and the purchase process is simulated with an alert.

As you learn more about JavaScript and web development, you can start adding these features and more to your e-commerce site. You might also want to look into using a library or framework, such as React or Vue.js, which can make it easier to build complex interfaces.

Please note that building a real, production-quality e-commerce site involves a lot more than this, including backend programming, database management, user authentication, security considerations, payment processing, and much more. But this example should give you a good starting point for a basic, front-end only e-commerce site. -->

E-commerce Site

Shoes 1

Category: Shoes

Comfortable running shoes.

Price: $100

| 1 |

Add to Cart

Hat 1

Category: Hats

Stylish baseball cap.

Price: $50

| 1 |

Add to Cart

T-shirt 1

Shoes 2

Category: Shoes

Comfortable running shoes.

476

```
<!DOCTYPE html>
<html>

<head>
  <title>E-commerce Site</title>
  <style>
    body {
      font-family: Arial, sans-serif;
      background-color: #F0F8FF;
    }

    #products {
      display: flex;
      flex-wrap: wrap;
      justify-content: space-around;
    }

    .product {
      margin: 1em;
      padding: 1em;
      border: 1px solid #000;
      border-radius: 10px;
      background-color: #FFF8DC;
```

```
      width: 30%;
      text-align: center;
    }

    .product img {
      width: 70%;
    }

    button {
      margin: 1em;
      padding: 0.5em 1em;
      background-color: #87CEFA;
      border: none;
      border-radius: 5px;
    }

    #cart {
      margin: 2em;
    }

    #checkout {
      display: block;
      margin: auto;
      padding: 1em 3em;
      background-color: #FF7F50;
      color: white;
      border: none;
      border-radius: 5px;
      font-size: 1.2em;
    }
  </style>
</head>

<body>
  <h1 style="text-align: center; color: #008B8B;">E-commerce
Site</h1>

  <div id="products">
    <!-- Products will be added here by JavaScript -->
  </div>
  <hr>
  <h2 style="text-align: center; color: #008B8B;">Shopping
Cart</h2>
  <ul id="cart">
```

```html
    <!-- Cart items will be added here by JavaScript -->
  </ul>
  <hr>
  <button id="checkout">Checkout</button>
  <hr>

  <script>
    let products = [
      { id: 1, name: 'Shoes 1', price: 100, category: 'Shoes',
image: 'e-shoes1.png', description: 'Comfortable running
shoes.' },
      { id: 2, name: 'Hat 1', price: 50, category: 'Hats', image: 'e-
hat1.png', description: 'Stylish baseball cap.' },
      { id: 3, name: 'T-shirt 1', price: 20, category: 'Clothes',
image: 'e-tshirt1.jpg', description: 'Cotton t-shirt.' },
      { id: 4, name: 'Shoes 2', price: 100, category: 'Shoes',
image: 'e-shoes2.jpg', description: 'Comfortable running
shoes.' },
      { id: 5, name: 'Hat 2', price: 50, category: 'Hats', image: 'e-
hat2.jpg', description: 'Stylish baseball cap.' },
      { id: 6, name: 'T-shirt 2', price: 20, category: 'Clothes',
image: 'e-tshirt2.jpg', description: 'Cotton t-shirt.' },
      // ... more products ...
    ];

    let cart = [];

    // Display products
    products.forEach(product => {
      let productElement = document.createElement('div');
      productElement.className = 'product';

      let imgElement = document.createElement('img');
      imgElement.src = product.image;
      productElement.appendChild(imgElement);

      let nameElement = document.createElement('h2');
      nameElement.innerText = product.name;
      productElement.appendChild(nameElement);

      let categoryElement = document.createElement('p');
      categoryElement.innerText = 'Category: ' +
product.category;
      productElement.appendChild(categoryElement);
```

478

```javascript
    let descriptionElement = document.createElement('p');
    descriptionElement.innerText = product.description;
    productElement.appendChild(descriptionElement);

    let priceElement = document.createElement('p');
    priceElement.innerText = 'Price: $' + product.price;
    productElement.appendChild(priceElement);

    let quantityElement = document.createElement('input');
    quantityElement.type = 'number';
    quantityElement.value = 1;
    quantityElement.min = 1;
    quantityElement.id = `quantity_${product.id}`;
    productElement.appendChild(quantityElement);

    let buttonElement = document.createElement('button');
    buttonElement.innerText = 'Add to Cart';
    buttonElement.addEventListener('click', function () {
      let quantity =
document.getElementById(`quantity_${product.id}`).value;
      addToCart(product, quantity);
    });
    productElement.appendChild(buttonElement);

    document.getElementById('products').appendChild(productEl
ement);
  });

  // Add to cart function
  function addToCart(product, quantity) {
    cart.push({ ...product, quantity });

    let cartItemElement = document.createElement('li');
    cartItemElement.innerText = product.name + ' (' + quantity
+ '): $' + product.price * quantity;
    document.getElementById('cart').appendChild(cartItemElem
ent);
  }

  // Checkout function
  document.getElementById('checkout').addEventListener('click',
function () {
    if (cart.length > 0) {
```

```
      let total = cart.reduce((total, product) => total +
product.price * product.quantity, 0);
      alert('Purchase made! Total cost: $' + total);
      cart = [];
      document.getElementById('cart').innerHTML = '';
    } else {
      alert('Your cart is empty!');
    }
  });
  </script>
</body>

</html>

<!-- The code above adds quantity input for each product, as well
as images, descriptions, and categories. Products are also
displayed in a colorful way to make the site more vibrant.
-->
```

480

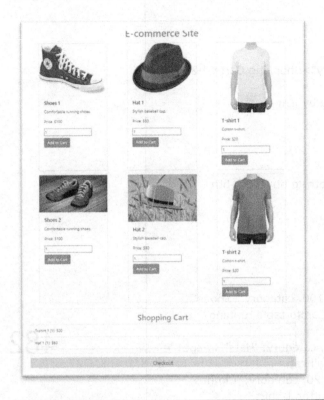

481

```
<!DOCTYPE html>
<html>

<head>
  <title>E-commerce Site</title>
  <link rel="stylesheet"
href="https://stackpath.bootstrapcdn.com/bootstrap/4.3.1/css/bo
otstrap.min.css">
  <script
src="https://ajax.googleapis.com/ajax/libs/jquery/3.4.1/jquery.m
in.js"></script>
</head>

<body class="container mt-3">
  <h1 class="text-center text-primary">E-commerce Site</h1>

  <div id="products" class="d-flex flex-wrap justify-content-
around">
    <!-- Products will be added here by jQuery -->
```

```html
  </div>

  <hr>

  <h2 class="text-center text-primary">Shopping Cart</h2>
  <ul id="cart" class="list-group">
    <!-- Cart items will be added here by jQuery -->
  </ul>

  <hr>

  <button id="checkout" class="btn btn-lg btn-block btn-
warning">Checkout</button>

  <hr>

  <script>
    let products = [
      { id: 1, name: 'Shoes 1', price: 100, category: 'Shoes',
image: 'e-shoes1.png', description: 'Comfortable running
shoes.' },
      { id: 2, name: 'Hat 1', price: 50, category: 'Hats', image: 'e-
hat1.png', description: 'Stylish baseball cap.' },
      { id: 3, name: 'T-shirt 1', price: 20, category: 'Clothes',
image: 'e-tshirt1.jpg', description: 'Cotton t-shirt.' },
      { id: 4, name: 'Shoes 2', price: 100, category: 'Shoes',
image: 'e-shoes2.jpg', description: 'Comfortable running
shoes.' },
      { id: 5, name: 'Hat 2', price: 50, category: 'Hats', image: 'e-
hat2.jpg', description: 'Stylish baseball cap.' },
      { id: 6, name: 'T-shirt 2', price: 20, category: 'Clothes',
image: 'e-tshirt2.jpg', description: 'Cotton t-shirt.' },
    ];

    let cart = [];

    $(document).ready(function () {
      // Display products
      products.forEach(product => {
        let productElement = $('<div/>', { "class": 'product card
m-2', "style": "width: 18rem;" }).appendTo('#products');
        $('<img/>', { "class": 'card-img-top', "src":
product.image }).appendTo(productElement);
```

482

```javascript
      let cardBody = $('<div/>', { "class": 'card-
body' }).appendTo(productElement);
      $('<h5/>', { "class": 'card-title', "text":
product.name }).appendTo(cardBody);
      $('<p/>', { "class": 'card-text', "text":
product.description }).appendTo(cardBody);
      $('<p/>', { "class": 'card-text', "text": 'Price: $' +
product.price }).appendTo(cardBody);
      let quantityInput = $('<input/>', { "type": "number",
"value": 1, "min": 1, "id":
`quantity_${product.id}` }).appendTo(cardBody);
      $('<button/>', { "class": 'btn btn-primary mt-2', "text":
'Add to Cart' }).click(function () {
        addToCart(product, quantityInput.val());
      }).appendTo(cardBody);
    });
  });

  // Add to cart function
  function addToCart(product, quantity) {
    cart.push({ ...product, quantity });

    let cartItemElement = $('<li/>', { "class": 'list-group-item',
"text": product.name + ' (' + quantity + '): $' + product.price *
quantity });
    $("#cart").append(cartItemElement);
  }
  // Checkout function
  $("#checkout").click(function () {
    if (cart.length > 0) {
      let total = cart.reduce((total, product) => total +
product.price * product.quantity, 0);
      alert('Purchase made! Total cost: $' + total);
      cart = [];
      $("#cart").empty();
    } else {
      alert('Your cart is empty!');
    }
  });
</script>
</body>
</html>
```

483

Weather Dashboard

| London | Search |

Current Weather for London

Temperature: 15.91°C

Weather: Clouds

Forecast for London

2023-07-21 00:00:00: 15.82°C, Clouds

2023-07-22 00:00:00: 14.8°C, Clouds

2023-07-23 00:00:00: 16.51°C, Rain

2023-07-24 00:00:00: 15.32°C, Clouds

2023-07-25 00:00:00: 13.52°C, Clouds

484

```html
<!DOCTYPE html>
<html>

<head>
  <title>Weather Dashboard</title>
  <!-- <link rel="stylesheet" type="text/css" href="styles.css"> -->
  <style>
    body {
      font-family: Arial, sans-serif;
    }

    form {
      margin-bottom: 2em;
    }

    #current-weather,
    #forecast {
      margin-top: 2em;
```

```
    }
  </style>
</head>

<body>
  <h1>Weather Dashboard</h1>

  <form id="search-form">
    <input type="text" id="search-input" placeholder="Search for
a city">
    <button type="submit">Search</button>
  </form>

  <div id="current-weather">
    <!-- Current weather will be inserted here by JavaScript -->
  </div>

  <div id="forecast">
    <!-- Weather forecast will be inserted here by JavaScript -->
  </div>

  <!-- <script src="script.js"></script> -->
  <script>
    // Replace this with your own API key
    let apiKey = '7608ff1b560bc531e31c2e640daee6**';

    document.getElementById('search-
form').addEventListener('submit', function (e) {
      e.preventDefault();

      let city = document.getElementById('search-input').value;
      getWeather(city);
    });

    function getWeather(city) {
      fetch('https://api.openweathermap.org/data/2.5/weather?q=
' + city + '&appid=' + apiKey + '&units=metric')
        .then(response => response.json())
        .then(data => {
          document.getElementById('current-weather').innerHTML
=
            '<h2>Current Weather for ' + data.name + '</h2>' +
            '<p>Temperature: ' + data.main.temp + '°C</p>' +
            '<p>Weather: ' + data.weather[0].main + '</p>';
```

```
        });

    fetch('https://api.openweathermap.org/data/2.5/forecast?q=
' + city + '&appid=' + apiKey + '&units=metric')
        .then(response => response.json())
        .then(data => {
          let forecastHTML = '<h2>Forecast for ' + city + '</h2>';
          for (let i = 0; i < data.list.length; i += 8) {
            forecastHTML +=
              '<p>' + data.list[i].dt_txt + ': ' +
data.list[i].main.temp + '°C, ' + data.list[i].weather[0].main +
'</p>';
          }
          document.getElementById('forecast').innerHTML =
forecastHTML;
        });
    }

  </script>
</body>

</html>

<!-- Building a weather dashboard is a great project to learn how
to work with APIs. For this, we'll be using the OpenWeatherMap
API. You will need to sign up for a free API key on their website:
https://openweathermap.org/

Here's an outline of what we'll do:

1. Design the layout: Plan how the dashboard will look like. You'll
need areas to display the current weather, the forecast, and a
search bar to find weather for different locations.

2. Create the HTML structure: Create the HTML structure based on
the design.

3. Style the application with CSS: Make the dashboard look good
with CSS.

4. Add functionality with JavaScript: Fetch weather data from the
API and display it on the page. Enable the search bar to fetch
weather data for different locations. -->
```

```
<!-- This is a very basic example and doesn't include error
checking, loading indicators, or detailed weather information. As
you learn more about JavaScript and web development, you can
add these features and more to your weather dashboard.

Remember that you'll need to replace 'your_api_key' with your
actual OpenWeatherMap API key. Also, the API requests in this
example are not secure because they are not using HTTPS, and
the API key is exposed in the client-side code, which is generally
not recommended. In a production application, you would want to
secure your API requests and hide your API key on the server
side. -->
```

Weather Dashboard

Seattle   Search

Current Weather for Seattle

Temperature: 29.22°C

Weather: Clear

Forecast for Seattle

2023-07-21 00:00:00: 29.29°C, Clear

2023-07-22 00:00:00: 28°C, Clear

2023-07-23 00:00:00: 28.37°C, Clear

2023-07-24 00:00:00: 24.53°C, Clouds

2023-07-25 00:00:00: 23.45°C, Clouds

488

```
<!DOCTYPE html>
<html>

<head>
  <title>Weather Dashboard</title>
  <link rel="stylesheet"
href="https://stackpath.bootstrapcdn.com/bootstrap/4.5.0/css/bo
otstrap.min.css">
  <script
src="https://ajax.googleapis.com/ajax/libs/jquery/3.5.1/jquery.m
in.js"></script>
</head>
```

```html
<body class="container">
  <h1 class="text-center my-4">Weather Dashboard</h1>

  <form id="search-form" class="form-inline justify-content-
center mb-4">
    <input type="text" id="search-input" class="form-control mr-
sm-2" placeholder="Search for a city">
    <button type="submit" class="btn btn-outline-primary my-2
my-sm-0">Search</button>
  </form>

  <div id="current-weather" class="card mb-4 p-4">
    <!-- Current weather will be inserted here by jQuery -->
  </div>

  <div id="forecast" class="card p-4">
    <!-- Weather forecast will be inserted here by jQuery -->
  </div>

  <script>
    // Replace this with your own API key
    let apiKey = '7608ff1b560bc531e31c2e640daee6**';

    $('#search-form').on('submit', function (e) {
      e.preventDefault();
      let city = $('#search-input').val();
      getWeather(city);
    });

    function getWeather(city) {
      fetch('https://api.openweathermap.org/data/2.5/weather?q=
' + city + '&appid=' + apiKey + '&units=metric')
        .then(response => response.json())
        .then(data => {
```

```
$('#current-weather').html(`
    <h2 class="card-title">Current Weather for
${data.name}</h2>
    <p class="card-text">Temperature:
${data.main.temp}°C</p>
    <p class="card-text">Weather:
${data.weather[0].main}</p>
    `);
});


fetch('https://api.openweathermap.org/data/2.5/forecast?q=
' + city + '&appid=' + apiKey + '&units=metric')
    .then(response => response.json())
    .then(data => {
    let forecastHTML = `<h2 class="card-title">Forecast for
${city}</h2>`;
    for (let i = 0; i < data.list.length; i += 8) {
        forecastHTML +=
        `<p class="card-text">${data.list[i].dt_txt}:
${data.list[i].main.temp}°C,
${data.list[i].weather[0].main}</p>`;
    }
    $('#forecast').html(forecastHTML);
    });
}
</script>
</body>

</html>
```

490

My Blog

Register Login

New Post

Title: [   ] Content: [   ]

[Post]

© 2023 My Blog

491

```html
<!DOCTYPE html>
<html>

<head>
  <title>My Blog</title>
  <!-- <link rel="stylesheet" type="text/css" href="styles.css"> --
>
  <style>
    body {
      font-family: Arial, sans-serif;
      margin: 0;
      padding: 0;
      box-sizing: border-box;
    }

    header {
      background-color: #f8f9fa;
      padding: 1em;
      border-bottom: 1px solid #dee2e6;
    }

    nav {
      margin-top: 1em;
    }

    nav a {
```

```css
      margin-right: 1em;
    }

    main {
      padding: 1em;
    }

    #blog-posts {
      margin-bottom: 2em;
    }

    #new-post-form {
      margin-top: 1em;
    }

    footer {
      background-color: #f8f9fa;
      padding: 1em;
      border-top: 1px solid #dee2e6;
      text-align: center;
      font-size: 0.8em;
    }

    button {
      margin: 20px;
    }
  </style>
</head>

<body>
  <header>
    <h1>My Blog</h1>
    <nav>
      <a href="/register">Register</a>
      <a href="/login">Login</a>
    </nav>
  </header>

  <main>
    <section id="blog-posts">
      <!-- Blog posts will be inserted here -->
    </section>

    <section id="new-post">
```

```html
    <h2>New Post</h2>
    <form id="new-post-form">
      <label for="title">Title:</label>
      <input type="text" id="title" required>

      <label for="content">Content:</label>
      <textarea id="content" required></textarea>
      <br>
      <button type="submit">Post</button>
    </form>
  </section>
</main>

<footer>
  &copy; 2023 My Blog
</footer>
</body>

</html>

<!-- This gives us a simple blog layout with a header, main
content area with a section for blog posts and a form to create a
new post, and a footer. The Register and Login links don't do
anything yet, and the form doesn't actually post anything because
we don't have a server-side to handle it.

Remember, this is just a starting point. You'll want to expand on
this to include features like displaying the logged-in user's name,
only showing the new post form to logged-in users, and so on. As
you learn more about HTML, CSS, and JavaScript, you can start
adding these features and more to your blog. -->
```

494

```
<!DOCTYPE html>
<html>

<head>
  <title>My Blog</title>
  <!-- <link rel="stylesheet" type="text/css" href="styles.css"> --
>
  <style>
    body {
      font-family: Arial, sans-serif;
      margin: 0;
      padding: 0;
      box-sizing: border-box;
      background-color: #f0f8ff;
      /* Light blue background */
      color: #333;
      /* Dark text color */
    }
```

```
header {
  background-color: #4682b4;
  /* Steel blue header */
  padding: 1em;
  border-bottom: 1px solid #dee2e6;
  color: #ffffff;
  /* White text color */
}

nav {
  display: flex;
  /* Align navigation items */
  justify-content: flex-end;
  /* Align items to the right */
  margin-top: 1em;
}

nav a {
  color: #ffffff;
  /* White link color */
  margin-right: 1em;
}

main,
section,
form {
  display: flex;
  /* Use Flexbox */
  flex-direction: column;
  /* Stack elements vertically */
  padding: 1em;
  gap: 1em;
  /* Add space between elements */
}

#new-post-form {
  margin-top: 1em;
}

footer {
  background-color: #4682b4;
  /* Steel blue footer */
  padding: 1em;
```

```
      border-top: 1px solid #dee2e6;
      text-align: center;
      font-size: 0.8em;
      color: #ffffff;
      /* White text color */
    }
  </style>
</head>

<body>
  <header>
    <h1>My Blog</h1>
    <nav>
      <a href="/register">Register</a>
      <a href="/login">Login</a>
    </nav>
  </header>

  <main>
    <section id="blog-posts">
      <!-- Blog posts will be inserted here -->
    </section>

    <section id="new-post">
      <h2>New Post</h2>
      <form id="new-post-form">
        <label for="title">Title:</label>
        <input type="text" id="title" required>

        <label for="content">Content:</label>
        <textarea id="content" required></textarea>

        <button type="submit">Post</button>
      </form>
    </section>
  </main>

  <footer>
    &copy; 2023 My Blog
  </footer>
</body>

</html>
```

```
<!-- You can use Flexbox to align items and add more colors to
your design. -->

<!-- In this updated CSS, I've added a light blue background to
the body and dark text color. The header and footer have a steel
blue background with white text. The navigation items are aligned
to the right using display: flex and justify-content: flex-end. In
the main section, I've used display: flex and flex-direction:
column to stack elements vertically and gap to add space between
elements.

Remember, these are just examples. You can customize the
colors, spacing, and alignment to suit your design preference. -->
```

My Blog

Register

Login

New Post

Title:

Content:

Post

© 2023 My Blog

498

```html
<!DOCTYPE html>
<html>

<head>
  <title>My Blog</title>

  <!-- Bootstrap CSS -->
  <link rel="stylesheet"
href="https://stackpath.bootstrapcdn.com/bootstrap/4.3.1/css/bo
otstrap.min.css">

  <style>
    body {
      font-family: Arial, sans-serif;
      padding: 0;
      box-sizing: border-box;
    }
```

```
  .navbar,
  .footer {
    background-color: #f8f9fa;
  }

  .new-post {
    margin-top: 1em;
  }

  .button {
    margin: 20px;
  }
  </style>
</head>

<body>
  <header>
    <nav class="navbar navbar-expand-lg">
      <h1 class="navbar-brand">My Blog</h1>
      <div class="navbar-nav ml-auto">
        <a class="nav-item nav-link"
href="/register">Register</a>
        <a class="nav-item nav-link" href="/login">Login</a>
      </div>
    </nav>
  </header>

  <main class="container">
    <section id="blog-posts" class="mt-3">
      <!-- Blog posts will be inserted here -->
    </section>

    <section class="new-post mt-3">
```

```
    <h2>New Post</h2>
    <form id="new-post-form">
      <div class="form-group">
        <label for="title">Title:</label>
        <input type="text" id="title" class="form-control"
required>
      </div>

      <div class="form-group">
        <label for="content">Content:</label>
        <textarea id="content" class="form-control" rows="3"
required></textarea>
      </div>

      <button type="submit" class="btn btn-primary
button">Post</button>
    </form>
  </section>
</main>

<footer class="footer py-3 text-center">
  &copy; 2023 My Blog
</footer>
</body>

</html>
```

500

Recipe App

Add Recipe

Name:

Ingredients:

Method:

Add Recipe

Classic Spaghetti with Tomato Sauce

Ingredients

Spaghetti pasta
Olive Oil
Onion
Tomatoes

Method

1. Bring a salted water to a boil.
2. Heat the olive oil in a saucepan.
3. Add the chopped onion,

Delete Recipe

501

```
<!DOCTYPE html>
<html>

<head>
  <title>Recipe App</title>
  <style>
    body {
      font-family: Arial, sans-serif;
      margin: 0;
      padding: 0;
      box-sizing: border-box;
      background-color: #f2f2f2;
    }

    nav {
      background-color: #333;
      position: fixed;
      top: 0;
      width: 100%;
      padding: 1em;
```

```css
  left: 0;
  color: white;
  text-align: center;
  z-index: 999;
}

.container {
  display: grid;
  grid-template-columns: 1fr 3fr;
  gap: 2em;
  margin: 5em;
}

form {
  display: grid;
  gap: 1em;
}

input[type="text"],
textarea {
  padding: .5em;
  border-radius: 5px;
  border: 1px solid #ccc;
}

button[type="submit"] {
  padding: 10px;
  background-color: #333;
  color: #fff;
  border: none;
  border-radius: 5px;
  cursor: pointer;
}

.delete-button {
  padding: 10px;
  background-color: #f00;
  color: #fff;
  border: none;
  border-radius: 5px;
  cursor: pointer;
```

502

```
      display: inline-block;
    }

    .recipe-card {
      border: 1px solid #ccc;
      padding: 1em;
      margin-bottom: 1em;
      background-color: #fff;
    }

    .recipe-card p {
      white-space: pre-wrap;
    }
  </style>
</head>

<body>
  <nav>
    <h1>Recipe App</h1>
  </nav>
  <div class="container">
    <div class="left-column">
      <h3>Add Recipe</h3>
      <form id="recipe-form">
        <label for="recipe-name">Name:</label>
        <input type="text" id="recipe-name" required>
        <label for="recipe-ingredients">Ingredients:</label>
        <textarea id="recipe-ingredients" rows="3"
required></textarea>
        <label for="recipe-method">Method:</label>
        <textarea id="recipe-method" rows="3"
required></textarea>
        <button type="submit">Add Recipe</button>
      </form>
    </div>
    <div class="right-column">
      <!-- Recipes will be displayed here -->
    </div>
  </div>

  <script>
```

```javascript
   const form = document.querySelector('form');
   const nameInput = document.querySelector('#recipe-name');
   const ingrInput = document.querySelector('#recipe-
ingredients');
   const methodInput = document.querySelector('#recipe-
method');
   const rightColumn = document.querySelector('.right-column');
   let recipes = [];

   function handleSubmit(event) {
     event.preventDefault();
     const name = nameInput.value.trim();
     const ingredients = ingrInput.value.trim().split(',').map(i =>
i.trim());
     const method = methodInput.value.trim();

     if (name && ingredients.length > 0 && method) {
       const newRecipe = { name, ingredients, method };
       recipes.push(newRecipe);
       nameInput.value = '';
       ingrInput.value = '';
       methodInput.value = '';
       displayRecipes();
     }
   }

   function displayRecipes() {
     rightColumn.innerHTML = '';
     recipes.forEach((recipe, index) => {
       const recipeHtml = `
         <div class="recipe-card">
           <h2>${recipe.name}</h2>
           <h3>Ingredients</h3>
           <p>${recipe.ingredients.join(', ')}</p>
           <h3>Method</h3>
           <p>${recipe.method}</p>
           <button class="delete-button" data-
index="${index}">Delete Recipe</button>
         </div>
       `;
       rightColumn.innerHTML += recipeHtml;
```

504

```
    });
    document.querySelectorAll('.delete-button').forEach(button
=> {
        button.addEventListener('click', deleteRecipe);
    });
    }

    function deleteRecipe(event) {
    const index = event.target.dataset.index;
    recipes.splice(index, 1);
    displayRecipes();
    }

    form.addEventListener('submit', handleSubmit);
  </script>
</body>

</html>
```

505

506

```
<!DOCTYPE html>
<html>

<head>
  <title>Recipe App</title>
  <style>
    body {
      font-family: sans-serif;
      background-color: #F8F2F4;
    }

    nav {
      background-color: #dc6c04;
      position: fixed;
      top: 0;
      width: 100%;
      padding: 20px;
      left: 0;
      color: white;
      text-align: center;
    }
```

```css
.container {
  display: flex;
  flex-direction: row;
  justify-content: space-between;
  margin: 150px 5%;
}

.left-column {
  width: 25%;
  background-color: #a2f6b3;
  padding: 20px;
  border-radius: 20px;
}

.right-column {
  width: 65%;
  background-color: #f3f8b4;
  padding: 20px;
  border-radius: 20px;
}

form {
  display: flex;
  flex-direction: column;
}

label {
  margin-bottom: 5px;
  font-weight: bold;
}

input[type="text"],
textarea {
  padding: 10px;
  margin-bottom: 10px;
  border-radius: 5px;
  border: 1px solid #ccc;
  width: 100%;
  box-sizing: border-box;
}

button[type="submit"] {
  padding: 10px;
  background-color: #1b29f5;
```

```css
  color: #fff;
  border: none;
  border-radius: 5px;
  cursor: pointer;
}

.recipe-card:nth-child(even) {
  margin-bottom: 20px;
  background-color: #f2f5f3;
}

.recipe-card:nth-child(odd) {
  margin-bottom: 20px;
  background-color: #dceff1;
}

.recipe-card {
  padding: 10px;
  border-radius: 10px;
}

.recipe-card h2 {
  color: #8f5805;
}

.recipe-card h3 {
  color: #119511;
}

.recipe-card p {
  color: #3c3c37;
}

.recipe-card button {
  margin: 10px;
  color: #fff;
  background-color: #f43b1f;
  border: none;
  border-radius: 5px;
  padding: 5px 10px;
  cursor: pointer;
}

.recipe-card p {
```

508

```
      white-space: pre-wrap;
    }
  </style>
</head>

<body>
  <nav>
   <h1>Recipe App</h1>
  </nav>
  <div class="container">
    <div class="left-column">
      <h3>Add Recipe</h3>
      <form>
        <label for="recipe-name">Name:</label>
        <input type="text" id="recipe-name" required>
        <label for="recipe-ingredients">Ingredients:</label>
        <textarea id="recipe-ingredients" rows="5"
required></textarea>
        <label for="recipe-method">Method:</label>
        <textarea id="recipe-method" rows="5"
required></textarea>
        <button type="submit">Add Recipe</button>
      </form>
    </div>
    <div class="right-column">
      <!-- Recipes will be displayed here -->
    </div>
  </div>

  <script>
    const form = document.querySelector('form');
    const nameInput = document.querySelector('#recipe-name');
    const ingrInput = document.querySelector('#recipe-
ingredients');
    const methodInput = document.querySelector('#recipe-
method');

    let recipes = JSON.parse(localStorage.getItem('recipes')) || [];

    window.onload = displayRecipes;

    form.addEventListener('submit', function (event) {
      event.preventDefault();
```

509

```javascript
    const name = nameInput.value.trim();
    const ingredients = ingrInput.value.trim().split(',').map(i =>
i.trim());
    const method = methodInput.value.trim();

    if (name && ingredients.length > 0 && method) {
      const newRecipe = { name, ingredients, method };
      recipes.push(newRecipe);

      localStorage.setItem('recipes', JSON.stringify(recipes));

      nameInput.value = '';
      ingrInput.value = '';
      methodInput.value = '';

      displayRecipes();
    }
  });

  function displayRecipes() {
    const rightColumn = document.querySelector('.right-
column');
    rightColumn.innerHTML = '';

    recipes.forEach((recipe, index) => {
      const recipeHtml = `
        <div class="recipe-card">
          <h2>${recipe.name}</h2>
          <h3>Ingredients</h3>
          <p>${recipe.ingredients.join(', ')}</p>
          <h3>Method</h3>
          <p>${recipe.method}</p>
          <button class="delete-button" data-
index="${index}">Delete Recipe</button>
        </div>
      `;

      rightColumn.innerHTML += recipeHtml;
    });

    document.querySelectorAll('.delete-button').forEach(button
=> {
      button.addEventListener('click', deleteRecipe);
    });
```

510

```
      }

   function deleteRecipe(event) {
      const index = event.target.dataset.index;

      recipes.splice(index, 1);

      localStorage.setItem('recipes', JSON.stringify(recipes));

      displayRecipes();
   }
  </script>
</body>

</html>

<!-- This version stores the recipes in localStorage so they persist
across page refreshes. It also has a more colorful style with
padding and border-radius to make the recipe cards look nicer. --
>

<!-- This code changes the color of each element inside
the .recipe-card to a different color. It also sets the background
color of the recipe cards to alternate between two different colors
depending on whether they are odd or even. This is done using
the :nth-child(even) and :nth-child(odd) selectors. -->
```

Fitness Tracker

Date: 연도-월-일 📅
Workout Type: [   ]
Duration (minutes): [   ]
[Log Workout]

2023-07-22: running for 20 minutes

2023-07-23: swimming for 30 minutes

2023-07-26: hiking for 60 minutes

512

```html
<!DOCTYPE html>
<html>

<head>
  <title>Fitness Tracker</title>
  <style>
    /* Add your custom CSS here */
  </style>
</head>

<body>
  <h1>Fitness Tracker</h1>

  <form id="workout-form">
    <label for="date">Date:</label>
    <input type="date" id="date" required>
    <br>
```

```html
    <label for="workout-type">Workout Type:</label>
    <input type="text" id="workout-type" required>
    <br>
    <label for="duration">Duration (minutes):</label>
    <input type="number" id="duration" required>
    <br>
    <button type="submit">Log Workout</button>
  </form>

  <div id="workout-log"></div>

  <!-- <script src="fitness-tracker.js"></script> -->

  <script>
    document.getElementById('workout-
form').addEventListener('submit', function (event) {
      // Prevent the form from submitting
      event.preventDefault();

      // Get the workout data
      var date = document.getElementById('date').value;
      var workoutType = document.getElementById('workout-
type').value;
      var duration = document.getElementById('duration').value;

      // Create a new workout log entry
      var logEntry = document.createElement('p');
      logEntry.textContent = date + ': ' + workoutType + ' for ' +
duration + ' minutes';

      // Add the log entry to the workout log
      document.getElementById('workout-
log').appendChild(logEntry);
```

```
    // Clear the form
    document.getElementById('date').value = '';
    document.getElementById('workout-type').value = '';
    document.getElementById('duration').value = '';
  });

  </script>
</body>

</html>

<!-- This is a basic example and does not include user
authentication, database storage, or data visualization. For a more
advanced application, you would likely need to learn additional
technologies, such as a backend framework (e.g., Node.js) and a
database system (e.g., MongoDB). -->

<!-- This will create a basic fitness tracker where users can log
their workouts by date, type, and duration. The workouts are
displayed in the workout log as soon as they are submitted. Note
that this application does not persist data, so the logs will be lost
if the page is refreshed. -->
```

Fitness Tracker

Date:

연도-월-일

Workout Type:

Duration (minutes):

Log Workout

2023-07-22: Jogging for 20 minutes

2023-07-23: Swimming for 30 minutes

2023-07-24: Aerobics for 30 minutes

2023-07-26: Yoga for 25 minutes

515

```
<!DOCTYPE html>
<html>

<head>
  <title>Fitness Tracker</title>
  <style>
   body {
     font-family: Arial, sans-serif;
     background-color: #f8f8f8;
     padding: 20px;
     color: #333;
   }

   h1 {
     text-align: center;
     color: #333;
```

```
    }

    form {
      display: flex;
      flex-direction: column;
      margin: auto;
      width: 50%;
      background-color: #fff;
      padding: 20px;
      border-radius: 10px;
      box-shadow: 0px 0px 10px rgba(0, 0, 0, 0.1);
    }

    label {
      margin-bottom: 10px;
      font-weight: bold;
    }

    input {
      margin-bottom: 20px;
      padding: 10px;
      border-radius: 5px;
      border: 1px solid #ccc;
      font-size: 16px;
    }

    button {
      padding: 10px;
      background-color: #007BFF;
      color: #fff;
      border: none;
      border-radius: 5px;
      cursor: pointer;
      font-size: 16px;
    }

    #workout-log {
      margin-top: 20px;
      width: 50%;
      margin: auto;
    }

    #workout-log p {
      padding: 10px;
```

```
      background-color: #fff;
      border-radius: 5px;
      margin-bottom: 10px;
      box-shadow: 0px 0px 10px rgba(0, 0, 0, 0.1);
    }
  </style>
</head>

<body>
  <h1>Fitness Tracker</h1>

  <form id="workout-form">
    <label for="date">Date:</label>
    <input type="date" id="date" required>

    <label for="workout-type">Workout Type:</label>
    <input type="text" id="workout-type" required>

    <label for="duration">Duration (minutes):</label>
    <input type="number" id="duration" required>

    <button type="submit">Log Workout</button>
  </form>

  <div id="workout-log"></div>

  <!-- <script src="fitness-tracker.js"></script> -->

  <script>
    document.getElementById('workout-
form').addEventListener('submit', function (event) {
      // Prevent the form from submitting
      event.preventDefault();

      // Get the workout data
      var date = document.getElementById('date').value;
      var workoutType = document.getElementById('workout-
type').value;
      var duration = document.getElementById('duration').value;

      // Create a new workout log entry
      var logEntry = document.createElement('p');
      logEntry.textContent = date + ': ' + workoutType + ' for ' +
duration + ' minutes';
```

517

```javascript
    // Add the log entry to the workout log
    document.getElementById('workout-
log').appendChild(logEntry);

    // Clear the form
    document.getElementById('date').value = '';
    document.getElementById('workout-type').value = '';
    document.getElementById('duration').value = '';
  });

 </script>
</body>

</html>
```

```
<!DOCTYPE html>
<html>

<head>
  <title>Music Player</title>
  <!-- <link rel="stylesheet" type="text/css" href="style.css"> --
>
  <style>
    body {
      display: flex;
      justify-content: center;
      align-items: center;
      height: 100vh;
      background-color: #f8f8f8;
    }

    #player {
      display: flex;
      flex-direction: column;
    }

    #controls {
      display: flex;
      justify-content: space-around;
      margin-top: 20px;
    }

    button {
      padding: 10px 20px;
      font-size: 16px;
```

```
      border: none;
      border-radius: 5px;
      cursor: pointer;
      background-color: #007BFF;
      color: #fff;
    }

    h2 {
      text-align: center;
    }
  </style>
</head>

<body>
  <div id="player">
    <h2>Music Player</h2>
    <audio id="audio" src="song.mp3"></audio>
    <div id="controls">
      <button id="play">Play</button>
      <button id="pause">Pause</button>
      <button id="skip">Skip</button>
      <button id="replay">Replay</button>
    </div>
  </div>
  <!-- <script src="script.js"></script> -->
  <script>
    window.onload = function () {
      var audio = document.getElementById('audio');
      var playButton = document.getElementById('play');
      var pauseButton = document.getElementById('pause');
      var skipButton = document.getElementById('skip');
      var replayButton = document.getElementById('replay');

      playButton.addEventListener('click', function () {
        audio.play();
      });

      pauseButton.addEventListener('click', function () {
        audio.pause();
      });

      skipButton.addEventListener('click', function () {
        audio.currentTime += 10;
      });
```

520

```
    replayButton.addEventListener('click', function () {
      audio.currentTime = 0;
      audio.play();
    });
  }

 </script>
</body>

</html>

<!-- I'll use a single song as an example.
```

Remember to replace song.mp3 in the src attribute of the audio tag with the path to your actual audio file. This simple music player has Play, Pause, Skip, and Replay functionality. The Skip button will move the audio forward by 10 seconds.

Please note that this is a very basic player. There's a lot more you can do with the HTML5 audio API, such as displaying the current time, adding a volume control, or creating a playlist. Feel free to expand upon this basic structure! -->

521

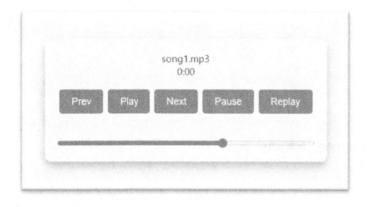

```
<!DOCTYPE html>
<html>
<head>
  <title>Music Player</title>
  <!-- <link rel="stylesheet" type="text/css" href="style.css"> --
>
  <style>
    body {
      display: flex;
      justify-content: center;
      align-items: center;
      height: 100vh;
      background-color: #fdf7f7;
    }
    #player {
      display: flex;
      flex-direction: column;
      align-items: center;
      box-shadow: 0px 8px 15px rgba(0, 0, 0, 0.3);
      padding: 20px;
      border-radius: 10px;
    }
    #controls {
      display: flex;
      justify-content: space-around;
      margin: 20px;
      width: 100%;
    }
```

522

```
    button {
      padding: 10px 20px;
      font-size: 16px;
      border: none;
      border-radius: 5px;
      cursor: pointer;
      background-color: #007BFF;
      color: #fff;
    }
    #volume {
      width: 100%;
      margin-top: 20px;
    }
  </style>
</head>
<body>
  <div id="player">
    <audio id="audio">
      <source id="source" src="song1.mp3">
    </audio>
    <div id="songTitle"></div>
    <div id="currentTime"></div>
    <div id="controls">
      <button id="prev">Prev</button>
      <button id="play">Play</button>
      <button id="next">Next</button>
      <button id="pause">Pause</button>
      <button id="replay">Replay</button>
    </div>
    <input type="range" id="volume" min="0" max="1"
step="0.01" value="1">
  </div>
  <!-- <script src="script.js"></script> -->
  <script>
    window.onload = function () {
      var audio = document.getElementById('audio');
      var source = document.getElementById('source');
      var playButton = document.getElementById('play');
      var nextButton = document.getElementById('next');
      var prevButton = document.getElementById('prev');
      var pauseButton = document.getElementById('pause');
      var replayButton = document.getElementById('replay');
      var volumeControl = document.getElementById('volume');
```

523

```javascript
    var currentTimeDisplay =
document.getElementById('currentTime');
    var songTitle = document.getElementById('songTitle');

    var songs = ['song1.mp3', 'song2.mp3', 'song3.mp3'];
    var currentSongIndex = 0;

    function loadSong() {
      source.src = songs[currentSongIndex];
      songTitle.textContent = songs[currentSongIndex];
      audio.load();
    }

    playButton.addEventListener('click', function () {
      audio.play();
    });

    nextButton.addEventListener('click', function () {
      currentSongIndex = (currentSongIndex + 1) %
songs.length;
      loadSong();
      audio.play();
    });

    prevButton.addEventListener('click', function () {
      currentSongIndex = (currentSongIndex - 1 +
songs.length) % songs.length;
      loadSong();
      audio.play();
    });

    pauseButton.addEventListener('click', function () {
      audio.pause();
    });

    replayButton.addEventListener('click', function () {
      audio.currentTime = 0;
      audio.play();
    });

    volumeControl.addEventListener('input', function () {
      audio.volume = this.value;
    });
```

524

```
    audio.ontimeupdate = function () {
      var minutes = Math.floor(audio.currentTime / 60);
      var seconds = Math.floor(audio.currentTime % 60);
      currentTimeDisplay.textContent = minutes + ':' + (seconds
< 10 ? '0' + seconds : seconds);
    }

    loadSong();
  }
  </script>
</body>
</html>
<!-- Here's an expanded version of the music player that includes
multiple songs, a volume control, and a current time display. -->

<!-- In this version, we've added a few features:
Multiple songs: The JavaScript keeps an array of songs and a
currentSongIndex to keep track of the current song. The Next and
Prev buttons will cycle through the songs.
Volume control: The input element with type="range" controls the
volume. As the user slides the control, the audio element's volume
property is updated.
Current time display: The ontimeupdate event of the audio
element is used to update a currentTimeDisplay element with the
current time of the song.
Remember to replace 'song1.mp3', 'song2.mp3', and 'song3.mp3'
with the paths to your actual audio files.

This player is still pretty basic and there's a lot more you can do!
Some ideas for further improvements could be adding a duration
display, a progress bar, or even fancy animations. Happy coding! -
->
```

525

song1.mp3

0:19

Prev | Play | Next | Pause | Replay

526

```html
<!DOCTYPE html>
<html>

<head>
  <title>Music Player</title>
  <!-- Link to Bootstrap CSS -->
  <link rel="stylesheet"
href="https://stackpath.bootstrapcdn.com/bootstrap/4.5.2/css/bo
otstrap.min.css">
</head>

<body class="d-flex align-items-center justify-content-center"
style="height: 100vh; background-color: #fdf7f7;">
  <div class="card text-center shadow" style="width: 18rem;">
    <div class="card-header" id="songTitle"></div>
    <div class="card-body">
      <audio id="audio" class="w-100">
        <source id="source" src="song1.mp3">
      </audio>
      <div id="currentTime" class="mt-3"></div>
      <div id="controls" class="d-flex justify-content-around mt-
3">
        <button id="prev" class="btn btn-primary">Prev</button>
        <button id="play" class="btn btn-danger">Play</button>
```

```html
      <button id="next" class="btn btn-
primary">Next</button>
      <button id="pause" class="btn btn-
warning">Pause</button>
      <button id="replay" class="btn btn-
primary">Replay</button>
    </div>
    <input type="range" id="volume" class="custom-range mt-
3" min="0" max="1" step="0.01" value="0.5">
  </div>
</div>

<!-- Link to jQuery and Bootstrap JavaScript -->
<script src="https://code.jquery.com/jquery-
3.5.1.slim.min.js"></script>
<script
src="https://stackpath.bootstrapcdn.com/bootstrap/4.5.2/js/boot
strap.bundle.min.js"></script>

<script>
  $(document).ready(function () {
    var audio = $('#audio')[0];
    var source = $('#source');
    var playButton = $('#play');
    var nextButton = $('#next');
    var prevButton = $('#prev');
    var pauseButton = $('#pause');
    var replayButton = $('#replay');
    var volumeControl = $('#volume');
    var currentTimeDisplay = $('#currentTime');
    var songTitle = $('#songTitle');

    var songs = ['song1.mp3', 'song2.mp3', 'song3.mp3'];
    var currentSongIndex = 0;

    function loadSong() {
      source.attr('src', songs[currentSongIndex]);
      songTitle.text(songs[currentSongIndex]);
      audio.load();
    }

    playButton.on('click', function () {
      audio.play();
    });
```

```javascript
    nextButton.on('click', function () {
      currentSongIndex = (currentSongIndex + 1) %
songs.length;
      loadSong();
      audio.play();
    });

    prevButton.on('click', function () {
      currentSongIndex = (currentSongIndex - 1 +
songs.length) % songs.length;
      loadSong();
      audio.play();
    });

    pauseButton.on('click', function () {
      audio.pause();
    });

    replayButton.on('click', function () {
      audio.currentTime = 0;
      audio.play();
    });

    volumeControl.on('input', function () {
      audio.volume = this.value;
    });

    audio.ontimeupdate = function () {
      var minutes = Math.floor(audio.currentTime / 60);
      var seconds = Math.floor(audio.currentTime % 60);
      currentTimeDisplay.text(minutes + ':' + (seconds < 10 ? '0'
+ seconds : seconds));
    }

    loadSong();
  });
  </script>
</body>

</html>
```

```
<!DOCTYPE html>
<html>

<head>
  <title>Quiz App</title>
  <!-- <link rel="stylesheet" href="style.css"> -->
  <style>
    body {
      display: flex;
      flex-direction: column;
      align-items: center;
      justify-content: center;
      height: 100vh;
      font-family: Arial, sans-serif;
    }

    #quiz {
      display: flex;
      flex-direction: column;
      margin-bottom: 20px;
    }

    button {
```

```
      margin-top: 10px;
      padding: 10px;
      font-size: 16px;
    }

    #scoreboard {
      margin-top: 20px;
      border: 1px solid #000;
      padding: 20px;
    }
  </style>
</head>

<body>
  <div id="quiz">
    <h1 id="question"></h1>
    <button id="btn0"></button>
    <button id="btn1"></button>
    <button id="btn2"></button>
    <button id="btn3"></button>
  </div>
  <div id="scoreboard">
    <h2>Scoreboard</h2>
    <p id="score"></p>
  </div>
  <button id="next">Next</button>
  <!-- <script src="script.js"></script> -->
  <script>
    var questions = [
      { question: "What is 2+2?", answers: ["4", "22", "222", "0"],
correct: 0 },
      { question: "What is the capital of France?", answers:
["Tokyo", "London", "Paris", "Berlin"], correct: 2 },
      { question: "What is 5*3?", answers: ["10", "15", "20",
"25"], correct: 1 },
      // Add more questions as needed
    ];

    var currentQuestion = 0;
    var score = 0;

    function loadQuestion() {
      if (currentQuestion < questions.length) {
```

530

```
      document.getElementById('question').innerText =
questions[currentQuestion].question;
       for (var i = 0; i < 4; i++) {
         document.getElementById('btn' + i).innerText =
questions[currentQuestion].answers[i];
       }
     } else {
       document.getElementById('quiz').style.display = 'none';
       document.getElementById('next').style.display = 'none';
     }
   }

   function checkAnswer(answer) {
     if (answer === questions[currentQuestion].correct) {
       score++;
       document.getElementById('score').innerText = "Score: " +
score;
     }
     currentQuestion++;
     loadQuestion();
   }

   for (var i = 0; i < 4; i++) {
     document.getElementById('btn' + i).addEventListener('click',
function (i) {
       return function () {
         checkAnswer(i);
       }
     }(i));
   }

   document.getElementById('next').addEventListener('click',
function () {
     currentQuestion++;
     loadQuestion();
   });

   loadQuestion();

 </script>
</body>

</html>
```

531

<!-- In this JavaScript code, we have an array of question objects. Each object has a question property, an answers array, and a correct property indicating the index of the correct answer in the answers array.

When the page loads, loadQuestion is called to load the first question and answers. When the user clicks an answer button, checkAnswer is called to check if the answer is correct and update the score if it is, then loadQuestion is called to load the next question.

If there are no more questions, loadQuestion hides the quiz and next button.

This is a very basic quiz app and there's a lot more you could add! Some ideas for further improvements could be adding a timer, allowing the user to select the number of questions, or adding different categories of questions. Happy coding! -->

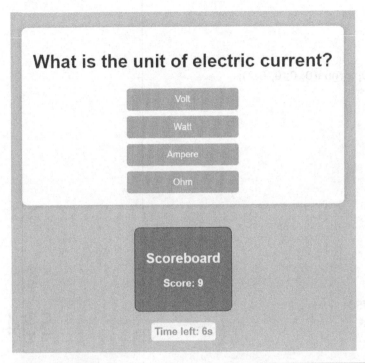

```
<!DOCTYPE html>
<html>

<head>
  <title>Quiz App</title>
  <style>
    body {
      display: flex;
      flex-direction: column;
      align-items: center;
      justify-content: center;
      height: 100vh;
      font-family: Arial, sans-serif;
      background-color: #fea204;
    }

    #quiz {
      display: flex;
      flex-direction: column;
```

```
  align-items: center;
  margin-bottom: 20px;
  background-color: #fff;
  padding: 20px;
  border-radius: 10px;
  box-shadow: 0px 0px 10px rgba(0, 0, 0, 0.2);
}

h1 {
  text-align: center;
  margin-bottom: 20px;
}

button {
  margin-top: 10px;
  padding: 10px;
  font-size: 16px;
  width: 200px;
  background-color: #4caf50;
  color: #fff;
  border: none;
  border-radius: 5px;
  cursor: pointer;
}

button:hover {
  background-color: #45a049;
}

#scoreboard {
  margin-top: 20px;
  border: 1px solid #000;
  padding: 20px;
  border-radius: 10px;
  background-color: #1058f5;
  color: white;
}

#score {
  text-align: center;
  font-size: 18px;
```

```
    font-weight: bold;
  }

  #next {
    display: none;
    margin-top: 20px;
  }

  #timer {
    margin-top: 20px;
    font-size: 18px;
    font-weight: bold;
    color: red;
    padding: 5px;
    border-radius: 5px;
    background-color: #fafafb;
  }
  </style>
</head>

<body>
  <div id="quiz">
    <h1 id="question"></h1>
    <button id="btn0"></button>
    <button id="btn1"></button>
    <button id="btn2"></button>
    <button id="btn3"></button>
  </div>
  <div id="scoreboard">
    <h2>Scoreboard</h2>
    <p id="score"></p>
  </div>
  <div id="timer"></div>
  <button id="next">Next</button>
  <script>
  var questions = [
    { category: "Math", question: "What is 2 + 2?", answers:
["4", "5", "6", "7"], correct: 0 },
    { category: "Geography", question: "What is the capital of
France?", answers: ["Tokyo", "London", "Paris", "Berlin"], correct:
2 },
```

{ category: "Math", question: "What is 5 * 3?", answers: ["10", "15", "20", "25"], correct: 1 },

{ category: "Science", question: "What is the chemical symbol for gold?", answers: ["Au", "Ag", "Fe", "Cu"], correct: 0 },

{ category: "History", question: "Who was the first President of the United States?", answers: ["Thomas Jefferson", "George Washington", "John Adams", "Abraham Lincoln"], correct: 1 },

{ category: "Science", question: "What is the largest planet in our solar system?", answers: ["Venus", "Mars", "Jupiter", "Saturn"], correct: 2 },

{ category: "History", question: "In which year did World War II end?", answers: ["1939", "1944", "1945", "1950"], correct: 2 },

{ category: "Geography", question: "What is the longest river in the world?", answers: ["Amazon River", "Nile River", "Yangtze River", "Mississippi River"], correct: 1 },

{ category: "Math", question: "What is the square root of 64?", answers: ["6", "7", "8", "9"], correct: 2 },

{ category: "Science", question: "What is the unit of electric current?", answers: ["Volt", "Watt", "Ampere", "Ohm"], correct: 2 },

{ category: "Geography", question: "Which country is home to the Great Barrier Reef?", answers: ["Australia", "Brazil", "India", "Canada"], correct: 0 },

{ category: "Science", question: "What is the chemical symbol for oxygen?", answers: ["O", "H", "C", "N"], correct: 0 },

{ category: "History", question: "Who painted the Mona Lisa?", answers: ["Leonardo da Vinci", "Pablo Picasso", "Vincent van Gogh", "Michelangelo"], correct: 0 },

{ category: "Math", question: "What is 10 divided by 2?", answers: ["3", "4", "5", "6"], correct: 2 },

{ category: "Geography", question: "What is the smallest country in the world?", answers: ["Vatican City", "Monaco", "Maldives", "Nauru"], correct: 0 },

{ category: "Science", question: "What is the largest organ in the human body?", answers: ["Heart", "Liver", "Lungs", "Skin"], correct: 3 },

{ category: "History", question: "Who wrote the play 'Romeo and Juliet'?", answers: ["William Shakespeare", "Charles Dickens", "Jane Austen", "Mark Twain"], correct: 0 },

```javascript
    { category: "Math", question: "What is the value of pi (π)?",
answers: ["3.14", "2.71", "1.62", "4.20"], correct: 0 },
    { category: "Geography", question: "Which city is known as
the 'Big Apple'?", answers: ["New York City", "Los Angeles",
"Chicago", "Houston"], correct: 0 },
    { category: "Science", question: "What is the freezing point
of water in Fahrenheit?", answers: ["32°F", "0°F", "100°F",
"212°F"], correct: 0 },
    { category: "History", question: "Which country was the first
to send a human to space?", answers: ["United States", "Russia",
"China", "Germany"], correct: 1 }
    // Add more questions as needed
  ];


  var currentQuestion = 0;
  var score = 0;
  var timer;
  var timeLeft = 10; // Default timer duration in seconds

  function startTimer() {
    clearInterval(timer);
    timeLeft = 10; // Reset timer duration
    document.getElementById('timer').innerText = "Time left: "
+ timeLeft + "s";
    timer = setInterval(function () {
      timeLeft--;
      document.getElementById('timer').innerText = "Time left: "
+ timeLeft + "s";
      if (timeLeft === 0) {
        clearInterval(timer);
        checkAnswer(-1); // Timeout answer
      }
    }, 1000);
  }

  function loadQuestion() {
    if (currentQuestion < questions.length) {
      document.getElementById('question').innerText =
questions[currentQuestion].question;
      for (var i = 0; i < 4; i++) {
```

537

```
        document.getElementById('btn' + i).innerText =
questions[currentQuestion].answers[i];
      }
      startTimer();
    } else {
      document.getElementById('quiz').style.display = 'none';
      document.getElementById('next').style.display = 'none';
      clearInterval(timer);
      document.getElementById('timer').innerText = "";
    }
  }

  function checkAnswer(answer) {
    clearInterval(timer);
    if (answer === questions[currentQuestion].correct) {
      score++;
      document.getElementById('score').innerText = "Score: " +
score;
    }
    currentQuestion++;
    loadQuestion();
  }

  for (var i = 0; i < 4; i++) {
    document.getElementById('btn' + i).addEventListener('click',
function (i) {
      return function () {
        checkAnswer(i);
      }
    }(i));
  }

  document.getElementById('next').addEventListener('click',
function () {
    currentQuestion++;
    loadQuestion();
  });

  loadQuestion();

  </script>
```

538

```
</body>

</html>

<!-- In this updated code, I've added categories to the questions
and introduced a timer feature. Each question is associated with a
category (e.g., Math, Geography, Science, History). The timer
starts with a default duration of 10 seconds for each question. If
the user does not answer within the given time, it will be
considered a timeout.

Feel free to add more questions to the questions array and
customize the design further to make it even more colorful and
visually appealing according to your preferences. -->
```

540

```html
<!DOCTYPE html>
<html>

<head>
  <title>Quiz App</title>
  <!-- Bootstrap CSS -->
  <link
href="https://stackpath.bootstrapcdn.com/bootstrap/4.3.1/css/bo
otstrap.min.css" rel="stylesheet">
</head>

<body class="bg-warning d-flex align-items-center justify-
content-center" style="height: 100vh;">
  <div class="card text-center p-4 shadow-sm">
    <h2 class="card-header" id="question"></h2>
    <div class="card-body">
      <button id="btn0" class="btn btn-primary m-1"></button>
      <button id="btn1" class="btn btn-primary m-1"></button>
      <button id="btn2" class="btn btn-primary m-1"></button>
      <button id="btn3" class="btn btn-primary m-1"></button>
    </div>
    <div class="card-footer text-muted">
      <h5 class="text-info" id="timer"></h5>
      <button id="next" class="btn btn-success m-1 d-
none">Next</button>
```

```
    <div id="scoreboard" class="alert alert-dark mt-2"
role="alert">
      <h4 class="alert-heading">Scoreboard</h4>
      <p id="score"></p>
    </div>
  </div>
</div>

<!-- jQuery and Bootstrap Bundle (includes Popper) -->
<script src="https://code.jquery.com/jquery-
3.4.1.slim.min.js"></script>
<script
src="https://stackpath.bootstrapcdn.com/bootstrap/4.3.1/js/boot
strap.bundle.min.js"></script>

<script>
  $(document).ready(function () {
    var questions = [
      { category: "Math", question: "What is 2 + 2?", answers:
["4", "5", "6", "7"], correct: 0 },
      { category: "Geography", question: "What is the capital of
France?", answers: ["Tokyo", "London", "Paris", "Berlin"], correct:
2 },
      { category: "Math", question: "What is 5 * 3?", answers:
["10", "15", "20", "25"], correct: 1 },
      { category: "Science", question: "What is the chemical
symbol for gold?", answers: ["Au", "Ag", "Fe", "Cu"], correct: 0 },
      { category: "History", question: "Who was the first
President of the United States?", answers: ["Thomas Jefferson",
"George Washington", "John Adams", "Abraham Lincoln"], correct:
1 },
      { category: "Science", question: "What is the largest planet
in our solar system?", answers: ["Venus", "Mars", "Jupiter",
"Saturn"], correct: 2 },
      { category: "History", question: "In which year did World
War II end?", answers: ["1939", "1944", "1945", "1950"], correct:
2 },
      { category: "Geography", question: "What is the longest
river in the world?", answers: ["Amazon River", "Nile River",
"Yangtze River", "Mississippi River"], correct: 1 },
      { category: "Math", question: "What is the square root of
64?", answers: ["6", "7", "8", "9"], correct: 2 },
```

```
      { category: "Science", question: "What is the unit of
electric current?", answers: ["Volt", "Watt", "Ampere", "Ohm"],
correct: 2 },
      { category: "Geography", question: "Which country is
home to the Great Barrier Reef?", answers: ["Australia", "Brazil",
"India", "Canada"], correct: 0 },
      { category: "Science", question: "What is the chemical
symbol for oxygen?", answers: ["O", "H", "C", "N"], correct: 0 },
      { category: "History", question: "Who painted the Mona
Lisa?", answers: ["Leonardo da Vinci", "Pablo Picasso", "Vincent
van Gogh", "Michelangelo"], correct: 0 },
      { category: "Math", question: "What is 10 divided by 2?",
answers: ["3", "4", "5", "6"], correct: 2 },
      { category: "Geography", question: "What is the smallest
country in the world?", answers: ["Vatican City", "Monaco",
"Maldives", "Nauru"], correct: 0 },
      { category: "Science", question: "What is the largest organ
in the human body?", answers: ["Heart", "Liver", "Lungs", "Skin"],
correct: 3 },
      { category: "History", question: "Who wrote the play
'Romeo and Juliet'?", answers: ["William Shakespeare", "Charles
Dickens", "Jane Austen", "Mark Twain"], correct: 0 },
      { category: "Math", question: "What is the value of pi
(π)?", answers: ["3.14", "2.71", "1.62", "4.20"], correct: 0 },
      { category: "Geography", question: "Which city is known as
the 'Big Apple'?", answers: ["New York City", "Los Angeles",
"Chicago", "Houston"], correct: 0 },
      { category: "Science", question: "What is the freezing point
of water in Fahrenheit?", answers: ["32°F", "0°F", "100°F",
"212°F"], correct: 0 },
      { category: "History", question: "Which country was the
first to send a human to space?", answers: ["United States",
"Russia", "China", "Germany"], correct: 1 }
      // Add more questions as needed
    ];
    var currentQuestion = 0;
    var score = 0;
    var timer;
    var timeLeft = 10; // Default timer duration in seconds

    function startTimer() {
      clearInterval(timer);
```

542

```javascript
    timeLeft = 10; // Reset timer duration
    $("#timer").text("Time left: " + timeLeft + "s");
    timer = setInterval(function () {
      timeLeft--;
      $("#timer").text("Time left: " + timeLeft + "s");
      if (timeLeft === 0) {
        clearInterval(timer);
        checkAnswer(-1); // Timeout answer
      }
    }, 1000);
  }

  function loadQuestion() {
    if (currentQuestion < questions.length) {
      $("#question").text(questions[currentQuestion].question)
;

      for (var i = 0; i < 4; i++) {
        $("#btn" +
i).text(questions[currentQuestion].answers[i]);
      }
      startTimer();
    } else {
      $("#quiz").css('display', 'none');
      $("#next").css('display', 'none');
      clearInterval(timer);
      $("#timer").text("");
    }
  }

  function checkAnswer(answer) {
    clearInterval(timer);
    if (answer === questions[currentQuestion].correct) {
      score++;
      $("#score").text("Score: " + score);
    }
    currentQuestion++;
    loadQuestion();
  }

  for (var i = 0; i < 4; i++) {
    $("#btn" + i).on('click', (function (i) {
      return function () {
```

```
            checkAnswer(i);
          }
        })(i));
      }

      $("#next").on('click', function () {
        currentQuestion++;
        loadQuestion();
      });

      loadQuestion();
    });
  </script>
</body>

</html>
```

```
<!DOCTYPE html>
<html>

<head>
  <title>Library Management System</title>
  <!-- <link rel="stylesheet" href="style.css"> -->
  <style>
    body {
      display: flex;
      flex-direction: column;
      align-items: center;
      font-family: Arial, sans-serif;
      padding: 20px;
    }

    .centered {
      display: flex;
      flex-direction: column;
      align-items: center;
      justify-content: center;
    }

    form {
```

```
      margin-bottom: 20px;
    }

    input,
    button {
      margin-top: 10px;
      padding: 10px;
      font-size: 16px;
    }
  </style>
</head>

<body>
  <div class="centered">
    <h1>Library Management System</h1>
    <form id="addBookForm">
      <input type="text" id="title" placeholder="Title" required>
      <input type="text" id="author" placeholder="Author"
required>
      <button type="submit">Add Book</button>
    </form>
  </div>
  <div id="bookList"></div>
  <!-- <script src="script.js"></script> -->
  <script>
    let library = [];

    document.getElementById("addBookForm").addEventListener(
"submit", function (event) {
      event.preventDefault();
      const title = document.getElementById("title").value;
      const author = document.getElementById("author").value;
      addBookToLibrary(title, author);
      displayBooks();
    });

    function addBookToLibrary(title, author) {
      library.push({ title: title, author: author, status:
'Available' });
    }

    function displayBooks() {
      const bookList = document.getElementById("bookList");
      bookList.innerHTML = '';
```

546

```
    for (let i = 0; i < library.length; i++) {
      const book = document.createElement("div");
      book.innerHTML = `<h2>${library[i].title}</h2>
                <h3>${library[i].author}</h3>
                <p>${library[i].status}</p>
                <button onclick="loanBook(${i})">Loan
Book</button>
                <button onclick="returnBook(${i})">Return
Book</button><hr>`;
      bookList.append(book);
    }
  }

  function loanBook(index) {
    library[index].status = 'Loaned Out';
    displayBooks();
  }

  function returnBook(index) {
    library[index].status = 'Available';
    displayBooks();
  }
 </script>
</body>
</html>
```

<!-- The issue here is that you're using height: 100vh on the body, which makes it occupy only the visible height of the viewport. When the content exceeds this height, it overflows but the body does not stretch to accommodate it. This can be fixed by removing the height: 100vh property.
Also, the use of justify-content: center is causing your form and title to be in the middle of the page, and move up as more books are added. I'd recommend moving these styles to a separate container if you want to keep the centered layout for the form and title, but don't want it to affect the book list. -->
<!-- In this update, I've wrapped the title and form in a div with the class centered, which applies the flex layout and centers them. The bookList is not part of this div, so it will start from where the form ends and will not push it upwards. I've also added some padding to the body to create some space around the content. -->

Library Management System

Book List:

Book Title:

Author:

Pages:

Status:

Available ▾

Add Book

RICH DAD POOR DAD

Author: Robert Kiyosaki

Pages: 345

Status: available

Delete

War and Peace

Author: LEO TOLSTOY

Pages: 1390

Status: loaned

Delete

548

```html
<!DOCTYPE html>
<html>

<head>
  <title>Library Management System</title>
  <style>
    body {
      display: flex;
      flex-direction: column;
      align-items: center;
      justify-content: center;
      font-family: Arial, sans-serif;
      padding: 20px;
      background-color: #f2f2f2;
    }

    .container {
      display: flex;
      align-items: flex-start;
      justify-content: space-between;
      width: 800px;
      max-width: 100%;
    }

    .left {
      width: 40%;
```

```
}

.right {
  width: 60%;
}

.centered {
  display: flex;
  flex-direction: column;
  align-items: center;
  justify-content: center;
}

form {
  margin-bottom: 20px;
}

input,
select,
button {
  margin: 10px;
  padding: 10px;
  font-size: 16px;
}

.book {
  margin: 10px 0;
  padding: 10px;
  border-bottom: 1px solid #ddd;
  background-color: #fff;
  box-shadow: 0px 0px 5px rgba(0, 0, 0, 0.2);
  border-radius: 5px;
}

.delete {
  background-color: #ff5252;
  color: #fff;
  border: none;
  border-radius: 5px;
  cursor: pointer;
}

.delete:hover {
  background-color: #e63946;
```

```
    }
  </style>
</head>

<body>
  <div class="container">
    <div class="left">
      <div class="centered">
        <h2>Library Management System</h2>
        <form id="book-form">
          <label for="title">Book Title:</label><br>
          <input type="text" id="title" name="title" required><br>
          <label for="author">Author:</label><br>
          <input type="text" id="author" name="author"
required><br>
          <label for="pages">Pages:</label><br>
          <input type="number" id="pages" name="pages"
required><br>
          <label for="status">Status:</label><br>
          <select id="status" name="status" required>
            <option value="available">Available</option>
            <option value="loaned">Loaned</option>
          </select><br>
          <input type="submit" value="Add Book">
        </form>
      </div>
    </div>
    <div class="right">
      <h2>Book List:</h2>
      <div id="book-list"></div>
    </div>
  </div>

  <script>
    document.getElementById("book-
form").addEventListener("submit", function (event) {
      event.preventDefault();

      const title = document.getElementById("title").value;
      const author = document.getElementById("author").value;
      const pages = document.getElementById("pages").value;
      const status = document.getElementById("status").value;

      const bookList = document.getElementById("book-list");
```

```javascript
      const bookDiv = document.createElement("div");
      bookDiv.className = "book";

      bookDiv.innerHTML = `
        <h3>${title}</h3>
        <p>Author: ${author}</p>
        <p>Pages: ${pages}</p>
        <p>Status: ${status}</p>
        <button class="delete">Delete</button>
      `;

      bookList.appendChild(bookDiv);
      // Clear the form
      document.getElementById("title").value = '';
      document.getElementById("author").value = '';
      document.getElementById("pages").value = '';
      document.getElementById("status").value = 'available';
    });
    // Delete book
    document.getElementById("book-
list").addEventListener("click", function (event) {
      if (event.target.className == "delete") {
        event.target.parentElement.remove();
      }
    });
  </script>
</body>
</html>
<!-- In this upgraded version, the layout has been modified to
place the book-form on the left side and the book-list on the right
side within a container element. The styles have been updated to
add colorful design elements, including a background color, box
shadows, and border radius.
Feel free to customize the styles further to match your desired
colorful design preferences. -->
```

```
<!DOCTYPE html>
<html>

<head>
  <title>Library Management System</title>
  <!-- Bootstrap CSS -->
  <link
href="https://stackpath.bootstrapcdn.com/bootstrap/4.3.1/css/bo
otstrap.min.css" rel="stylesheet">
</head>

<body class="bg-light">
  <div class="container py-5">
    <h2 class="text-center mb-4">Library Management
System</h2>
    <div class="row">
      <div class="col-md-6">
        <form id="book-form">
          <div class="form-group">
            <label for="title">Book Title:</label>
            <input type="text" id="title" class="form-control"
required>
```

```
        </div>
        <div class="form-group">
          <label for="author">Author:</label>
          <input type="text" id="author" class="form-control"
required>
        </div>
        <div class="form-group">
          <label for="pages">Pages:</label>
          <input type="number" id="pages" class="form-control"
required>
        </div>
        <div class="form-group">
          <label for="status">Status:</label>
          <select id="status" class="form-control" required>
            <option value="available">Available</option>
            <option value="loaned">Loaned</option>
          </select>
        </div>
        <button type="submit" class="btn btn-primary">Add
Book</button>
      </form>
    </div>
    <div class="col-md-6">
      <h3>Book List:</h3>
      <div id="book-list"></div>
    </div>
  </div>
</div>

<!-- jQuery and Bootstrap Bundle (includes Popper) -->
<script src="https://code.jquery.com/jquery-
3.4.1.slim.min.js"></script>
<script
src="https://stackpath.bootstrapcdn.com/bootstrap/4.3.1/js/boot
strap.bundle.min.js"></script>

<script>
  $(document).ready(function () {
    $("#book-form").on("submit", function (event) {
      event.preventDefault();

      var title = $("#title").val();
      var author = $("#author").val();
      var pages = $("#pages").val();
```

```
        var status = $("#status").val();

        var bookDiv = $('<div class="card mb-4 p-3">').html(`
          <h5 class="card-title">${title}</h5>
          <h6 class="card-subtitle mb-2 text-
muted">${author}</h6>
          <p class="card-text">Pages: ${pages}</p>
          <p class="card-text">Status: ${status}</p>
          <button class="btn btn-danger delete">Delete</button>
        `);

        bookDiv.find(".delete").on("click", function () {
          $(this).parent().remove();
        });

        $("#book-list").append(bookDiv);

        // Clear the form
        $("#book-form").trigger("reset");
      });
    });
  </script>
</body>

</html>

<!-- In this version, the script has been converted to use jQuery
for handling events and manipulating the DOM. When a book is
added, a Bootstrap card is created, and the delete button has an
event handler attached using jQuery's .on() method.

Bootstrap styles have been applied to the form and buttons to
give them a clean, modern look. Also, the form is reset using
$("#book-form").trigger("reset"); after a book is added.

As a result, your Library Management System will have a more
refined and responsive interface, with the functionality remaining
consistent. -->
```

```
<!DOCTYPE html>
<html>

<head>
  <title>Interactive Map</title>
  <link rel="stylesheet"
href="https://unpkg.com/leaflet@1.9.4/dist/leaflet.css"
    integrity="sha256-
p4NxAoJBhIIN+hmNHrzRCf9tD/miZyoHS5obTRR9BMY="
crossorigin="" />
  <script src="https://unpkg.com/leaflet@1.9.4/dist/leaflet.js"
    integrity="sha256-
20nQCchB9co0qIjJZRGuk2/Z9VM+kNiyxNV1lvTlZBo="
crossorigin=""></script>
</head>

<body>
  <h2>Interactive Map</h2>
  <div id="mapid" style="height: 600px;"></div>

  <script>
  var mymap = L.map('mapid').setView([51.505, -0.09], 13);

    L.tileLayer('https://tile.openstreetmap.org/{z}/{x}/{y}.png',
{
```

555

```
      maxZoom: 19,
      attribution: '&copy; <a
href="http://www.openstreetmap.org/copyright">OpenStreetMap
</a>'
    }).addTo(mymap);

    var marker = L.marker([51.5, -0.09]).addTo(mymap);
  </script>

</body>

</html>
```

<!-- The above coordinates are for London. Seoul is at latitude
37.541 degrees and longitude 126.986 degrees.
Let's try changing the coordinates for the 'mymap' at the top and
the 'marker' at the bottom of script. -->

<!-- Creating an interactive map with features like adding
markers, searching for locations, and displaying information based
on location typically involves using a mapping library or service,
such as Leaflet.js or Google Maps API. Here, I'll show you a basic
example using Leaflet.js, as it's an open-source library.

First, you need to include the Leaflet.js library and CSS in your
HTML file. -->

<!-- This code sets up a basic interactive map centered at the
coordinates [51.505, -0.09] with a zoom level of 13. The
L.tileLayer call adds the actual map imagery from Mapbox's
"streets" style. The L.marker call adds a marker to the map at the
coordinates [51.5, -0.09].

This is a very basic example. Creating a full-featured interactive
map with features like adding markers, searching for locations,
displaying information based on location etc. would require a more
in-depth understanding of the Leaflet.js library or the Google
Maps API, and possibly server-side programming to persist data
between sessions.

Here's what I've found:

1. Leaflet.js: Leaflet.js is a powerful open-source JavaScript
library for interactive maps. The library is designed to be

556

lightweight, easy to use, and mobile-friendly. It's very flexible and customizable, which makes it a good choice for your project. You can find a beginner's guide on how to use Leaflet.js to create an interactive map in the Leaflet.js tutorial.
https://leafletjs.com/examples/quick-start/

2. Google Maps JavaScript API: The Google Maps JavaScript API allows you to embed Google Maps in your website. The API provides a wide range of functionality, including the ability to add markers, search for locations, and display location-based information. Here is the official Google Maps JavaScript API tutorial.
https://developers.google.com/maps/documentation/javascript/overview?hl=ko

To achieve the functionality you're looking for (adding markers, searching for locations, displaying information based on location), you would need to use features from these libraries. I'd recommend checking out the official documentation for both Leaflet.js and the Google Maps JavaScript API for more information on how to implement these features. -->

558

```
<!DOCTYPE html>
<html>

<head>
  <title>Interactive Map</title>
  <link rel="stylesheet"
href="https://unpkg.com/leaflet@1.7.1/dist/leaflet.css" />
</head>

<body>
  <h2>Interactive Map</h2>
  <div id="map" style="height: 600px; width: 100%;"></div>
  <script
src="https://unpkg.com/leaflet@1.7.1/dist/leaflet.js"></script>

  <script>
    // Coordinates for Seoul, South Korea
    const seoul = [37.5665, 126.9780];

    // Initialize the map centered on Seoul with a zoom level of 13
    const map = L.map('map').setView(seoul, 13);
```

```
    // Add tile layer to the map (Map data © OpenStreetMap
contributors)
    L.tileLayer('https://{s}.tile.openstreetmap.org/{z}/{x}/{y}.p
ng', {
      attribution: '&copy; <a
href="https://www.openstreetmap.org/copyright">OpenStreetMa
p</a> contributors'
    }).addTo(map);

    // Add a marker for Seoul
    const marker = L.marker(seoul).addTo(map);

    // Add a popup to the marker
    marker.bindPopup('<b>Seoul</b><br>South
Korea').openPopup();
  </script>
</body>

</html>

<!-- This will create an interactive map centered on Seoul, South
Korea, and place a marker on it. When you click on the marker, a
popup will appear with the text "Seoul, South Korea".

To allow users to search for locations and add their own markers,
you will need to add more JavaScript and possibly use some
additional plugins or APIs. The Leaflet.js documentation provides
a lot of examples and tutorials that can help you with this.

If you want to display additional information based on location,
you might need to look into using a geocoding service or other
data source, and how to integrate that into your map. -->
```

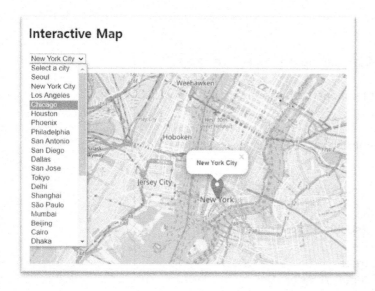

560

```
<!DOCTYPE html>
<html>

<head>
  <title>Interactive Map</title>
  <link rel="stylesheet"
href="https://unpkg.com/leaflet@1.7.1/dist/leaflet.css" />
  <script src="https://code.jquery.com/jquery-
3.5.1.min.js"></script>
</head>

<body>
  <h2>Interactive Map</h2>
  <select id="city-select">
    <option>Select a city</option>
  </select>
  <hr>
  <div id="map" style="height: 550px; width: 100%;"></div>
  <script
src="https://unpkg.com/leaflet@1.7.1/dist/leaflet.js"></script>

  <script>
    const cities = {
      "Seoul": [37.5665, 126.9780],
      "New York City": [40.7128, -74.0060],
```

```
    "Los Angeles": [34.0522, -118.2437],
    "Chicago": [41.8781, -87.6298],
    "Houston": [29.7604, -95.3698],
    "Phoenix": [33.4484, -112.0740],
    "Philadelphia": [39.9526, -75.1652],
    "San Antonio": [29.4241, -98.4936],
    "San Diego": [32.7157, -117.1611],
    "Dallas": [32.7767, -96.7970],
    "San Jose": [37.3382, -121.8863],
    "Tokyo": [35.6528, 139.8395],
    "Delhi": [28.7041, 77.1025],
    "Shanghai": [31.2304, 121.4737],
    "São Paulo": [-23.5505, -46.6333],
    "Mumbai": [19.0760, 72.8777],
    "Beijing": [39.9042, 116.4074],
    "Cairo": [30.0444, 31.2357],
    "Dhaka": [23.8103, 90.4125],
    "Mexico City": [19.4326, -99.1332],
    "Osaka": [34.6937, 135.5023],
    "Karachi": [24.8607, 67.0011],
    "Chongqing": [29.4316, 106.9123],
    "Istanbul": [41.0082, 28.9784],
    "Buenos Aires": [-34.6037, -58.3816],
    "Kolkata": [22.5726, 88.3639],
    "Lagos": [6.5244, 3.3792],
    "Rio de Janeiro": [-22.9068, -43.1729],
    "Manila": [14.5995, 120.9842],
    "Tianjin": [39.3434, 117.3616],
    "Jakarta": [-6.2088, 106.8456],
    // Add more cities as needed
  };

  // Initialize the map centered on Seoul with a zoom level of 13
  const map = L.map('map').setView(cities["Seoul"], 13);

  // Add tile layer to the map (Map data © OpenStreetMap
contributors)
  L.tileLayer('https://{s}.tile.openstreetmap.org/{z}/{x}/{y}.p
ng', {
    attribution: '&copy; <a
href="https://www.openstreetmap.org/copyright">OpenStreetMa
p</a> contributors'
  }).addTo(map);
```

561

```
    // Add a marker for Seoul
    let marker = L.marker(cities["Seoul"]).addTo(map);

    // Add a popup to the marker
    marker.bindPopup('<b>Seoul</b><br>South
Korea').openPopup();

    // Populate the select form with cities
    $.each(cities, function (key) {
      $('#city-select').append($('<option>', {
        value: key,
        text: key
      }));
    });

    // Change the map view and marker when a city is selected
    $('#city-select').on('change', function () {
      const city = this.value;
      const coordinates = cities[city];

      map.setView(coordinates, 13);
      marker.setLatLng(coordinates);
      marker.bindPopup(`<b>${city}</b>`).openPopup();
    });
  </script>
</body>

</html>
```

562

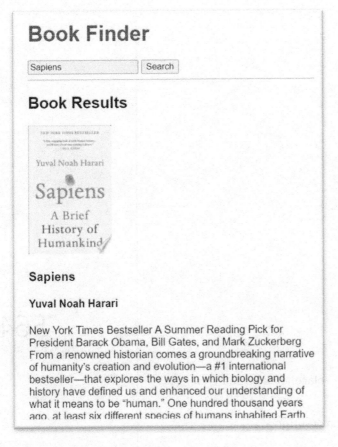

563

```
<!DOCTYPE html>
<html>

<head>
  <title>Book Finder</title>
  <!-- Insert your CSS link here -->
  <style>
    body {
      font-family: Arial, sans-serif;
      margin: 20px;
    }
```

```css
    #book-form {
      margin-bottom: 20px;
    }

    #result {
      margin-top: 20px;
    }

    h1 {
      color: blue;
    }

  </style>
</head>
```

564

```html
<body>
  <h1>Book Finder</h1>
  <form id="book-form">
    <input type="text" id="search" placeholder="Search for books">
    <button type="submit">Search</button>
    <hr>
  </form>
  <div id="result"></div>
  <!-- <script src="app.js"></script> -->
  <script>
    document.getElementById('book-form').addEventListener('submit', fetchBooks);

    function fetchBooks(e) {
      e.preventDefault();

      // Get the search term
      let searchTerm = document.getElementById('search').value;
```

```javascript
    // Call the Google Books API
    getBooks(searchTerm);
  }

  function getBooks(searchTerm) {
    let url =
`https://www.googleapis.com/books/v1/volumes?q=${searchTer
m}`;

    fetch(url)
      .then(response => response.json())
      .then(data => {
        let output = '<h2>Book Results</h2>';
        data.items.forEach(book => {
          let title = book.volumeInfo.title;
          let authors = book.volumeInfo.authors;
          let description = book.volumeInfo.description;
          let imgLink = book.volumeInfo.imageLinks ?
book.volumeInfo.imageLinks.thumbnail : "Image Not Available";

          output += `
          <div>
              <img src="${imgLink}" alt="book-image">
              <h3>${title}</h3>
              <h4>${authors}</h4>
              <p>${description}</p>
          </div><br>`;
        });
        document.getElementById('result').innerHTML = output;
      })
      .catch(err => console.log(err));
  }
```

565

```
  </script>
</body>

</html>

<!-- You can definitely create a book finder using HTML, CSS,
JavaScript, and the Google Books API.

Here's a basic example of how you can set this up:

1. Create your HTML structure. We'll create a simple form for the
book search and a div to display the results.

2. Create your CSS for styling. This is a very simple example.

3. In your JavaScript file, set up an event listener for the form
submission. When the form is submitted, prevent the default form
action, get the search term from the form input, and call a
function to search the Google Books API.

If you need further information, you can get it from following site.

https://developers.google.com/books/docs/v1/using?hl=ko#APIK
ey

This script fetches data from the Google Books API based on the
search term. The response from the API is processed and
displayed in the result div.

Note: Error handling is very basic in this example. In a real-world
application, you would want to enhance this, and also handle the
case where the search returns no results. -->
```

```
<!DOCTYPE html>
<html>

<head>
  <title>Book Finder</title>
  <link rel="stylesheet"
href="https://stackpath.bootstrapcdn.com/bootstrap/4.5.0/css/bo
otstrap.min.css">
  <script src="https://code.jquery.com/jquery-
3.5.1.min.js"></script>
  <style>
    body {
```

```
      font-family: Arial, sans-serif;
      padding: 20px;
    }
  </style>
</head>

<body>
  <div class="container">
    <h1 class="text-primary text-center">Book Finder</h1>
    <form id="book-form" class="form-inline">
      <input type="text" id="search" class="form-control mr-sm-
2" placeholder="Search for books">
      <button type="submit" class="btn btn-outline-success my-2
my-sm-0">Search</button>
    </form>
    <hr>
    <div id="result"></div>
  </div>

  <script>
    $('#book-form').on('submit', function (e) {
      e.preventDefault();

      // Get the search term
      let searchTerm = $('#search').val();

      // Call the Google Books API
      getBooks(searchTerm);
    });

    function getBooks(searchTerm) {
      let url =
`https://www.googleapis.com/books/v1/volumes?q=${searchTer
m}`;
```

568

```
    $.getJSON(url, function (data) {
      let output = '<h2 class="text-center">Book Results</h2>';
      data.items.forEach(book => {
        let title = book.volumeInfo.title;
        let authors = book.volumeInfo.authors;
        let description = book.volumeInfo.description;
        let imgLink = book.volumeInfo.imageLinks ?
book.volumeInfo.imageLinks.thumbnail : "Image Not Available";


        output += `
          <div class="media my-4">
            <img src="${imgLink}" class="mr-3" alt="book-
image">
            <div class="media-body">
              <h5 class="mt-0">${title}</h5>
              <h6>${authors}</h6>
              <p>${description}</p>
            </div>
          </div><hr>`;
      });
      $('#result').html(output);
    }).fail(function () {
      console.log("An error has occurred.");
    });
  }
  </script>
</body>

</html>
```

569

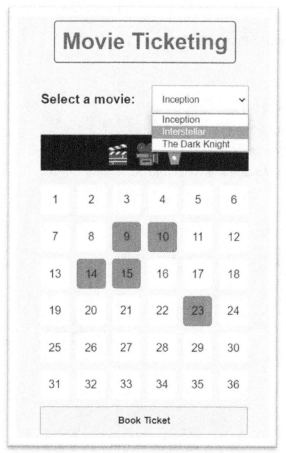

570

```
<!DOCTYPE html>
<html>

<head>
  <style>
    body {
      display: flex;
      justify-content: center;
      align-items: center;
      flex-direction: column;
      height: 100vh;
      margin: 0;
      background-color: #f5f5f5;
```

```
  font-family: Arial, sans-serif;
}

h1 {
  color: #4a4a4a;
  border: 2px solid #4a4a4a;
  padding: 10px;
  border-radius: 5px;
}

.movie-selection {
  display: flex;
  justify-content: space-between;
  width: 60vmin;
  margin-bottom: 20px;
}

.screen {
  width: 60vmin;
  height: 10vmin;
  margin-bottom: 20px;
  display: flex;
  justify-content: center;
  align-items: center;
  font-size: 2em;
  background-color: #000;
  color: #fff;
}

.container {
  display: grid;
  grid-template-columns: repeat(6, 1fr);
  grid-template-rows: repeat(6, 1fr);
  grid-gap: 10px;
  width: 60vmin;
  height: 60vmin;
}

.seat {
  display: flex;
  justify-content: center;
  align-items: center;
  background-color: #fff;
  cursor: pointer;
```

```
      border-radius: 5px;
    }

    .seat.selected {
      background-color: #f00;
    }

    select,
    button {
      padding: 10px;
      margin: 10px 0;
    }

    button {
      width: 60vmin;
    }
  </style>
</head>

<body>
  <h1>Movie Ticketing</h1>
  <div class="movie-selection">
    <label for="movie-select">
      <h3>Select a movie:</h3>
    </label>
    <select id="movie-select">
      <option>Inception</option>
      <option>Interstellar</option>
      <option>The Dark Knight</option>
    </select>
  </div>
  <div class="screen">🎬🍿🎟</div>
  <div class="container" id="seat-container"></div>
  <button id="book-button"><strong>Book
Ticket</strong></button>
  <hr>
  <script>
    // Number of seats in the grid
    const numSeats = 36;

    // Container for the seats
    const container = document.getElementById('seat-container');

    // Create seats and add them to the container
```

```
for (let i = 0; i < numSeats; i++) {
  const seat = document.createElement('div');
  seat.className = 'seat';
  seat.textContent = i + 1;
  container.appendChild(seat);
}

// Add event listener to each seat
document.querySelectorAll('.seat').forEach(seat => {
  seat.addEventListener('click', () => {
    seat.classList.toggle('selected');
  });
});

// Add event listener to the book button
document.getElementById('book-
button').addEventListener('click', () => {
  const selectedSeats =
document.querySelectorAll('.seat.selected');
  alert(`You've selected ${selectedSeats.length} seats for
${document.getElementById('movie-select').value}`);
});
</script>
</body>

</html>
```

Movie Ticketing

Select a movie: Inception

1	2	3	4	5	6
7	8	9	10	11	12
13	14	15	16	17	18
19	20	21	22	23	24
25	26	27	28	29	30
31	32	33	34	35	36

Book Ticket

Reset Selection

574

```
<!DOCTYPE html>
<html>

<head>
  <style>
    body {
      display: flex;
      justify-content: center;
      align-items: center;
      flex-direction: column;
      height: 100vh;
      margin: 0;
```

```css
  background-color: #f5f5f5;
  font-family: Arial, sans-serif;
}

h1 {
  color: #4a4a4a;
  border: 2px solid #4a4a4a;
  padding: 10px;
  border-radius: 5px;
}

.movie-selection {
  display: flex;
  justify-content: space-between;
  width: 60vmin;
  margin-bottom: 20px;
}

.screen {
  width: 60vmin;
  height: 10vmin;
  margin-bottom: 20px;
  display: flex;
  justify-content: center;
  align-items: center;
  font-size: 2em;
  background-color: #000;
  color: #fff;
  overflow: hidden;
}

.screen-content {
  display: inline-block;
  position: relative;
  animation: marquee 5s linear infinite;
}

@keyframes marquee {
  0% {
    transform: translateX(0%);
  }

  50% {
    transform: translateX(-50%);
```

```
      }
      100% {
        transform: translateX(0%);
      }
    }

    .container {
      display: grid;
      grid-template-columns: repeat(6, 1fr);
      grid-template-rows: repeat(6, 1fr);
      grid-gap: 10px;
      width: 60vmin;
      height: 60vmin;
    }

    .seat {
      display: flex;
      justify-content: center;
      align-items: center;
      background-color: #fff;
      cursor: pointer;
      border-radius: 5px;
    }

    .seat.selected {
      background-color: #f00;
    }

    select,
    button {
      padding: 10px;
      margin: 10px 0;
    }

    button {
      width: 60vmin;
    }
  </style>
</head>

<body>
  <h1>Movie Ticketing</h1>
  <div class="movie-selection">
```

```html
    <label for="movie-select">
      <h3>Select a movie:</h3>
    </label>
    <select id="movie-select">
      <option>Inception</option>
      <option>Interstellar</option>
      <option>The Dark Knight</option>
    </select>
  </div>
  <div class="screen">
    <div class="screen-content">🎬🍿🥤🎬🍿🥤</div>
  </div>
  <div class="container" id="seat-container"></div>
  <button id="book-button"><strong>Book
Ticket</strong></button>
  <button id="reset-button"><strong>Reset
Selection</strong></button>
  <hr>
  <script>
    // Number of seats in the grid
    const numSeats = 36;

    // Container for the seats
    const container = document.getElementById('seat-container');

    // Create seats and add them to the container
    for (let i = 0; i < numSeats; i++) {
      const seat = document.createElement('div');
      seat.className = 'seat';
      seat.textContent = i + 1;
      container.appendChild(seat);
    }

    // Add event listener to each seat
    document.querySelectorAll('.seat').forEach(seat => {
      seat.addEventListener('click', () => {
        seat.classList.toggle('selected');
      });
    });

    // Add event listener to the book button
    document.getElementById('book-
button').addEventListener('click', () => {
```

```
      const selectedSeats =
document.querySelectorAll('.seat.selected');
      alert(`You've selected ${selectedSeats.length} seats for
${document.getElementById('movie-select').value}`);
    });

    // Add event listener to the reset button
    document.getElementById('reset-
button').addEventListener('click', () => {
      document.querySelectorAll('.seat.selected').forEach(seat =>
{
        seat.classList.remove('selected');
      });
    });
  </script>
</body>

</html>

<!-- Here, a reset button is added just below the 'Book Ticket'
button. This new button will deselect all currently selected seats
when clicked. This is accomplished by adding a new event listener
to the reset button that removes the 'selected' class from all
seats. -->

<!-- Now the emojis on the screen move back and forth, creating
a simple animation. I've added a 'screen-content' div inside the
'screen' div to achieve this. The animation is controlled using the
'@keyframes' CSS rule with the name 'marquee'. -->
```

578

579

```
<!DOCTYPE html>
<html>

<head>
  <!-- <link rel="stylesheet" href="styles.css"> -->
  <style>
body {
  margin: 20px;
}

    h2 {
      color: #4a4a4a;
      border: 2px solid #4a4a4a;
      padding: 5px;
      border-radius: 5px;
      text-align: center;
      width: 200px;
    }

    .galleryImage {
      width: 100%;
```

```
      max-width: 200px;
      height: auto;
      cursor: pointer;
    }

    .modal {
      display: none;
      position: fixed;
      z-index: 1;
      padding-top: 100px;
      left: 0;
      top: 0;
      width: 100%;
      height: 100%;
      overflow: auto;
      background-color: rgba(0, 0, 0, 0.9);
    }

    .modal-content {
      margin: auto;
      display: block;
      width: 80%;
      max-width: 700px;
    }

    .close {
      position: absolute;
      top: 15px;
      right: 35px;
      color: #f1f1f1;
      font-size: 40px;
      font-weight: bold;
      transition: 0.3s;
    }

    .close:hover,
    .close:focus {
      color: #bbb;
      text-decoration: none;
      cursor: pointer;
    }
  </style>
</head>
```

```
<body>
  <h2>Image Gallery</h2>
  <div id="imageGallery">
    <img src="image1.jpg" alt="image1" class="galleryImage">
    <img src="image2.jpg" alt="image2" class="galleryImage">
    <img src="image3.jpg" alt="image3" class="galleryImage">
    <img src="image5.jpg" alt="image1" class="galleryImage">
    <img src="image6.jpg" alt="image2" class="galleryImage">
    <img src="image7.jpg" alt="image3" class="galleryImage">
    <!-- Add more images as needed -->
  </div>

  <div id="modal" class="modal">
    <span class="close">&times;</span>
    <img class="modal-content" id="img01">
    <div id="caption"></div>
  </div>

  <!-- <script src="script.js"></script> -->
  <script>
    const modal = document.getElementById('modal');
    const modalImg = document.getElementById('img01');
    const captionText = document.getElementById('caption');
    const galleryImages =
document.querySelectorAll('.galleryImage');
    const close = document.getElementsByClassName('close')[0];

    galleryImages.forEach(img => {
      img.onclick = function () {
        modal.style.display = "block";
        modalImg.src = this.src;
        captionText.innerHTML = this.alt;
      }
    });

    close.onclick = function () {
      modal.style.display = "none";
    };

  </script>
</body>

</html>
```

581

```
<!-- This is a basic example of a responsive image gallery that
allows users to view images in a modal/lightbox.

In this code, we have a gallery of images and a modal box. The
JavaScript code will open the modal box and display the clicked
image along with its alt text whenever a gallery image is clicked.
The modal box can be closed by clicking on the close button.

Please replace "image1.jpg", "image2.jpg", "image3.jpg" … with
actual image paths or URLs.

If you want to add features like sorting or filtering, you'll likely
need to use some additional JavaScript or a library that provides
those capabilities. For a more advanced or specific solution, you
might consider using a library or framework like jQuery or React. -
->
```

```
<!DOCTYPE html>
<html>

<head>
  <!-- <link rel="stylesheet" href="style.css"> -->
  <style>
   #menu {
     display: flex;
     flex-wrap: wrap;
     justify-content: space-around;
   }

   .menuItem {
     border: 1px solid #000;
     margin: 10px;
     padding: 10px;
```

```css
      width: calc(33.33% - 20px);
    }

    form {
      display: flex;
      flex-direction: column;
      max-width: 300px;
      margin: 0 auto;
    }

    input,
    button {
      margin-bottom: 10px;
    }

    h1 {
      color: #e1770c;
      text-align: center;
    }

  </style>
</head>
```

```html
<body>
  <h1>Menu Manager</h1>
  <div id="menu">
    <!-- Menu items will be rendered here -->
  </div>

  <form id="addItemForm">
    <input type="text" id="itemName" placeholder="Item name">
    <input type="text" id="itemCategory" placeholder="Item
category">
    <input type="text" id="itemPrice" placeholder="Item price">
    <button type="submit">Add Item</button>
  </form>

  <!-- <script src="script.js"></script> -->
  <script>
    let menu = [
      { name: 'Burger', category: 'main course', price: '$10' },
      { name: 'Salad', category: 'starter', price: '$5' },
      { name: 'Ice Cream', category: 'dessert', price: '$3' },
      // Add more items as needed
```

```
    ];

    function renderMenu() {
      const menuContainer = document.getElementById('menu');
      menuContainer.innerHTML = '';
      menu.forEach((item, index) => {
        const itemElement = document.createElement('div');
        itemElement.classList.add('menuItem');
        itemElement.innerHTML = `
      <h2>${item.name}</h2>
      <p>Category: ${item.category}</p>
      <p>Price: ${item.price}</p>
      <button
onclick="removeItem(${index})">Remove</button>
  `;
        menuContainer.appendChild(itemElement);
      });
    }

    function addItem(event) {
      event.preventDefault();
      const name = document.getElementById('itemName').value;
      const category =
document.getElementById('itemCategory').value;
      const price = document.getElementById('itemPrice').value;
      menu.push({ name, category, price });
      renderMenu();
    }

    function removeItem(index) {
      menu.splice(index, 1);
      renderMenu();
    }

    document.getElementById('addItemForm').addEventListener('s
ubmit', addItem);
    renderMenu();

  </script>
</body>

</html>
```

585

<!-- To create the Restaurant Menu Manager with the functionality
that a restaurant owner can add, update, and remove items from
their menu, you would need a back-end server and database to
store the menu items that the restaurant owner can modify.
However, for simplicity, we can create a mock-up of this project
using local JavaScript data.

Here's a basic layout using HTML/CSS for the page and some
simple JavaScript to demonstrate the idea. Please note that this is
a simplified version, and in a real-world scenario, you would also
need to handle form validation and display appropriate messages
to the user.

In this example, we have a list of menu items stored in the menu
array. We have a renderMenu function that creates HTML for each
menu item and appends it to the #menu div. The addItem
function is called when the form is submitted, and it adds a new
item to the menu. The removeItem function is used to remove
items from the menu.

Again, this is a simplified example and may not reflect a complete
and robust implementation suitable for a production environment.
For instance, the removal of items is simply based on the index in
this case, which might not be a good approach for a real-world
application.

Moreover, adding real backend support would need the use of
AJAX/fetch for server communication or the use of a full-stack
library/framework like Express.js for Node.js on the backend and
a library like React or Angular on the frontend. You would also
need to consider security and data validation, among other things.
-->

```
<!DOCTYPE html>
<html>

<head>
  <link rel="stylesheet"
href="https://stackpath.bootstrapcdn.com/bootstrap/4.3.1/css/bo
otstrap.min.css">
  <script src="https://code.jquery.com/jquery-
3.4.1.min.js"></script>
  <script
src="https://stackpath.bootstrapcdn.com/bootstrap/4.3.1/js/boot
strap.min.js"></script>
</head>

<body>
  <h1 class="text-center text-primary my-4">Menu
Manager</h1>
```

```
<div class="container">
  <div id="menu" class="row">
    <!-- Menu items will be rendered here -->
  </div>

  <form id="addItemForm" class="my-4">
    <div class="form-group">
      <input type="text" id="itemName" placeholder="Item
name" class="form-control">
    </div>
    <div class="form-group">
      <input type="text" id="itemCategory" placeholder="Item
category" class="form-control">
    </div>
    <div class="form-group">
      <input type="text" id="itemPrice" placeholder="Item
price" class="form-control">
    </div>
    <div class="form-group">
      <input type="text" id="itemImage" placeholder="Image
URL" class="form-control">
    </div>
    <button type="submit" class="btn btn-primary">Add
Item</button>
  </form>
</div>

<script>
  let menu = [
    { name: 'Burger', category: 'main course', price: '$10',
image: 'menu_burger.jpg' },
    { name: 'Salad', category: 'starter', price: '$5', image:
'menu_salad.jpg' },
    { name: 'Ice Cream', category: 'dessert', price: '$3', image:
'menu_icecream.jpg' },
  ];

  function renderMenu() {
    const menuContainer = $('#menu');
    menuContainer.html('');
    menu.forEach((item, index) => {
      const itemElement = $(`<div class="col-sm-4 my-2">
        <div class="card">
```

```
        <img src="${item.image}" class="card-img-top"
alt="${item.name}">
        <div class="card-body">
          <h5 class="card-title">${item.name}</h5>
          <p class="card-text">Category:
${item.category}</p>
          <p class="card-text">Price: ${item.price}</p>
          <button class="btn btn-danger remove-button" data-
index="${index}">Remove</button>
        </div>
      </div>
    </div>`);
    menuContainer.append(itemElement);
  });
  $('.remove-button').click(function () {
    const index = $(this).data('index');
    removeItem(index);
  });
  }

  $('#addItemForm').submit(function (event) {
    event.preventDefault();
    const name = $('#itemName').val();
    const category = $('#itemCategory').val();
    const price = $('#itemPrice').val();
    const image = $('#itemImage').val();
    menu.push({ name, category, price, image });
    $(this)[0].reset();
    renderMenu();
  });

  function removeItem(index) {
    menu.splice(index, 1);
    renderMenu();
  }

  renderMenu();
 </script>
</body>

</html>
```

589

590

```
<!DOCTYPE html>
<html>

<head>
  <title>Canvas Drawing App</title>
  <!-- <link rel="stylesheet" type="text/css" href="style.css"> --
>
  <style>
    body {
      display: flex;
      flex-direction: column;
      align-items: center;
    }

    canvas {
      border: 1px solid black;
      margin-top: 10px;
    }
  </style>
</head>

<body>
```

```html
<label for="colorPicker">Color:</label>
<input type="color" id="colorPicker">

<label for="brushSize">Brush Size:</label>
<input type="range" id="brushSize" min="1" max="100"
value="30">

<button id="clear">Clear</button>

<canvas id="drawArea" width="600" height="400"></canvas>

<!-- <script src="app.js"></script> -->
<script>
  const canvas = document.querySelector('#drawArea');
  const ctx = canvas.getContext('2d');

  let drawing = false;

  let brushColor = '#000000';
  let brushSize = 10;

  canvas.addEventListener('mousedown', start);
  canvas.addEventListener('mouseup', stop);
  canvas.addEventListener('mousemove', draw);

  document.querySelector('#colorPicker').addEventListener('cha
nge', changeColor);
  document.querySelector('#brushSize').addEventListener('chan
ge', changeSize);
  document.querySelector('#clear').addEventListener('click',
clearCanvas);

  function start(e) {
    drawing = true;
    draw(e);
  }

  function stop() {
    drawing = false;
    ctx.beginPath();
  }

  function draw(e) {
    if (!drawing) return;
```

```
    ctx.lineWidth = brushSize;
    ctx.lineCap = 'round';
    ctx.strokeStyle = brushColor;

    ctx.lineTo(e.clientX - canvas.offsetLeft, e.clientY -
canvas.offsetTop);
    ctx.stroke();
    ctx.beginPath();
    ctx.moveTo(e.clientX - canvas.offsetLeft, e.clientY -
canvas.offsetTop);
  }

  function changeColor(e) {
    brushColor = e.target.value;
  }

  function changeSize(e) {
    brushSize = e.target.value;
  }

  function clearCanvas() {
    ctx.clearRect(0, 0, canvas.width, canvas.height);
  }
  </script>
</body>
</html>
<!-- This is a basic example of a drawing app using HTML canvas
with the ability to change colors and brush sizes.
```

In this app, you can draw on the canvas by clicking and dragging the mouse. You can change the color of the brush with a color picker input and the size of the brush with a range input. There is also a Clear button to clear the canvas.

Saving the drawing as an image can be done by right-clicking on the canvas and choosing 'Save image as...', but implementing an actual save button would require server-side support to handle the image data, which goes beyond the scope of this simple example. -->

```
<!DOCTYPE html>
<html>

<head>
  <title>Canvas Drawing App</title>
  <style>
   :root {
     --primary-color: #3498db;
     --secondary-color: #2ecc71;
     --bg-color: #ecf0f1;
   }

   body {
     display: flex;
     flex-direction: column;
     align-items: center;
     justify-content: center;
     height: 100vh;
     background: var(--bg-color);
     background: linear-gradient(135deg, var(--primary-color),
var(--secondary-color));
     color: white;
```

```
      font-family: Arial, sans-serif;
    }

    label {
      margin: 10px;
    }

    input[type="range"],
    button {
      cursor: pointer;
      margin: 10px;
    }

    canvas {
      border: 2px solid white;
      border-radius: 5px;
    }

    #controls {
      display: flex;
      justify-content: center;
      margin-bottom: 10px;
    }
  </style>
</head>

<body>
  <h1>Canvas Drawing App</h1>

  <div id="controls">
    <label for="colorPicker">Color:</label>
    <input type="color" id="colorPicker">

    <label for="brushSize">Brush Size:</label>
    <input type="range" id="brushSize" min="1" max="100"
value="30">

    <button id="randomColor">Random Color</button>
    <button id="clear">Clear</button>
    <button id="save">Save</button>
  </div>

  <canvas id="drawArea" width="700" height="500"></canvas>
```

```
<script>
  const canvas = document.querySelector('#drawArea');
  const ctx = canvas.getContext('2d');

  let drawing = false;

  let brushColor = '#000000';
  let brushSize = 10;

  canvas.addEventListener('mousedown', start);
  canvas.addEventListener('mouseup', stop);
  canvas.addEventListener('mousemove', draw);

  document.querySelector('#colorPicker').addEventListener('change', changeColor);
  document.querySelector('#brushSize').addEventListener('change', changeSize);
  document.querySelector('#clear').addEventListener('click', clearCanvas);
  document.querySelector('#randomColor').addEventListener('click', randomColor);
  document.querySelector('#save').addEventListener('click', saveCanvas);

  function start(e) {
    drawing = true;
    draw(e);
  }

  function stop() {
    drawing = false;
    ctx.beginPath();
  }

  function draw(e) {
    if (!drawing) return;
    ctx.lineWidth = brushSize;
    ctx.lineCap = 'round';
    ctx.strokeStyle = brushColor;

    ctx.lineTo(e.clientX - canvas.offsetLeft, e.clientY - canvas.offsetTop);
    ctx.stroke();
    ctx.beginPath();
```

```
    ctx.moveTo(e.clientX - canvas.offsetLeft, e.clientY -
canvas.offsetTop);
  }

  function changeColor(e) {
    brushColor = e.target.value;
  }

  function changeSize(e) {
    brushSize = e.target.value;
  }

  function clearCanvas() {
    ctx.clearRect(0, 0, canvas.width, canvas.height);
  }

  function randomColor() {
    brushColor = '#' + Math.floor(Math.random() *
16777215).toString(16);
    document.querySelector('#colorPicker').value = brushColor;
  }

  function saveCanvas() {
    var link = document.createElement('a');
    link.download = 'drawing.png';
    link.href = canvas.toDataURL();
    link.click();
  }
 </script>
</body>
</html>
<!-- In this code, the saveCanvas function allows users to
download their drawings as PNG files. The randomColor function
changes the brush color to a random color when the 'Random
Color' button is clicked. -->
```

596

Markdown Previewer

```
# Hello World!
This is a sample markdown.
## This is a sub-heading
**This text will be bold**
_This text will be italic_
- This is a list item
[This is a link]
(http://www.example.com)
```
This is a code block
```
> This is a quote
```

Hello World!

This is a sample markdown.

This is a sub-heading

This text will be bold

This text will be italic

- This is a list item

This is a link

This is a code block

This is a quote

```
<!DOCTYPE html>
<html>

<head>
  <title>Markdown Previewer</title>
  <!-- <link rel="stylesheet" type="text/css" href="style.css"> -->
  <style>
    body {
      display: flex;
      flex-direction: column;
      align-items: center;
      justify-content: center;
      height: 100vh;
      margin: 10px;
      background-color: #f0f0f0;
      font-family: Arial, sans-serif;
    }

    h1 {
```

```css
    margin-bottom: 10px;
  }

  .container {
    display: flex;
    justify-content: space-between;
    width: 80%;
    height: 80%;
    background-color: #fff;
    padding: 20px;
    box-shadow: 0px 0px 10px rgba(0, 0, 0, 0.1);
  }

  #editor {
    width: 45%;
    height: 100%;
    padding: 10px;
    box-sizing: border-box;
    border: 1px solid #ddd;
  }

  #preview {
    width: 45%;
    height: 100%;
    padding: 10px;
    box-sizing: border-box;
    border: 1px solid #ddd;
    overflow-y: auto;
  }
</style>
<script
src="https://cdn.jsdelivr.net/npm/marked@3.0.8/marked.min.js"
defer></script>
```

```
</head>

<body>
  <h1>Markdown Previewer</h1>
  <div class="container">
    <textarea id="editor" placeholder="Write markdown
here..."></textarea>
    <div id="preview"></div>
  </div>
  <!-- <script src="app.js"></script> -->
  <script>
    const editor = document.getElementById('editor');
    const preview = document.getElementById('preview');

    editor.addEventListener('input', updatePreview);

    function updatePreview() {
      const markdown = editor.value;
      preview.innerHTML = marked(markdown);
    }

  </script>
</body>

</html>

<!-- This is a simple Markdown Previewer. The user can type
Markdown into the textarea, and the preview area updates in real-
time, rendering the Markdown as HTML.

Please note that this is a basic example and does not include any
handling for invalid Markdown. You would need to add error
handling in a production-level application. -->
```

<!-- Usage of Markdown Previewer :
1. You should see a split screen, with an input area (the textarea) on the left and a preview area on the right.

2. Click into the textarea on the left and start typing Markdown. Markdown is a lightweight markup language for creating formatted text. Here are a few basic examples of Markdown syntax:

Headers: # H1, ## H2, ### H3, etc.
Bold: **bold text**
Italic: *italicized text*
Bullet list: - item 1, - item 2, - item 3
Numbered list: 1. item 1, 2. item 2, 3. item 3
Link: [title](https://www.example.com)
Image: ![alt text](image.jpg)
Blockquote: > blockquote
Inline code: `code`
Code block: ```code```
Line Break: two spaces at the end of a line

3. As you type in Markdown on the left, you should see the right side of the screen automatically update with the formatted HTML.

Remember, the above code is a simple Markdown Previewer. For more complex Markdown syntax (like tables, footnotes, etc.), you may need to configure the marked.js library or use additional libraries. -->

```
<!DOCTYPE html>
<html>

<head>
  <title>Markdown Previewer</title>
  <style>
   body {
     display: flex;
     flex-direction: column;
     align-items: center;
     justify-content: center;
     height: 100vh;
     margin: 0;
     background-color: #f0f0f0;
     font-family: Arial, sans-serif;
   }

   h1 {
     margin-bottom: 10px;
```

```
}

.container {
  display: flex;
  justify-content: space-between;
  width: 80%;
  height: 80%;
  background-color: #fff;
  padding: 20px;
  box-shadow: 0px 0px 10px rgba(0, 0, 0, 0.1);
}

#editor {
  width: 45%;
  height: 100%;
  padding: 10px;
  box-sizing: border-box;
  border: 1px solid #ddd;
}

#preview {
  width: 45%;
  height: 100%;
  padding: 10px;
  box-sizing: border-box;
  border: 1px solid #ddd;
  overflow-y: auto;
}

#button-container {
  width: 80%;
  display: flex;
  justify-content: space-between;
  margin-top: 10px;
}

button {
  padding: 10px;
  cursor: pointer;
}

#instructions {
  width: 80%;
  margin-top: 10px;
```

```
      text-align: center;
    }
  </style>
  <script
src="https://cdn.jsdelivr.net/npm/marked@3.0.8/marked.min.js"
defer></script>
</head>

<body>
  <h1>Markdown Previewer</h1>
  <div class="container">
    <textarea id="editor" placeholder="Write markdown
here..."></textarea>
    <div id="preview"></div>
  </div>
  <div id="button-container"><button id="loadSample">Load
Sample</button>
    <button id="clear">Clear</button>
  </div>
  <div id="instructions">
    <p>You can use Markdown syntax to style your text. For
example, **bold text** will become <b>bold</b>, *italic text*
    will become <i>italic</i>, and so on. You can learn more
about Markdown syntax <a
      href="https://www.markdownguide.org/basic-syntax/"
target="_blank">here</a>.</p>
  </div>
  <script>
    const editor = document.getElementById('editor');
    const preview = document.getElementById('preview');

    editor.addEventListener('input', updatePreview);

    function updatePreview() {
      const markdown = editor.value;
      preview.innerHTML = marked(markdown);
    }

    document.getElementById('loadSample').addEventListener('cli
ck', loadSampleMarkdown);
    document.getElementById('clear').addEventListener('click',
clearMarkdown);

    function loadSampleMarkdown() {
```

```
    const sampleMarkdown = `
# Hello World!

This is a sample markdown.

## This is a sub-heading

**This text will be bold**

_This text will be italic_

- This is a list item

[This is a link](http://www.example.com)

\`\`\`
This is a code block
\`\`\`

> This is a quote
`;
    ;
    editor.value = sampleMarkdown;
    updatePreview();
  }

  function clearMarkdown() {
    editor.value = '';
    updatePreview();
  }

  </script>
</body>

</html>
```

<!-- This updated code contains two new features, each activated
by a button. The "Load Sample" button populates the editor with
some sample Markdown text. The "Clear" button erases all text
from both the editor and the previewer. -->

<!-- The sample Markdown above includes:

Header tags (using `#` and `##`)

Bold text (using `**`)
Italic text (using `_`)
Unordered list (using `-`)
Link (using `[]()` syntax)
Code block (using ``` syntax)
Blockquote (using `>`)

With this sample, users can learn how to use the basic syntax of
Markdown. -->

606

```
<!DOCTYPE html>
<html>

<head>
  <title>Markdown Previewer</title>
  <link rel="stylesheet"
href="https://maxcdn.bootstrapcdn.com/bootstrap/4.0.0/css/boot
strap.min.css">
  <script src="https://code.jquery.com/jquery-
3.5.1.slim.min.js"></script>
  <script
src="https://cdn.jsdelivr.net/npm/marked@3.0.8/marked.min.js"
></script>
</head>

<body class="p-5">
  <h1 class="text-center mb-4">Markdown Previewer</h1>
```

```html
<div class="container">
  <div class="row">
    <div class="col">
      <textarea id="editor" class="form-control" rows="15"
placeholder="Write markdown here..."></textarea>
    </div>
    <div class="col">
      <div id="preview" class="border p-3 h-100"></div>
    </div>
  </div>
  <div class="mt-3">
    <button id="loadSample" class="btn btn-primary">Load
Sample</button>
    <button id="clear" class="btn btn-secondary float-
right">Clear</button>
  </div>
</div>

<script>
  $(document).ready(function () {
    function updatePreview() {
      const markdown = $('#editor').val();
      $('#preview').html(marked(markdown));
    }

    $('#editor').on('input', updatePreview);

    $('#loadSample').on('click', function () {
      const sampleMarkdown = `
# Hello World!

This is a sample markdown.

## This is a sub-heading
```

```
**This text will be bold**

_This text will be italic_

- This is a list item

[This is a link](http://www.example.com)

\`\`\`
This is a code block
\`\`\`

> This is a quote
`;
    $('#editor').val(sampleMarkdown);
    updatePreview();
  });

  $('#clear').on('click', function () {
    $('#editor').val('');
    updatePreview();
  });
});
</script>
</body>

</html>
```

609

```
<!DOCTYPE html>
<html>

<head>
  <style>
   body {
     display: flex;
     flex-direction: column;
     align-items: center;
     justify-content: center;
     height: 100vh;
     background-color: #f2f2f2;
   }

   .currency-converter {
     display: flex;
     flex-direction: column;
     padding: 20px;
     background-color: white;
     border-radius: 5px;
     box-shadow: 0 0 10px rgba(0, 0, 0, 0.1);
```

```
      width: 300px;
    }

    .currency-converter input,
    .currency-converter select {
      margin: 10px 0;
      padding: 10px;
      border-radius: 5px;
      border: 1px solid #ccc;
    }

    #result {
      margin-top: 20px;
    }

    p {
      margin: 0;
      padding: 0;
    }
  </style>
</head>

<body>
  <h2>Currency Converter</h2>
  <div class="currency-converter">
    <p>Amount</p>
    <input type="number" id="amount" placeholder="Enter
amount">
    <p>From</p>
    <select id="from-currency">
      <!-- The option values will be filled with JavaScript -->
    </select>
    <p>To</p>
    <select id="to-currency">
      <!-- The option values will be filled with JavaScript -->
    </select>
    <button onclick="convertCurrency()">Currency
Convert</button>
    <p id="result"></p>
  </div>

  <script>
    const fromCurrencySelect = document.getElementById('from-
currency');
```

```
    const toCurrencySelect = document.getElementById('to-
currency');
    const amountInput = document.getElementById('amount');
    const resultParagraph = document.getElementById('result');
    let exchangeRates;

    // Fetch the latest exchange rates
    fetch('https://v6.exchangerate-
api.com/v6/aaf53da1eba53d98819909**/latest/USD')
      .then(response => response.json())
      .then(data => {
        exchangeRates = data.conversion_rates;

        // Populate the select elements with the currency options
        Object.keys(exchangeRates).forEach(currency => {
          fromCurrencySelect.innerHTML += `<option
value="${currency}">${currency}</option>`;
          toCurrencySelect.innerHTML += `<option
value="${currency}">${currency}</option>`;
        });
      });

    function convertCurrency() {
      const fromCurrency = fromCurrencySelect.value;
      const toCurrency = toCurrencySelect.value;
      const amount = amountInput.value;

      const result = amount / exchangeRates[fromCurrency] *
exchangeRates[toCurrency];
      resultParagraph.innerText = `${new
Intl.NumberFormat().format(amount)} ${fromCurrency} = ${new
Intl.NumberFormat().format(result)} ${toCurrency}`;
    }
  </script>
</body>

</html>

<!-- You can create a currency converter using HTML, CSS, and
JavaScript by connecting to a currency API. Please replace your-
api-key with your actual API key.

This code creates a simple currency converter. It fetches the
latest exchange rates from the ExchangeRate-API and populates
```

two select elements with the available currencies. When the "Convert" button is clicked, it gets the selected currencies and the entered amount, performs the conversion, and displays the result.

Remember to replace your-api-key with your actual API key. The Intl.NumberFormat object is used to format the result with a thousands separator.

This code only fetches the exchange rates once when the page is loaded. If you want to get the most recent rates every time you perform a conversion, you can move the fetch request into the convertCurrency function. Also, make sure you handle potential errors, such as a failed fetch request or invalid input. -->

Currency Converter

Amount

10000

From

USD

To

KRW

Currency Convert

Reverse Currencies

10,000 USD = 12,843,471 KRW

613

```
<!DOCTYPE html>
<html>

<head>
  <link rel="stylesheet"
href="https://maxcdn.bootstrapcdn.com/bootstrap/4.0.0/css/boot
strap.min.css">
</head>

<body class="bg-light d-flex flex-column justify-content-center
align-items-center h-100">
  <h2 class="mb-4">Currency Converter</h2>
  <div class="currency-converter bg-white p-4 rounded shadow">
    <div class="form-group">
      <label>Amount</label>
      <input type="number" id="amount" class="form-control"
placeholder="Enter amount">
```

```
    </div>
    <div class="form-group">
      <label>From</label>
      <select id="from-currency" class="form-control"></select>
    </div>
    <div class="form-group">
      <label>To</label>
      <select id="to-currency" class="form-control"></select>
    </div>
    <button onclick="convertCurrency()" class="btn btn-primary
btn-block">Currency Convert</button>
    <button onclick="reverseCurrencies()" class="btn btn-
secondary btn-block mt-2">Reverse Currencies</button>
    <p id="result" class="mt-3 text-center"></p>
  </div>

  <script>
    const fromCurrencySelect = document.getElementById('from-
currency');
    const toCurrencySelect = document.getElementById('to-
currency');
    const amountInput = document.getElementById('amount');
    const resultParagraph = document.getElementById('result');
    let exchangeRates;

    // Please replace your-api-key with your actual API key.
    fetch('https://v6.exchangerate-
api.com/v6/aaf53da1eba53d98819909**/latest/USD')
      .then(response => response.json())
      .then(data => {
        exchangeRates = data.conversion_rates;

        Object.keys(exchangeRates).forEach(currency => {
          fromCurrencySelect.innerHTML += `<option
value="${currency}">${currency}</option>`;
          toCurrencySelect.innerHTML += `<option
value="${currency}">${currency}</option>`;
        });
      });

    function convertCurrency() {
      const fromCurrency = fromCurrencySelect.value;
      const toCurrency = toCurrencySelect.value;
      const amount = Number(amountInput.value);
```

614

```javascript
    if (amount <= 0) {
      resultParagraph.innerText = "Please enter a positive
amount.";
      resultParagraph.className = 'text-danger';
      return;
    }

    const result = amount / exchangeRates[fromCurrency] *
exchangeRates[toCurrency];
    resultParagraph.innerText = `${new
Intl.NumberFormat().format(amount)} ${fromCurrency} = ${new
Intl.NumberFormat().format(result)} ${toCurrency}`;
    resultParagraph.className = '';
  }

  function reverseCurrencies() {
    const fromCurrency = fromCurrencySelect.value;
    const toCurrency = toCurrencySelect.value;

    fromCurrencySelect.value = toCurrency;
    toCurrencySelect.value = fromCurrency;

    convertCurrency();
  }
  </script>
</body>

</html>
```

<!-- This enhanced version of your application includes Bootstrap
for better user interface styling. A "Reverse Currencies" button is
added to swap the "from" and "to" currency values, and error
checking is added for the input amount to ensure it's a positive
number. -->

<!-- Please replace your-api-key with your actual API key. -->

Job Board

Comprador/a Material Indirecto (Temporal) (m/f/d) Apply Now	**Welder, Rail Manufacturing** Apply Now	**Senior Project Manager EPS - Syracuse(NY)** Apply Now
Abschlussarbeit (Bachelor) im Bereich industrielle Kommunikation - OPC UA - strukturierte Daten bis in die Cloud Apply Now	**DoD SkillBridge Internship - Technician/Specialist - Salt Lake City, UT** Apply Now	**Senior Electrical Engineer** Apply Now
Supplier Quality Engineer Apply Now	**Software Developer Power Electronics (f/m/d)** Apply Now	**IC Packaging Engineer, Silicon Technology (Starlink)** Apply Now

616

```
<!DOCTYPE html>
<html lang="en">

<head>
  <meta charset="UTF-8">
  <title>Job Board</title>
  <style>
    body {
      font-family: Arial, sans-serif;
      background-color: #f0f0f0;
      padding: 10px;
    }

    #job-list {
      display: flex;
      flex-wrap: wrap;
    }
```

```
    .job {
      background-color: #fff;
      padding: 10px;
      margin: 10px;
      border-radius: 5px;
      box-shadow: 0px 0px 10px rgba(0, 0, 0, 0.1);
      width: calc(25% - 20px);
    }


    .job h2 {
      margin: 0;
    }


    .job a {
      color: blue;
      text-decoration: none;
    }
  </style>
</head>

<body>
  <h1>Job Board</h1>
  <div id="job-list"></div>

  <script>
    fetch('https://www.themuse.com/api/public/jobs?page=1')
      .then(response => response.json())
      .then(data => {
        let jobList = document.getElementById('job-list');
        data.results.forEach(job => {
          let jobDiv = document.createElement('div');
          jobDiv.classList.add('job');
```

617

```
        jobDiv.innerHTML = `<h2>${job.name}</h2><a
href="${job.refs.landing_page}" target="_blank">Apply
Now</a>`;
        jobList.appendChild(jobDiv);
      });
    })
    .catch(error => console.error('Error:', error));
  </script>
</body>

</html>
```

<!-- GitHub has closed their jobs site in 2021. However, there are
many other job-related APIs available to use. One such API is The
Muse's job API, which you can find more details at
https://www.themuse.com/developers/api/v2. This is just an
example, and I'm sure there are many other options out there.

Thhis is an example of how you might use The Muse's API in your
code.

In this example, we're pulling the first page of jobs from The
Muse's API. The job's title is accessed via job.name and the job's
link is accessed via job.refs.landing_page.

Please note, depending on the API you choose, you may need to
adjust the URLs and property names accordingly. Also, be aware
that you may run into CORS (Cross-Origin Resource Sharing)
issues when using certain APIs directly from a front-end script. In
that case, you'd need to set up a back-end proxy to make the API
request. -->

Job Board

Software Developer	Data Analyst	Product Manager
New York	San Francisco	Austin
Apply Now	Apply Now	Apply Now

```
<!DOCTYPE html>
<html lang="en">

<head>
  <meta charset="UTF-8">
  <title>Job Board</title>
  <style>
    body {
      font-family: Arial, sans-serif;
      background-color: #f0f0f0;
      padding: 10px;
    }

    #job-list {
      display: flex;
      flex-wrap: wrap;
    }

    .job {
      background-color: #fff;
      padding: 10px;
      margin: 10px;
      border-radius: 5px;
      box-shadow: 0px 0px 10px rgba(0, 0, 0, 0.1);
      width: calc(25% - 20px);
    }

    .job h2 {
      margin: 0;
    }
```

619

```
    .job a {
      color: blue;
      text-decoration: none;
    }
  </style>
</head>

<body>
  <h1>Job Board</h1>
  <div id="job-list"></div>

  <script>

    fetch('https://my-json-server.typicode.com/SanghyunNa-
web/jobboard/jobs')
      .then(response => response.json())
      .then(data => {
        let jobList = document.getElementById('job-list');
        data.forEach(job => {
          let jobDiv = document.createElement('div');
          jobDiv.classList.add('job');
          jobDiv.innerHTML =
`<h2>${job.title}</h2><p>${job.location}</p><a
href="${job.url}" target="_blank">Apply Now</a>`;
          jobList.appendChild(jobDiv);
        });
      })
      .catch(error => console.error('Error:', error));
  </script>
</body>

</html>

<!-- First, sign up for GitHub and create an account. -->

<!-- Let's use My JSON Server which is a fake online REST API for
testing and prototyping. It's powered by JSON Server.

First, we'll create a db.json file. For example:

{
  "jobs": [
    {
```

620

```
    "id": 1,
    "title": "Software Developer",
    "location": "New York",
    "url": "https://www.example.com"
  },
  {
    "id": 2,
    "title": "Data Analyst",
    "location": "San Francisco",
    "url": "https://www.example.com"
  },
  {
    "id": 3,
    "title": "Product Manager",
    "location": "Austin",
    "url": "https://www.example.com"
  }
  // add more jobs as you wish (If you create this db.json file on
GitHub, delete the comment line on the left (add...wish).)
  ]
}
```

Now, let's say you host this on GitHub. The base URL for your API would be https://my-json-server.typicode.com/{your-username}/{your-repo}.

Now let's create our job board. Replace {your-username}/{your-repo} with your actual GitHub username and repository name.

This is a simple job board using a mock API. You might want to add more functionalities, such as search and filter, to make it more interactive.

Remember to replace {your-username} and {your-repo} with your actual GitHub username and repository name. -->

Travel Planner

Destination

연도-월-일 📅

Add Trip

Tokyo (2023-07-23) Delete

Hawaii (2023-07-29) Delete

Los Angeles (2023-08-05) Delete

622

```html
<!DOCTYPE html>
<html>

<head>
  <title>Travel Planner</title>
  <style>
    body {
      display: flex;
      justify-content: center;
      align-items: center;
      height: 100vh;
      margin: 0;
      background-color: #f0f0f0;
      font-family: Arial, sans-serif;
    }

    .container {
      display: flex;
      flex-direction: column;
      justify-content: center;
      align-items: center;
      padding: 20px;
      box-shadow: 0px 0px 10px rgba(0, 0, 0, 0.2);
      border-radius: 10px;
      width: 500px;
      background-color: #fff;
    }
```

```
    input {
      margin: 5px;
    }

    .trip {
      display: flex;
      justify-content: space-between;
      width: 100%;
      margin: 10px 0;
    }

    .trip button {
      margin-left: 10px;
    }
  </style>
</head>

<body>
  <div class="container">
    <h1>Travel Planner</h1>
    <input id="destination" type="text" placeholder="Destination"
/>
    <input id="date" type="date" />
    <button onclick="addTrip()">Add Trip</button>
    <div id="trips"></div>
  </div>

  <script>
    const trips = [];

    function addTrip() {
      const destination =
document.getElementById('destination').value;
      const date = document.getElementById('date').value;

      if (destination && date) {
        const trip = { destination, date };
        trips.push(trip);
        document.getElementById('destination').value = '';
        document.getElementById('date').value = '';
        renderTrips();
      } else {
        alert('Please enter a destination and date');
```

```
      }
    }

    function deleteTrip(index) {
      trips.splice(index, 1);
      renderTrips();
    }

    function renderTrips() {
      const tripsDiv = document.getElementById('trips');
      tripsDiv.innerHTML = '';
      trips.forEach((trip, index) => {
        tripsDiv.innerHTML += `<div
class="trip"><span>${trip.destination}
(${trip.date})</span><button
onclick="deleteTrip(${index})">Delete</button></div>`;
      });
    }
  </script>
</body>

</html>
```

624

```
<!-- Creating a Travel Planner can be quite complex, especially
when you want to suggest activities based on location. Here, I will
provide a simplified version of the travel planner that allows users
to add, view, and delete trips (destination and dates only) in a
list.

In this code, the user enters a destination and a date. When the
user clicks the 'Add Trip' button, these values are added to the
'trips' array, and the list of trips is re-rendered.

Note that this is a very basic example. You may want to add error
checking, such as ensuring the user doesn't enter a date in the
past, or a destination that doesn't exist. For a more advanced
app, you could use a mapping or location API to suggest activities
or locations. -->
```

```
<!DOCTYPE html>
<html>

<head>
  <title>Travel Planner</title>
  <style>
    body {
      display: flex;
      justify-content: center;
      align-items: center;
      height: 100vh;
      margin: 0;
      background-color: #f0f0f0;
      font-family: Arial, sans-serif;
    }

    .container {
      display: flex;
      flex-direction: column;
```

```
      justify-content: center;
      align-items: center;
      padding: 20px;
      box-shadow: 0px 0px 10px rgba(0, 0, 0, 0.2);
      border-radius: 10px;
      width: 500px;
      background-color: #fff;
    }

    input {
      margin: 5px;
    }

    .trip {
      display: flex;
      justify-content: space-between;
      width: 100%;
      margin: 10px 0;
    }

    .trip button {
      margin-left: 10px;
    }

    #map {
      height: 300px;
      width: 100%;
    }
  </style>

  <!-- load Google Maps JavaScript API -->
  <!-- <script
src="https://maps.googleapis.com/maps/api/js?key=YOUR_API_K
EY"></script> -->
  <script
src="https://maps.googleapis.com/maps/api/js?key=****SyAll1i
p-R2G9Sp9FXZ5Msr8OHThPoo****"></script>
</head>

<body>
  <div class="container">
    <h1>Travel Planner</h1>
    <input id="destination" type="text" placeholder="Destination"
/>
```

```
    <input id="date" type="date" />
    <button onclick="addTrip()">Add Trip</button>
    <div id="trips"></div>
    <div id="map"></div>
  </div>

  <script>
    let map;
    const trips = [];

    function initMap() {
      const center = { lat: 0, lng: 0 };
      map = new
google.maps.Map(document.getElementById('map'), {
        center,
        zoom: 2,
      });
    }

    function addTrip() {
      const destination =
document.getElementById('destination').value;
      const date = document.getElementById('date').value;

      if (destination && date) {
        const trip = { destination, date };
        trips.push(trip);
        document.getElementById('destination').value = '';
        document.getElementById('date').value = '';
        renderTrips();
      } else {
        alert('Please enter a destination and date');
      }

      //
fetch(`https://maps.googleapis.com/maps/api/geocode/json?addr
ess=${destination}&key=YOUR_API_KEY`)
      fetch(`https://maps.googleapis.com/maps/api/geocode/json
?address=${destination}&key=****SyAll1ip-
R2G9Sp9FXZ5Msr8OHThPoo****`)
        .then(response => response.json())
        .then(data => {
          if (data.results[0]) {
            const location = data.results[0].geometry.location;
```

627

```
        map.setCenter(new google.maps.LatLng(location.lat,
location.lng));
            new google.maps.Marker({
              position: location,
              map: map,
            });
          }
        });
      }

    function deleteTrip(index) {
      trips.splice(index, 1);
      renderTrips();
    }

    function renderTrips() {
      const tripsDiv = document.getElementById('trips');
      tripsDiv.innerHTML = '';
      trips.forEach((trip, index) => {
        tripsDiv.innerHTML += `<div
class="trip"><span>${trip.destination}
(${trip.date})</span><button
onclick="deleteTrip(${index})">Delete</button></div>`;
      });
    }

    window.onload = initMap;
  </script>
</body>
</html>
```

628

<!-- Integrating a location or mapping API could greatly improve
your travel planner app. For example, you could use the Google
Places API to suggest popular attractions or activities based on the
entered destination. Google Maps JavaScript API could be used to
show a visual map of the destination.
This is a simple example of how you could integrate Google Maps
into your existing code to display a map of the destination.
Please replace YOUR_API_KEY with your actual API key. This
example uses the Google Maps Geocoding API to convert the
destination into latitude and longitude coordinates, which are then
used to center the map and add a marker.

In a real-world application, you would also want to handle errors and edge cases, like what happens if the geocoding API can't find the destination.

Please note that using Google Maps API services are not free and you would need to have billing enabled for your Google Cloud project. For more details, check their pricing details. -->

<!-- "API keys with referer restrictions cannot be used with this API."

This error means that your current API key is set up with HTTP referer restrictions. HTTP referers are a security measure to ensure that your API key is only used on specific websites or pages. However, some APIs, like the Geocoding API used here, do not accept API keys with referer restrictions.

Here is what you can do to solve this issue:

Go to the Google Cloud Platform Console: https://console.cloud.google.com/.

Click the project drop-down and select or create the project that you have used to generate your API key.

From the menu bar, go to APIs & Services > Credentials.

On the Credentials page, look for the API key that you are using in your request.

Click the edit (pencil) button.

Under Key restrictions > Application restrictions, select the "None" option. If you select the "None" option, be aware that your key will work with any APIs that you have enabled and can be used from any referrer. This can make your application more vulnerable.

Click the Save button at the bottom of the page.

After making these changes, please try again with your request. If you're still facing issues, you might want to consider creating a new unrestricted API key to test if the problem persists.

Remember to secure your API keys to prevent unauthorized usage. For production applications, it's not recommended to leave the API key unrestricted. Instead, set up a backend server to make secure calls to Google APIs. -->

629

```
<!DOCTYPE html>
<html>

<head>
  <title>Virtual Pet Game</title>
  <style>
    body {
      display: flex;
      flex-direction: column;
      align-items: center;
      justify-content: center;
      height: 100vh;
      background-color: #f5f5f5;
      font-family: Arial, sans-serif;
    }

    .pet {
      font-size: 100px;
    }

    .controls {
      display: flex;
```

```
      justify-content: space-around;
      width: 100%;
    }

    .controls button {
      padding: 10px 20px;
      font-size: 20px;
      border-radius: 5px;
      border: none;
      background-color: #007BFF;
      color: #fff;
      cursor: pointer;
    }

    .controls button:disabled {
      background-color: #ccc;
    }
  </style>
</head>

<body>
  <!-- To find an emoji, press the Windows key and period at the
same time, then click on the emoji you want. -->
  <div class="pet">🐶</div>
  <div class="controls">
    <button onclick="feedPet()">Feed</button>
    <button onclick="playWithPet()">Play</button>
  </div>
  <p>The status of the pet dog can be observed in the console
window.</p>
  <p>(Windows: Press either `Ctrl + Shift + J` or `F12`)<br>
  (Mac: Press `Cmd + Option + J`)</p>
  <script>
    let petHunger = 0;
    let petBoredom = 0;

    // The status of the pet dog can be observed in the console
window. This method is inconvenient and needs to be improved.
    function feedPet() {
      petHunger -= 10;
      if (petHunger < 0) petHunger = 0;
      console.log(`Pet hunger: ${petHunger}`);
    }
```

631

```
    function playWithPet() {
      petBoredom -= 10;
      if (petBoredom < 0) petBoredom = 0;
      console.log(`Pet boredom: ${petBoredom}`);
    }

    setInterval(() => {
      petHunger += 1;
      petBoredom += 1;
      if (petHunger > 50 || petBoredom > 50) {
        console.log("Your pet is unhappy. Please feed or play with
your pet.");
      }
    }, 1000);
  </script>
</body>

</html>

<!-- Building a fully featured virtual pet game can be quite
complex, but I'll help you get started with a basic version that
includes feeding and playing with the pet. Here is the basic
structure in HTML, CSS, and JavaScript.

In this basic example, your virtual pet gets hungrier and more
bored every second. If either value goes over 50, the console will
display a message asking you to take care of your pet. You can
feed or play with your pet to decrease these values. This is only a
very simple example and doesn't have any graphical elements,
but you can expand upon this by adding images, animations,
more actions, and more statistics for your pet. -->

<!-- In the code I provided, the pet is represented by a dog emoji
in a div with the class pet. A div (short for division) is a block-
level element that can be used as a container for other HTML
elements.

If you want to use an image as the pet, you can replace the emoji
with an img tag. The img tag is used in HTML to embed images in
web pages. Here's an example of how you can do this:
<div class="pet">
  <img src="pet_image.jpg" alt="Your pet image" width="300px"
height="300px">
</div>
```

In this code, replace "pet_image.jpg" with the path to your image file. The alt attribute provides alternative information for an image if a user for some reason cannot view it (because of slow connection, an error in the src attribute, or if the user uses a screen reader). -->

<!-- Emojis are small digital images or icons that express an idea or emotion. They are very popular in text messages and social media posts. You can include emojis in your HTML code just like regular text.

You can usually open your operating system's emoji picker with the following shortcuts:

Windows: Win + . or Win + ;
(This is a shortcut key combination for accessing the emoji keyboard in Windows.

Win + . (Windows key and period): This opens the emoji picker over your current window, allowing you to select and insert emojis into any text field.

Win + ; (Windows key and semicolon): This is an alternative shortcut that does the exact same thing as Win + ..

Once the emoji picker is open, you can select any emoji to insert into your text. The emojis are organized by category and you can also search for a specific emoji by typing its name or a keyword associated with it.

Remember to have your text cursor in the place where you want to insert the emoji before you open the emoji picker.) -->

<!-- From the emoji picker, you can select an emoji and it will be inserted where your text cursor is. For example, you can open the emoji picker while your text cursor is in your code editor to insert an emoji into your code.

Here are 10 popular emojis:

😂 - Face with Tears of Joy
♡ - Red Heart
😍 - Smiling Face with Heart-Eyes
🤣 - Rolling on the Floor Laughing

😊 - Smiling Face with Smiling Eyes
🙏 - Folded Hands
💗 - Two Hearts
😭 - Loudly Crying Face
😘 - Face Blowing a Kiss
👍 - Thumbs Up

You can include these in your HTML code like this:
<p>😂 💗 😍 🤣 😊 🙏 💗 😭 😘 👍</p>

When your HTML file is viewed in a web browser, these emojis will be displayed. Emojis are standard and should be displayed consistently across different devices and platforms. However, the exact design of an emoji can vary between different operating systems and apps. -->

634

```
<!DOCTYPE html>
<html>

<head>
  <title>Virtual Pet Game</title>
  <style>
    body {
      display: flex;
      flex-direction: column;
      align-items: center;
      justify-content: center;
      height: 100vh;
      background-color: #f5f5f5;
      font-family: Arial, sans-serif;
    }

    .pet {
      font-size: 100px;
    }

    .controls {
      display: flex;
      justify-content: space-around;
      width: 100%;
    }
```

635

```css
    .controls button {
      padding: 10px 20px;
      font-size: 20px;
      border-radius: 5px;
      border: none;
      background-color: #007BFF;
      color: #fff;
      cursor: pointer;
    }

    .controls button:disabled {
      background-color: #ccc;
    }

    .status {
      text-align: center;
      margin: 20px;
      font-size: 20px;
    }
  </style>
</head>
```

```html
<body>
  <h1>Virtual Pet Game</h1>
  <div id="status" class="status">Status:</div>
  <div class="pet" id="pet">🐶</div>
  <div class="controls">
    <button onclick="feedPet()">Feed</button>
    <button onclick="playWithPet()">Play</button>
  </div>
  <script>
    let petHunger = 0;
    let petBoredom = 0;
    const statusDiv = document.getElementById('status');
    const petDiv = document.getElementById('pet');

    function feedPet() {
      petHunger -= 10;
      if (petHunger < 0) petHunger = 0;
      updateStatus();
    }

    function playWithPet() {
      petBoredom -= 10;
```

636

```
      if (petBoredom < 0) petBoredom = 0;
      updateStatus();
    }

    function updateStatus() {
      statusDiv.textContent = `Pet hunger: ${petHunger}, Pet
boredom: ${petBoredom}`;
      if (petHunger > 10) {
        petDiv.textContent = "🐕💭🦴🍖"; // Hungry dog
dreaming of a bone
      } else if (petBoredom > 20) {
        petDiv.textContent = "🐕💭🎡🧸🎾"; // Bored dog
dreaming of a ball
      } else {
        petDiv.textContent = "🐕"; // Happy dog
      }
    }

    setInterval(() => {
      petHunger += 1;
      petBoredom += 1;
      updateStatus();
    }, 1000);
  </script>
</body>

</html>

<!-- We can also dynamically change the pet's emoji based on its
state (i.e., happy, hungry, or bored).
```

In this code, I have added a status div to display the pet's hunger
and boredom. I also added a function updateStatus() that updates
the status div and the pet emoji according to the pet's state. The
pet emoji changes based on the levels of hunger and boredom.
This function is called whenever the pet's status changes. -->

```
<!DOCTYPE html>
<html>

<head>
  <title>Virtual Pet Game</title>
  <link
href="https://stackpath.bootstrapcdn.com/bootstrap/4.5.0/css/bo
otstrap.min.css" rel="stylesheet" />
</head>

<body class="d-flex flex-column align-items-center justify-
content-center vh-100 bg-light text-center">
  <h1 class="mb-4">Virtual Pet Game</h1>
  <div id="status" class="mb-3 h3">Status:</div>
  <div class="pet display-1 mb-4" id="pet">🐶</div>
  <div class="controls btn-group">
    <button class="btn btn-primary btn-lg"
onclick="feedPet()">Feed</button>
    <button class="btn btn-primary btn-lg"
onclick="playWithPet()">Play</button>
```

```
    <button class="btn btn-primary btn-lg"
onclick="napPet()">Nap</button>
  </div>

  <script>
    let petHunger = 0;
    let petBoredom = 0;
    const statusDiv = document.getElementById('status');
    const petDiv = document.getElementById('pet');

    function feedPet() {
      petHunger -= 10;
      if (petHunger < 0) petHunger = 0;
      updateStatus();
    }

    function playWithPet() {
      petBoredom -= 10;
      if (petBoredom < 0) petBoredom = 0;
      updateStatus();
    }

    function napPet() {
      petBoredom -= 15;
      if (petBoredom < 0) petBoredom = 0;
      updateStatus();
    }

    function updateStatus() {
      statusDiv.textContent = `Pet hunger: ${petHunger}, Pet
boredom: ${petBoredom}`;
      if (petHunger > 20) {
        petDiv.textContent = "🐶💭🦴🍖"; // Hungry dog
dreaming of food
```

```
    } else if (petBoredom > 20) {
      petDiv.textContent = "🐶💭🐸🐾🐾"; // Bored dog
dreaming of play
    } else {
      petDiv.textContent = "🐶"; // Happy dog
    }
  }

  setInterval(() => {
    petHunger += 1;
    petBoredom += 1;
    updateStatus();
  }, 1000);
  </script>
</body>

</html>

<!-- This version of your code uses Bootstrap to enhance the
layout and provide some basic styling to your buttons. I've also
added a `napPet` function, which lets you decrease your pet's
boredom by an additional amount. It's represented by a "Nap"
button on the screen. -->
```

Online Poll App

Which is your favorite pet?

 Dog   🐫 Cat

Dog: 42   Cat: 24

641

```
<!DOCTYPE html>
<html>

<head>
  <title>Online Poll App</title>
  <style>
    body {
      display: flex;
      flex-direction: column;
      align-items: center;
      justify-content: center;
      min-height: 100vh;
      background-color: #f5f5f5;
      font-family: Arial, sans-serif;
    }

    .poll {
      margin-top: 20px;
    }

    .poll button {
      margin: 10px;
    }
```

```
    .buttons {
      display: flex;
      justify-content: center;
    }

    .results {
      margin: 20px;
      display: flex;
      justify-content: space-around;
      width: 30%;
    }

    .results p {
      margin: 10px;
    }
  </style>
</head>

<body>
  <h1>Online Poll App</h1>
  <div class="poll">
    <h3>Which is your favorite pet?</h3>
    <div class="buttons">
      <button onclick="vote('Dog')"> 🐕 Dog</button>
      <button onclick="vote('Cat')"> 🐈 Cat</button>
    </div>
  </div>
  <div id="results" class="results"></div>

  <script>
    let pollResults = {
      Dog: 0,
      Cat: 0
    };

    function vote(option) {
      pollResults[option]++;
      displayResults();
    }

    function displayResults() {
      const resultsDiv = document.getElementById('results');
      resultsDiv.innerHTML = '';
      for (let option in pollResults) {
```

642

```
        resultsDiv.innerHTML += `<p>${option}:
${pollResults[option]}</p>`;
      }
    }
  </script>
</body>

</html>

<!-- This application allows users to vote between two options and
displays the results.

In this example, a user can vote for either 'Dog' or 'Cat' by
clicking the respective button. Each time a vote is cast, the vote()
function is called, which increments the vote count for the chosen
option and updates the display.

Please note, this is a simple version of an online poll application.
It doesn't support multiple polls, doesn't save results between
page reloads, and all users view and vote on the same poll. For a
more complex and functional version, you would probably need to
use a backend to store data and potentially user authentication to
track votes. This might involve using a framework or server-side
language such as Node.js, and a database to store the poll data. -
->
```

643

```
<!DOCTYPE html>
<html>

<head>
  <title>Online Poll App</title>
  <style>
    body {
      display: flex;
      flex-direction: column;
      align-items: center;
      justify-content: center;
      min-height: 100vh;
      background-color: #f4f4f4;
      font-family: Arial, sans-serif;
      color: #333;
    }

    .poll {
      margin-top: 20px;
    }

    .buttons {
      display: flex;
      justify-content: center;
    }

    .poll button {
```

644

```css
      margin: 0 10px;
      padding: 10px;
      background-color: #007BFF;
      color: #fff;
      border: none;
      border-radius: 5px;
      cursor: pointer;
    }

    .results {
      margin-top: 20px;
      width: 100%;
      display: flex;
      justify-content: center;
    }

    .bar {
      height: 20px;
      margin: 5px 0;
      background-color: #c70831;
      color: #fff;
      text-align-last: center;
      border-radius: 10px;
      transition: width 0.4s ease;
    }
  </style>
</head>

<body>
  <h1>Online Poll App</h1>
  <div class="poll">
    <h3>Which is your favorite pet?</h3>
    <div class="buttons">
      <button onclick="vote('Dog')">🐕 Dog🐶</button>
      <button onclick="vote('Cat')">🐈 Cat🐱</button>
    </div>
  </div>
  <div id="results" class="results"></div>

  <script>
    let pollResults = {
      Dog: 0,
      Cat: 0
    };
```

```
   function vote(option) {
     pollResults[option]++;
     displayResults();
   }

   function displayResults() {
     const resultsDiv = document.getElementById('results');
     resultsDiv.innerHTML = '';
     for (let option in pollResults) {
       const bar = document.createElement('div');
       bar.className = 'bar';
       bar.style.width = (pollResults[option] * 4) + '%';
       bar.textContent = `${option}: ${pollResults[option]}`;
       resultsDiv.appendChild(bar);
     }
   }
 </script>
</body>

</html>

<!-- This version of your code now includes a horizontal bar graph
representation for each poll option. The length of each bar
corresponds to the number of votes that option has received. Each
bar's length is updated in real time as new votes are cast. The
colors and fonts have been adjusted to provide a more modern
and friendly appearance. -->
```

646

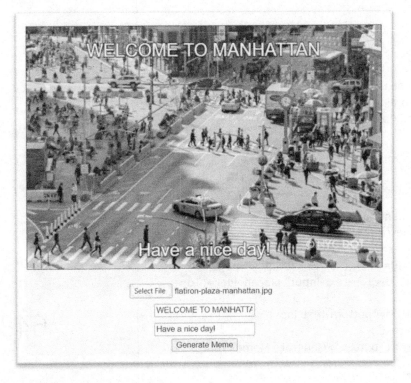

```
<!DOCTYPE html>
<html>

<head>
  <title>Meme Generator</title>
  <style>
    body {
      display: flex;
      justify-content: center;
      align-items: center;
      height: 100vh;
      background-color: #fafafa;
      font-family: Arial, sans-serif;
    }

    .meme-generator {
      display: flex;
      flex-direction: column;
      align-items: center;
```

```
    }

    input {
      margin: 5px;
    }

    .meme-generator canvas {
      border: 1px solid black;
      margin-bottom: 20px;
    }
  </style>
</head>

<body>
  <div class="meme-generator">
    <canvas id="meme-canvas" width="600"
height="400"></canvas>
    <input type="file" id="image-input" accept="image/*">
    <input type="text" id="top-text-input" placeholder="Top
text">
    <input type="text" id="bottom-text-input"
placeholder="Bottom text">
    <button id="generate-button">Generate Meme</button>
  </div>
  <script>
    const canvas = document.getElementById('meme-canvas');
    const ctx = canvas.getContext('2d');

    const img = new Image();
    let topText = '';
    let bottomText = '';

    document.getElementById('image-
input').addEventListener('change', function (e) {
      const reader = new FileReader();
      reader.onload = function (event) {
        img.onload = renderMeme;
        img.src = event.target.result;
      };
      reader.readAsDataURL(e.target.files[0]);
    });

    document.getElementById('top-text-
input').addEventListener('input', function (e) {
```

648

```
    topText = e.target.value;
    renderMeme();
  });

  document.getElementById('bottom-text-
input').addEventListener('input', function (e) {
    bottomText = e.target.value;
    renderMeme();
  });

  document.getElementById('generate-
button').addEventListener('click', function () {
    const dataUrl = canvas.toDataURL('image/png');
    const newTab = window.open('about:blank', 'image from
canvas');
    newTab.document.write("<img src='" + dataUrl + "'
alt='Meme'/>");
  });

  function renderMeme() {
    ctx.clearRect(0, 0, canvas.width, canvas.height);
    ctx.drawImage(img, 0, 0, canvas.width, canvas.height);
    ctx.font = '30px Arial';
    ctx.textAlign = 'center';
    ctx.strokeStyle = 'black';
    ctx.lineWidth = 3;
    ctx.strokeText(topText, canvas.width / 2, 50);
    ctx.strokeText(bottomText, canvas.width / 2, canvas.height -
20);
    ctx.fillStyle = 'white';
    ctx.fillText(topText, canvas.width / 2, 50);
    ctx.fillText(bottomText, canvas.width / 2, canvas.height -
20);
  }
  </script>
</body>

</html>

<!-- Creating a Meme Generator involves manipulation of images
and text. We'll be using the canvas element to draw the image
and text, and FileReader to load the image. -->
```

649

<!-- This simple Meme Generator will let the user select an image, input text for the top and bottom of the meme, and generate the meme. The "Generate Meme" button will open the generated meme in a new tab, where the user can then save the image. This is a very basic implementation, and there's a lot more you could do to improve it, such as adding the ability to adjust the size and position of the text, adding more fonts, etc. -->

<!-- A Meme Generator is a type of online tool that allows users to create their own memes. Memes are humorous images, videos, or pieces of text that are copied and spread rapidly by Internet users, often with slight variations.

In the context of a Meme Generator, users typically have the ability to:

1. Choose a template: Many meme generators come pre-loaded with popular meme templates - recognizable images that have a certain associated humor or meaning within Internet culture.

2. Add text: Once a template is chosen, users can add their own text. Often, meme formats have specific places where text is added, such as at the top and/or bottom of an image. The text is what personalizes the meme and makes it relevant to different situations.

3. Customize the meme: Some meme generators allow further customization, like changing the text color or font, adding stickers, or even uploading your own images to use as templates.

4. Share or download the meme: After the meme is created, users can usually download the image to their device or directly share it on social media platforms.

Building a Meme Generator as a coding project can be an interesting way to practice manipulating images and text on a canvas with HTML, CSS, and JavaScript. -->

650

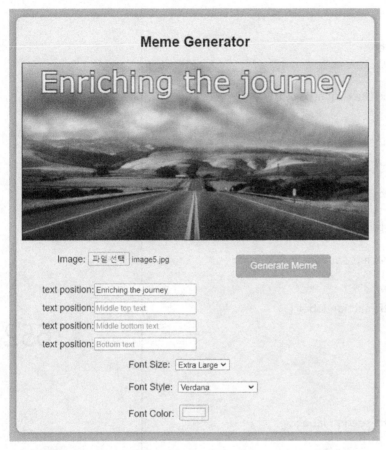

```
<!DOCTYPE html>
<html>

<head>
  <title>Meme Generator</title>
  <style>
    body {
      display: flex;
      justify-content: center;
      align-items: center;
      height: auto;
      background-color: #a9a3e6;
      font-family: Arial, sans-serif;
    }

    .meme-generator {
```

```css
  display: flex;
  flex-direction: column;
  align-items: center;
  background: #eeeeee;
  padding: 10px;
  border-radius: 10px;
  box-shadow: 0px 0px 10px rgba(0, 0, 0, 0.4);
  margin: 20px;
}

.meme-generator .input-section {
  display: flex;
  flex-direction: column;
  align-items: flex-start;
  /* Move input forms to the left side */
  width: 50%;
  /* Adjust width for the left section */
}

.meme-generator .input-section label {
  display: flex;
  justify-content: left;
  align-items: center;
  width: 100%;
}

.meme-generator .input-section label,
.meme-generator button {
  margin: 5px;
}

.meme-generator .centered {
  display: flex;
  justify-content: center;
  width: 100%;
}

.meme-generator canvas {
  border: 1px solid black;
  margin-bottom: 20px;
}

button {
  background-color: #4CAF50;
```

```css
    border: none;
    color: white;
    padding: 10px 24px;
    text-align: center;
    text-decoration: none;
    display: inline-block;
    font-size: 16px;
    margin: 4px 2px;
    cursor: pointer;
    border-radius: 5px;
  }

  .meme-generator .input-section {
    width: 90%;
    /* Adjust width for the left section */
  }

  .meme-generator .centered {
    width: 90%;
    /* Adjust width for the centered section */
  }

  /* Add a container for the right section */
  .meme-generator .right-section {
    display: flex;
    flex-direction: column;
    align-items: flex-start;
    width: 40%;
    /* Adjust width for the right section */
  }

  /* Align the right section to the right */
  .meme-generator .right-section label {
    justify-content: flex-end;
  }

  /* Add some spacing between the right section elements */
  .meme-generator .right-section label,
  .meme-generator .right-section select,
  .meme-generator .right-section input {
    margin: 5px;
  }
  </style>
</head>
```

653

```
<body>
  <div class="meme-generator">
    <h2>Meme Generator</h2>
    <canvas id="meme-canvas" width="600"
height="300"></canvas>
    <div class="centered">
      <label for="image-input">Image:
      <input type="file" id="image-input"
accept="image/*"></label>
      <button id="generate-button">Generate Meme</button>
    </div>
    <div class="input-section">
      <label for="top-text-input">text position:
        <input type="text" id="top-text-input" placeholder="Top
text"></label>
      <label for="middle-top-text-input">text position:
        <input type="text" id="middle-top-text-input"
placeholder="Middle top text"></label>
      <label for="middle-bottom-text-input">text position:
        <input type="text" id="middle-bottom-text-input"
placeholder="Middle bottom text"></label>
      <label for="bottom-text-input">text position:
        <input type="text" id="bottom-text-input"
placeholder="Bottom text"></label>
    </div>
    <div class="right-section">
      <label for="font-size-input">Font Size:
        <select id="font-size-input">
          <option value="10">Extra Small</option>
          <option value="20">Small</option>
          <option value="30" selected>Medium</option>
          <option value="40">Large</option>
          <option value="50">Extra Large</option>
        </select></label>
      <label for="font-style-input">Font Style:
        <select id="font-style-input">
          <option value="Arial" selected>Arial</option>
          <option value="Courier">Courier</option>
          <option value="Georgia">Georgia</option>
          <option value="Times New Roman">Times New
Roman</option>
          <option value="Verdana">Verdana</option>
        </select></label>
```

654

```
      <label for="color-input">Font Color:
        <input type="color" id="color-input" value="#ffffff">
    </div></label>

  </div>
  <script>
    const canvas = document.getElementById('meme-canvas');
    const ctx = canvas.getContext('2d');

    const img = new Image();
    let topText = '';
    let middleTopText = '';
    let middleBottomText = '';
    let bottomText = '';
    let fontSize = '30px';
    let fontStyle = 'Arial';
    let fontColor = '#ffffff';

    document.getElementById('image-
input').addEventListener('change', function (e) {
      const reader = new FileReader();
      reader.onload = function (event) {
        img.onload = renderMeme;
        img.src = event.target.result;
      };
      reader.readAsDataURL(e.target.files[0]);
    });

    document.getElementById('top-text-
input').addEventListener('input', function (e) {
      topText = e.target.value;
      renderMeme();
    });

    document.getElementById('middle-top-text-
input').addEventListener('input', function (e) {
      middleTopText = e.target.value;
      renderMeme();
    });

    document.getElementById('middle-bottom-text-
input').addEventListener('input', function (e) {
      middleBottomText = e.target.value;
      renderMeme();
```

```javascript
    });

    document.getElementById('bottom-text-
input').addEventListener('input', function (e) {
        bottomText = e.target.value;
        renderMeme();
    });

    document.getElementById('font-size-
input').addEventListener('change', function (e) {
        fontSize = e.target.value + 'px';
        renderMeme();
    });

    document.getElementById('font-style-
input').addEventListener('change', function (e) {
        fontStyle = e.target.value;
        renderMeme();
    });

    document.getElementById('color-
input').addEventListener('change', function (e) {
        fontColor = e.target.value;
        renderMeme();
    });

    document.getElementById('generate-
button').addEventListener('click', function () {
        const dataUrl = canvas.toDataURL('image/png');
        const newTab = window.open('about:blank', 'image from
canvas');
        newTab.document.write("<img src='" + dataUrl + "'
alt='Meme'/>");
    });

    function renderMeme() {
      ctx.clearRect(0, 0, canvas.width, canvas.height);
      ctx.drawImage(img, 0, 0, canvas.width, canvas.height);
      ctx.font = fontSize + ' ' + fontStyle;
      ctx.textAlign = 'center';
      ctx.strokeStyle = 'black';
      ctx.lineWidth = 3;
      ctx.strokeText(topText, canvas.width / 2, 50);
```

```
    ctx.strokeText(middleTopText, canvas.width / 2,
canvas.height / 2 - 20);
    ctx.strokeText(middleBottomText, canvas.width / 2,
canvas.height / 2 + 20);
    ctx.strokeText(bottomText, canvas.width / 2, canvas.height -
20);
    ctx.fillStyle = fontColor;
    ctx.fillText(topText, canvas.width / 2, 50);
    ctx.fillText(middleTopText, canvas.width / 2, canvas.height /
2 - 20);
    ctx.fillText(middleBottomText, canvas.width / 2,
canvas.height / 2 + 20);
    ctx.fillText(bottomText, canvas.width / 2, canvas.height -
20);
    }
  </script>
</body>

</html>
```

```
<!DOCTYPE html>
<html>

<head>
  <title>Meme Generator</title>
  <!-- Add Bootstrap CSS link -->
  <link rel="stylesheet"
href="https://maxcdn.bootstrapcdn.com/bootstrap/4.5.2/css/boot
strap.min.css">
  <style>
   body {
     background-color: #a3e6a6;
     font-family: Arial, sans-serif;
   }

   .meme-generator {
     background: #eeeeee;
     padding: 10px;
     border-radius: 10px;
     box-shadow: 0px 0px 10px rgba(0, 0, 0, 0.4);
```

```css
      margin: 20px;
    }

    .meme-generator canvas {
      border: 1px solid black;
      margin-bottom: 20px;
    }

    .input-section label,
    button {
      margin: 5px;
    }

    .right-section label,
    .right-section select,
    .right-section input {
      margin: 5px;
    }

    .centered {
      text-align: center;
    }
  </style>
</head>

<body>
  <div class="container meme-generator">
    <h2 class="text-center mb-4">Meme Generator</h2>
    <div class="centered mb-4">
      <label for="image-input">Image:
        <input type="file" id="image-input" accept="image/*">
      </label>
      <button id="generate-button" class="btn btn-
success">Generate Meme</button>
    </div>
    <div class="row">
      <div class="col-md-6 input-section">
        <label for="top-text-input">Top Text:
          <input type="text" id="top-text-input" class="form-
control" placeholder="Top text">
        </label>
        <label for="middle-top-text-input">Middle Top Text:
          <input type="text" id="middle-top-text-input"
class="form-control" placeholder="Middle top text">
```

```html
        </label>
        <label for="middle-bottom-text-input">Middle Bottom
Text:
          <input type="text" id="middle-bottom-text-input"
class="form-control" placeholder="Middle bottom text">
        </label>
        <label for="bottom-text-input">Bottom Text:
          <input type="text" id="bottom-text-input" class="form-
control" placeholder="Bottom text">
        </label>
      </div>
      <div class="col-md-6 right-section">
        <label for="font-size-input">Font Size:
          <select id="font-size-input" class="form-control">
            <option value="10">Extra Small</option>
            <option value="20">Small</option>
            <option value="30" selected>Medium</option>
            <option value="40">Large</option>
            <option value="50">Extra Large</option>
          </select>
        </label>
        <label for="font-style-input">Font Style:
          <select id="font-style-input" class="form-control">
            <option value="Arial" selected>Arial</option>
            <option value="Courier">Courier</option>
            <option value="Georgia">Georgia</option>
            <option value="Times New Roman">Times New
Roman</option>
            <option value="Verdana">Verdana</option>
          </select>
        </label>
        <label for="color-input">Font Color:
          <input type="color" id="color-input" class="form-control"
value="#ffffff">
        </label>
      </div>
    </div>
    <div class="centered">
      <canvas id="meme-canvas" width="500"
height="250"></canvas>
    </div>
  </div>

  <!-- Add jQuery and Bootstrap JS scripts -->
```

```
  <script src="https://code.jquery.com/jquery-
3.6.0.min.js"></script>
  <script
src="https://maxcdn.bootstrapcdn.com/bootstrap/4.5.2/js/bootstr
ap.min.js"></script>

  <script>
    const canvas = document.getElementById('meme-canvas');
    const ctx = canvas.getContext('2d');

    const img = new Image();
    let topText = '';
    let middleTopText = '';
    let middleBottomText = '';
    let bottomText = '';
    let fontSize = '30px';
    let fontStyle = 'Arial';
    let fontColor = '#ffffff';

    document.getElementById('image-
input').addEventListener('change', function (e) {
      const reader = new FileReader();
      reader.onload = function (event) {
        img.onload = renderMeme;
        img.src = event.target.result;
      };
      reader.readAsDataURL(e.target.files[0]);
    });

    document.getElementById('top-text-
input').addEventListener('input', function (e) {
      topText = e.target.value;
      renderMeme();
    });

    document.getElementById('middle-top-text-
input').addEventListener('input', function (e) {
      middleTopText = e.target.value;
      renderMeme();
    });

    document.getElementById('middle-bottom-text-
input').addEventListener('input', function (e) {
      middleBottomText = e.target.value;
```

```
      renderMeme();
   });

   document.getElementById('bottom-text-
input').addEventListener('input', function (e) {
      bottomText = e.target.value;
      renderMeme();
   });

   document.getElementById('font-size-
input').addEventListener('change', function (e) {
      fontSize = e.target.value + 'px';
      renderMeme();
   });

   document.getElementById('font-style-
input').addEventListener('change', function (e) {
      fontStyle = e.target.value;
      renderMeme();
   });

   document.getElementById('color-
input').addEventListener('change', function (e) {
      fontColor = e.target.value;
      renderMeme();
   });

   document.getElementById('generate-
button').addEventListener('click', function () {
      const dataUrl = canvas.toDataURL('image/png');
      const newTab = window.open('about:blank', 'image from
canvas');
      newTab.document.write("<img src='" + dataUrl + "'
alt='Meme'/>");
   });

   function renderMeme() {
     ctx.clearRect(0, 0, canvas.width, canvas.height);
     ctx.drawImage(img, 0, 0, canvas.width, canvas.height);
     ctx.font = fontSize + ' ' + fontStyle;
     ctx.textAlign = 'center';
     ctx.strokeStyle = 'black';
     ctx.lineWidth = 3;
     ctx.strokeText(topText, canvas.width / 2, 50);
```

```
    ctx.strokeText(middleTopText, canvas.width / 2,
canvas.height / 2 - 20);
    ctx.strokeText(middleBottomText, canvas.width / 2,
canvas.height / 2 + 20);
    ctx.strokeText(bottomText, canvas.width / 2, canvas.height -
20);
    ctx.fillStyle = fontColor;
    ctx.fillText(topText, canvas.width / 2, 50);
    ctx.fillText(middleTopText, canvas.width / 2, canvas.height /
2 - 20);
    ctx.fillText(middleBottomText, canvas.width / 2,
canvas.height / 2 + 20);
    ctx.fillText(bottomText, canvas.width / 2, canvas.height -
20);
    }
  </script>
</body>

</html>
```

URL Shortener

https://www.naver.com

Shorten

rebrand.ly/ok3ubhu

```
<!DOCTYPE html>
<html>

<head>
  <title>URL Shortener</title>
  <style>
    body {
      display: flex;
      flex-direction: column;
      align-items: center;
      justify-content: center;
      height: 100vh;
      margin: 0;
      padding: 0;
      background-color: #f0f0f0;
      font-family: Arial, sans-serif;
    }

    #url-input,
    button {
      width: 70%;
      margin: 5px;
      padding: 10px;
      box-sizing: border-box;
      font-size: 18px;
      border-radius: 5px;
    }

    #url-input {
      border: 1px solid #ddd;
```

664

```
    }

    button {
      color: #fff;
      background-color: #007BFF;
      border: none;
      cursor: pointer;
    }

    #result {
      margin-top: 20px;
      padding: 10px;
      width: 65%;
      text-align: center;
      box-shadow: 0px 0px 10px rgba(0, 0, 0, 0.2);
      border-radius: 5px;
    }

    a {
      text-decoration: none;
      color: #007BFF;
    }
  </style>
</head>

<body>
  <h1>URL Shortener</h1>
  <input type="text" id="url-input" placeholder="Enter URL">
  <button onclick="shortenUrl()">Shorten</button>
  <div id="result"></div>

  <script>
    function shortenUrl() {
      const urlInput = document.getElementById('url-input').value;
      fetch('https://api.rebrandly.com/v1/links', {
        method: 'POST',
        headers: {
          'Content-Type': 'application/json',
          'apikey': '0153da865bf04e59839143493c1f76**',
        },
        body: JSON.stringify({
          destination: urlInput
        })
```

```
      })
      .then(response => response.json())
      .then(data => {
        document.getElementById('result').innerHTML = `<a
href="https://${data.shortUrl}"
target="_blank">${data.shortUrl}</a>`;
      })
      .catch(error => {
        console.error('Error:', error);
      });
  }
 </script>
</body>

</html>

<!-- Please replace 'YOUR_REBRANDLY_API_KEY' with your actual
Rebrandly API key. This will now display the shortened URL as a
clickable link that opens in a new tab. -->
```

667

```
<!DOCTYPE html>
<html>

<head>
  <title>URL Shortener</title>
  <!-- Add Bootstrap CSS link -->
  <link rel="stylesheet"
href="https://maxcdn.bootstrapcdn.com/bootstrap/4.5.2/css/boot
strap.min.css">
  <style>
    body {
      height: 100vh;
      background-color: #f0f0f0;
      font-family: Arial, sans-serif;
    }

    .container {
      display: flex;
      flex-direction: column;
      align-items: center;
      justify-content: center;
```

```css
      height: 100%;
    }

    #url-input,
    button {
      width: 70%;
      margin: 5px;
      padding: 10px;
      box-sizing: border-box;
      font-size: 18px;
      border-radius: 5px;
    }

    #url-input {
      border: 1px solid #ddd;
    }

    button {
      color: #fff;
      background-color: #007BFF;
      border: none;
      cursor: pointer;
    }

    #result {
      margin-top: 20px;
      padding: 10px;
      width: 65%;
      text-align: center;
      box-shadow: 0px 0px 10px rgba(0, 0, 0, 0.2);
      border-radius: 5px;
    }

    a {
      text-decoration: none;
      color: #007BFF;
    }
  </style>
</head>

<body>
```

```html
<div class="container">
  <h1>URL Shortener</h1>
  <input type="text" id="url-input" class="form-control"
placeholder="Enter URL">
  <button id="shorten-btn" class="btn btn-
primary">Shorten</button>
  <div id="result"></div>
</div>

<!-- Add Bootstrap and jQuery scripts -->
<script src="https://code.jquery.com/jquery-
3.6.0.min.js"></script>
<script
src="https://maxcdn.bootstrapcdn.com/bootstrap/4.5.2/js/bootstr
ap.min.js"></script>

<script>
  $(document).ready(function () {
    $('#shorten-btn').click(function () {
      shortenUrl();
    });
  });

  function shortenUrl() {
    const urlInput = $('#url-input').val();
    fetch('https://api.rebrandly.com/v1/links', {
      method: 'POST',
      headers: {
        'Content-Type': 'application/json',
        'apikey': '0153da865bf04e59839143493c1f76**',
      },
      body: JSON.stringify({
        destination: urlInput
      })
    })
      .then(response => response.json())
      .then(data => {
        if (data.shortUrl) {
          $('#result').html(`
            <div class="alert alert-success">
```

```
            Shortened URL: <a href="https://${data.shortUrl}"
target="_blank">${data.shortUrl}</a>
                <button class="btn btn-primary ml-2"
onclick="copyToClipboard('${data.shortUrl}')">Copy to
Clipboard</button>
            </div>
          `);
        } else {
          $('#result').html(`
            <div class="alert alert-danger">
              Failed to shorten the URL. Please try again.
            </div>
          `);
        }
      })
      .catch(error => {
        console.error('Error:', error);
      });
  }

  function copyToClipboard(text) {
    const input = document.createElement('input');
    input.value = text;
    document.body.appendChild(input);
    input.select();
    document.execCommand('copy');
    document.body.removeChild(input);

    $('#result').append('<div class="alert alert-success mt-
2">URL copied to clipboard!</div>');
    setTimeout(() => {
      $('.alert-success').remove();
    }, 2000);
  }
  </script>
</body>

</html>

<!-- Please replace 'YOUR_REBRANDLY_API_KEY' with your actual
Rebrandly API key. -->
```

670

<!-- In the upgraded code, we have replaced the onclick attribute in the "Shorten" button with a jQuery click event listener to call the shortenUrl() function. We also added the "Copy to Clipboard" button, and when the short URL is successfully generated, we display the button along with a success message. The copyToClipboard() function handles copying the short URL to the clipboard and displays a success message.

We've also added Bootstrap classes to improve the layout and make the URL Shortener look more visually appealing. The modified code uses Bootstrap's alert classes for success and error messages.

Now, the URL Shortener is more user-friendly with a colorful layout and additional functionality to copy the shortened URL easily. -->

671

```
<!DOCTYPE html>
<html>

<head>
  <title>Flashcards</title>
  <!-- <link rel="stylesheet" type="text/css" href="style.css"> --
>
  <style>
    body {
      display: flex;
      justify-content: center;
      align-items: center;
      height: 100vh;
      background-color: #f0f0f0;
      font-family: Arial, sans-serif;
    }

    .flashcard-grid {
      display: grid;
      grid-template-columns: repeat(3, 1fr);
      grid-gap: 40px;
      justify-items: center;
    }

    .card {
      width: 200px;
      height: 100px;
      perspective: 1000px;
```

```
      }

   .card-front,
   .card-back {
     position: absolute;
     width: 100%;
     height: 100%;
     backface-visibility: hidden;
     display: flex;
     justify-content: center;
     align-items: center;
     padding: 10px;
     box-shadow: 0px 0px 5px rgba(0, 0, 0, 0.3);
     border-radius: 10px;
     transition: transform 0.5s;
   }

   .card-front {
     background-color: #007BFF;
     color: white;
   }

   .card-back {
     background-color: #28a745;
     color: white;
     transform: rotateY(180deg);
   }

   .card-flipped .card-front {
     transform: rotateY(180deg);
   }

   .card-flipped .card-back {
     transform: rotateY(360deg);
   }
 </style>
</head>

<body>
 <!-- The sample questions are middle school level science
problems. What's your skill level? -->
 <div class="flashcard-grid">
   <div class="card" onclick="flipCard(this)">
     <div class="card-front">
```

```
      <p>Question: What are the building blocks of
proteins?</p>
    </div>
    <div class="card-back">
      <p>Answer: amino acids</p>
    </div>
  </div>
  <div class="card" onclick="flipCard(this)">
    <div class="card-front">
      <p>Question: What are the four largest planets in our solar
system called?</p>
    </div>
    <div class="card-back">
      <p>Answer: Jupiter, Saturn, Uranus, and Neptune</p>
    </div>
  </div>
  <div class="card" onclick="flipCard(this)">
    <div class="card-front">
      <p>Question: What is the name of our galaxy?</p>
    </div>
    <div class="card-back">
      <p>Answer: the Milky Way</p>
    </div>
  </div>
  <div class="card" onclick="flipCard(this)">
    <div class="card-front">
      <p>Question: What is the process by which plants make
their own food called?</p>
    </div>
    <div class="card-back">
      <p>Answer: photosynthesis</p>
    </div>
  </div>
  <div class="card" onclick="flipCard(this)">
    <div class="card-front">
      <p>Question: What is the smallest unit of life in all living
organisms called?</p>
    </div>
    <div class="card-back">
      <p>Answer: cell</p>
    </div>
  </div>
  <div class="card" onclick="flipCard(this)">
    <div class="card-front">
```

```html
      <p>Question: What are the three states of matter?</p>
    </div>
    <div class="card-back">
      <p>Answer: solid, liquid, and gas</p>
    </div>
  </div>
  <div class="card" onclick="flipCard(this)">
    <div class="card-front">
      <p>Question: What is the chemical symbol for the element
Oxygen?</p>
    </div>
    <div class="card-back">
      <p>Answer: O</p>
    </div>
  </div>
  <div class="card" onclick="flipCard(this)">
    <div class="card-front">
      <p>Question: What is the force that pulls objects towards
each other called?</p>
    </div>
    <div class="card-back">
      <p>Answer: gravity</p>
    </div>
  </div>
  <div class="card" onclick="flipCard(this)">
    <div class="card-front">
      <p>Question: What is the law of conservation of
energy?</p>
    </div>
    <div class="card-back">
      <p>Answer: Energy cannot be created or destroyed, only
transferred or transformed from one form to another.</p>
    </div>
  </div>

  <!-- Add more flashcards here... -->

</div>
<!-- <script src="script.js"></script> -->
<script>
  function flipCard(card) {
    card.classList.toggle('card-flipped');
  }
```

```
   </script>
</body>

</html>

<!-- I created a grid layout with 9 flashcards and add a transition
for the flip animation to make it slower.

In this version, I've added a .flashcard-grid div that uses CSS grid
to lay out the flashcards in 3 columns. You can add more .card
divs inside the .flashcard-grid to create more flashcards. I've also
added a transition property to the .card-front and .card-back
classes to slow down the flip animation. -->

<!-- In this example, clicking on the card will trigger the flipCard
function which toggles the card-flipped class. When this class is
present, the .card-front and .card-back will rotate around the Y-
axis, creating a flip effect.

For a more complex and functional flashcard app, you would
probably want to use a framework like React or Vue, and a
database to store the flashcards. The above example is quite
simplified and is intended as a starting point. -->
```

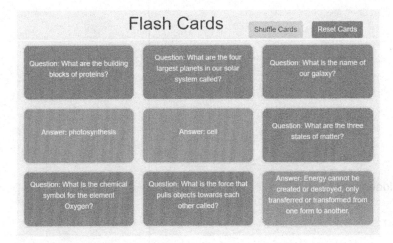

```
<!DOCTYPE html>
<html>

<head>
  <title>Flashcards</title>
  <!-- Add Bootstrap CSS link -->
  <link rel="stylesheet"
href="https://maxcdn.bootstrapcdn.com/bootstrap/4.5.2/css/boot
strap.min.css">
  <style>
    body {
      display: flex;
      justify-content: center;
      align-items: center;
      height: 100%;
      background-color: #f0f0f0;
      font-family: Arial, sans-serif;
    }

    .flashcard-grid {
      display: grid;
      grid-template-columns: repeat(3, 1fr);
      grid-gap: 20px;
      justify-items: center;
    }
```

```css
.card {
  width: 250px;
  height: 120px;
  perspective: 1000px;
}

.card-front,
.card-back {
  position: absolute;
  width: 100%;
  height: 100%;
  backface-visibility: hidden;
  display: flex;
  justify-content: center;
  align-items: center;
  padding: 10px;
  box-shadow: 0px 0px 5px rgba(0, 0, 0, 0.3);
  border-radius: 10px;
  transition: transform 0.5s;
}

.card-front {
  background-color: #007BFF;
  color: white;
}

.card-back {
  background-color: #28a745;
  color: white;
  transform: rotateY(180deg);
}

.card-flipped .card-front {
  transform: rotateY(180deg);
}

.card-flipped .card-back {
  transform: rotateY(360deg);
}

.button-container {
```

```
      position: absolute;
      top: 20px;
      left: 50%;
      transform: translateX(57%);
    }
  </style>
</head>

<body>
  <div class="container text-center">
    <h1 class="my-4">Flash Cards</h1>
    <div class="flashcard-grid">
      <div class="card" onclick="flipCard(this)">
        <div class="card-front">
         <p>Question: What are the building blocks of
proteins?</p>
        </div>
        <div class="card-back">
          <p>Answer: amino acids</p>
        </div>
      </div>
      <div class="card" onclick="flipCard(this)">
        <div class="card-front">
         <p>Question: What are the four largest planets in our
solar system called?</p>
        </div>
        <div class="card-back">
          <p>Answer: Jupiter, Saturn, Uranus, and Neptune</p>
        </div>
      </div>
      <div class="card" onclick="flipCard(this)">
        <div class="card-front">
          <p>Question: What is the name of our galaxy?</p>
        </div>
        <div class="card-back">
          <p>Answer: the Milky Way</p>
        </div>
      </div>
      <div class="card" onclick="flipCard(this)">
        <div class="card-front">
```

679

```
      <p>Question: What is the process by which plants make
their own food called?</p>
      </div>
      <div class="card-back">
       <p>Answer: photosynthesis</p>
      </div>
     </div>
     <div class="card" onclick="flipCard(this)">
      <div class="card-front">
       <p>Question: What is the smallest unit of life in all living
organisms called?</p>
      </div>
      <div class="card-back">
       <p>Answer: cell</p>
      </div>
     </div>
     <div class="card" onclick="flipCard(this)">
      <div class="card-front">
       <p>Question: What are the three states of matter?</p>
     </div>
      <div class="card-back">
       <p>Answer: solid, liquid, and gas</p>
      </div>
     </div>
     <div class="card" onclick="flipCard(this)">
      <div class="card-front">
       <p>Question: What is the chemical symbol for the
element Oxygen?</p>
      </div>
      <div class="card-back">
       <p>Answer: O</p>
      </div>
     </div>
     <div class="card" onclick="flipCard(this)">
      <div class="card-front">
       <p>Question: What is the force that pulls objects towards
each other called?</p>
      </div>
      <div class="card-back">
       <p>Answer: gravity</p>
      </div>
```

```
    </div>
    <div class="card" onclick="flipCard(this)">
      <div class="card-front">
        <p>Question: What is the law of conservation of
energy?</p>
      </div>
      <div class="card-back">
        <p>Answer: Energy cannot be created or destroyed, only
transferred or transformed from one form to another.
        </p>
      </div>
    </div>
    <div class="mt-4 button-container">
      <button class="btn btn-warning mx-2"
onclick="shuffleCards()">Shuffle Cards</button>
      <button class="btn btn-secondary mx-2"
onclick="resetCards()">Reset Cards</button>
    </div>
  </div>

  <!-- Add Bootstrap and jQuery scripts -->
  <script src="https://code.jquery.com/jquery-
3.6.0.min.js"></script>
  <script
src="https://maxcdn.bootstrapcdn.com/bootstrap/4.5.2/js/bootstr
ap.min.js"></script>

  <script>
  function flipCard(card) {
    card.classList.toggle('card-flipped');
  }

  function shuffleCards() {
    const flashcards = document.querySelectorAll('.flashcard-
grid .card');
    const shuffledCards = Array.from(flashcards).sort(() =>
Math.random() - 0.5);
    shuffledCards.forEach((card, index) => {
      card.style.order = index;
      card.classList.remove('card-flipped');
    });
```

```
        }

    function resetCards() {
        const flashcards = document.querySelectorAll('.flashcard-
grid .card');
        flashcards.forEach(card => {
            card.classList.remove('card-flipped');
        });
    }
    </script>
</body>

</html>
```

Geocoding App

| Seoul | | Search |

- 서울, 대한민국

- **Latitude:** 37.5666791
- **Longitude:** 126.9782914

```html
<!DOCTYPE html>
<html>

<head>
  <title>Geocoding App</title>
  <!-- <link rel="stylesheet" type="text/css" href="style.css"> -->
  <style>
    body {
      font-family: Arial, sans-serif;
      margin: 20px;
    }

    form {
      margin-bottom: 1em;
    }

    #result {
      margin-top: 1em;
      font-size: 1.2em;
    }
  </style>

  <script
src="https://cdn.jsdelivr.net/npm/axios/dist/axios.min.js"></script>
```

```html
</head>

<body>
  <h1>Geocoding App</h1>

  <form id="geocode-form">
    <input type="text" id="location-input" placeholder="Enter an
address or coordinates">
    <button type="submit">Search</button>
  </form>

  <div id="result"></div>

  <!-- <script src="app.js"></script> -->
  <script>
    document.getElementById('geocode-
form').addEventListener('submit', geocode);

    function geocode(e) {
      // Prevent actual submit
      e.preventDefault();

      var location = document.getElementById('location-
input').value;

      axios.get('https://api.opencagedata.com/geocode/v1/json', {
        params: {
          q: location,
          key: 'eb22ceb9c80844b0b227a0a4260494**' // replace
this with your API key
        }
      })
        .then(function (response) {
          // Log full response
          console.log(response);

          // Formatted Address
          var formattedAddress =
response.data.results[0].formatted;
          var formattedAddressOutput = `
      <ul class="list-group">
        <li class="list-group-item">${formattedAddress}</li>
      </ul>
```

684

```
     `;

         // Geometry
         var lat = response.data.results[0].geometry.lat;
         var lng = response.data.results[0].geometry.lng;

         var geometryOutput = `
     <ul class="list-group">
       <li class="list-group-item"><strong>Latitude:</strong>
${lat}</li>
       <li class="list-group-item"><strong>Longitude:</strong>
${lng}</li>
     </ul>
     `;

         // Output to app
         document.getElementById('result').innerHTML =
formattedAddressOutput + geometryOutput;
       })
       .catch(function (error) {
         console.log(error);
       });
     }

   </script>
</body>

</html>
```

<!-- To create a Geocoding application, you'll need to make use of
APIs that offer geocoding services. One popular and reliable
choice is Google Maps Geocoding API, but it's not free. If you want
to use a free API, you can use OpenCage Geocoding API which
offers a generous free tier.

This is a simple guide to help you create your application.

1. Setting up the HTML and CSS:
You'll need a form where users can input the address or the
latitude/longitude, and a space to display the result.

2. CSS (style.css)

3. Creating the JavaScript logic (app.js):

Firstly, you'll have to register for an API key from the OpenCage Data website. After obtaining your key, here's how you can setup your JavaScript file.

Remember to replace 'YOUR_OPENCAGE_API_KEY' with your own API key.

This code adds an event listener to your form that listens for a submit event. When the form is submitted, it prevents the page from refreshing (which is the default behavior), grabs the user's input, and sends a GET request to the OpenCage Data API. The API will return a response containing the geocoding data, which you can then display in your app.

This is a very basic example and there's a lot more you can do with geocoding, like showing the location on a map or providing autocomplete suggestions as the user types. But this should get you started. -->

<!-- Please note: You'll need to include the Axios library for the HTTP request in this example. You can include it in your HTML like so:

<script src="https://cdn.jsdelivr.net/npm/axios/dist/axios.min.js"></script>

Or install it with npm if you're using a build system:

npm install axios

Axios is a popular, promise-based HTTP client that sports an easy-to-use API and can be used in both the browser and Node.js. If you prefer to use the built-in fetch function in the browser instead of Axios, you can absolutely do that.

Lastly, always be aware that handling sensitive data like API keys on the client-side JavaScript exposes them to potential misuse. It's best to handle sensitive data server-side whenever possible. This might not be a big concern when you're just playing around or building something for learning purposes, but it's definitely something to keep in mind for serious projects. -->

Geocoding App

40.7, -74.0   Search   Clear

Pier 2, Brooklyn Bridge Park Greenway, 뉴욕, 뉴욕 11201, 미국

Latitude: 40.6995099

Longitude: -73.9988963

Copy Formatted Address

687

```
<!DOCTYPE html>
<html>

<head>
  <title>Geocoding App</title>
  <!-- Add Bootstrap CSS link -->
  <link rel="stylesheet"
href="https://maxcdn.bootstrapcdn.com/bootstrap/4.5.2/css/boot
strap.min.css">

  <style>
    body {
      font-family: Arial, sans-serif;
      margin: 20px;
    }

    form {
      margin-bottom: 1em;
    }

    #result {
      margin-top: 1em;
      font-size: 1.2em;
    }
```

```
  </style>

  <script
src="https://cdn.jsdelivr.net/npm/axios/dist/axios.min.js"></scri
pt>
  <!-- Add jQuery -->
  <script src="https://code.jquery.com/jquery-
3.6.0.min.js"></script>
</head>

<body>
  <div class="container">
    <h1 class="my-4">Geocoding App</h1>

    <form id="geocode-form">
      <div class="input-group mb-3">
        <input type="text" id="location-input" class="form-
control" placeholder="Enter an address or coordinates">
        <div class="input-group-append">
          <button type="submit" class="btn btn-
primary">Search</button>
        </div>
        <div class="input-group-append">
          <button type="button" class="btn btn-secondary"
id="clear-button">Clear</button>
        </div>
      </div>
    </form>

    <div id="result"></div>
    <button type="button" class="btn btn-success mt-3"
id="copy-button">Copy Formatted Address</button>
  </div>

  <script>
    $(document).ready(function () {
      // Event listener for the form submission
      $('#geocode-form').submit(function (e) {
        e.preventDefault();

        var location = $('#location-input').val();

        axios.get('https://api.opencagedata.com/geocode/v1/json',
{
```

```
        params: {
          q: location,
          key: 'eb22ceb9c80844b0b227a0a426049458' // replace
this with your API key
        }
      })
        .then(function (response) {
          var formattedAddress =
response.data.results[0].formatted;
          var lat = response.data.results[0].geometry.lat;
          var lng = response.data.results[0].geometry.lng;

          var formattedAddressOutput = `
    <ul class="list-group">
      <li class="list-group-item">${formattedAddress}</li>
    </ul>
  `;

          var geometryOutput = `
    <ul class="list-group">
      <li class="list-group-item"><strong>Latitude:</strong>
${lat}</li>
      <li class="list-group-item"><strong>Longitude:</strong>
${lng}</li>
    </ul>
  `;

          $('#result').html(formattedAddressOutput +
geometryOutput);
        })
        .catch(function (error) {
          console.log(error);
        });
    });

    // Event listener for the clear button
    $('#clear-button').click(function () {
      $('#location-input').val('');
      $('#result').html('');
    });

    // Event listener for the copy button
    $('#copy-button').click(function () {
```

689

```
      var formattedAddress = $('#result').find('.list-group-
item').first().text();
      copyToClipboard(formattedAddress);
    });

    // Function to copy the text to the clipboard
    function copyToClipboard(text) {
      var tempInput = $('<input>');
      $('body').append(tempInput);
      tempInput.val(text).select();
      document.execCommand('copy');
      tempInput.remove();
      alert('Formatted address copied to clipboard!');
    }
  });
 </script>
</body>

</html>

<!-- In this updated version of the Geocoding App, we have used
Bootstrap classes for styling, added a "Clear" button to reset the
input and results, and introduced a "Copy" button to copy the
formatted address to the clipboard. The jQuery library is utilized
for smooth interaction with the buttons and form submission. -->
```

Password Generator

2en6khca

Password length:

8

Include uppercase letters

☐

Include numbers

☑

Include symbols

☐

Generate Password

691

```html
<!DOCTYPE html>
<html>

<head>
  <title>Password Generator</title>
  <!-- <link rel="stylesheet" href="style.css">
</head> -->
  <style>
    body {
      font-family: Arial, sans-serif;
      width: 80%;
      margin: 0 auto;
    }

    #passwordDisplay {
      margin-top: 20px;
      font-size: 2em;
      word-wrap: break-word;
      color: blue;
```

```
    }

    #passwordGeneratorControls {
      margin-top: 20px;
    }

    #passwordGeneratorControls label,
    #passwordGeneratorControls input {
      margin-top: 10px;
      display: block;
    }

    button {
      margin-top: 20px;
      padding: 10px;
    }
  </style>

<body>
  <h1>Password Generator</h1>

  <div id="passwordDisplay"></div>

  <div id="passwordGeneratorControls">
    <label for="passwordLength">Password length:</label>
    <input type="number" id="passwordLength" min="8"
max="128" value="12">

    <label for="includeUppercase">Include uppercase
letters</label>
    <input type="checkbox" id="includeUppercase" checked>

    <label for="includeNumbers">Include numbers</label>
    <input type="checkbox" id="includeNumbers" checked>

    <label for="includeSymbols">Include symbols</label>
    <input type="checkbox" id="includeSymbols" checked>

    <button id="generateButton">Generate Password</button>
  </div>

  <!-- <script src="main.js"></script> -->
  <script>
```

```
    const passwordDisplay =
document.getElementById('passwordDisplay');
    const passwordLength =
document.getElementById('passwordLength');
    const includeUppercase =
document.getElementById('includeUppercase');
    const includeNumbers =
document.getElementById('includeNumbers');
    const includeSymbols =
document.getElementById('includeSymbols');
    const generateButton =
document.getElementById('generateButton');

    const upperCaseCharCodes = arrayFromLowToHigh(65, 90)
    const lowerCaseCharCodes = arrayFromLowToHigh(97, 122)
    const numberCharCodes = arrayFromLowToHigh(48, 57)
    const symbolCharCodes = arrayFromLowToHigh(33,
47).concat(
    arrayFromLowToHigh(58, 64)
  ).concat(
    arrayFromLowToHigh(91, 96)
  ).concat(
    arrayFromLowToHigh(123, 126)
  )

    generateButton.addEventListener('click', generatePassword)

    function generatePassword() {
      const length = passwordLength.value;
      const includeUpper = includeUppercase.checked;
      const includeNums = includeNumbers.checked;
      const includeSyms = includeSymbols.checked;

      let charCodes = lowerCaseCharCodes;
      if (includeUpper) charCodes =
charCodes.concat(upperCaseCharCodes);
      if (includeNums) charCodes =
charCodes.concat(numberCharCodes);
      if (includeSyms) charCodes =
charCodes.concat(symbolCharCodes);

      const passwordCharacters = [];
      for (let i = 0; i < length; i++) {
```

```
      const character = charCodes[Math.floor(Math.random() *
charCodes.length)];
      passwordCharacters.push(String.fromCharCode(character))
;
    }
    passwordDisplay.innerText = passwordCharacters.join('');
  }

  function arrayFromLowToHigh(low, high) {
    const array = [];
    for (let i = low; i <= high; i++) {
      array.push(i);
    }
    return array;
  }

 </script>
</body>

</html>

<!-- Creating a Password Generator is a fun and useful project.
```

In this HTML, we're defining a series of controls for the user to select their password criteria, as well as a button to generate the password. The generated password will be displayed in the passwordDisplay div.

This CSS is quite basic. It just ensures that all of the elements on the page are laid out nicely.

This JavaScript first grabs all of the elements we'll need from the DOM, including our controls and the password display. Then it generates arrays of charCodes for uppercase letters, lowercase letters, numbers, and symbols. These will be used as potential characters in our password. The button's event listener triggers the generatePassword function when the button is clicked.

The generatePassword function gets the user's password criteria, generates an array of character codes to pull from based on these criteria, and then constructs a password of the specified length from these characters.

694

The arrayFromLowToHigh function is a helper function that generates an array of numbers from the low to the high inclusive. This is used to generate our arrays of character codes.

Remember to replace the dummy text in the passwordDisplay div with the generated password.

This is a pretty basic password generator. It's certainly possible to add more complex features, like different classes of symbols, non-sequential characters, etc. But this should give you a good foundation to build upon. -->

Password Generator

5tk1HgsQHJuY

Password length:

12

Include uppercase letters

☑

Include numbers

☑

Include symbols

☐

Generate Password   Copy Password   Reset

696

```
<!DOCTYPE html>
<html>

<head>
  <title>Password Generator</title>
  <!-- Add Bootstrap CSS link -->
  <link rel="stylesheet"
href="https://maxcdn.bootstrapcdn.com/bootstrap/4.5.2/css/boot
strap.min.css">

  <style>
    body {
      font-family: Arial, sans-serif;
      width: 80%;
      margin: 0 auto;
    }

    #passwordDisplay {
```

```
      margin-top: 20px;
      font-size: 2em;
      word-wrap: break-word;
      color: blue;
    }

    #passwordGeneratorControls {
      margin-top: 20px;
    }

    #passwordGeneratorControls label,
    #passwordGeneratorControls input {
      margin-top: 10px;
      display: block;
    }

    button {
      margin-top: 20px;
      padding: 10px;
    }
  </style>
</head>

<body>
  <div class="container">
    <h1 class="my-4">Password Generator</h1>

    <div id="passwordDisplay"></div>

    <div id="passwordGeneratorControls">
      <label for="passwordLength">Password length:</label>
      <input type="number" id="passwordLength" min="8"
max="128" value="12">

      <label for="includeUppercase">Include uppercase
letters</label>
      <input type="checkbox" id="includeUppercase" checked>

      <label for="includeNumbers">Include numbers</label>
      <input type="checkbox" id="includeNumbers" checked>

      <label for="includeSymbols">Include symbols</label>
      <input type="checkbox" id="includeSymbols" checked>
```

```
    <button id="generateButton" class="btn btn-
primary">Generate Password</button>
    <button id="copyButton" class="btn btn-success">Copy
Password</button>
    <button id="resetButton" class="btn btn-
danger">Reset</button>
  </div>
 </div>

 <script>
  const passwordDisplay =
document.getElementById('passwordDisplay');
  const passwordLength =
document.getElementById('passwordLength');
  const includeUppercase =
document.getElementById('includeUppercase');
  const includeNumbers =
document.getElementById('includeNumbers');
  const includeSymbols =
document.getElementById('includeSymbols');
  const generateButton =
document.getElementById('generateButton');
  const copyButton = document.getElementById('copyButton');
  const resetButton = document.getElementById('resetButton');

  const upperCaseCharCodes = arrayFromLowToHigh(65, 90);
  const lowerCaseCharCodes = arrayFromLowToHigh(97, 122);
  const numberCharCodes = arrayFromLowToHigh(48, 57);
  const symbolCharCodes = arrayFromLowToHigh(33,
47).concat(
    arrayFromLowToHigh(58, 64)
  ).concat(
    arrayFromLowToHigh(91, 96)
  ).concat(
    arrayFromLowToHigh(123, 126)
  );

  generateButton.addEventListener('click', generatePassword);
  copyButton.addEventListener('click', copyPassword);
  resetButton.addEventListener('click', resetPassword);

  function generatePassword() {
    const length = passwordLength.value;
    const includeUpper = includeUppercase.checked;
```

```javascript
    const includeNums = includeNumbers.checked;
    const includeSyms = includeSymbols.checked;

    let charCodes = lowerCaseCharCodes;
    if (includeUpper) charCodes =
charCodes.concat(upperCaseCharCodes);
    if (includeNums) charCodes =
charCodes.concat(numberCharCodes);
    if (includeSyms) charCodes =
charCodes.concat(symbolCharCodes);

    const passwordCharacters = [];
    for (let i = 0; i < length; i++) {
      const character = charCodes[Math.floor(Math.random() *
charCodes.length)];
      passwordCharacters.push(String.fromCharCode(character))
;
    }
    const generatedPassword = passwordCharacters.join('');
    passwordDisplay.innerText = generatedPassword;
  }

  function copyPassword() {
    const generatedPassword = passwordDisplay.innerText;
    if (!generatedPassword) {
      alert("No password generated to copy!");
      return;
    }

    const tempInput = document.createElement('textarea');
    document.body.appendChild(tempInput);
    tempInput.value = generatedPassword;
    tempInput.select();
    document.execCommand('copy');
    document.body.removeChild(tempInput);
    alert('Password copied to clipboard!');
  }

  function resetPassword() {
    passwordDisplay.innerText = '';
  }

  function arrayFromLowToHigh(low, high) {
    const array = [];
```

```
      for (let i = low; i <= high; i++) {
        array.push(i);
      }
      return array;
    }

  </script>
</body>

</html>

<!-- In this updated version of the Password Generator, we have
used Bootstrap classes for styling, added a "Copy" button to copy
the generated password to the clipboard, and a "Reset" button to
clear the generated password and reset the input fields. The
JavaScript code has been enhanced to handle the new functions,
making the Password Generator more interactive and user-
friendly. -->
```

Product Inventory

Product Name	Product Description	
Product Price	Product Quantity	Add Product

Product 1 - This is product 1 - $10.99 - Quantity: 100 [Delete]

Product 2 - This is product 2 - $20.99 - Quantity: 200 [Delete]

Product 3 - This is product 3 - $10.99 - Quantity: 1200 [Delete]

Hat - This is summer hat. - $5.99 - Quantity: 2000 [Delete]

Tent - Made in South Korea - $120.99 - Quantity: 1200 [Delete]

701

```
<!DOCTYPE html>
<html>

<head>
  <title>Product Inventory</title>
  <!-- <link rel="stylesheet" href="style.css"> -->
  <style>
    body {
      font-family: Arial, sans-serif;
      margin: 20px;
    }

    form {
      margin-bottom: 1em;
    }

    ul {
      list-style-type: none;
      padding-left: 0;
    }

    li {
      margin-bottom: 0.5em;
      background-color: #f0f0f0;
      padding: 0.5em;
```

```
    }

    button {
      margin-left: 1em;
    }
  </style>
</head>

<body>
  <h1>Product Inventory</h1>
  <form id="product-form">
    <input type="hidden" id="productId">
    <input type="text" id="productName" placeholder="Product
Name">
    <input type="text" id="productDescription"
placeholder="Product Description">
    <input type="number" id="productPrice" placeholder="Product
Price">
    <input type="number" id="productQuantity"
placeholder="Product Quantity">
    <button>Add Product</button>
  </form>
  <ul id="product-list"></ul>

  <!-- <script src="app.js"></script> -->
  <script>
    const form = document.getElementById('product-form');
    const nameInput =
document.getElementById('productName');
    const descriptionInput =
document.getElementById('productDescription');
    const priceInput = document.getElementById('productPrice');
    const quantityInput =
document.getElementById('productQuantity');
    const productList = document.getElementById('product-list');
    const API_URL = 'https://my-json-
server.typicode.com/SanghyunNa-web/inventory/products';

    // Fetch initial products
    fetch(API_URL)
      .then((response) => response.json())
      .then((products) => {
        products.forEach((product) => {
          addProductToPage(product);
```

702

```javascript
    });
  });

  // Form submission
  form.addEventListener('submit', (event) => {
    event.preventDefault();

    const product = {
      name: nameInput.value,
      description: descriptionInput.value,
      price: parseFloat(priceInput.value),
      quantity: parseInt(quantityInput.value),
    };

    // In real-world scenario, you would send POST request to
API here
    addProductToPage(product);

    // Clear the input fields
    nameInput.value = '';
    descriptionInput.value = '';
    priceInput.value = '';
    quantityInput.value = '';
  });

  function addProductToPage(product) {
    const listItem = document.createElement('li');
    listItem.textContent = `${product.name} -
${product.description} - $${product.price} - Quantity:
${product.quantity}`;

    const deleteButton = document.createElement('button');
    deleteButton.textContent = 'Delete';
    deleteButton.addEventListener('click', () => {
      // In real-world scenario, you would send DELETE request
to API here
      productList.removeChild(listItem);
    });

    listItem.appendChild(deleteButton);
    productList.appendChild(listItem);
  }

</script>
```

703

```
</body>

</html>

<!-- This is a great project idea! Before we start, you should have
a basic understanding of how to use GitHub, including creating
repositories and files. If you're not familiar with this, there are
many resources online to help you learn.

For this example, we will be using JSON Server which is a Node
Module that you can use to create demo REST JSON webservices.
-->

<!-- 1. Setting up the Mock API
Create a new repository on GitHub.
Create a new file in the repository and name it db.json.
Inside db.json, add your initial data. Here's an example:

{
  "products": [
    {
      "id": 1,
      "name": "Product 1",
      "description": "This is product 1",
      "price": 10.99,
      "quantity": 100
    },
    {
      "id": 2,
      "name": "Product 2",
      "description": "This is product 2",
      "price": 20.99,
      "quantity": 200
    }
  ]
}
```

704

Sign up on GitHub and create a username, and within that
username, create a repository. In that repository, create a file
called db.json, and paste the "products" code into this file. You
can add more if you'd like.

We will use My JSON Server service to serve this file as a REST API. Your API endpoint would be `https://my-json-server.typicode.com/<username>/<repository>/products`. -->

<!-- 2. Creating the HTML and CSS
In this step, you need to set up your basic HTML structure and CSS. -->

<!-- 3. Creating the JavaScript
In the JavaScript file, you'll need to fetch data from the API and dynamically add it to the page. You'll also need to add functionality to add, update, and delete products.

Please note that My JSON Server is a fake server for prototyping and doesn't support all kinds of HTTP requests. In a real-world scenario, you would send POST, PUT, and DELETE requests to add, update, and delete products. -->

<!-- In this JavaScript file, we fetch the initial list of products from the API and add them to the page. We also add an event listener to the form that adds a new product to the page when the form is submitted. In a real-world scenario, we would also send a POST request to the API when adding a product and a DELETE request when deleting a product. -->

<!-- Please note that this is a simple, prototype example. In a real-world application, you would likely need more complex functionality, error handling, and security measures. For example, you may need to validate the form inputs to ensure they're not empty and are in the correct format. You would also likely need a way to handle network errors, such as if the API is down or the user is offline. -->

706

```
<!DOCTYPE html>
<html>

<head>
  <title>Product Inventory</title>
  <!-- Add Bootstrap CSS link -->
  <link rel="stylesheet"
href="https://maxcdn.bootstrapcdn.com/bootstrap/4.5.2/css/boot
strap.min.css">

  <style>
    body {
      font-family: Arial, sans-serif;
      margin: 20px;
    }

    form {
      margin-bottom: 1em;
    }

    ul {
      list-style-type: none;
```

```
    padding-left: 0;
  }

  li {
    margin-bottom: 0.5em;
    background-color: #f0f0f0;
    padding: 0.5em;
  }

  button {
    margin-left: 1em;
  }
 </style>
</head>

<body>
  <div class="container">
    <h1 class="my-4">Product Inventory</h1>
    <form id="product-form">
      <input type="hidden" id="productId">
      <input type="text" id="productName" class="form-control"
placeholder="Product Name">
      <input type="text" id="productDescription" class="form-
control" placeholder="Product Description">
      <input type="number" id="productPrice" class="form-
control" placeholder="Product Price">
      <input type="number" id="productQuantity" class="form-
control" placeholder="Product Quantity">
      <button class="btn btn-primary mt-2">Add
Product</button>
    </form>
    <ul id="product-list"></ul>
  </div>

  <!-- <script src="app.js"></script> -->
  <script>
    const form = document.getElementById('product-form');
    const nameInput =
document.getElementById('productName');
    const descriptionInput =
document.getElementById('productDescription');
    const priceInput = document.getElementById('productPrice');
    const quantityInput =
document.getElementById('productQuantity');
```

```
const productList = document.getElementById('product-list');
const API_URL = 'https://my-json-
server.typicode.com/SanghyunNa-web/inventory/products';

// Fetch initial products
fetch(API_URL)
  .then((response) => response.json())
  .then((products) => {
    products.forEach((product) => {
      addProductToPage(product);
    });
  });

// Form submission
form.addEventListener('submit', (event) => {
  event.preventDefault();

  const product = {
    name: nameInput.value,
    description: descriptionInput.value,
    price: parseFloat(priceInput.value),
    quantity: parseInt(quantityInput.value),
  };

  // In real-world scenario, you would send POST request to
API here
  addProductToPage(product);

  // Clear the input fields
  nameInput.value = '';
  descriptionInput.value = '';
  priceInput.value = '';
  quantityInput.value = '';
});

function addProductToPage(product) {
  const listItem = document.createElement('li');
  listItem.textContent = `${product.name} -
${product.description} - $${product.price} - Quantity:
${product.quantity}`;

  const editButton = document.createElement('button');
  editButton.textContent = 'Edit';
  editButton.classList.add('btn', 'btn-info', 'mr-2');
```

708

```
    editButton.addEventListener('click', () => {
      // In real-world scenario, you would implement the edit
functionality here
      alert('Edit functionality is not implemented in this demo.');
    });

    const deleteButton = document.createElement('button');
    deleteButton.textContent = 'Delete';
    deleteButton.classList.add('btn', 'btn-danger');
    deleteButton.addEventListener('click', () => {
      // In real-world scenario, you would send DELETE request
to API here
      const confirmDelete = confirm('Are you sure you want to
delete this product?');
      if (confirmDelete) {
        productList.removeChild(listItem);
      }
    });

    listItem.appendChild(editButton);
    listItem.appendChild(deleteButton);
    productList.appendChild(listItem);
  }

  </script>
</body>

</html>

<!-- In this updated version of the Product Inventory, we have
used Bootstrap classes for styling, added an "Edit" button (without
full edit functionality) for each product to demonstrate its use, and
added a confirmation alert before deleting a product. The Product
Inventory now looks more visually appealing and is more
interactive with the added buttons and alert. -->
```

709

Contact Management

| Name | Email |
| Phone | Address | Add Contact |

John Doe - john@gmail.com - 123-456-7890 - 123 Main St, New York, NY 10001 [Delete]

Jane Doe - jane@gmail.com - 987-654-3210 - 456 Elm St, Los Angeles, CA 90001 [Delete]

Hugimori - fhju2@yahoo.co.jp - 012-987-5678 - 123 Ichonoe Chiyigu Tokyo, Japan [Delete]

710

```html
<!DOCTYPE html>
<html>

<head>
  <title>Contact Management</title>
  <!-- <link rel="stylesheet" href="style.css"> -->
  <style>
    body {
      font-family: Arial, sans-serif;
      margin: 20px;
    }

    form {
      margin-bottom: 1em;
    }

    ul {
      list-style-type: none;
      padding-left: 0;
    }

    li {
      margin-bottom: 0.5em;
      background-color: #f0f0f0;
      padding: 0.5em;
    }
```

```
  button {
    margin-left: 1em;
  }
  </style>
</head>

<body>
  <h1>Contact Management</h1>
  <form id="contact-form">
    <input type="hidden" id="contactId">
    <input type="text" id="contactName" placeholder="Name">
    <input type="text" id="contactEmail" placeholder="Email">
    <input type="text" id="contactPhone" placeholder="Phone">
    <input type="text" id="contactAddress"
placeholder="Address">
    <button>Add Contact</button>
  </form>
  <ul id="contact-list"></ul>

  <!-- <script src="app.js"></script> -->
  <script>
    const form = document.getElementById('contact-form');
    const nameInput = document.getElementById('contactName');
    const emailInput = document.getElementById('contactEmail');
    const phoneInput =
document.getElementById('contactPhone');
    const addressInput =
document.getElementById('contactAddress');
    const contactList = document.getElementById('contact-list');
    const API_URL = 'https://my-json-
server.typicode.com/SanghyunNa-web/contactmanage/contacts';

    // Fetch initial contacts
    fetch(API_URL)
      .then((response) => response.json())
      .then((contacts) => {
        contacts.forEach((contact) => {
          addContactToPage(contact);
        });
      });

    // Form submission
    form.addEventListener('submit', (event) => {
      event.preventDefault();
```

```
      const contact = {
        name: nameInput.value,
        email: emailInput.value,
        phone: phoneInput.value,
        address: addressInput.value,
      };

      // In a real-world scenario, you would send POST request to
API here
      addContactToPage(contact);

      // Clear the input fields
      nameInput.value = '';
      emailInput.value = '';
      phoneInput.value = '';
      addressInput.value = '';
    });

    function addContactToPage(contact) {
      const listItem = document.createElement('li');
      listItem.textContent = `${contact.name} - ${contact.email}
- ${contact.phone} - ${contact.address}`;

      const deleteButton = document.createElement('button');
      deleteButton.textContent = 'Delete';
      deleteButton.addEventListener('click', () => {
        // In a real-world scenario, you would send DELETE request
to API here
        contactList.removeChild(listItem);
      });

      listItem.appendChild(deleteButton);
      contactList.appendChild(listItem);
    }
  </script>
</body>
</html>

<!-- This is a fantastic idea for a project! Similar to the Product
Inventory system.
We can create a contact management system using GitHub, JSON
Server, and My JSON Server.
```

1. Setting up the Mock API
Create a new repository on GitHub.
Create a new file in the repository and name it db.json.
Inside db.json, add your initial data. Here's an example:

```json
{
  "contacts": [
    {
      "id": 1,
      "name": "John Doe",
      "email": "john@gmail.com",
      "phone": "123-456-7890",
      "address": "123 Main St, New York, NY 10001"
    },
    {
      "id": 2,
      "name": "Jane Doe",
      "email": "jane@gmail.com",
      "phone": "987-654-3210",
      "address": "456 Elm St, Los Angeles, CA 90001"
    }
  ]
}
```

713

Your API endpoint would be https://my-json-server.typicode.com/<username>/<repository>/contacts.

2. Creating the HTML and CSS
3. Creating the JavaScript

Please note that in a real-world application, you would likely need more complex functionality, error handling, and security measures. For example, you may need to validate the form inputs to ensure they're not empty and are in the correct format. You would also likely need a way to handle network errors, such as if the API is down or the user is offline. -->

Contact Management

Name

Email

Phone

Address

Add Contact

Search by Name or Email

John Doe - john@gmail.com - 123-456-7890 - 123 Main St, New York, NY 10001   Edit   Delete

Jane Doe - jane@gmail.com - 987-654-3210 - 456 Elm St, Los Angeles, CA 90001   Edit   Delete

Trump Joe - buiding@daum.net - 001-9223-2468 - 175 5th Ave, New York, NY 10010, United States   Edit   Delete

714

```
<!DOCTYPE html>
<html>

<head>
  <title>Contact Management</title>
  <!-- Add Bootstrap CSS link -->
  <link rel="stylesheet"
href="https://maxcdn.bootstrapcdn.com/bootstrap/4.5.2/css/boot
strap.min.css">

  <style>
    body {
      font-family: Arial, sans-serif;
      margin: 20px;
    }

    form {
```

```
      margin-bottom: 1em;
    }

    ul {
      list-style-type: none;
      padding-left: 0;
    }

    li {
      margin-bottom: 0.5em;
      background-color: #f0f0f0;
      padding: 0.5em;
    }

    button {
      margin-left: 1em;
    }
  </style>
</head>

<body>
  <div class="container">
    <h1 class="my-4">Contact Management</h1>
    <form id="contact-form">
      <input type="hidden" id="contactId">
      <input type="text" id="contactName" class="form-control"
placeholder="Name">
      <input type="text" id="contactEmail" class="form-control"
placeholder="Email">
      <input type="text" id="contactPhone" class="form-control"
placeholder="Phone">
      <input type="text" id="contactAddress" class="form-control"
placeholder="Address">
      <button class="btn btn-primary mt-2">Add
Contact</button>
    </form>
    <div class="form-group">
      <input type="text" id="searchInput" class="form-control mt-
4" placeholder="Search by Name or Email">
    </div>
    <ul id="contact-list"></ul>
  </div>

  <!-- <script src="app.js"></script> -->
```

```
<script>
  const form = document.getElementById('contact-form');
  const nameInput = document.getElementById('contactName');
  const emailInput = document.getElementById('contactEmail');
  const phoneInput =
document.getElementById('contactPhone');
  const addressInput =
document.getElementById('contactAddress');
  const contactList = document.getElementById('contact-list');
  const searchInput = document.getElementById('searchInput');
  const API_URL = 'https://my-json-
server.typicode.com/SanghyunNa-web/contactmanage/contacts';

  // Fetch initial contacts
  fetch(API_URL)
    .then((response) => response.json())
    .then((contacts) => {
      contacts.forEach((contact) => {
        addContactToPage(contact);
      });
    });

  // Form submission
  form.addEventListener('submit', (event) => {
    event.preventDefault();

    const contact = {
      name: nameInput.value,
      email: emailInput.value,
      phone: phoneInput.value,
      address: addressInput.value,
    };

    // In a real-world scenario, you would send POST request to
API here
    addContactToPage(contact);

    // Clear the input fields
    nameInput.value = '';
    emailInput.value = '';
    phoneInput.value = '';
    addressInput.value = '';
  });
```

```javascript
    // Add contact to the page
    function addContactToPage(contact) {
      const listItem = document.createElement('li');
      listItem.textContent = `${contact.name} - ${contact.email}
- ${contact.phone} - ${contact.address}`;

      const editButton = document.createElement('button');
      editButton.textContent = 'Edit';
      editButton.classList.add('btn', 'btn-info', 'mr-2');
      editButton.addEventListener('click', () => {
        // In a real-world scenario, you would implement the edit
functionality here
        alert('Edit functionality is not implemented in this demo.');
      });

      const deleteButton = document.createElement('button');
      deleteButton.textContent = 'Delete';
      deleteButton.classList.add('btn', 'btn-danger');
      deleteButton.addEventListener('click', () => {
        // In a real-world scenario, you would send DELETE request
to API here
        const confirmDelete = confirm('Are you sure you want to
delete this contact?');
        if (confirmDelete) {
          contactList.removeChild(listItem);
        }
      });

      listItem.appendChild(editButton);
      listItem.appendChild(deleteButton);
      contactList.appendChild(listItem);
    }

    // Search functionality
    searchInput.addEventListener('input', () => {
      const searchText = searchInput.value.toLowerCase();
      const contacts = contactList.getElementsByTagName('li');
      for (const contact of contacts) {
        const contactText = contact.textContent.toLowerCase();
        if (contactText.includes(searchText)) {
          contact.style.display = 'block';
        } else {
          contact.style.display = 'none';
        }
```

```
      }
   });

  </script>
</body>

</html>

<!-- In this updated version of the Contact Management, we have
used Bootstrap classes for styling, added an "Edit" button (without
full edit functionality) for each contact to demonstrate its use, and
added a search feature to filter contacts by name or email. The
Contact Management now looks more visually appealing and is
more interactive with the added search functionality. -->
```

Project Management Dashboard

Project 1

Description: This is project 1

Status: In Progress

Team: Alice, Bob

Project 2

Description: This is project 2

Status: Completed

Team: Charlie, Dave

719

```html
<!DOCTYPE html>
<html>

<head>
  <title>Project Management Dashboard</title>
  <!-- <link rel="stylesheet" href="style.css"> -->
  <style>
    body {
      font-family: Arial, sans-serif;
      display: flex;
      flex-direction: column;
      align-items: center;
      margin: 0;
      padding: 0;
      background-color: #f0f0f0;
    }

    h1 {
      color: #333;
```

```
      }

    .project {
      width: 80%;
      background-color: #fff;
      margin: 1em 0;
      padding: 1em;
      box-shadow: 0px 0px 10px 0px rgba(0, 0, 0, 0.1);
      border-radius: 5px;
    }

    .project h2 {
      color: #333;
    }

    .project p {
      color: #666;
    }

    #project-list {
      width: 80%;
      display: flex;
      flex-direction: column;
      align-items: center;
    }
  </style>
</head>

<body>
  <h1>Project Management Dashboard</h1>
  <div id="project-list"></div>

  <!-- <script src="app.js"></script> -->
  <script>
    const projectList = document.getElementById('project-list');

    // Our local data
    const projects = [
      {
        name: 'Project 1',
        description: 'This is project 1',
        status: 'In Progress',
        teamMembers: ['Alice', 'Bob']
      },
```

720

```
    {
      name: 'Project 2',
      description: 'This is project 2',
      status: 'Completed',
      teamMembers: ['Charlie', 'Dave']
    },
    // Add more projects as needed
  ];

  projects.forEach((project) => {
    const projectDiv = document.createElement('div');
    projectDiv.classList.add('project');

    const projectName = document.createElement('h2');
    projectName.textContent = project.name;
    projectDiv.appendChild(projectName);

    const projectDescription = document.createElement('p');
    projectDescription.textContent = `Description:
${project.description}`;
    projectDiv.appendChild(projectDescription);

    const projectStatus = document.createElement('p');
    projectStatus.textContent = `Status: ${project.status}`;
    projectDiv.appendChild(projectStatus);

    const projectTeam = document.createElement('p');
    projectTeam.textContent = `Team:
${project.teamMembers.join(', ')}`;
    projectDiv.appendChild(projectTeam);

    projectList.appendChild(projectDiv);
  });

  </script>
</body>

</html>
```

721

```
<!-- Great! If you want to move away from a mock API and
db.json file, we can create a simple local data structure in
JavaScript for this example. This will be a simple static dashboard
```

where you can't dynamically add, update, or delete projects. But it will still display the list of projects from our local data.

This is a very basic project management dashboard. It doesn't have any interactive features yet. To add these, you'll need to learn more about JavaScript event handling and possibly server-side programming if you want to save changes across sessions. But this should give you a good foundation to build upon. -->

722

723

```
<!DOCTYPE html>
<html>

<head>
  <title>Project Management Dashboard</title>
  <!-- Add Bootstrap CSS link -->
  <link rel="stylesheet"
href="https://maxcdn.bootstrapcdn.com/bootstrap/4.5.2/css/boot
strap.min.css">

  <style>
    body {
      font-family: Arial, sans-serif;
      display: flex;
      flex-direction: column;
      align-items: center;
      margin: 0;
      padding: 0;
      background-color: #f0f0f0;
```

```
      }

    h1 {
      color: #333;
      }

    .project {
      width: 80%;
      background-color: #fff;
      margin: 1em 0;
      padding: 1em;
      box-shadow: 0px 0px 10px 0px rgba(0, 0, 0, 0.1);
      border-radius: 5px;
      }

    .project h2 {
      color: #333;
      }

    .project p {
      color: #666;
      }

  </style>
</head>

<body>
  <div class="container">
    <h1 class="my-4">Project Management Dashboard</h1>

    <!-- Add new project form -->
    <form id="project-form" class="mb-4">
      <div class="form-group">
        <label for="projectName">Project Name:</label>
        <input type="text" id="projectName" class="form-control"
required>
      </div>
      <div class="form-group">
        <label for="projectDescription">Project
Description:</label>
        <input type="text" id="projectDescription" class="form-
control" required>
      </div>
      <div class="form-group">
```

```html
      <label for="projectStatus">Project Status:</label>
      <select id="projectStatus" class="form-control" required>
        <option value="In Progress">In Progress</option>
        <option value="Completed">Completed</option>
      </select>
    </div>
    <div class="form-group">
      <label for="projectTeam">Team Members (comma-
separated):</label>
        <input type="text" id="projectTeam" class="form-control"
required>
    </div>
    <button type="submit" class="btn btn-primary">Add
Project</button>
  </form>

  <div id="project-list"></div>
  </div>

  <!-- <script src="app.js"></script> -->
  <script>
  const projectList = document.getElementById('project-list');
  const projectForm = document.getElementById('project-
form');

  // Our local data
  const projects = [
    {
      name: 'Project 1',
      description: 'This is project 1',
      status: 'In Progress',
      teamMembers: ['Alice', 'Bob']
    },
    {
      name: 'Project 2',
      description: 'This is project 2',
      status: 'Completed',
      teamMembers: ['Charlie', 'Dave']
    },
    // Add more projects as needed
  ];

  // Function to display projects
  function displayProjects(projects) {
```

725

```
    projectList.innerHTML = '';

    projects.forEach((project) => {
      const projectDiv = document.createElement('div');
      projectDiv.classList.add('project');

      const projectName = document.createElement('h2');
      projectName.textContent = project.name;
      projectDiv.appendChild(projectName);

      const projectDescription = document.createElement('p');
      projectDescription.textContent = `Description:
${project.description}`;
      projectDiv.appendChild(projectDescription);

      const projectStatus = document.createElement('p');
      projectStatus.textContent = `Status: ${project.status}`;
      projectDiv.appendChild(projectStatus);

      const projectTeam = document.createElement('p');
      projectTeam.textContent = `Team:
${project.teamMembers.join(', ')}`;
      projectDiv.appendChild(projectTeam);

      projectList.appendChild(projectDiv);
    });
  }

  // Initial display of projects
  displayProjects(projects);

  // Form submission to add a new project
  projectForm.addEventListener('submit', (event) => {
    event.preventDefault();

    const projectName =
document.getElementById('projectName').value;
    const projectDescription =
document.getElementById('projectDescription').value;
    const projectStatus =
document.getElementById('projectStatus').value;
    const projectTeam =
document.getElementById('projectTeam').value.split(',').map(item
=> item.trim());
```

```javascript
    const newProject = {
      name: projectName,
      description: projectDescription,
      status: projectStatus,
      teamMembers: projectTeam,
    };

    // Add the new project to the projects array
    projects.push(newProject);

    // Refresh the display with updated projects
    displayProjects(projects);

    // Clear the form fields
    projectForm.reset();
  });

  </script>
</body>

</html>
```

727

```html
<!-- In this updated version of the Project Management
Dashboard, we have incorporated Bootstrap for styling and added
a form to dynamically add new projects. The Project Management
Dashboard now has a more interactive and colorful layout, making
it easier to manage projects and visualize their status and team
members. -->
```

728

```
<!DOCTYPE html>
<html>

<head>
  <title>Blog Post App</title>
  <!-- <link rel="stylesheet" href="style.css"> -->
  <style>
    body {
      font-family: Arial, sans-serif;
      display: flex;
      flex-direction: column;
      align-items: center;
      background-color: #f0f0f0;
    }

    h1 {
      color: #333;
    }

    form {
      display: flex;
```

```css
      flex-direction: column;
      margin-bottom: 1em;
      width: 80%;
    }

    form input,
    form textarea {
      margin-bottom: 0.5em;
      padding: 0.5em;
    }

    .post {
      width: 80%;
      background-color: #fff;
      margin: 1em 0;
      padding: 1em;
      box-shadow: 0px 0px 10px 0px rgba(0, 0, 0, 0.1);
      border-radius: 5px;
    }

    .post h2 {
      color: #333;
    }

    .post p {
      color: #666;
    }

    #post-list {
      width: 90%;
      display: flex;
      flex-direction: column;
      align-items: center;
    }
  </style>
</head>

<body>
  <h1>Blog Post App</h1>
  <form id="post-form">
    <input type="text" id="postTitle" placeholder="Title">
    <textarea id="postBody" placeholder="Body"></textarea>
    <button>Add Post</button>
  </form>
```

```
<div id="post-list"></div>

<!-- <script src="app.js"></script> -->
<script>
  const form = document.getElementById('post-form');
  const titleInput = document.getElementById('postTitle');
  const bodyInput = document.getElementById('postBody');
  const postList = document.getElementById('post-list');
  const API_URL = 'https://my-json-
server.typicode.com/SanghyunNa-web/blogmanage/posts';

  // Fetch initial posts
  fetch(API_URL)
    .then((response) => response.json())
    .then((posts) => {
      posts.forEach((post) => {
        addPostToPage(post);
      });
    });

  // Form submission
  form.addEventListener('submit', (event) => {
    event.preventDefault();

    const post = {
      title: titleInput.value,
      body: bodyInput.value,
    };

    // In a real-world scenario, you would send POST request to
API here
    addPostToPage(post);

    // Clear the input fields
    titleInput.value = '';
    bodyInput.value = '';
  });

  function addPostToPage(post) {
    const postDiv = document.createElement('div');
    postDiv.classList.add('post');

    const postTitle = document.createElement('h2');
    postTitle.textContent = post.title;
```

```
    postDiv.appendChild(postTitle);

    const postBody = document.createElement('p');
    postBody.textContent = post.body;
    postDiv.appendChild(postBody);

    const deleteButton = document.createElement('button');
    deleteButton.textContent = 'Delete';
    deleteButton.addEventListener('click', () => {
        // In a real-world scenario, you would send DELETE request
to API here
        postList.removeChild(postDiv);
    });

    postDiv.appendChild(deleteButton);
    postList.appendChild(postDiv);
    }

  </script>
</body>

</html>
```

```
<!-- This is a basic Blog Post App using a mock API, which can
add, delete, and display posts.
```

Create a new file named db.json for your mock API. Add some initial data:

```json
{
  "posts": [
    {
      "id": 1,
      "title": "First post",
      "body": "This is the first post"
    },
    {
      "id": 2,
      "title": "Second post",
      "body": "This is the second post"
    }
  ]
}
```

You can use My JSON Server, a project which serves this db.json file as a mock API.

Please note that My JSON Server is a read-only API. That means your POST and DELETE requests will look like they're working correctly, but they won't persist any changes. You need a real backend server for a fully functioning blog post app. -->

732

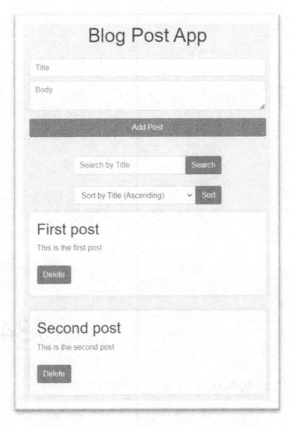

733

```
<!DOCTYPE html>
<html>

<head>
  <title>Blog Post App</title>
  <!-- Add Bootstrap CSS link -->
  <link rel="stylesheet"
href="https://maxcdn.bootstrapcdn.com/bootstrap/4.5.2/css/boot
strap.min.css">

  <style>
    body {
      font-family: Arial, sans-serif;
      display: flex;
      flex-direction: column;
      align-items: center;
      background-color: #f0f0f0;
```

```
    }

    h1 {
      color: #333;
    }

    form {
      display: flex;
      flex-direction: column;
      margin-bottom: 1em;
      width: 80%;
    }

    form input,
    form textarea {
      margin-bottom: 0.5em;
      padding: 0.5em;
    }

    .post {
      width: 80%;
      background-color: #fff;
      margin: 1em 0;
      padding: 1em;
      box-shadow: 0px 0px 10px 0px rgba(0, 0, 0, 0.1);
      border-radius: 5px;
    }

    .post h2 {
      color: #333;
    }

    .post p {
      color: #666;
    }

    #post-list {
      width: 100%;
      display: flex;
      flex-direction: column;
      align-items: center;
    }
  </style>
</head>
```

734

```html
<body>
  <h1 class="my-4">Blog Post App</h1>
  <form id="post-form">
    <input type="text" id="postTitle" class="form-control"
placeholder="Title">
    <textarea id="postBody" class="form-control"
placeholder="Body"></textarea>
    <button class="btn btn-primary mt-2">Add Post</button>
  </form>
  <div class="input-group my-4 w-50">
    <input type="text" id="searchTitle" class="form-control"
placeholder="Search by Title">
    <div class="input-group-append">
      <button class="btn btn-secondary"
onclick="searchPosts()">Search</button>
    </div>
  </div>
  <div class="input-group w-50">
    <select id="sortPosts" class="form-control">
      <option value="asc">Sort by Title (Ascending)</option>
      <option value="desc">Sort by Title (Descending)</option>
    </select>
    <div class="input-group-append">
      <button class="btn btn-secondary"
onclick="sortPosts()">Sort</button>
    </div>
  </div>
  <div id="post-list"></div>

  <!-- <script src="app.js"></script> -->
  <script>
    const form = document.getElementById('post-form');
    const titleInput = document.getElementById('postTitle');
    const bodyInput = document.getElementById('postBody');
    const searchTitleInput =
document.getElementById('searchTitle');
    const sortPostsInput = document.getElementById('sortPosts');
    const postList = document.getElementById('post-list');
    const API_URL = 'https://my-json-
server.typicode.com/SanghyunNa-web/blogmanage/posts';

    // Fetch initial posts
    fetch(API_URL)
```

```
    .then((response) => response.json())
    .then((posts) => {
      posts.forEach((post) => {
        addPostToPage(post);
      });
    });

  // Form submission
  form.addEventListener('submit', (event) => {
    event.preventDefault();

    const post = {
      title: titleInput.value,
      body: bodyInput.value,
    };

    // In a real-world scenario, you would send POST request to
API here
    addPostToPage(post);

    // Clear the input fields
    titleInput.value = '';
    bodyInput.value = '';
  });

  function addPostToPage(post) {
    const postDiv = document.createElement('div');
    postDiv.classList.add('post');

    const postTitle = document.createElement('h2');
    postTitle.textContent = post.title;
    postDiv.appendChild(postTitle);

    const postBody = document.createElement('p');
    postBody.textContent = post.body;
    postDiv.appendChild(postBody);

    const deleteButton = document.createElement('button');
    deleteButton.textContent = 'Delete';
    deleteButton.classList.add('btn', 'btn-danger', 'my-2');
    deleteButton.addEventListener('click', () => {
      // In a real-world scenario, you would send DELETE request
to API here
      postList.removeChild(postDiv);
```

```
        });

      postDiv.appendChild(deleteButton);
      postList.appendChild(postDiv);
    }

    function searchPosts() {
      const searchTerm = searchTitleInput.value.toLowerCase();
      const posts = postList.querySelectorAll('.post');

      posts.forEach((post) => {
        const title =
post.querySelector('h2').textContent.toLowerCase();
        if (title.includes(searchTerm)) {
          post.style.display = 'block';
        } else {
          post.style.display = 'none';
        }
      });
    }

    function sortPosts() {
      const sortOrder = sortPostsInput.value;
      const posts = Array.from(postList.querySelectorAll('.post'));

      posts.sort((a, b) => {
        const titleA =
a.querySelector('h2').textContent.toLowerCase();
        const titleB =
b.querySelector('h2').textContent.toLowerCase();
        if (sortOrder === 'asc') {
          return titleA.localeCompare(titleB);
        } else {
          return titleB.localeCompare(titleA);
        }
      });

      posts.forEach((post) => {
        postList.appendChild(post);
      });
    }

  </script>
</body>
```

737

```
</html>
```

<!-- In this updated version of the Blog Post App, we have
incorporated Bootstrap for styling, added a search feature to filter
posts based on the title, and a sorting feature to sort posts by title
in ascending or descending order. The Blog Post App now has a
more user-friendly and interactive layout, making it easier to
manage blog posts and find specific posts quickly. -->

738

Task Management App

Task Title

Add Task

delectus aut autem [Delete]

quis ut nam facilis et officia qui [Delete]

fugiat veniam minus [Delete]

~~et porro tempora~~ [Delete]

laboriosam mollitia et enim quasi adipisci quia provident illum
[Delete]

qui ullam ratione quibusdam voluptatem quia omnis [Delete]

illo expedita consequatur quia in [Delete]

quo adipisci enim quam ut ab [Delete]

739

```html
<!DOCTYPE html>
<html>

<head>
  <title>Task Management App</title>
  <!-- <link rel="stylesheet" href="style.css"> -->
  <style>
    body {
      font-family: Arial, sans-serif;
      display: flex;
      flex-direction: column;
      align-items: center;
      background-color: #f0f0f0;
    }

    h1 {
      color: #333;
    }

    form {
      display: flex;
      flex-direction: column;
      margin-bottom: 1em;
```

```
      width: 80%;
    }

    form input {
      margin-bottom: 0.5em;
      padding: 0.5em;
    }

    ul {
      width: 80%;
      padding: 0;
      list-style-type: none;
    }

    li {
      background-color: #fff;
      margin: 0.5em 0;
      padding: 0.5em;
      box-shadow: 0px 0px 10px 0px rgba(0, 0, 0, 0.1);
      border-radius: 5px;
    }

    li.completed {
      text-decoration: line-through;
    }

    button {
      margin-left: 1em;
    }
  </style>
</head>

<body>
  <h1>Task Management App</h1>
  <form id="task-form">
    <input type="text" id="taskTitle" placeholder="Task Title">
    <button>Add Task</button>
  </form>
  <ul id="task-list"></ul>

  <!-- <script src="app.js"></script> -->
  <script>
    const form = document.getElementById('task-form');
    const titleInput = document.getElementById('taskTitle');
```

740

```
const taskList = document.getElementById('task-list');
const API_URL = 'https://jsonplaceholder.typicode.com/todos';

// Fetch initial tasks
fetch(API_URL)
  .then((response) => response.json())
  .then((tasks) => {
    tasks.forEach((task) => {
      addTaskToPage(task);
    });
  });

// Form submission
form.addEventListener('submit', (event) => {
  event.preventDefault();

  const task = {
    title: titleInput.value,
    completed: false
  };

  // In a real-world scenario, you would send POST request to
API here
  addTaskToPage(task);

  // Clear the input field
  titleInput.value = '';
});

function addTaskToPage(task) {
  const taskItem = document.createElement('li');
  taskItem.textContent = task.title;

  if (task.completed) {
    taskItem.classList.add('completed');
  }

  const deleteButton = document.createElement('button');
  deleteButton.textContent = 'Delete';
  deleteButton.addEventListener('click', () => {
    // In a real-world scenario, you would send DELETE request
to API here
    taskList.removeChild(taskItem);
  });
```

```
    taskItem.appendChild(deleteButton);
    taskList.appendChild(taskItem);
  }

  </script>
</body>

</html>

<!-- We'll use JSONPlaceholder, which is a simple mock REST API
for testing and prototyping, to handle our mock API requests.
We'll also add some simple CSS for styling.

Please note that JSONPlaceholder is a mock API, so POST and
DELETE requests will not actually change the data on the server.
However, it does simulate the responses you would get from a
real REST API. For a real-world task management app, you would
need to use a real backend. -->
```

Task Management App

| Task Title |
| Add Task |

| 5 | Set Number of Tasks |

delectus aut autem [Delete]

quis ut nam facilis et officia qui [Delete]

fugiat veniam minus [Delete]

~~et porro tempora~~ [Delete]

laboriosam mollitia et enim quasi adipisci quia provident illum
[Delete]

743

```html
<!DOCTYPE html>
<html>

<head>
  <title>Task Management App</title>
  <style>
    body {
      font-family: Arial, sans-serif;
      display: flex;
      flex-direction: column;
      align-items: center;
      background-color: #f0f0f0;
    }

    h1 {
      color: #333;
    }

    form {
      display: flex;
      flex-direction: column;
      margin-bottom: 1em;
      width: 80%;
    }
```

```css
    form input {
      margin-bottom: 0.5em;
      padding: 0.5em;
    }

    ul {
      width: 80%;
      padding: 0;
      list-style-type: none;
    }

    li {
      background-color: #fff;
      margin: 0.5em 0;
      padding: 0.5em;
      box-shadow: 0px 0px 10px 0px rgba(0, 0, 0, 0.1);
      border-radius: 5px;
    }

    li.completed {
      text-decoration: line-through;
    }

    button {
      margin-left: 1em;
    }
  </style>
</head>

<body>
  <h1>Task Management App</h1>
  <form id="task-form">
    <input type="text" id="taskTitle" placeholder="Task Title">
    <button>Add Task</button>
  </form>
  <div>
    <input type="number" id="taskNumber" min="1"
value="10">
    <button id="setTaskNumber">Set Number of Tasks</button>
  </div>
  <ul id="task-list"></ul>

  <script>
```

```
    const form = document.getElementById('task-form');
    const titleInput = document.getElementById('taskTitle');
    const taskNumberInput =
document.getElementById('taskNumber');
    const setTaskNumberButton =
document.getElementById('setTaskNumber');
    const taskList = document.getElementById('task-list');
    const API_URL = 'https://jsonplaceholder.typicode.com/todos';

    // Fetch initial tasks
    function fetchTasks() {
      fetch(API_URL)
        .then((response) => response.json())
        .then((tasks) => {
          taskList.innerHTML = '';
          tasks.slice(0, taskNumberInput.value).forEach((task) =>
{
            addTaskToPage(task);
          });
        });
    }

    fetchTasks();

    // Set number of tasks
    setTaskNumberButton.addEventListener('click', (event) => {
      event.preventDefault();
      fetchTasks();
    });

    // Form submission
    form.addEventListener('submit', (event) => {
      event.preventDefault();

      const task = {
        title: titleInput.value,
        completed: false
      };

      // Add task at the top of the list
      addTaskToPage(task, true);

      // Clear the input field
      titleInput.value = '';
```

```
    });

    function addTaskToPage(task, prepend = false) {
      const taskItem = document.createElement('li');
      taskItem.textContent = task.title;

      if (task.completed) {
        taskItem.classList.add('completed');
      }

      const deleteButton = document.createElement('button');
      deleteButton.textContent = 'Delete';
      deleteButton.addEventListener('click', () => {
        // In a real-world scenario, you would send DELETE request
to API here
        taskList.removeChild(taskItem);
      });

      taskItem.appendChild(deleteButton);

      // Prepend or append the task item to the list based on the
"prepend" parameter
      if (prepend) {
        taskList.prepend(taskItem);
      } else {
        taskList.appendChild(taskItem);
      }
    }
  </script>
</body>
</html>
<!-- I added a "Set" button next to the number input, allowing
users to specify the number of tasks to be fetched from the API.
This version of the code provides an additional "Set Number of
Tasks" button next to the number input field. When clicked, it
fetches the number of tasks specified by the user from the API
and displays them in the list. -->
```

746

Task Management App

Task Title		Add Task

10	Set Number of Tasks

Completed	⌄

~~et porro tempora~~	Delete

~~quo adipisci enim quam ut ab~~	Delete

~~illo est ratione doloremque quia maiores aut~~	
	Delete

747

```
<!DOCTYPE html>
<html>

<head>
  <title>Task Management App</title>
  <link rel="stylesheet"
href="https://maxcdn.bootstrapcdn.com/bootstrap/4.5.2/css/boot
strap.min.css">
  <style>
    body {
      font-family: Arial, sans-serif;
      display: flex;
      flex-direction: column;
      align-items: center;
      background-color: #f0f0f0;
    }

    h1 {
      color: #333;
    }
```

```
    form {
      display: flex;
      flex-direction: column;
      margin-bottom: 1em;
      width: 80%;
    }

    form input {
      margin-bottom: 0.5em;
      padding: 0.5em;
    }

    ul {
      width: 80%;
      padding: 0;
      list-style-type: none;
    }

    li {
      background-color: #fff;
      margin: 0.5em 0;
      padding: 0.5em;
      box-shadow: 0px 0px 10px 0px rgba(0, 0, 0, 0.1);
      border-radius: 5px;
      cursor: pointer;
    }

    li.completed {
      text-decoration: line-through;
    }

    button {
      margin-left: 1em;
    }
  </style>
</head>

<body>
  <div class="container">
    <h1 class="my-4">Task Management App</h1>
```

```html
<form id="task-form" class="form-inline mb-3">
    <input type="text" id="taskTitle" class="form-control mr-2"
placeholder="Task Title">
    <button type="submit" class="btn btn-primary">Add
Task</button>
  </form>
  <div class="input-group mb-3">
    <input type="number" id="taskNumber" class="form-
control" min="1" value="10">
    <div class="input-group-append">
     <button id="setTaskNumber" class="btn btn-
secondary">Set Number of Tasks</button>
    </div>
  </div>
  <select id="task-status-filter" class="form-control mb-3">
    <option value="all">All</option>
    <option value="completed">Completed</option>
    <option value="incomplete">Incomplete</option>
  </select>
  <ul id="task-list" class="list-group"></ul>
</div>
```

749

```html
<script>
  const form = document.getElementById('task-form');
  const titleInput = document.getElementById('taskTitle');
  const taskNumberInput =
document.getElementById('taskNumber');
  const setTaskNumberButton =
document.getElementById('setTaskNumber');
  const taskStatusFilter = document.getElementById('task-
status-filter');
  const taskList = document.getElementById('task-list');
  const API_URL = 'https://jsonplaceholder.typicode.com/todos';

  // Fetch initial tasks
  function fetchTasks() {
   fetch(API_URL)
     .then((response) => response.json())
     .then((tasks) => {
       taskList.innerHTML = '';
```

```
        tasks.slice(0, taskNumberInput.value).forEach((task) =>
{
            addTaskToPage(task);
        });
      });
    }

    fetchTasks();

    // Set number of tasks
    setTaskNumberButton.addEventListener('click', (event) => {
      event.preventDefault();
      fetchTasks();
    });

    // Form submission
    form.addEventListener('submit', (event) => {
      event.preventDefault();

      const task = {
        title: titleInput.value,
        completed: false
      };

      // Add task at the top of the list
      addTaskToPage(task, true);

      // Clear the input field
      titleInput.value = '';
    });

    // Mark a task as completed
    taskList.addEventListener('click', (event) => {
      const target = event.target;
      if (target.classList.contains('task-item')) {
        target.classList.toggle('completed');
      }
    });

    // Filter tasks by status
    taskStatusFilter.addEventListener('change', (event) => {
```

```
    const selectedStatus = event.target.value;
    const taskItems = taskList.querySelectorAll('.task-item');

    if (selectedStatus === 'all') {
      taskItems.forEach(item => item.style.display = 'block');
    } else {
      taskItems.forEach(item => {
        item.style.display =
item.classList.contains(selectedStatus) ? 'block' : 'none';
      });
    }
  });

  function addTaskToPage(task, prepend = false) {
    const taskItem = document.createElement('li');
    taskItem.textContent = task.title;
    taskItem.classList.add('list-group-item', 'task-item');

    if (task.completed) {
      taskItem.classList.add('completed');
    }

    const deleteButton = document.createElement('button');
    deleteButton.textContent = 'Delete';
    deleteButton.classList.add('btn', 'btn-danger', 'btn-sm',
'float-right');
    deleteButton.addEventListener('click', () => {
      // In a real-world scenario, you would send DELETE request
to API here
      taskItem.remove();
    });

    taskItem.appendChild(deleteButton);

    // Prepend or append the task item to the list based on the
"prepend" parameter
    if (prepend) {
      taskList.prepend(taskItem);
    } else {
      taskList.appendChild(taskItem);
    }
```

```
      }
  </script>
</body>

</html>

<!-- With these changes, the Task Management App now has a
more colorful layout, Bootstrap-styled buttons and form elements,
and two additional functionalities - marking tasks as completed by
clicking on them and filtering tasks by status using a dropdown
menu.

Note: Since the Task Management App is a front-end only app
using dummy data from the JSONPlaceholder API, the changes for
marking tasks as completed won't persist beyond the session, and
the filtering functionality won't filter tasks based on server-side
data. For a complete and persistent solution, you would need to
integrate the app with a back-end server and database. -->
```

Event Countdown

My birthday

2023-08-31 오후 06:00

Start Countdown

Countdown to My birthday:

37d 21h 54m 50s

```
<!DOCTYPE html>
<html>

<head>
  <title>Event Countdown</title>
  <!-- <link rel="stylesheet" href="style.css"> -->
  <style>
    body {
      font-family: Arial, sans-serif;
      display: flex;
      flex-direction: column;
      align-items: center;
      background-color: #f0f0f0;
    }

    h1 {
      color: #333;
    }

    form {
      display: flex;
      flex-direction: column;
      margin-bottom: 1em;
      width: 80%;
    }
```

```css
    form input {
      margin-bottom: 0.5em;
      padding: 0.5em;
    }

    h2 {
      color: #666;
    }

    p {
      color: #f70606;
      font-size: 20px;
    }
  </style>
</head>
```

```html
<body>
  <h1>Event Countdown</h1>
  <form id="event-form">
    <input type="text" id="eventName" placeholder="Event Name">
    <input type="datetime-local" id="eventTime">
    <button>Start Countdown</button>
  </form>
  <h2 id="countdown-title"></h2>
  <p id="countdown"></p>

  <!-- <script src="app.js"></script> -->
  <script>
    const form = document.getElementById('event-form');
    const nameInput = document.getElementById('eventName');
    const timeInput = document.getElementById('eventTime');
    const countdownTitle =
document.getElementById('countdown-title');
    const countdownEl = document.getElementById('countdown');

    let countdownInterval;

    // Form submission
    form.addEventListener('submit', (event) => {
      event.preventDefault();

      const eventName = nameInput.value;
      const eventTime = new Date(timeInput.value);
```

```javascript
    countdownTitle.textContent = `Countdown to
${eventName}:`;

    // Clear any existing countdown
    clearInterval(countdownInterval);

    // Start new countdown
    countdownInterval = setInterval(() => {
      const now = new Date();
      const distance = eventTime - now;

      const days = Math.floor(distance / (1000 * 60 * 60 * 24));
      const hours = Math.floor((distance % (1000 * 60 * 60 *
24)) / (1000 * 60 * 60));
      const minutes = Math.floor((distance % (1000 * 60 * 60))
/ (1000 * 60));
      const seconds = Math.floor((distance % (1000 * 60)) /
1000);

      countdownEl.textContent = `${days}d ${hours}h
${minutes}m ${seconds}s`;

      // When countdown is over
      if (distance < 0) {
        clearInterval(countdownInterval);
        countdownEl.textContent = "Event has started!";
      }
    }, 1000);
  });
  </script>
</body>
</html>
<!-- This is a simple countdown that updates every second. When
the event time is reached, the countdown stops and a message is
displayed. Note that type="datetime-local" might not be
supported in all browsers. It allows users to select a date and time
with no time zone. In a production application, you might want to
use a JavaScript library for a more robust date/time picker. -->
```

Event Countdown

| Test for real estate agents | 2023-10-28 오전 08:01📅 | Start Countdown |

Countdown to Test for real estate agents:

95d 11h 51m 0s

```
<!DOCTYPE html>
<html>

<head>
  <title>Event Countdown</title>
  <!-- <link rel="stylesheet" href="style.css"> -->
  <style>
    body {
      font-family: Arial, sans-serif;
      display: flex;
      flex-direction: column;
      align-items: center;
      justify-content: center;
      height: 100vh;
      background-color: #f0f0f0;
    }

    h1 {
      color: #663399;
      text-align: center;
      width: 100%;
    }

    form {
      display: flex;
      justify-content: space-between;
      align-items: center;
```

756

```css
    margin-bottom: 1em;
    width: 80%;
  }

  form input {
    width: 400px;
    margin-right: 0.5em;
    padding: 0.5em;
  }

  form button {
    width: 200px;
    background-color: #28a745;
    color: white;
    padding: 10px;
    border: none;
    cursor: pointer;
  }

  h2 {
    color: #333;
  }

  p {
    color: #dc3545;
    font-size: 20px;
  }

  .countdown {
    display: flex;
    flex-direction: column;
    align-items: center;
    padding: 10px;
    background-color: #f8f9fa;
    border-radius: 5px;
    color: #333;
  }
  </style>
</head>

<body>
  <h1>Event Countdown</h1>
  <form id="event-form">
```

```html
    <input type="text" id="eventName" placeholder="Event
Name">
    <input type="datetime-local" id="eventTime">
    <button>Start Countdown</button>
  </form>
  <div class="countdown">
   <h2 id="countdown-title"></h2>
   <p id="countdown"></p>
  </div>

  <!-- <script src="app.js"></script> -->
  <script>
   const form = document.getElementById('event-form');
   const nameInput = document.getElementById('eventName');
   const timeInput = document.getElementById('eventTime');
   const countdownTitle =
document.getElementById('countdown-title');
   const countdownEl = document.getElementById('countdown');

   let countdownInterval;

   // Form submission
   form.addEventListener('submit', (event) => {
     event.preventDefault();

     const eventName = nameInput.value;
     const eventTime = new Date(timeInput.value);

     countdownTitle.textContent = `Countdown to
${eventName}:`;

     // Clear any existing countdown
     clearInterval(countdownInterval);

     // Start new countdown
     countdownInterval = setInterval(() => {
       const now = new Date();
       const distance = eventTime - now;

       const days = Math.floor(distance / (1000 * 60 * 60 * 24));
       const hours = Math.floor((distance % (1000 * 60 * 60 *
24)) / (1000 * 60 * 60));
       const minutes = Math.floor((distance % (1000 * 60 * 60))
/ (1000 * 60));
```

```
      const seconds = Math.floor((distance % (1000 * 60)) /
1000);

      countdownEl.textContent = `${days}d ${hours}h
${minutes}m ${seconds}s`;

      // When countdown is over
      if (distance < 0) {
        clearInterval(countdownInterval);
        countdownEl.textContent = "Event has started!";
      }
    }, 1000);
  });
</script>
</body>

</html>
```

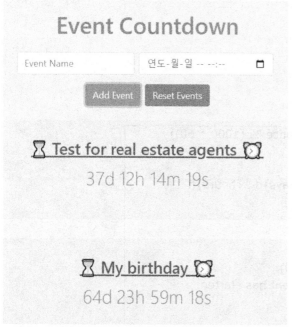

760

```
<!DOCTYPE html>
<html>

<head>
  <title>Event Countdown</title>

  <!-- Add Bootstrap CSS -->
  <link rel="stylesheet"
href="https://stackpath.bootstrapcdn.com/bootstrap/4.3.1/css/bo
otstrap.min.css">

  <!-- Custom CSS -->
  <style>
    h3 {
      color: blue;
      text-decoration: underline;
    }

    .countdown-number {
      font-size: 2.0em;
    }
  </style>
```

```html
<!-- Add jQuery -->
<script src="https://code.jquery.com/jquery-
3.3.1.min.js"></script>

</head>

<body class="d-flex align-items-center justify-content-center"
style="height: 100vh; background-color: #f0f0f0;">

  <div class="container text-center">
    <h1 class="text-primary mb-4">Event Countdown</h1>

    <form id="event-form" class="form-inline justify-content-
center mb-4">
      <div class="form-group mr-2">
        <input class="form-control" type="text" id="eventName"
placeholder="Event Name">
      </div>
      <div class="form-group mr-2">
        <input class="form-control" type="datetime-local"
id="eventTime">
      </div>
      <button class="btn btn-success mr-2">Add Event</button>
      <button class="btn btn-danger" id="reset">Reset
Events</button>
    </form>

    <div id="events-list">
    <!-- Event countdowns will be added here -->
    </div>
  </div>

  <script>
  $('#event-form').on('submit', function (event) {
    event.preventDefault();

    let eventName = $('#eventName').val();
    let eventTime = new Date($('#eventTime').val());

    if (!eventName || !eventTime) {
      alert("Both fields are required!");
      return;
    }
```

```
    if (eventTime < new Date()) {
      alert("Event time cannot be in the past!");
      return;
    }

    // Create new event countdown
    let countdownDiv = $('<div class="jumbotron"></div>');
    countdownDiv.append(`<h3>⏳ ${eventName} 🕐</h3>`);
    countdownDiv.append('<p class="lead text-danger
countdown-number"></p>');

    // Add to events list
    $('#events-list').append(countdownDiv);

    let countdownEl = countdownDiv.find('.countdown-number');

    // Start countdown
    let countdownInterval = setInterval(function () {
      let now = new Date();
      let distance = eventTime - now;

      let days = Math.floor(distance / (1000 * 60 * 60 * 24));
      let hours = Math.floor((distance % (1000 * 60 * 60 * 24))
/ (1000 * 60 * 60));
      let minutes = Math.floor((distance % (1000 * 60 * 60)) /
(1000 * 60));
      let seconds = Math.floor((distance % (1000 * 60)) / 1000);

      countdownEl.text(`${days}d ${hours}h ${minutes}m
${seconds}s`);

      // When countdown is over
      if (distance < 0) {
        clearInterval(countdownInterval);
        countdownEl.text("Event has started!");
      }
    }, 1000);

    // Reset input fields
    $('#eventName').val('');
    $('#eventTime').val('');
  });
```

```
    $('#reset').on('click', function (event) {
      event.preventDefault();

      // Clear all events
      $('#events-list').empty();
    });
  </script>

  <!-- Add Bootstrap JS -->
  <script
src="https://stackpath.bootstrapcdn.com/bootstrap/4.3.1/js/boot
strap.min.js"></script>

</body>

</html>

<!-- This code creates a new countdown for each event, adds
them to a list in the DOM, and clears the input fields after an
event is added. The countdowns are independent of each other
and run concurrently. The "Reset Events" button clears all events.
-->
```

763

097_WEBCALCULATOR1

```
<!DOCTYPE html>
<html>

<head>
  <title>Complex Web Calculator</title>
  <style>
    body {
      font-family: Arial, sans-serif;
      display: flex;
      justify-content: center;
      align-items: center;
      height: 100vh;
      background-color: #f0f0f0;
    }

    .calculator {
      display: flex;
      flex-direction: column;
      align-items: center;
      width: 300px;
      border: 2px solid #a9a9a9;
      border-radius: 5px;
      padding: 20px;
```

```
      background-color: #fff;
      box-shadow: 0px 0px 15px rgba(0, 0, 0, 0.1);
    }

    #display {
      width: 100%;
      height: 50px;
      margin-bottom: 10px;
      text-align: right;
      padding: 0 10px;
      box-sizing: border-box;
    }

    button {
      width: 60px;
      height: 40px;
      margin: 5px;
      font-size: 18px;
      border: none;
      background-color: #ddd;
      border-radius: 5px;
    }

    #equals {
      background-color: #ff6347;
    }

    #clear {
      background-color: #a9a9a9;
    }
  </style>
</head>

<body>
  <div class="calculator">
    <input type="text" id="display" disabled>
    <div class="buttons">
      <button data-number="1">1</button>
      <button data-number="2">2</button>
      <button data-number="3">3</button>
      <button data-number="4">4</button>
      <button data-number="5">5</button>
      <button data-number="6">6</button>
      <button data-number="7">7</button>
```

```html
      <button data-number="8">8</button>
      <button data-number="9">9</button>
      <button data-number="0">0</button>
      <button data-decimal>.</button>
      <button data-sign>±</button>
      <button data-percent>%</button>
      <button data-operator="+">+</button>
      <button data-operator="-">-</button>
      <button data-operator="*">*</button>
      <button data-operator="/">/</button>
      <button data-sqrt>√</button>
      <button data-square>x²</button>
      <button id="equals" data-equal>=</button>
      <button id="clear" data-clear>Clear</button>
    </div>
  </div>
  <script>
    const display = document.querySelector("#display");

    document.querySelectorAll("button").forEach((button) => {
      button.addEventListener("click", () => {
        if (button.hasAttribute("data-number") ||
button.hasAttribute("data-operator") || button.hasAttribute("data-
decimal")) {
          display.value += button.textContent;
        } else if (button.hasAttribute("data-equal")) {
          try {
            display.value = eval(display.value);
          } catch {
            display.value = "Error";
          }
        } else if (button.hasAttribute("data-clear")) {
          display.value = "";
        } else if (button.hasAttribute("data-sign")) {
          if (display.value) {
            display.value = parseFloat(display.value) * -1;
          }
        } else if (button.hasAttribute("data-percent")) {
          if (display.value) {
            display.value = parseFloat(display.value) / 100;
          }
        } else if (button.hasAttribute("data-sqrt")) {
          if (display.value) {
```

```
          display.value =
Math.sqrt(parseFloat(display.value)).toFixed(2);
        }
      } else if (button.hasAttribute("data-square")) {
        if (display.value) {
          display.value = Math.pow(parseFloat(display.value), 2);
        }
      }
    });
  });
  </script>
</body>

</html>
```

767

768

```
<!DOCTYPE html>
<html>

<head>
  <title>Complex Web Calculator</title>
  <style>
    body {
      font-family: Arial, sans-serif;
      display: flex;
      justify-content: center;
      align-items: center;
      height: 100vh;
      background-color: #f0f0f0;
    }

    .calculator {
      display: flex;
      flex-direction: column;
      align-items: center;
```

```
  width: 300px;
  border: 2px solid #a9a9a9;
  /* Add border */
  border-radius: 5px;
  /* Add border radius */
  padding: 20px;
  /* Add padding */
  background-color: #ffffff;
  /* Add background color */
  box-shadow: 0px 0px 15px rgba(0, 0, 0, 0.1);
  /* Add shadow */
}

#display {
  width: 100%;
  height: 50px;
  margin-bottom: 10px;
  text-align: right;
  padding: 0 10px;
  box-sizing: border-box;
}

.buttons {
  display: grid;
  grid-template-columns: repeat(4, 1fr);
  gap: 10px;
  width: 100%;
}

button {
  height: 50px;
  font-size: 1.5em;
  border: none;
  background-color: #ddd;
  border-radius: 5px;
}

[data-operator] {
  background-color: #ffa500;
}

[data-equal] {
  background-color: #ff6347;
  grid-column: span 2;
```

```
      }

    [data-clear],
    [data-sign],
    [data-percent] {
      background-color: #a9a9a9;
    }
  </style>
</head>

<body>
  <div class="calculator">
    <input type="text" id="display" disabled>
    <div class="buttons">
      <button data-clear>Clear</button>
      <button data-sign>±</button>
      <button data-percent>%</button>
      <button data-operator="/">/</button>
      <button data-number="7">7</button>
      <button data-number="8">8</button>
      <button data-number="9">9</button>
      <button data-operator="*">*</button>
      <button data-number="4">4</button>
      <button data-number="5">5</button>
      <button data-number="6">6</button>
      <button data-operator="-">-</button>
      <button data-number="1">1</button>
      <button data-number="2">2</button>
      <button data-number="3">3</button>
      <button data-operator="+">+</button>
      <button data-number="0">0</button>
      <button data-decimal>.</button>
      <button data-sqrt>√</button>
      <button data-square>x²</button>
      <button data-equal>=</button>
    </div>
  </div>

  <script>
  const display = document.querySelector("#display");

document.querySelectorAll("button").forEach((button) => {
  button.addEventListener("click", () => {
```

```
    if (button.hasAttribute("data-number") ||
button.hasAttribute("data-operator") || button.hasAttribute("data-
decimal")) {
        display.value += button.textContent;
    } else if (button.hasAttribute("data-equal")) {
        try {
            display.value = eval(display.value);
        } catch {
            display.value = "Error";
        }
    } else if (button.hasAttribute("data-clear")) {
        display.value = "";
    } else if (button.hasAttribute("data-sign")) {
        if (display.value) {
            display.value = parseFloat(display.value) * -1;
        }
    } else if (button.hasAttribute("data-percent")) {
        if (display.value) {
            display.value = parseFloat(display.value) / 100;
        }
    } else if (button.hasAttribute("data-sqrt")) {
        if (display.value) {
            display.value =
Math.sqrt(parseFloat(display.value)).toFixed(2);
        }
    } else if (button.hasAttribute("data-square")) {
        if (display.value) {
            display.value = Math.pow(parseFloat(display.value), 2);
        }
    }
  });
});
  </script>
</body>

</html>
```

771

Newsletter Signup

Name:

Peter

Email:

google@gmail.com

Interests:

science AI

Sign Up

772

```
<!DOCTYPE html>
<html>

<head>
  <title>Newsletter Signup</title>
  <!-- <link rel="stylesheet" type="text/css" href="styles.css"> --
>
  <style>
    body {
      display: flex;
      justify-content: center;
      align-items: center;
      height: 100vh;
      background-color: #f2f2f2;
    }

    .container {
      background-color: #fff;
      border-radius: 10px;
      box-shadow: 0 2px 5px rgba(0, 0, 0, 0.3);
      padding: 20px;
```

```
      width: 400px;
    }

    h1 {
      text-align: center;
      color: #333;
    }

    .form-group {
      display: flex;
      flex-direction: column;
      margin-bottom: 15px;
    }

    label {
      margin-bottom: 5px;
      color: #666;
    }

    input[type="text"],
    input[type="email"] {
      padding: 8px;
      border-radius: 4px;
      border: 1px solid #ccc;
    }

    button[type="submit"] {
      padding: 10px;
      border-radius: 4px;
      background-color: #333;
      color: #fff;
      border: none;
      cursor: pointer;
      transition: background-color 0.3s;
    }

    button[type="submit"]:hover {
      background-color: #555;
    }
  </style>
</head>

<body>
  <div class="container">
```

```html
    <h1>Newsletter Signup</h1>
    <form id="signup-form" onsubmit="submitForm(event)">
      <div class="form-group">
        <label for="name">Name:</label>
        <input type="text" id="name" required>
      </div>
      <div class="form-group">
        <label for="email">Email:</label>
        <input type="email" id="email" required>
      </div>
      <div class="form-group">
        <label for="interests">Interests:</label>
        <input type="text" id="interests" required>
      </div>
      <button type="submit">Sign Up</button>
    </form>
  </div>

  <!-- <script src="script.js"></script> -->
  <script>
    function submitForm(event) {
      event.preventDefault(); // Prevent form submission
      // Get form values
      var name = document.getElementById('name').value;
      var email = document.getElementById('email').value;
      var interests = document.getElementById('interests').value;

      // Perform form validation or additional processing if needed
      // ...

      // Display a success message
      alert('Thank you for signing up!');
      // Clear form fields
      document.getElementById('name').value = '';
      document.getElementById('email').value = '';
      document.getElementById('interests').value = '';
    }

  </script>
</body>

</html>
```

774

```
<!-- Creating a newsletter signup form in HTML, CSS, and
JavaScript is a great start. However, to actually store and manage
the data entered by your users, you would need a back-end
server or a service to handle the form data.

There are two primary ways you could approach this:

1. Use a Third-Party Service: There are various services like
MailChimp, Sendinblue, or Constant Contact that provide an
integrated solution for creating and managing newsletter
subscriptions. These services have in-built signup forms that can
be easily integrated into your website. They handle everything
from storing email addresses to sending out newsletters, and
often provide additional functionality like analytics, A/B testing,
etc.

2. Develop Your Own Back-End Service: This requires more
technical know-how but gives you more control. You would need
to set up a server, using something like Node.js, Python (with
Django or Flask), or Ruby on Rails. This server would have
endpoints that your front-end could send data to. You would also
need a database (like PostgreSQL, MySQL, or MongoDB) to store
the email addresses.

Keep in mind that managing user data requires careful attention
to security and privacy. It is important to handle the data
according to the data protection laws applicable in your region
(like the GDPR in the European Union). You should securely store
the data and inform your users about how their data will be used.
-->
```

775

Newsletter Signup

Name:

Peter

Email:

google@gmail.com

Password:

1111

☑ Show Password

Interests:

science AI

Sign Up

776

```
<!DOCTYPE html>
<html>

<head>
  <title>Newsletter Signup</title>
  <!-- Bootstrap CSS -->
  <link
href="https://stackpath.bootstrapcdn.com/bootstrap/4.3.1/css/bo
otstrap.min.css" rel="stylesheet">

  <!-- jQuery -->
  <script src="https://code.jquery.com/jquery-
3.3.1.min.js"></script>
</head>
```

```html
<body class="d-flex justify-content-center align-items-center vh-100 bg-light">

  <div class="container bg-white p-4 rounded shadow-sm w-50">
    <h1 class="text-center text-dark mb-4">Newsletter Signup</h1>
    <form id="signup-form">
      <div class="form-group">
        <label for="name">Name:</label>
        <input type="text" id="name" class="form-control" required>
      </div>
      <div class="form-group">
        <label for="email">Email:</label>
        <input type="email" id="email" class="form-control" required>
      </div>
      <div class="form-group">
        <label for="password">Password:</label>
        <input type="password" id="password" class="form-control" required>
        <input type="checkbox" id="show-password"> Show Password
      </div>
      <div class="form-group">
        <label for="interests">Interests:</label>
        <input type="text" id="interests" class="form-control" required>
      </div>
      <button type="submit" class="btn btn-dark w-100">Sign Up</button>
    </form>
  </div>

  <script>
    $('#signup-form').on('submit', function (event) {
      event.preventDefault(); // Prevent form submission

      // Get form values
      var name = $('#name').val();
      var email = $('#email').val();
      var interests = $('#interests').val();
```

```
    var emailPattern = /^([\w-\.]+@([\w-]+\.)+[\w-]{2,4})?$/;
// Basic email pattern

    if (!emailPattern.test(email)) {
      alert('Please enter a valid email address');
      return false;
    }

    // Display a success message
    alert('Thank you for signing up!');

    // Clear form fields
    $('#name').val('');
    $('#email').val('');
    $('#interests').val('');
    $('#password').val('');
  });

  // Show or hide password
  $('#show-password').on('click', function () {
    var passwordField = $('#password');
    var passwordFieldType = passwordField.attr('type');
    if (passwordFieldType == 'password') {
      passwordField.attr('type', 'text');
    } else {
      passwordField.attr('type', 'password');
    }
  });
</script>

<!-- Bootstrap JS -->
<script
src="https://stackpath.bootstrapcdn.com/bootstrap/4.3.1/js/boot
strap.min.js"></script>

</body>

</html>
```

778

```
<!DOCTYPE html>
<html>

<head>
  <title>Image Carousel</title>
  <style>
    .carousel-container {
      display: flex;
      justify-content: center;
      align-items: center;
      height: 100vh;
      background-color: #f2f2f2;
    }

    .carousel {
      position: relative;
      width: 100%;
      height: 500px;
      /* Adjust this to your desired height */
      overflow: hidden;
      border-radius: 10px;
      box-shadow: 0 2px 5px rgba(0, 0, 0, 0.3);
    }

    .carousel-image {
      position: absolute;
      top: 0;
```

779

```css
      left: 0;
      width: 100%;
      height: 100%;
      object-fit: cover;
      /* Resizes the image to fill the container without distorting
the aspect ratio */
      transition: transform 1s;
      opacity: 0;
    }

    .carousel-image.active {
      opacity: 1;
    }

    .carousel-nav {
      margin-top: 10px;
      text-align: center;
    }

    .carousel-prev,
    .carousel-next {
      padding: 5px 10px;
      border-radius: 4px;
      background-color: #333;
      color: #fff;
      border: none;
      cursor: pointer;
      transition: background-color 0.3s;
    }

    .carousel-prev {
      margin-right: 10px;
    }

    .carousel-prev:hover,
    .carousel-next:hover {
      background-color: #555;
    }
  </style>
</head>

<body>
  <div class="carousel-container">
    <div class="carousel">
```

```
        <img class="carousel-image active" src="image1.jpg"
alt="Image 1">
        <img class="carousel-image" src="image2.jpg" alt="Image
2">
        <img class="carousel-image" src="image3.jpg" alt="Image
3">
        <img class="carousel-image" src="image4.png" alt="Image
4">
        <img class="carousel-image" src="image5.jpg" alt="Image
5">
        <img class="carousel-image" src="image6.jpg" alt="Image
6">
        <img class="carousel-image" src="image7.jpg" alt="Image
7">
        <img class="carousel-image" src="image8.jpg" alt="Image
8">
        <img class="carousel-image" src="image9.jpg" alt="Image
9">
    </div>
    <div class="carousel-nav">
        <button class="carousel-prev" onclick="changeSlide(-
1)">&#10094;</button>
        <button class="carousel-next"
onclick="changeSlide(1)">&#10095;</button>
    </div>
  </div>
  <script>
    let currentIndex = 0;
    let carouselImages =
Array.from(document.getElementsByClassName('carousel-
image'));
    let numSlides = carouselImages.length;
    let intervalId;

    // Auto-rotate images every 3 seconds
    intervalId = setInterval(() => {
      changeSlide(1);
    }, 3000);

    function changeSlide(n) {
      if ((currentIndex === numSlides - 1 && n === 1) ||
(currentIndex === 0 && n === -1)) {
        // Do not move past the last or before the first slide
```

```
      clearInterval(intervalId); // stop auto-rotate when the last
image is reached
        return;
      }
      currentIndex += n;
      showSlide();
    }

    function showSlide() {
      carouselImages.forEach((image, i) => {
        image.classList.remove("active");
        if (i === currentIndex) {
          image.classList.add("active");
        }
      });
    }

    // This ensures that the showSlide function is called once the
DOM is fully loaded
    document.addEventListener("DOMContentLoaded",
showSlide);
  </script>
</body>
</html>
<!-- There are several websites that offer free images that can be
used for both personal and commercial projects. Here are some of
them:
1. Unsplash: Offers a large collection of high-resolution photos.

2. Pixabay: Provides a vast range of high-quality photos, vector
graphics, and art illustrations.

3. Pexels: Offers high-quality and completely free stock photos.

4. Freepik: Besides high-quality photos, Freepik also offers a large
collection of vector images.

5. Burst by Shopify: Provides free stock photos for entrepreneurs.

6. Gratisography: Offers free high-resolution pictures you can use
on your personal and commercial projects.

7. StockSnap.io: Offers a large selection of high resolution photos.
-->
```

782

```
<!DOCTYPE html>
<html>

<head>
  <title>Image Carousel</title>

  <!-- Bootstrap CSS -->
  <link
href="https://stackpath.bootstrapcdn.com/bootstrap/4.3.1/css/bo
otstrap.min.css" rel="stylesheet">

  <!-- jQuery -->
  <script src="https://code.jquery.com/jquery-
3.3.1.min.js"></script>
</head>

<body class="d-flex justify-content-center align-items-center vh-
100 bg-light">
```

783

```html
<div id="carouselExampleIndicators" class="carousel slide w-
50" data-ride="carousel">
  <ol class="carousel-indicators">
    <li data-target="#carouselExampleIndicators" data-slide-
to="0" class="active"></li>
    <li data-target="#carouselExampleIndicators" data-slide-
to="1"></li>
    <li data-target="#carouselExampleIndicators" data-slide-
to="2"></ll>
    <li data-target="#carouselExampleIndicators" data-slide-
to="3"></li>
    <li data-target="#carouselExampleIndicators" data-slide-
to="4"></li>
    <li data-target="#carouselExampleIndicators" data-slide-
to="5"></li>
    <li data-target="#carouselExampleIndicators" data-slide-
to="6"></li>
    <li data-target="#carouselExampleIndicators" data-slide-
to="7"></li>
    <li data-target="#carouselExampleIndicators" data-slide-
to="8"></li>
    <!-- Add more <li> elements based on the number of
images -->
  </ol>
  <div class="carousel-inner">
    <div class="carousel-item active">
      <img src="image1.jpg" class="d-block w-100" alt="...">
    </div>
    <div class="carousel-item">
      <img src="image2.jpg" class="d-block w-100" alt="...">
    </div>
    <div class="carousel-item">
      <img src="image3.jpg" class="d-block w-100" alt="...">
    </div>
```

```
    <div class="carousel-item">
      <img src="image4.png" class="d-block w-100" alt="...">
    </div>
    <div class="carousel-item">
      <img src="image5.jpg" class="d-block w-100" alt="...">
    </div>
    <div class="carousel-item">
      <img src="image6.jpg" class="d-block w-100" alt="...">
    </div>
    <div class="carousel-item">
      <img src="image7.jpg" class="d-block w-100" alt="...">
    </div>
    <div class="carousel-item">
      <img src="image8.jpg" class="d-block w-100" alt="...">
    </div>
    <div class="carousel-item">
      <img src="image9.jpg" class="d-block w-100" alt="...">
    </div>
    <!-- Add more .carousel-item elements based on the number
of images -->
  </div>
  <a class="carousel-control-prev"
href="#carouselExampleIndicators" role="button" data-
slide="prev">
    <span class="carousel-control-prev-icon" aria-
hidden="true"></span>
    <span class="sr-only">Previous</span>
  </a>
  <a class="carousel-control-next"
href="#carouselExampleIndicators" role="button" data-
slide="next">
    <span class="carousel-control-next-icon" aria-
hidden="true"></span>
    <span class="sr-only">Next</span>
```

```
    </a>
  </div>

  <script>
    $(document).ready(function () {
      $('#carouselExampleIndicators').carousel({
        interval: 3000,
        pause: false,
      });

      $('.carousel-control-prev, .carousel-control-
next').click(function () {
          $('#carouselExampleIndicators').carousel('pause');
          setTimeout(function () {
            $('#carouselExampleIndicators').carousel('cycle');
          }, 5000);
        });
      });
  </script>

  <!-- Bootstrap JS -->
  <script
src="https://stackpath.bootstrapcdn.com/bootstrap/4.3.1/js/boot
strap.min.js"></script>
</body>
</html>
<!-- This new version now uses Bootstrap for a more attractive
and interactive carousel, and jQuery for simpler and cleaner
JavaScript code. The carousel now includes a dot indicator
showing the number of images and the current image. Also, the
carousel will pause when the user interacts with it and resume
after 5 seconds. -->
```

Typing Speed per Minute

JavaScript code can be embedded inline into an HTML
document by using the dedicated HTML tag <script>.
This HTML tag wraps around the JS code. The
<script> tag can be placed either in the <head>
section of your HTML or in the <body> section. The
placement entirely depends on when you want the JS
code to load.

Start

Reset

0

You typed at 57 words per minute.

787

```
<!DOCTYPE html>
<html>

<head>
  <title>Typing Speed Tester</title>
  <style>
    body {
      display: flex;
      flex-direction: column;
      align-items: center;
      justify-content: center;
      height: 100vh;
      background-color: #f2f2f2;
      color: #333;
      font-family: Arial, sans-serif;
      margin: 0;
      padding: 0;
      box-sizing: border-box;
```

```css
    }
    textarea {
      width: 50%;
      height: 150px;
      margin: 20px 0;
      padding: 10px;
      box-shadow: 0 2px 5px rgba(0, 0, 0, 0.3);
      border-radius: 5px;
    }

    button {
      padding: 10px 20px;
      margin: 5px;
      background-color: #008CBA;
      color: #fff;
      border: none;
      border-radius: 5px;
      cursor: pointer;
      box-shadow: 0 2px 5px rgba(0, 0, 0, 0.3);
    }

    button:hover {
      background-color: #007B9A;
    }
    .timer {
      color: red;
      margin-top: 10px;
      font-size: 20px;
    }
    .result {
      margin-top: 20px;
    }
  </style>
</head>

<body>
  <h1>Typing Speed per Minute</h1>
  <textarea id="test-text" placeholder="Start typing here..."
disabled></textarea>
  <button id="start-btn" onclick="startTest()">Start</button>
  <button id="reset-btn" onclick="resetTest()">Reset</button>
  <div class="timer" id="timer">60</div>
  <div class="result" id="result"></div>
```

```
<script>
  let testText = document.getElementById('test-text');
  let result = document.getElementById('result');
  let timer = document.getElementById('timer');
  let startBtn = document.getElementById('start-btn');
  let intervalId;
  let timeRemaining = 60;

  function startTest() {
    startBtn.disabled = true;
    testText.disabled = false;
    testText.focus();
    timer.textContent = timeRemaining;
    intervalId = setInterval(countdown, 1000);
  }

  function countdown() {
    timeRemaining--;
    timer.textContent = timeRemaining;
    if (timeRemaining === 0) {
      clearInterval(intervalId);
      calculateSpeed();
    }
  }

  function calculateSpeed() {
    let totalWords = testText.value.split(' ').length;
    result.textContent = `You typed at ${totalWords} words per
minute.`;
    testText.disabled = true;
  }

  function resetTest() {
    clearInterval(intervalId);
    testText.value = '';
    result.textContent = '';
    startBtn.disabled = false;
    testText.disabled = true;
    timeRemaining = 60;
    timer.textContent = timeRemaining;
  }
</script>
</body>
```

789

```
</html>

<!-- This is a modified version of our Typing Speed Tester that
includes a countdown timer from 60 seconds.

In this updated version, a timer is displayed on the page which
starts counting down from 60 seconds as soon as the start button
is clicked. The test textarea is disabled until the start button is
clicked. When the timer reaches 0, the speed calculation is made,
the textarea is disabled, and the interval is cleared. The reset
button resets everything back to the initial state.

You can adjust this to meet your needs. -->
```

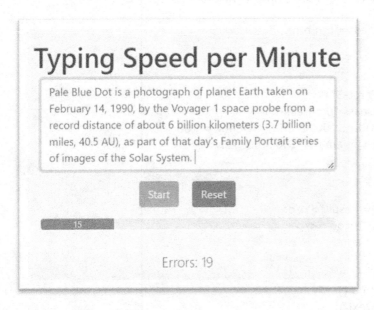

```
<!DOCTYPE html>
<html>

<head>
  <title>Typing Speed Tester</title>

  <!-- Bootstrap CSS -->
  <link
href="https://stackpath.bootstrapcdn.com/bootstrap/4.3.1/css/bo
otstrap.min.css" rel="stylesheet">

  <!-- jQuery -->
  <script src="https://code.jquery.com/jquery-
3.3.1.min.js"></script>
</head>

<body class="d-flex flex-column align-items-center justify-
content-center vh-100 bg-light text-dark">

  <h1>Typing Speed per Minute</h1>
  <textarea id="test-text" class="form-control w-50" rows="5"
placeholder="Start typing here..." disabled></textarea>

  <div class="mt-3">
```

```
    <button id="start-btn" class="btn btn-primary mr-
3">Start</button>
    <button id="reset-btn" class="btn btn-
danger">Reset</button>
  </div>

  <div class="progress w-50 mt-3">
    <div id="progress-bar" class="progress-bar"
role="progressbar" style="width: 100%" aria-valuenow="100"
      aria-valuemin="0" aria-valuemax="100">60</div>
  </div>

  <div class="mt-3">
    <p class="result lead" id="result"></p>
    <p class="error lead" id="error"></p>
  </div>

  <script>
    $(document).ready(function () {
      let testText = $('#test-text');
      let result = $('#result');
      let progressBar = $('#progress-bar');
      let startBtn = $('#start-btn');
      let intervalId;
      let timeRemaining = 60;
      let errorCount = 0;

      startBtn.click(function () {
        startBtn.prop('disabled', true);
        testText.prop('disabled', false).focus();
        progressBar.text(timeRemaining);
        intervalId = setInterval(countdown, 1000);
      });

      $('#reset-btn').click(function () {
        clearInterval(intervalId);
        testText.val('');
        result.text('');
        errorCount = 0;
        $('#error').text('');
        startBtn.prop('disabled', false);
        testText.prop('disabled', true);
        timeRemaining = 60;
        progressBar.css('width', '100%').text(timeRemaining);
```

```
    });

    testText.keydown(function (event) {
      if (event.keyCode === 8) {
        errorCount++;
        $('#error').text(`Errors: ${errorCount}`);
      }
    });

    function countdown() {
      timeRemaining--;
      progressBar.css('width', `${(timeRemaining / 60) *
100}%`).text(timeRemaining);
      if (timeRemaining === 0) {
        clearInterval(intervalId);
        calculateSpeed();
      }
    }

    function calculateSpeed() {
      let totalWords = testText.val().split(' ').length;
      result.text(`You typed at ${totalWords} words per
minute.`);
      testText.prop('disabled', true);
    }
  });
</script>

<!-- Bootstrap JS -->
<script
src="https://stackpath.bootstrapcdn.com/bootstrap/4.3.1/js/boot
strap.min.js"></script>

</body>

</html>

<!-- In this updated version, Bootstrap is used to make the
```

interface more engaging and responsive. jQuery simplifies the
JavaScript part of the code, making it easier to read and maintain.
The timer is now shown as a progress bar that depletes as time
passes, giving the user a more intuitive understanding of the
remaining time. Moreover, the application now counts and

displays the number of typing errors made by the user, providing more detailed feedback. -->

<!--
   1. Timer functionality using a Progress Bar: This will visually represent the time remaining for the user. The progress bar will deplete as the time decreases.

   2. Error counting: We will add a functionality that counts how many times the user presses the backspace key, as this usually indicates a typing error. -->

"You did well. Congratulations."

How to download 235 task files related to 100 projects:

1. Open page 276 of this book.
2. Enter the word(d...r) in the center of the top picture into the asterisk(*) place in step 3.
3. Input the following address into the URL field of Chrome or Edge, then press enter.

http://www.mij.co.kr/*****/235task-files.zip   (or)

mijkor.dothome.co.kr/*****/235task-files.zip

4. Once the download is complete, unzip the files, open the folder in Visual Studio Code, and utilize them.

Author : Sanyhyun Na

1. House husband
2. Person who does not have a job
3. Family: one wife and one son
4. Residence: Incheon, South Korea

&

1. Domestic Champion, ruling the roost with finesse.
2. A free-spirited explorer in the vast expanse of life's opportunities, currently untethered by conventional employment.
3. The proud patriarch of a tight-knit family, blessed with an inspiring wife and an energetic son.

+

1. "The author has been involved in studying 20 coding books, viewing hundreds of YouTube videos, executing hundreds of Google searches, and engaging in hundreds of conversations with ChatGPT. This book is the culmination of those experiences."

2. "Having read through 20 coding books, sifted through hundreds of YouTube videos, carried out hundreds of Google searches, and held hundreds of dialogues with ChatGPT, the author presents this book as the result of those endeavors."

3. "The author, after digesting the content of 20 coding books, watching hundreds of YouTube videos, performing hundreds of Google searches, and interacting hundreds of times with ChatGPT, has produced this book as an outcome of all that work."   =

4. "20 coding books read, hundreds of YouTube videos watched, hundreds of Google searches conducted, and hundreds of conversations held with ChatGPT - all of these led the author to the creation of this book."

"Take on 100 projects with HTML, CSS, and JavaScript. Experience a total of 216 coding tasks. There's no set order. Start with the project you want to challenge first. Think of Bootstrap and jQuery as a bonus."

1. "Embark on 100 projects using HTML, CSS, and JavaScript. Encounter 216 unique coding tasks. There's no particular sequence. Initiate with any project that sparks your interest. Consider Bootstrap and jQuery as an added advantage."

2. "Challenge yourself with 100 projects encompassing HTML, CSS, and JavaScript. Delve into 216 diverse coding tasks. The order doesn't matter. Begin with a project that appeals to you. Regard Bootstrap and jQuery as bonus tools."

3. "Undertake 100 projects incorporating HTML, CSS, and JavaScript. Get a hands-on experience with 216 different coding tasks. The sequence is not pre-determined. You can choose to start with the project that intrigues you the most. Treat Bootstrap and jQuery as a plus."

796

4. "Engage in 100 projects with HTML, CSS, and JavaScript at the core. Get to know 216 distinctive coding tasks. There's no rigid order. Pick the project you're most excited about to start with. View Bootstrap and jQuery as supplementary gifts."

5. "Dive into 100 projects centered around HTML, CSS, and JavaScript. Explore 216 unique coding activities. There's no predetermined sequence. Start with the project that catches your eye. Consider Bootstrap and jQuery as extra benefits."

Thank you so much.

July 31, 2023

mijkor@naver.com

©®™♥♥♡♥♥♥♥♥♥♥♥♥

797

Made in the USA
Monee, IL
28 October 2023

45344528R00444